# Seasonality and Sedentism

## Archaeological Perspectives from Old and New World Sites

Peabody Museum Bulletin 6

T0384964

## CONTRIBUTORS

*Karen R. Adams*
*Ofer Bar-Yosef*
*Peter Bleed*
*Vorsila L. Bohrer*
*Gary W. Crawford*
*Robert L. Kelly*
*Daniel E. Lieberman*
*Preston T. Miracle*
*Katherine M. Moore*
*Arturo Morales Muñiz*
*Christopher J. O'Brien*
*Augusto Oyuela-Caycedo*
*James L. Phillips*
*Thomas R. Rocek*
*Michael Russo*
*François R. Valla*

# Seasonality and Sedentism

## Archaeological Perspectives from Old and New World Sites

Thomas R. Rocek and Ofer Bar-Yosef

EDITORS

Peabody Museum of Archaeology and Ethnology

Harvard University

Cambridge, Massachusetts, U.S.A.

1998

Cover illustrations: line drawing adapted from "*Boonea impressa* seasonal modal size classes"
by Michael Russo; photograph of San Jacinto by Augusto Oyuela-Caycedo.
Original design by Janis Owens.
Adaptation of design and layout by Amy Hirschfeld.
Printing and binding by Thomson-Shore, Inc.


"Foraging and Sedentism" excerpted from *The Foraging Spectrum*
by Robert L. Kelly, published by the Smithsonian Institution Press,
Washington, D.C.; copyright © 1995. Used by permission of the publisher.

COPYRIGHT © 1998 BY THE PRESIDENT AND FELLOWS OF HARVARD COLLEGE
ISBN 0-87365-956-2
LIBRARY OF CONGRESS CATALOG CARD NUMBER 97-69904
MANUFACTURED IN THE UNITED STATES OF AMERICA

# Contents

## CHAPTER 9. Measuring Sedentism with Fauna: Archaic Cultures Along the Southwest Florida Coast          143

*Michael Russo*

## CHAPTER 10. Seasonality in the Tropical Lowlands of Northwestern South America: The Case of San Jacinto 1, Colombia          165

*Augusto Oyuela-Caycedo*

## CHAPTER 11. Measures of Mobility and Occupational Intensity in Highland Peru          181

*Katherine M. Moore*

# Figures

## CHAPTER 11. Measures of Mobility and Occupational Intensity in Highland Peru

## CHAPTER 12. Pithouses and Pueblos on Two Continents: Interpretations of Sedentism and Mobility in the Southwestern United States and Southwest Asia

# Tables

CHAPTER 1 # Introduction

*Ofer Bar-Yosef, Harvard University*

*Thomas R. Rocek, University of Delaware*

Human society in general is quite mobile. Every society, whether observed over one human generation or numerous generations, uses a territorial range. In fact, the concept of sedentary, permanent settlement is only a matter of definition, in the prehistoric past as well as now. Thus both ethnographic and archaeological studies must seek to identify settlement patterns. The study of a single site as representative of a society's economic, social, or ritual activities is misleading.

The papers in this volume examine the ways in which archaeologists worldwide have begun to grapple with the critical dimension of mobility in human adaptations. Both from a theoretical and a methodological perspective, it has become clear that trying to divide societies into categories of "sedentary" and "mobile" is unproductive. The fact is that *all* societies have a mobility component; the issue is what the form of that mobility is, not whether it exists. Thus analysis of mobility is not a specialty restricted to hunter-gatherer or nomad studies, but rather is a critical variable in the study of any society.

During the last two decades, prehistoric archaeologists have invested major efforts in identifying and reconstructing settlement patterns (e.g., Mortensen 1972; Monks 1981; Vogt and Leventhal 1983; Rafferty 1985; Fish and Kowalewski 1990; Kelly 1992). Diachronic reconstruction of settlement patterns enables us to identify the history of human adaptations within their environments. In some cases, different mobility patterns were suggested in order to explain the differences between Neanderthals and modern humans in the Levant (Lieberman and Shea 1994). In addition, we may discover that a given society (identified archaeologically or ethnohistorically) failed, sur-

vived, or flourished while confronted by internal sociopolitical stresses, natural vagaries, human enemies, or changes in its habitat's carrying capacity.

However, one of the major obstacles to archaeological research is that we may not always recognize and reconstruct the entire settlement pattern. Sites of human activity, whether ephemeral or permanent, whether representing the remains of a task force or a passing member of the society, are not always well preserved or archaeologically visible. In addition, site formation and postdepositional processes may play an important role in determining the degree of preservation and conservation of portions of or even the entire settlement pattern (e.g., Bar-Yosef 1993; Schiffer 1987). Natural processes that hamper our goals are numerous. Surface erosion causes the destruction of sites. Collapsed ceilings cover cave occupations. Inundation by sea water due to glacial melting or movement of sand dunes are all responsible in one way or another for the destruction and/or disappearance of archaeological remains.

Human activities are also responsible for eliminating options for settlement pattern studies. For example, 10,000 years of cultivation in the Near East has caused incredible damage to earlier sites. By felling trees for building, quarrying, building terraces, plowing, building houses, and herding, human activities have generated rapid alluviation (Goldberg 1994; Miller Rosen 1995; Bar-Yosef 1986). Numerous Late Pleistocene and Neolithic to Bronze Age sites are buried, sometimes under a thick mantle of colluvium and alluvium. Damage has been accelerated in the twentieth century by modern development. Construction of dams, new towns and villages, highways, and so forth, carried out

1

without the necessary salvage projects, has already eliminated a large number of sites. Even desertic areas that appear pristine are highly susceptible to modern damage. Large areas have become militarized zones (Marks 1976; Bar-Yosef and Phillips 1977). The use of tanks and other heavy equipment, as well as agricultural development (e.g., in the Nile Valley), has caused permanent destruction in many arid regions.

Despite great efforts to improve field techniques and prompt reporting, archaeological research is also a destructive process. Excavations over the last 200 years have destroyed or removed large portions of important mounds and the deposits of major caves and rockshelters. All of these factors limit our ability to reconstruct past settlement patterns. Therefore we must do our best with current excavation data and old collections.

Due to increasingly limited funds and high costs of field research, archaeologists often concentrate on the study of one or two sites in a given region. Even when a regionally oriented project is organized to sample sites based on topography, micro-climate, or vegetal association and when multiple sites are tested, there is no assurance that a synchronic settlement pattern will emerge. Therefore the reconstruction of a settlement pattern becomes a complex operation, and it would perhaps be better to view each site as part of an unknown settlement system. Study of the site itself provides data on a *portion* of the annual or decadal range of human activities, and the likelihood of recovering all of the sites in a settlement round is vanishingly small. This means that from the start, we must give up the ideal of reconstructing the entire settlement pattern. We usually have to be satisfied with the study of one or a few sites to determine if each settlement was partially permanent, fully sedentary, ephemeral, seasonal, and so on.

In the following pages we briefly review the essential elements of various settlement patterns. There are differences in mobility patterns among hunter-gatherer groups depending on region, topography, climate, and vegetation. Differences are common also among farming societies and most obviously among those who combine different subsistence strategies according to seasonal options. Interaction between societies with different adaptations affects the settlement patterns of both.

The annual activities of a small group of hunter-gatherers or of small-scale, mildly hierarchical farmers may cover a relatively large territory. These activities create and leave behind a series of sites, some more permanently occupied than others. Mobility between sites creates different types of settlement patterns, known in the Near East as radial, circular, or combinations of

these (see Mortensen 1972). Binford's (1980) concepts of residential and logistical mobility are also to be understood as mixtures of different patterns. The anticipated mobility between base camps and ephemeral seasonal camps is perhaps the easier factor to identify archaeologically. One may construct various expectations based on ethnohistorical information or even current observations (Kent and Vierich 1989). More difficult to answer is the question of whether a site was occupied by a sedentary group. Thus the question of "sedentism" is among the main issues with which the papers in this volume deal.

In the study of seasonality, archaeologists generally employ the same scale as is common in the ethnographic literature (see Murdock 1967). In this scale, a sedentary, year-round settlement may be the only substantial site in an entire settlement system. On the other end of the continuum are highly mobile groups that may leave behind the remains of as many as 30 to 35 camps in a given year. The advantage of ethnographic studies is that with the help of historical documents, interviews with informants, and observations throughout the year, it is possible to find out for how long each site was occupied.

Unfortunately, most of this evidence concerning hunters and gatherers derives from marginal environments. Most hunter-gatherer studies concern the Khoisan-speaking groups of the Kalahari (e.g., Yellen 1977), Eskimo-speaking groups of the Arctic, or the Australian aborigines (Kelly 1995). In a few cases we have evidence from native North Americans and South Americans. However, no data are available concerning hunter-gatherers or simply organized horticultural societies from environments comparable to those found in mid-latitude regions such as the Near East during the Late Pleistocene or Early Holocene. Further, even where contemporary analogs are available, we must avoid the "tyranny of the ethnographic record" (Wobst 1978), or imposing the ethnographically observed patterns or time scales on processes observed archaeologically. Finally, less is known about mobility of farmers, although it is clear that farmers are mobile as well (Amiran 1953; Kent 1989).

In order to identify the seasonal pattern in a given territory, we have to understand the following: (1) the multiple aspects of mobility: frequency of moves, number or percentage of people moving, distance of moves, degree of interannual reuse of locations, as well as interaction of these variables (for instance, how many people traveled on which moves); (2) the economic needs that required mobility and the degree and form of mobility that these required; (3) the social, reproductive, and cultural needs, including ritual, that encouraged full or partial mobility by either the entire group or individuals within a given territory; and (4) the main elements in the archaeological finds or contexts that would enable us to identify the seasons during which the human group or portion of the group stayed or moved. Identifying the main activities that took place at a site is therefore helpful in determining the season of occupation.

Since each site potentially represents only a portion of its occupants' pattern of annual mobility, we must identify the duration and the season of its use in order to place it within the settlement system. In the process, we need to consider the above factors, isolating the related variables, such as the degree of interannual site reuse and group size, that covary and interact with patterns of seasonal mobility.

Thus the goal of archaeological research on settlement systems involves three facets: (1) a conceptual facet of understanding the multiple factors noted above defining settlement variability (frequency of moves, distance of moves, number of occupants moving, etc.); (2) a methodological issue of identifying season, duration, and extent of occupation; and (3) a theoretical facet of understanding the factors (economic, social, and ideological) that shape this movement.

These three areas are inherently interrelated, but may be emphasized to different degrees. The approaches to all three areas have been diverse, and a major goal of this volume is to provide an opportunity to develop links among some of these approaches taken in regional archaeological traditions in different parts of the world. The chapters here least explicitly address the first issue (the conceptual), though the very process of examining seasonality and sedentism brings out the range of implicit or explicit concepts of settlement systems. The papers show that approaches vary substantially, with some emphasizing a fairly restricted contrast of sedentary versus mobile patterns and others breaking this contrast down into a bundle of cross-cutting continua of variation. The works of Rafferty (1985) and Kelly (1992) provide surveys of some of these approaches.

The third issue (theoretical understanding of the factors conditioning mobility) is also not a central focus of this volume, though aspects of it, particularly the economic ones, are addressed in Kelly's paper (see also Kelly 1992, 1995). The theoretical questions about the *reasons* for settlement variation provide the underlying significance of all of the concentration of methodological effort on the question of recognizing seasonality and mobility patterns.

The second, methodological topic is the major emphasis of this volume. Here a wealth of innovative techniques have been and continue to be developed worldwide. Monks (1981) provides a broad overview of major methodological approaches to seasonality assessment. Monks divides techniques into two broad groups: direct methods (biologically based, using the presence or absence of particular seasonal taxa, physiological events in plants or animals, incremental growth structures, faunal population structure, or oxygen isotope analysis of biological material) and indirect methods (any other approaches such as those based on the physical characteristics of site sediments or season-specific cultural patterning). Both classes of approaches are represented in the papers in this volume. Rather than a survey of alternative techniques, the papers here demonstrate applications of these techniques, often emphasizing the benefit of combining multiple lines of evidence. An overview of the approaches taken in each paper follows.

Kelly presents a framework within which to consider the issues of sedentism and mobility as a whole. Unlike most of the succeeding papers, his contribution is not concerned with archaeological methodological issues, but rather with the question of why people (hunter-gatherers in particular) become sedentary in the first place. Kelly lays out some of the basic parameters that shape mobility and sedentism and points out the many variables that enter into settlement decisions by a hunting-gathering group (Kelly 1995).

Equally important for the purposes of this volume, the factors guiding hunter-gatherer settlement choices are also critical in defining the very concept of mobility—variables such as frequency of moves, composition of the moving group (who goes and who stays), and distance of moves. Using an optimal foraging approach, Kelly shows how these parameters may vary and how some simple intuitive ideas about mobility and sedentism (such as that resource abundance leads directly to sedentism) are invalid. His framework shows why the range of sophisticated approaches to interpreting seasonality and settlement variability outlined in the succeeding papers are critical.

Morales introduces a critical area of seasonality data and its interpretation for the assessment of mobility. Using avian faunal remains from the Spanish cave sites of Cueva de Nerja and Zafarraya, he shows on the one hand how careful analysis of such data can yield valuable information. On the other hand, he explores how even these high quality faunal data on migratory species do not yield a magic "fix" for the questions of seasonality and settlement. Not all species are equally predictable in their migratory behavior, nor are all faunal seasonal indicators equally reliable. The abundance of various migratory birds differs among sites not only as a function of season of occupation, but simply as a result of local environment as well. Migratory species can change behavior over time and in response to environmental shifts, and similarly human hunting strategies can alter over time independent of (or along with) changes in settlement. While clearly illustrating all of these complications and potential pitfalls, his message is not one of despair at the value of biological seasonality indicators. Instead he offers a strong call for the importance of combining multiple lines of evidence and avoiding simplistic interpretations of limited data.

Miracle and O'Brien's paper lays out a systematic research strategy for investigating settlement. They begin with a discussion of the environmental parameters that were likely to influence settlement patterns in their study area and consider the site of Badanj, Bosnia-Herzegovina in the context of the likely overall settlement system. They then discuss the methodology of two alternative approaches to seasonality assessment, one based on analysis of the fetal bone component of the ungulate faunal assemblage and another based on cementum increments in red deer. The two approaches provide interesting and complementary results. While both emphasize the seasonal, primarily cold-season occupation of the Badanj locality, the two approaches show variation in the degree of seasonality and a shift over the course of occupation of the site. Like Morales's paper, their analyses show how different approaches to seasonality may provide complementary rather than redundant information and demonstrate the necessity of caution in interpreting any single source of seasonality information.

Miracle and O'Brien carefully detail methodological issues, the complexities of the analysis, and the impact of small sample sizes. The sample size problem is the price paid for segregating the assemblages by level rather than treating the site as a single, several-thousand-year occupation—only by breaking the site down this way are we able to see the limited season of use and the shifts in seasonality over time. They point out the potential impact of human activity patterns (such as seasonal hunting patterns), as well as seasonality of settlement per se, in determining the seasonality of the faunal assemblages.

Lieberman shows how biological seasonality data may be used to address a major theoretical issue in archaeology. He uses cementum increment analysis to investigate the timing of sedentism in relation to the development of agriculture in southwest Asia. He examines a sample of gazelles from a series of Natufian sites to see if previously noted evidence of high occupation intensity (such as the heavy accumulation of occupational debris and the presence of substantial architecture, storage features, and human burials at several Natufian sites) corresponds to multiseason occupation. His results confirm reduced mobility at a number of Natufian sites originally considered as base camps (Bar-Yosef 1983). This offers the strongest support available for previous interpretations of Natufian settlement based on faunal (fish, migratory birds, gazelle kill age structure, and the self-domestication of human commensals) and limited floral data.

Aside from the methodological rigor of his approach, perhaps the most powerful aspect of his analysis is his use of a comparative approach. By examining multiple Natufian and pre-Natufian sites, he can conclusively show that there is a profound change toward increased sedentism around the start of the Natufian as seen in the enamel increment pattern, which stands in marked contrast to the enamel increment pattern at earlier sites. Regardless of questions about the precise interpretation of seasonality, the evidence of *change* in the Natufian is conclusive. He also documents variation within the Natufian pattern. Finally, his results show that despite a general match between the indirect indicators that have been used to argue for sedentism (such as the presence of visible architecture) and the increment data, the correspondence is less than perfect. This underscores the importance of comparing alternative sources of evidence and of using direct biological seasonality data.

Valla approaches the Natufian question from a different perspective, complementary to Lieberman's. Rather than focusing on a particular methodological approach to resolve the seasonality issue, Valla uses an overview from a range of sources such as fauna, flora, and architecture to examine the overall Natufian settlement pattern. In so doing, he considers both the range of particular site remains as well as theoretical expectations and comparative ethnographic cases. Not surprisingly, he finds that the question of Natufian settlement as usually phrased is too simplistic, ignoring three critical variables.

First is the simplistic notion of "sedentism" itself; he points to the potential range of variation subsumed under this term and like Lieberman, suggests that even sites with compelling direct evidence of multiseason use can still encompass a range of mobility. Second, he points to the range of variation among sites and particularly between regions. The Natufian does not represent a single settlement system and both its different regional expressions and the range of sites within them have to be examined individually if we are to make meaningful statements about mobility patterns. Third, the Natufian shows evidence of change over time—and this change varies from region to region. In short, Valla's paper shows that although precise seasonality data are clearly needed, they do not in themselves answer questions about settlement. Settlement systems must be understood as the variable and dynamic results of compromise among ecological and social factors that they are.

Crawford and Bleed complete the group of Old World case studies with an examination of settlement variability in the Japanese archaeological record. They focus on the issues of changing subsistence and scheduling decisions affecting settlement in the Early Jomon through post-Jomon Ezo-Haji periods, as well as comparing these with ethnographic Ainu data. Recovery of organic remains, particularly bone (but until recently plant material as well), has been limited in Japan. So Crawford and Bleed approach the question of mobility from a variety of perspectives, using indirect arguments based on resource availability and ethnographic analogy, as well as the new body of faunal and particularly botanical data that they provide. They show an interesting nonlinear trend, with mobility increasing and then decreasing again. Their case is also interesting in that it incorporates societies combining hunting and gathering with horticulture; they find an *increase* in mobility in their early horticultural sample, followed by a reduction in mobility during the subsequent, more fully agricultural period.

Adams and Bohrer survey the literature of botanically based settlement and seasonality assessment in the U. S. Southwest. In addition to providing a compendium of useful approaches to seasonality and mobility, they also consider the efficacy of botanical approaches. They describe both direct indicators of seasonality, such as seasonally available pollen, fruits, or other plant parts, as well as indirect indicators of settlement patterns, such as weedy plants that colonize disturbed ground. Much like Morales's results for avian faunal data, they show that simple reliance on a normative assignment of seasonality to particular taxa is potentially misleading. The degree of seasonality exhibited by plant species varies (they distinguish flora exhibiting true seasonality, qualified seasonality, shifting seasonality, and aseasonality), and equally importantly, the representation of plant remains in archeological sites is the result of the interaction of the biology of the plants, climate, and both human and nonhuman mechanisms of transport and preservation.

Their account shows the value of floral seasonality assessment but also shows the importance of the *combination* of paleobotanical data with a detailed understanding of the biology of the plant species, the cultural context of their use, and other complementary indicators of settlement. Biological data are critical but must be used in conjunction with, not as a substitute for, alternative sources of information on settlement.

In his paper, Russo develops the case for the year-round occupation of the southwest Florida coastal site of Horr's Island during the Middle to Late Archaic. This is a period that most traditional interpretations suggest precedes sedentary settlement, and coastal sites have been interpreted as seasonal extensions of inland settlement systems. Indirect measures of settlement permanence and seasonality (such as storage features, architecture, and midden accumulation) are inconclusive. Russo turns to biological seasonality indicators from marine mollusks and fish to resolve the issue.

Russo divides biological measures of seasonality into three categories: presence/absence, modal size classes, and incremental growth structures. Like Morales, he points out that presence/absence data can be misleading and concentrates on the latter two kinds of data. Annual growth increments in clams, size classes of mollusks and fish eaten by the prehistoric inhabitants (scallops, catfish, pinfish, and herring), and a parasitic gastropod associated with oysters at a nearby site provide estimates of the season when these resources were collected. Russo samples multiple proveniences at the site and uses the range of marine faunal seasonality signatures to suggest a multiseasonal mosaic of resource use.

As he acknowledges, some of his seasonality measures require further testing and refinement, but his approach shows the value of combining data from a variety of taxa to build up an understanding of the seasonal round. Biological as well as cultural factors influence seasonal patterns of collection of plants and animals. Thus, even when a species that is available year-round can be shown to be collected on a seasonal basis, we must consider the possibility that collection shifted to other species in the same area rather than that the people left. Again, multiple sources of data are vastly preferable to reliance on any single seasonality indicator. On the other hand, the danger of palimpsests of multiple occupations and of shifts in the season indicated by one species relative to another must also be considered.

Oyuela-Caycedo investigates one of the behavioral correlates of mobility patterns: the spatial layout of site features. He develops a series of predications about two sets of patterns: (1) assemblage redundancy and feature density in relation to the range of activities carried out at a site (the contrast between permanent and base camps versus special purpose sites) and (2) spatial patterning of features in relation to the degree of permanence of occupation (sedentary versus periodically revisited sites). He thus tries to tease apart two of the commonly confounded elements of shifts in mobility: seasonal prolongation of use versus increased multiyear reuse.

His study is based in the tropical lowlands of northern Columbia. Oyuela-Caycedo suggests that the seasonal distribution of rainfall and the resulting flooding is critical in determining settlement choices. He points out that these factors severely bias the archaeological sample since sites in low-lying flood-prone areas, which are suitable for dry-season occupation by mobile populations, are rapidly covered by alluvium or destroyed. They are likely to be discovered only under rare fortuitous circumstances. Thus the available site sample is biased towards settlements located in higher settings, which represent primarily rainy season encampments of mobile groups and relatively permanent sites of less mobile populations.

Oyuela-Caycedo tests his expectations at the site of San Jacinto I, a deeply buried valley-bottom site whose discovery was a rare exception to the problem of site bias. On the basis of his analysis, he suggests that the site represents the relatively mobile pattern that is expected in this low-lying setting. San Jacinto I shifts over time from a short-term, dry-season special-purpose site to a dry-season logistical base camp. The analysis shows the value of examining the environmental context and human behavior patterns in interpreting seasonality and mobility and in attacking the multiple dimensions of mobility.

Moore uses faunal evidence to investigate changes in the use of Panaulauca, a cave site in the high puna of Andean Peru. Her goal is to examine the degree to which such a site in this high elevation region was occupied on a seasonal as opposed to nonseasonal and periodic versus long-term basis. Thus she explicitly breaks down the issue of mobility into multiple dimensions of kind and degree.

She applies biological measures of seasonality including camelid and deer dental wear, deer antlers, and the age (as well as presence) of migratory fowl to identify season of occupation. Going beyond these data, however, she also examines evidence of cultural behavior to interpret the pattern of human settlement. For this purpose, she investigates the degree of bone fragmentation and burning (as a measure of intensity

of processing and further secondary damage), the density of bone as well as of artifacts, the quantity of bone, and finally the distribution of the different size categories and conditions (burnt/unburnt) of bone across the site. This analysis takes advantage of a body of data, unidentifiable bone fragments, that is typically ignored (or not even recovered) in many excavations.

The result of her approach is that she is able to examine mobility in its multiple aspects and show that Panaulauca was initially visited for short periods for wet-season hunting and then shifted to more extended, multiseason use. Subsequently, the site once again became a short-term, mostly wet-season hunting (and herding) station marked now by even lower intensities of bone processing than in the earliest period of use. The value of combining multiple biological measures of season *and* measures of cultural behavior is clear.

Rocek explores some of the commonly used indirect measures of mobility (site size, midden depth and distribution, house type, and storage feature placement) from the explicitly comparative perspective of the U.S. Southwest and Southwest Asia. He points out a number of methodological issues that limit the comparability of these variables and discusses limitations in mobility interpretations based solely on site structure. Still, he argues that even these crude measures of site form help constrain interpretations of possible mobility patterns and should not be ignored. Site form viewed from a comparative perspective (between regions such as Southwest and North America and Southwest Asia, but also between sites *within* a study area or between time periods of a study) can be combined with biological measures of seasonality to provide a more detailed understanding of a settlement system.

Finally, Phillips provides a critical overview of the papers in the volume as a whole. We hope that the volume will serve to encourage the exchange of ideas and techniques in the analysis of seasonality and settlement systems. The papers in this volume make it clear that there are no simple one-step solutions to settlement analysis. However, they also show the value of bringing multiple lines of data, analysis, and theory to bear on the topic.

Bringing researchers from the Old and New Worlds together allows us to strengthen the approach to this material by combining the complementary strengths of different archaeological traditions. While scientific techniques such as observation of cementum annuli and growth increments in shell are the same everywhere, the approach to prehistoric societies as a subject of study is somewhat different. With certain exceptions (such as some Africanists and Australians), many New World archaeologists are more familiar with the intricacies of hunter-gatherer mobility and related concepts. Old World archaeologists generally deal with longer periods of socioeconomic change than their New World counterparts and work in regions lacking ethnohistoric evidence. We felt that bringing both parties together would help to balance their approaches, and we organized a symposium on seasonality and sedentism from New and Old World perspectives held in April of 1992 at the 57th annual meetings of the Society for American Archaeology in Pittsburgh, Pennsylvania. With the omission of a few papers that were not available and the addition of several others, this volume derives from that symposium.

## Acknowledgments

Many thanks to Naomi Ornstein, Margaret Courtney, and Amy Hirschfeld for help editing the manuscripts and producing the book. We would also like to thank the American School of Prehistoric Research for financial support for this volume.

## BIBLIOGRAPHY

Amiran, D. H. K.
1953 "The Pattern of Settlement in Palestine." *Israel Exploration Journal* 3:65–78, 192–209, 250–260.

Bar-Yosef, O.
1983 "The Natufian in the Southern Levant," in *The Hilly Flanks: Essays on the Prehistory of Southwestern Asia*, T. C. Young, P. Smith, and P. Mortensen, eds., pp. 11–42. The Oriental Institute, Chicago.
1986 "The Walls of Jericho: An Alternative Interpretation." *Current Anthropology* 27:157–162.

Bar-Yosef, O., and J. Phillips
1977 *Prehistoric Investigations in Jebel Meghara, Northern Sinai*. Hebrew University, Jerusalem.

Binford, L. R.
1980 "Willow Smoke and Dogs' Tails: Hunter-Gatherer Settlement Systems and Archaeological Site Formation." *American Antiquity* 45(1):4–20.

Fish, S. K., and S. A. Kowalewski, eds.
1990 *The Archaeology of Regions; The Case for Full-Coverage Survey*. Smithsonian Institution Press, Washington, D.C.

Goldberg, P.
1994 "Interpreting Late Quaternary Continental Sequences in Israel," in *Late Quaternary Chronology and Paleoclimates of the Eastern Mediterranean*, O. Bar-Yosef and R. Kra, eds., pp. 89–102. Radiocarbon and the Peabody Museum of Archaeology and Ethnology, Harvard University, Tucson and Cambridge.

Kelly, R. L.
1992 "Mobility/Sedentism: Concepts, Archaeological Measures, and Effects." *Annual Review of Anthropology* 21:43–66.

Kelly, R.
1995 *The Foraging Spectrum: Diversity in Hunter-Gatherer Lifeways*. Smithsonian Institution Press, Washington, D.C.

Kent, S., ed.
1989 *Farmers as Hunters; The Implications of Sedentism*. Cambridge University Press, New York.

Kent, S., and H. Vierich
1989 "The Myth of Ecological Determinism—Anticipated Mobility and Site Spatial Organization," in *Farmers as Hunters; The Implications of Sedentism*, S. Kent, ed., pp. 96–130. Cambridge University Press, New York.

Lieberman, D. E., and J. J. Shea
1994 "Behavioral Differences Between Archaic and Modern Humans in the Levantine Mousterian." *American Anthropologist* 96:300–332.

Marks, A. E.
1976 *Prehistory and Palaeoenvironments in the Central Negev, Israel*, vol. 2. SMU Press, Dallas.

Miller Rosen, A.
1995 "The Social Response to Environmental Change in Early Bronze Age Canaan." *Journal of Anthropological Archaeology* 14:26–44.

Monks, G. G.
1981 "Seasonality Studies," in *Advances in Archaeological Method and Theory*, vol. 4, M. B. Schiffer, ed., pp. 177–240. Academic Press, New York.

Mortensen, P.
1972 "Seasonal Camps and Early Villages in the Zagros," in *Man, Settlement and Urbanism*, P. J. Ucko, R. Tringham, and G. W. Dimbleby, eds., pp. 293–297. Duckworth, London.

Murdock, G. P.
1967 *Ethnographic Atlas*. University of Pittsburgh Press, Pittsburgh.

Rafferty, J. E.
1985 "The Archaeological Record on Sedentariness: Recognition, Development, and Implications," in *Advances in Archaeological Method and Theory*, vol. 8, M. B. Schiffer, ed., pp. 113–156. Academic Press, New York.

Vogt, E. Z., and R. M. Leventhal, eds.
1983 *Prehistoric Settlement Patterns: Essays in Honor of Gordon R. Willey*. University of New Mexico Press, Albuquerque.

Wobst, H. M.
1978 "The Archaeo-Ethnology of Hunter-Gatherers or the Tyranny of the Ethnographic Record in Archaeology." *American Antiquity* 43:303–309.

Yellen, J. E.
1977 *Archeological Approaches to the Present*. Academic Press, New York.

CHAPTER 2　Foraging and Sedentism

*Robert L. Kelly*
*University of Louisville*

Contributors to this volume are concerned with the sedentization process and its relationship to resource seasonality. Sedentism was once seen as the straightforward outcome of resource abundance; people settled down when there was sufficient food in one place to permit it (Beardsley et al. 1956). Clearly, people cannot be sedentary and remain foragers if there is not a sufficient amount of food to permit it. Yet prehistoric foragers often did not avail themselves of such opportunities quickly (Price and Brown 1985), and ethnographic data show that even if a residential group occupies a single site year-round, individuals keep moving logistically, sometimes moving even more frequently or for longer distances than when they were "mobile." Sedentization does not entail a cessation of movement, but instead a reorganization of an individual's use of energy between foraging, camp movement, and other tasks. This process is critical because it is frequently the context for population growth, sociopolitical inequality, gender inequality, slavery, warfare, and other important sociocultural and demographic transitions (Kelly 1992, 1995). In this paper, I wish to explore some simple relationships between individual foraging and group (family) movement that are involved in a shift toward sedentism.

## INDIVIDUAL FORAGING AND GROUP MOVEMENT

Among hunter-gatherers, food resources are gathered by individuals or small groups who foray out from a residence, collect food, and return. Other variables (e.g., a family death) come into play, but the decision to move a residence or not is based largely on the costs and benefits of foraging. As Sahlins (1972:33) pointed out, the hunting and gathering economy

> is seriously afflicted by the imminence of diminishing returns . . . an initial success seems only to develop the probability that further efforts will yield smaller benefits. This describes the typical curve of food-getting within a particular locale. A modest number of people usually sooner than later reduce the food resources within convenient range of camp. Thereafter, they may stay on only by absorbing an increase in real costs or a decline in real returns: rise in costs if the people choose to search farther and farther afield, decline in returns if they are satisfied to live on the shorter supplies or inferior foods in easier reach. The solution, of course, is to go elsewhere.

Group movements, in other words, are related to the environment through foraging behavior. The case of the central Kalahari ≠Kade provides one example. Here, women "begin to gather food near the campsite [and] they can complete their work in a trip of 1 to 2 km during the first few days of their stay. Then, gradually, as they consume the plants near camp, they must go farther. If the round trip for gathering food plants exceeds 10 km or so, convenience dictates that they move themselves with all their belongings to virgin territory" (Tanaka 1980:66; see Kelly 1995 for other examples). Ethnographic data suggest that 10–15 km is the maximum daily foraging radius (i.e., the distance at which a forager can gather food and still return to camp before nightfall). Yet foragers rarely travel this far and rarely deplete a foraging area of food. The Hadza, for example, move camp "long before shortages have become in any way serious" (Woodburn 1968:106). Since foraging distances affect the length of time a camp is occupied, what conditions how far a person will walk in daily foraging?

The distance from a residential camp at which a forager can procure resources at an energetic gain is limited by the return rates of those resources. Figure 1 shows the results of a simple model of foraging (Kelly 1990, 1991, 1995). In this model, we assume that the family requires a total of 14,000 kcal/day, that the forager walks at a leisurely pace of 3 km/hr at 300 kcal/hr, that the cost of walking increases by 30 percent when

returning home with food (Jones and Madsen 1989), and that foraging activities, including traveling, harvesting, and processing food, are confined to eight hours a day. The daily return to foraging is:

$$\text{Net Return} = [(8-2T)R] - (300T + 390T)$$

where T = travel time to foraging patch (distance/ 3 km/hr) and R = overall environmental return rate (varied here from 1,000 to 4,000 kcal/hr).

The daily net return is a function of the overall environmental return rate (A–D) and it decreases far-

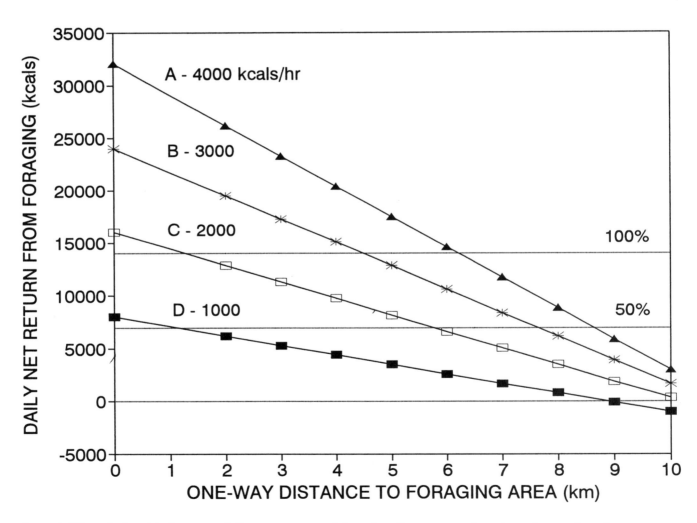

**Figure 1.** The relationship between daily net return and foraging distance as a function of mean foraging return rate. Horizontal lines indicate the calories that a forager must provide: 50 percent if a family has two foragers, 100 percent if a family has only one. As foragers expend more time and effort traveling, the mean daily return declines. As a forager provides more of the family's food needs, and/or as the return rate from the environment declines, the distance at which he or she can forage from camp becomes shorter.

ther from camp as the forager spends more time and energy traveling to and from the foraging area relative to the time spent collecting and processing food. The two horizontal lines in figure 1 indicate the amount of energy needed per day by the family depending on whether one or two foragers are responsible for the family's daily food needs (if two, then each collects 50 percent). The distance at which the forager brings home at least a day's worth of food, the intersection between one of the net return lines (A–D) and one of the horizontal caloric needs lines, becomes shorter as the return rate decreases and/or as a forager's contribution increases. Let's say that our forager lives in environment C. He or she can forage up to about 1.25 km from camp. If two foragers collect food, then food can be collected at a net gain up to 5.75 km from camp. The *effective foraging radius* therefore is affected by the return rates of the available resources, the number of foragers per family, and a family's caloric needs. As average return rates decline, the effective foraging radius becomes shorter and families must move more frequently. This is an oversimplification, of course, for any environment contains a range of resources of different return rates. Diet-breadth models can predict which foods will be taken, but the range can be expected to decrease at greater distances from camp.

The amount of food a forager needs to collect is obviously related to family size but also to the amount of foraging that children do. In some foraging societies, children collect much of their own food; in others, they collect very little (see Blurton Jones et al. 1994). When children collect food, adults can devote time to other activities or can forage at longer distances from camp for higher-return-rate (but possibly more risky) resources. This has implications for fertility and population growth, as well as residential mobility rates.

A decision to remain in one location, however, is based not only on what is available at that location but also on what is available elsewhere. As Sahlins pointed out, hunter-gatherers balance the cost of remaining where they are and foraging out farther and farther (or using closer but lower-return-rate resources) against the cost of moving to a new, unexploited area.

Imagine one of our families living in an environment where a 4,000 kcal/hr resource is homogeneously distributed across the landscape. The family relies upon a single forager to collect food for it in an eight-hour day. Therefore the forager must gather the resource at a minimum return rate of $14,000/8 = 1,750$ kcal/hr. Making the same assumptions as above, the net return rate (RR) decreases with increasing one-way foray distance (fig. 2):

$$RR = \frac{4000\,(8-2T) - (300T + 390T)}{8}$$

Thus the family lives in a "patch" defined by a maximum foraging radius of 6 km.

We can also compute the return rate if the family were to move to a new foraging area after exploiting the resources within a given radius of the site. We assume that the family uses food at progressively greater distances from camp over time. At any given moment, therefore, a residential move means moving twice the current foraging radius. The after-move return rate of the individual forager, allowing an hour for camp breakdown and setup (more on this variable below) is:

$$RR = \frac{4000\,(7-2T) - 300(2T)}{8}$$

(We assume that the after-move foraging and travel time are both zero—they would not be, but they would be minimal. Adding them would only move the "after-move" line in figure 2 down a bit.) At a return rate of just under 3,000 kcal/hour (achieved at a foraging distance of about 3 km) the after-move return rate is equal to the within-patch return rate and is higher at greater within-patch foraging distances. After having eaten everything within about 3 km of camp, foragers would do better to move their families to the center of a new foraging area (6 km away). Even with the move, the forager would achieve a higher return rate for that day than if they had remained where they were and will return to a 4,000 kcal/hr rate the following day.

This simple model assumes only that hunter-gatherers move as families, not necessarily as bands. From ethnographic data we know that some hunter-gatherer bands have extremely fluid composition, with individuals and families moving on different schedules. Anthropologists frequently attribute this fluidity to the need to relieve social tension. Subsistence can often be the source of this tension. Agta band members intensely debate whether to move or not, with decisions taking hours or even days (Rai 1990:59). This is understandable, for large families will reach the point of diminishing returns more quickly than small families; other factors being equal, large and small families should move on different schedules resulting in fluid band composition. Family size will become a less important factor, however, as everyone's subsistence becomes more closely tied to the same resource (e.g., fish runs, communal hunting).

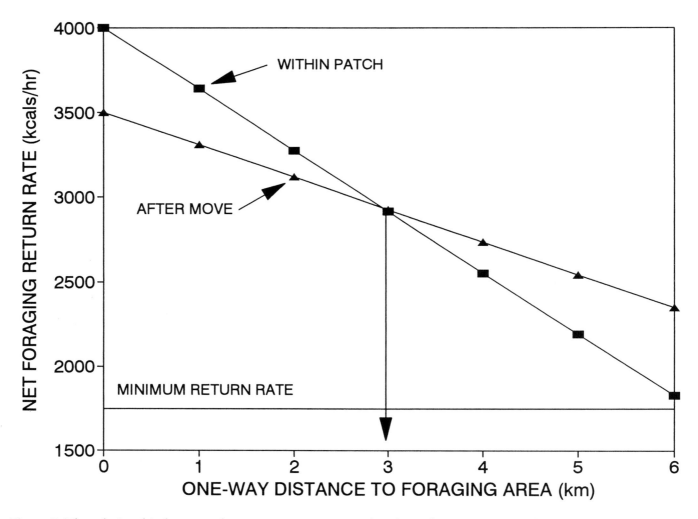

**Figure 2.** The relationship between the return rate experienced within a foraging area (within patch) relative to that which could be expected if the foragers moved to a new area (after move) as a function of the radius of the currently occupied camp. The model predicts camp movement when foragers travel about 3 km from camp to find food.

Also, since many plant foods provide returns lower than those of large game, the effective foraging distance for plants is shorter, in general, than it is for large game. Since large game is usually procured by men, women's foraging should by and large determine when (and where) camp is moved. Among the Agta, for example, since "hunting depends on mobile animals, it is not an important consideration [in determining moves]. Men and women freely voice their opinion on residence change, but women, who must carry out the most gathering, have the final say" (Rai 1990:59).

At the heart of the relationship between daily foraging and group movement are the perceived "costs"

of camp movement and foraging. In the above model, we assumed that the location of the next camp was a function of the location of the current camp. But campsites can be determined by many different factors such as water sources, firewood, shade, shelter, or insects. In figure 3, the distance to the next patch is not a function of the current foraging radius, as it was in figure 2, but is held constant at 5 and then 7 km (thus the slopes of the after-move lines are zero). As we would expect, if the next camp is 5 km away, a forager should exploit everything within nearly 4 km of camp before moving; if the next camp is 7 km away, he or she should eat everything within nearly 5 km of camp. The predicted

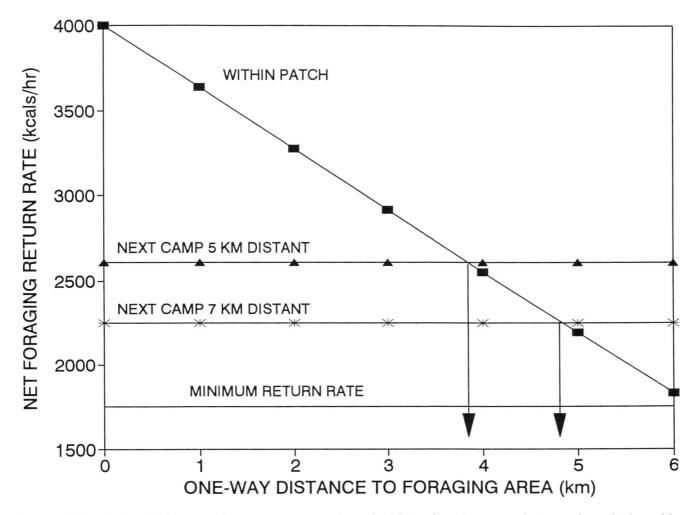

**Figure 3.** The relationship between the return rate experienced within a foraging area relative to that which could be expected if the foragers moved to a new area 5 or 7 km away. As the distance to the next patch increases, we could expect the current foraging patch to be occupied for longer and longer periods.

differences in foraging distance may seem to be minor, but note that increasing the effective foray distance from 3 to 4 km increases the foraging area, and the length of time a camp can be occupied, by 77 percent. (And, in these two cases, foragers would actually use some of the food within the effective foraging radius of the second camp while still in the first.)

The difficulty of traversing the terrain must also figure into calculations. For example, a kilometer of muskeg in the spring is much harder to cross than a kilometer of savanna. Increasing the walking cost to 1,200 kcal/hr in the model while leaving the foraging walking cost at 300 kcal/hr predicts camp movement

after foraging a 4 rather than a 3-km radius. This will be affected not only by the terrain to be crossed but also by whether draft animals and transportation technology are available, for example, dogsleds or horses (Binford 1990). Also, if the anticipated patch is already occupied, the cost of moving would have to include the cost of displacing current residents, perhaps through warfare.

Housing also affects the cost of moving. The above model used a one-hour camp breakdown/setup time. Camp breakdowns could be slower for Arctic peoples due to differences in the amount of material goods carried (see Burch [1988:107] for an example of

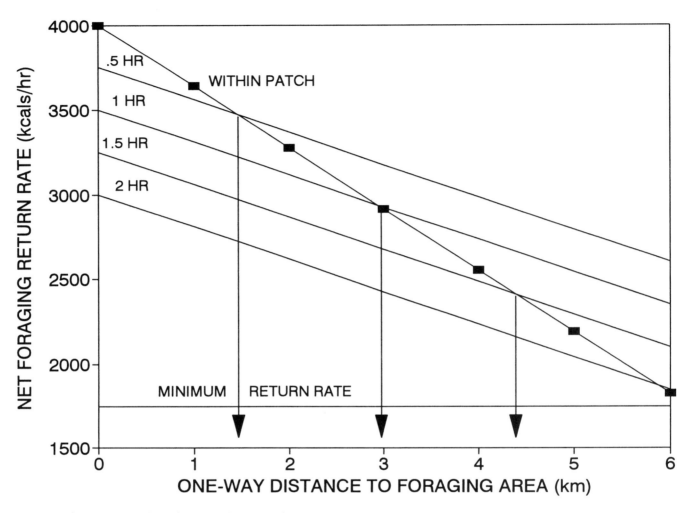

**Figure 4.** The same graph as figure 2, but with four lines generated using camp breakdown times of .5, 1, 1.5, and 2 hours. As camp breakdown and setup time increases (i.e., as the amount of material goods that need to be moved increases), the current camp should be occupied for increasingly longer periods of time as suggested by the increase in the foraging radius.

a one-hour camp setup time for an Arctic group). We can see, however, that increasing or decreasing this time greatly alters the mobility "solution" (fig. 4): a camp breakdown time of two hours makes movement prior to exploitation of food within a 6-km radius not worthwhile, while a breakdown/setup time of one-half hour predicts movement at a 1.5-km foraging radius. As the movement of camp itself becomes more difficult and time-consuming, hunter-gatherers will remain in their current foraging area for longer periods of time, trading the cost of moving for lower foraging return rates. Conversely, if a group must be mobile for ener-

getic reasons (low return rates that result in a short effective foray distance), their housing should be tailored to their mobility needs. Housing and mobility are related to one another (Binford 1990). If housing must be substantial, for example, in the Arctic, then mobility decreases; if on the other hand mobility must be high (as it sometimes is in the Arctic), then housing must be easily transportable (e.g., skin tents) or readily fashioned from local materials (e.g., brush shelters). The decision depends in part on the materials available for housing and/or transport.

## Other Variables: Resource Return Rates, Length of Foraging Day, Time Frames, Risk, and Storage

Referring back to the equations used to generate figure 2 we can see that the within-patch and after-move return rates always equal one another at a foraging radius of about 3 km. Changes in the return rate used (from 4,000 to 1,000, or 10,000) do not alter the predicted outcome even if, as is true for a return rate of 1,000 kcal/hr, it is not possible to forage at an energetic gain at a distance of 3 km. Under circumstances of low return rates, camp breakdown time (and the amount of material possessions) would have to be extremely low. In these cases, foragers might act less like central-place foragers and feed "as they go," behaving in a way that is more in concert with simple optimal foraging models.

We should also note that the rate of decrease in a resource's net return correlates with the slope of the net return line. That is, in figure 1, net returns from collecting the 4,000 kcal/hr resource decrease more rapidly relative to foraging distance than they do for the 3,000 or 1,000 kcal/hr resource. Simms (1987:50–55) found the same relationship in his harvesting experiments. This fact might mean that foragers are more likely to perceive and respond to changes in the availability of high-ranked resources—most likely large game—before they respond to changes in low-ranked resources—most likely plants. This is also a basic prediction of the diet-breadth model. And it means that if women primarily gather plants and men primarily hunt large game, then their respective choices are based on two sets of resources that can lead to different gender-linked mobility decisions.

The length of the foraging day can also affect daily net returns. As high-return-rate resources become more rare, a group of foragers must either move or, as the diet-breadth model predicts, include lower-ranked resources in their diet. The strategy taken depends on the cost and benefits of alternatives. Montagnais hunters, for example, when faced by a low-snowfall winter that made it difficult to track moose (and effectively lowered moose density), broke into smaller groups and increased their residential mobility (Leacock 1954). However, increased mobility can be an expensive option. Take, for example, the effect of unsuccessful moose-hunting among the Beaver Indians of western Canada:

> The first day a hunter without food starts out with a fair prospect of being able to kill a moose. He is able to travel twenty or thirty miles and has a good chance of finding the track of a moose, which he may follow to success. The second day the chances are considerably less and by the third or fourth day the exertion and cold without a supply of food has completely worn him out (Goddard 1916:215).

In this particular case, the Beaver eventually reduced residential mobility and turned to lower-ranked resources by establishing base camps near lakes and taking fish and waterfowl (Goddard 1916:216).

In our model, the foragers could remain in their camp, rather than move, as Sahlins pointed out, and take the lower-return-rate resources. To do so, they would have to spend more and more time collecting and processing food to maintain the same net return. By increasing the work day to 10 hours, for example, a 2,000 kcal/hr resource becomes collectable within a 4-km rather than 1-km radius of camp. However, the longer foragers forage, the less time they have to devote to kin and other nonsubsistence concerns. Thus there is a constant need to evaluate the trade offs involved in foraging more or less. Computer simulations by Winterhalder et al. (1988), for example, suggest that even a small increase in the length of the foraging day may eventually upset the reproductive vitality of the entire foraging band by reducing resources too quickly and by reducing foragers' time allotted to reproduction.

In the model, we assumed that some foraging is done on the day of the move. But this may not be true in many cases. Where no foraging is done on the day of the move, the post-move return rate of the day of a move would be zero. According to the model used here, this would mean that the forager should not move until eating everything within the 6-km radius of camp. In other words, the effective foraging patch should be completely depleted before moving (violating optimal foraging theory's marginal value theorem). This is not supported by ethnographic data (see above and Kelly 1995:132–133).

The answer may lie in the time frame used. In the model used here we assumed hourly return-rate maximization. However, an hour is probably not the relevant time period. Recognizing that there is always some daily variance in returns and that food may not be gathered everyday, foragers probably evaluate resource returns over several days, or even weeks. While moving before exploiting everything within a 3-km radius of camp may result in return-rate depression for a single day, hunter-gatherers may accept this temporary loss knowing that the day after the move the return rate will (in our model) return to 4,000 kcal/hr. Let's assume that the forager achieves a 4,000 kcal/hr

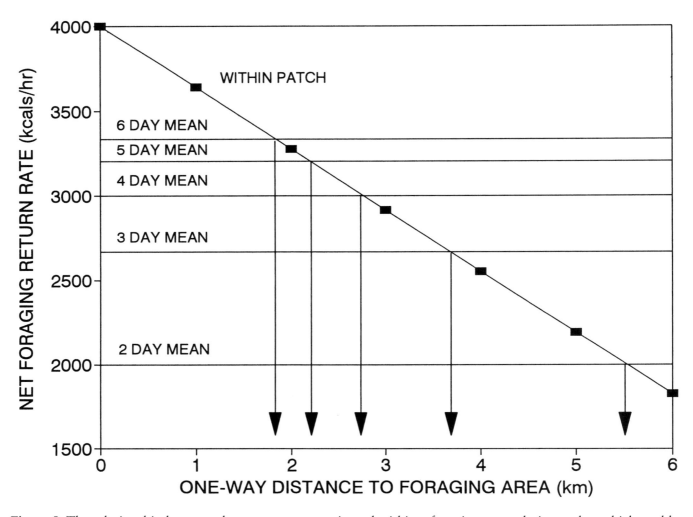

**Figure 5.** The relationship between the return rate experienced within a foraging area relative to that which could be expected if the foragers moved to a new area with after-move return rates averaged over two- to six-day periods. As the period over which after-move return rates are averaged increases, the predicted foraging radius and camp occupation time decreases.

return rate for up to six days after moving but does not forage on the day of the move. As figure 5 shows, depending on the time period over which rates are averaged, the forager stays for different lengths of time than those predicted by a model assuming foraging on the day of the move. For example, if post-move returns are averaged over only two days (0 for the day of the move + 4,000 kcal/hr for the next = 2,000 kcal/hr), the forager should remain at the current camp until consuming everything within 5.5 km of camp. If a four day average is used, then the mean return is increased to 3,000 kcal/hr, and the forager would remain in the cur-

rent camp for a much shorter period of time. Ethnographic data, unfortunately, do not provide much assistance in deciding the appropriate time frame.

The model used here also assumes that hunter-gatherers have a perfect knowledge of the environment and know the state and return rate of anticipated resources. This is, of course, rarely true in reality, and the "cost of moving" should also be weighted in terms of a risk factor. If it is uncertain whether the anticipated resource will be present, then the cost of moving will, in effect, be higher, and we could expect hunter-gatherers to stay longer in their current camp. Many

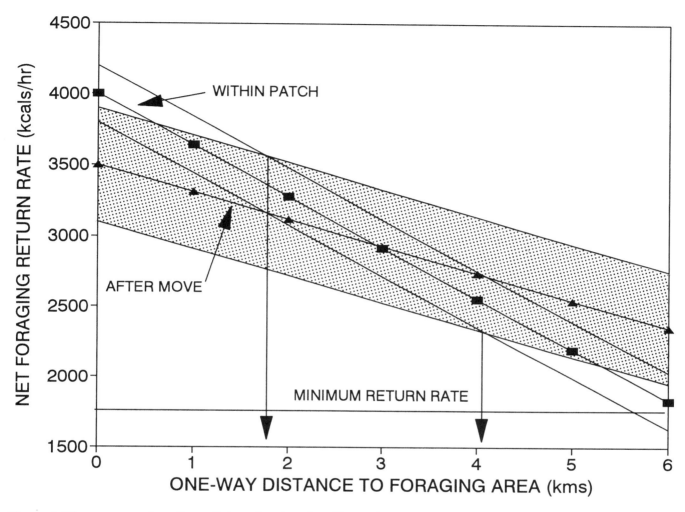

**Figure 6.** The same graph as figure 2, but showing the effects of return-rate variance on decisions to remain in the current camp or move. To maintain as high a return rate as possible, the forager should remain in the current camp until the lower variance limit of the after-move rate equals the lower variance limit of the within-patch rate. Alternatively, to seek risky resources, the forager may move much sooner, when the upper variance limit of the after-move rate exceeds that of the within-patch rate.

desert hunter-gatherers, for example, elect to remain at a water source at the expense of decreasing foraging return rates because they are uncertain of the status of other water holes. They may remain at the current waterhole either until it runs out or the status of other water sources is ascertained. Some Australian Aborigines, in fact, will accept caloric intakes as low as 800 kcal/day and forage up to 15 km from camp rather than move from a secure water source (Cane 1987).

An issue related to risk is return-rate variance. Holding resource type, density, and even forager capa-

bilities constant, there can be a great deal of variability in daily return rates (see, e.g., Cane's 1987 data on lizard return rates for individual Aborigines). How low must a return rate be before foragers move, knowing that variance in the after-move return rate can also be expected? Figure 6 shows the within-patch and after-move return rate lines of figure 1 with a hypothetical ±200 kcal/hr variance limit around the within-patch line and ±400 kcal/hr variance around the after-move line. Thus there is greater variance in the after-move returns, although the mean is the same as the within-patch return. Note that at a foraging radius of 4 km, the lower variance limit of the within-patch rate is equal to the lower limit of the after-move rate. We know very little about whether foragers judge resources in terms of mean return rates or their variance. But if they wanted to maintain as high a rate as possible, foragers might elect to remain in the current patch until after using all resources within 4, rather than 3 km of camp. If correct, this would suggest that as the variance in the next resource or resource area increases relative to that already being exploited, then hunter-gatherers should remain longer in their current camp. On the other hand, we know that foragers, especially males, sometimes seek "risky" resources, ones with high variances because they offer the potential of "bonanzas" that can be shared. If such is the case, they may seek out resources with higher variance (see Gragson 1993; Hawkes 1993) and may consequently move after using resources within only 1.75 km of camp.

Linked to the issue of resource variability is the issue of storage. Storage obviously results in the accumulation of food at one or more locations, thereby increasing the "patchiness" of an environment and according to the model presented here, should encourage decreased residential mobility. Food storage among hunter-gatherers is principally a way to cope with resource seasonality; data show that the volume of stored resources increases with latitude (Binford 1980; Keeley 1988). As was true for resource abundance, however, stored food resources are not a sufficient condition for sedentism. In fact, by assuring some level of food supply, storage can allow foragers to seek out more risky resources. The decision to reside at the location where food is stored or to transport the resources to another location, however, depends on the return from moving one set of resources versus the return rate expected from each area's local resources (Jones and Madsen 1989; Rhode 1990). As we saw above, it also depends on the variance of the return rate of the next anticipated resource. Figure 6 suggests that, given a choice of several resources with similar return rates, hunter-gatherers may move from their current foraging area to that of the resource with the least variance— and there is no variance in the rate of "acquisition" of a food that is already stored. As resource variability increases (which can be the result of a climatic change or an increase in population causing some groups to use more variable resources), hunter-gatherers may invest more in storage and decrease mobility (see Rowley-Conwy and Zvelebil 1989).

We have already noted that technology (e.g., boats, dog sleds, etc.) can reduce the costs of moving and encourage mobility. Changes in technology or subsistence tactics can also alter the return rate of resources and thus affect mobility decisions. The use of pottery for boiling, for example, may increase the benefit of gathering small seeds; preservatives such as pemmican may extend the shelf life of a food; traps may increase the return rate of rodent hunting. By increasing return rates, technology can indirectly reduce or increase mobility. Of course, the trade offs of manufacturing this technology must be considered—for time devoted to technology is time not devoted to something else. Nets, for example, can vastly increase returns from fishing (Lindström 1996) but have high up-front costs (especially small mesh nets) and high maintenance costs. Models of the sedentization process must consider the trade offs between mobility, technology, and social activities.

Finally, we must note that not all residential movements are directly controlled by subsistence. People may move to gain access to firewood, raw materials, or because insects have become intolerable at the current camp. Movements can be socially or politically motivated as well, as people seek spouses, allies, or shamans or seek to distance themselves from sorcery, death, and political forces. People may move to relieve social tension, to visit friends and relatives, trade, gamble, participate in rituals, or just catch up on news (see Kelly 1995:147–148). Some movements made for social reasons, however, can ultimately be related to foraging. For example, during a period of drought-induced food stress, some /Xia/xai Bushmen finally said that they were going elsewhere to trade, but this was after two weeks of bickering over food (Wiessner 1982). Leaving ostensibly to trade gave the Bushmen a socially acceptable excuse for moving, because leaving for lack of food might have implicitly accused others of stinginess.

Furthermore, residential mobility itself may be culturally valued. There are, in fact, a few cases of hunter-gatherers who move despite the fact that they could be sedentary (see, e.g., Meehan 1982). Members of modern or formerly mobile hunter-gatherer societies often express a strong desire to move around in order to visit friends, to see what's happening elsewhere, or to relieve boredom (see Kelly 1995:153). Among the Hare, traveling is a metaphor for freedom (Savishinsky 1974:120), and the Kaska did not like "sitting one place all the time like white men" (Honigmann 1949:102). On the other hand, the sedentary coastal Tlingit used dance to parody interior boreal forest peoples who, in their opinion, wandered about in a pathetic search for food (McClellan 1975:96), and the recently settled G//ana of the Kalahari likewise "speak disparagingly of residents of the Central Reserve who have no fixed home base as 'moving around like animals'" (Cashdan 1984:323). Most people are unfortunately ethnocentric, and they value their lifestyle over others. Cultural norms valuing movement might encourage mobility even where it is possible to be sedentary. Such norms may help perpetuate cultural and niche differences between populations of horticulturalists and hunter-gatherers/pastoralists, since mobility can be a strategy to maintain cultural autonomy. However, the desire to remain mobile does not account for large-scale evolutionary changes, since being mobile must be adaptive at some level for the population.

## DISCUSSION

Many factors affect individual foraging and consequently the decision to move as families or other social groups. How do these factors relate to sedentism, the concern of this volume?

Two basic hypotheses have been proposed to explain hunter-gatherer sedentism that Price and Brown (1985) label the "pull" and "push" hypotheses. In the "pull" hypothesis, the presence of abundant resources ipso facto results in sedentism: abundant resources are necessary and sufficient conditions of a sedentary lifestyle. Alternatively, the "push" hypothesis proposes that foragers are forced into sedentism because of subsistence stress. In this case, as efficiently gathered resources become scarce, previously unutilized secondary or "starvation" foods become more central to foraging efforts. Here, hunter-gatherers trade increased resource harvesting costs for residential mobility.

In the model above (fig. 2), the length of time foragers could remain at the current camp depends on the density of the food resource relative to band size. Assuming that the 4,000 kcal/hr resource once harvested and processed provides .25 kcal/m², then the 6-km-radius patch could potentially be occupied by a 25 member band for $[(3.14 * 6000^2) * .25]/(3 * 14,000) = 673$ days—nearly two years. But by leaving after foraging within a 3-km radius, as predicted, the band occupies the patch for 168 days, and the option to be sedentary is ignored. We can also predict that if a seasonal resource appears elsewhere that provides a return rate higher than 4,000 kcal/hr, the group would move even more quickly, namely, when the new resource's return rate minus the cost of moving was higher than the return rate in the current camp.

Changing the after-move return rate in the equations to only 4,500 kcal/hr (while leaving the within-patch return rate at 4,000 kcal/hr) predicts that foragers should leave after using the resources within only a .5-km radius of the current camp.

In sum, even though foragers could remain in a patch and forage from a single camp for well over a year, they should still leave that camp long before patch depletion occurs—and long before the maximum time the camp could be occupied is reached—if they wish to maintain a high daily return rate. Even in an area that could support a group of hunter-gatherers for a year or more, and leaving aside other factors that could encourage movement, foragers should still move. Eric Smith (1991), in fact, suggests that the marginal value theorem predicts that foragers should be more residentially mobile in an environment of high-return-rate resources than in one of low return rates. *In an environment of homogeneously distributed resources, even if the resources have high return rates, the only apparent reason hunter-gatherers would not move is if there was no place to move to.* I imagine that the conditions under which this would happen are ones in which population growth reaches a point where movements become limited. This could be expected to happen in environments requiring only a few hours of foraging each day to meet daily needs. Where this is the case, people can devote more time to reproduction and child rearing, which generate more offspring and allow a greater percentage of those born to survive (Winterhalder et al. 1988). If foraging is not arduous and food plentiful, then physiological constraints on female fecundity will be relaxed, including long-term energy balance, the effects of extreme aerobic work efforts, and the early cessation of breast-feeding (see Kelly 1995:chap. 6), increasing fecundity and possibly the population growth rate.

Where resources are not homogeneously distributed, sedentism could result from a combination of factors including the distance between potential foraging areas (which will be affected by population growth, for if a foraging area is already occupied, then the distance to the next foraging area is even farther, and we would predict an increased length of occupation of the current camp). Likewise, if there is a large amount of material goods to be moved (e.g., if housing material will likely not be available at the next potential site), or if difficult terrain must be crossed, or if the foragers cannot be sure of the reliability of the anticipated resources at the next camp, then the current camp will be occupied longer.

In sum, we may state that residential movement should cease if the anticipated return rate of the next patch minus the cost of moving is greater than the anticipated return rate of the patch currently occupied and, of course, if it is feasible for the forager to remain in the current patch (either because it provides a continuous supply of resources or because a storable resource is present). Put in more simple terms, *sedentism is also a product of local abundance in a context of effective regional scarcity.* But a number of variables enter into what constitutes local abundance and regional scarcity and whether or not a group decides to move itself to a new location. The use of marine resources by high-latitude hunter-gatherers, resources that in many instances are available only at particular locations, may encourage decreased residential mobility (see Renouf 1987; Rowley-Conwy and Zvelebil 1989). The situation of Arctic groups is exacerbated by high mobility costs at particular times of the year due to housing and traveling costs. The villages along North America's Northwest Coast may also be an example of sedentism as a product of local abundance (salmon, marine mammals, shellfish) in the context of low effective regional (terrestrial) return rates created by the dense forests and rugged terrain of the interior (Kelly 1991, 1995). Sedentary Natufian villages of the Epi-Paleolithic in the Levant may also be a product of patchily distributed wild grains (see Bar-Yosef 1987). It is not just the "abundance" of these resources that matters, but their return rates (which are affected by technology and tactics) and the cost of moving from one location to another (of which distance between patches is only one variable).

While hunter-gatherers require a continuously available local food base in order to be sedentary (and remain foragers), and while population/resource imbalances may lead to sedentism, it is insufficient to say that sedentism is a function of either resource stress or resource abundance; neither the Pull nor the Push hypothesis fully captures the sedentization process. In areas of homogeneously distributed high-return-rate resources, slow population growth may eventually result in population packing and density-dependent sedentism. In areas of patchily distributed resources, sedentism could result from a combination of population growth and/or environmental conditions affecting camp move times and the cost of foraging versus moving.

In both instances, and in terms of "archaeological time," sedentism should occur instantaneously over fairly large areas. Since the movements of one group are predicated on the movements of others, once one group elects to remain sedentary, their foraging patch is taken out of the effective environment, thus making the environment more patchy (see Rowley-Conwy and Zvelebil 1989:56) even in a region of homogeneously distributed food resources. Like dominoes, one sedentary community may force others into similar lifeways. On the other hand, if a sufficient number of communities become sedentary, then others may be forced into mobile foraging in the interstices between these communities. We should not expect to see in any case a simple progression from nomadic to sedentary communities, but we can expect some cases to show progressive movement in that direction while others show oscillations between sedentism and mobility (Ames 1991), and all show a complex geographic network of nomadic and sedentary peoples (with horticulture eventually entering the picture in many areas).

While it is likely that the conditions resulting in sedentism also promote increased fertility and decreased infant mortality, resulting in population growth and its attendant problems (Kelly 1995), these are differently related to the two general scenarios outlined here. In the first case, sedentism is a product of population increase and should be immediately (again, in archaeological time) accompanied by other behaviors that are linked to high population density. In the second case, these may take some time to appear, as population growth will occur after sedentism, and we should not find evidence of density-dependent behaviors in the initial phases of sedentization.

Analyses of archaeological cases of sedentary hunter-gatherers concentrate on descriptions of locally available resources, often hailing the abundance and efficiency of their collection. Yet abundance and efficiency can only be measured relative to their alternatives. Understanding sedentism requires that we study the resources *not* harvested by prehistoric sedentary foragers as well as those that were used. It also requires modeling the relationships between foraging in one location versus moving and foraging in another area.

If sedentism has implications for sociopolitical organization, and ethnographic data strongly indicate that is does (Keeley 1988), then sedentism resulting from different conditions may have different implications for the evolution of other aspects of forager economy, society, and politics. Following the older argument that sedentism is a product of resource abundance, several authors suggest that sedentary hunter-gatherers simply have more time and resources to devote to what Gould (1982) calls "aggrandizing" behavior. Ethnographically known sedentary hunter-gatherers do devote much time to prestige competition, but it is unlikely that they do so because of more time or resource wealth. More likely, this competition is a response to the conditions imposed on them by sedentism (this idea is developed in more detail in Kelly 1995). Sedentism does not lift the constraints of a mobile lifestyle as much as it replaces them with new ones. Since sedentism occurs when, or eventually results in situations where, mobility is no longer a viable option, sedentary hunter-gatherers must use other mechanisms to cope with resource failure (Cohen 1981). These may include warfare, increased household storage, restricted sharing networks, slavery, control of wives' labor (and increased gender inequality), and manipulation of sisters'/daughters' marriages and the exploitation of their spouses. While it is quite common to discuss nonegalitarian hunter-gatherers today as a single group, usually termed "complex" hunter-gatherers, discussion here suggests that we should anticipate variability within this category. Understanding the factors bearing upon residential mobility is critical to understanding the important evolutionary transition from egalitarian to nonegalitarian societies.

## Acknowledgments

I thank Ofer Bar-Yosef, Eric Ingbar, Tom Rocek, Steve Simms, and John Speth for their comments on earlier versions of this paper and Elizabeth Cashdan and Eric Smith for providing me with the opportunity to present an earlier version at the Sixth International Conference on Hunting and Gathering Societies in Fairbanks, Alaska, June 1, 1990. None of them are responsible for any of the paper's shortcomings. A more detailed version of this chapter can be found in Kelly (1995).

# BIBLIOGRAPHY

Ames, K. M.
  1991 "Sedentism: A Temporal Shift or a Transitional Change in Hunter-Gatherer Mobility Patterns," in *Between Bands and States*, S. A. Gregg, ed., pp. 108–134. Center for Archaeological Investigations Occasional Paper 9. Southern Illinois University Press, Carbondale, Illinois.

Bar-Yosef, O.
  1987 "Late Pleistocene Adaptation in the Levant," in *The Pleistocene Old World*, O. Soffer, ed., pp. 219–236. Plenum Press, New York.

Beardsley, R. K., P. Holder, A. Krieger, M. Meggers, J. Rinaldo, and P. Kutsche
  1956 "Functional and Evolutionary Implications of Community Patterning." *American Antiquity* 22(2):129–157. Seminars in Archaeology, 1955. Society for American Archaeology Memoir 11. Reprint. Bobbs-Merrill Reprint Series in the Social Sciences, Indianapolis, 1956.

Binford, L. R.
  1980 "Willow Smoke and Dogs' Tails: Hunter-Gatherer Settlement Systems and Archaeological Site Formation." *American Antiquity* 45:4–20.
  1990 "Mobility, Housing, and Environment: A Comparative Study." *Journal of Anthropological Research* 46:119–152.

Blurton Jones, N. G., K. Hawkes, and P. Draper
  1994 "Differences Between Hadza and !Kung Children's Work: Original Affluence or Practical Reason?" in *Key Issues in Hunter-Gatherer Research*, E. S. Burch, Jr. and L. Ellanna, eds., pp. 189–215. Berg, Oxford.

Burch, E.
  1988 "Models of Exchange in North-West Alaska," in *Hunters and Gatherers*. Vol. 2, *Property, Power and Ideology*, T. Ingold, D. Riches, and J. Woodburn, eds., pp. 95–109. Berg, Oxford.

Cane, S.
  1987 "Australian Aboriginal Subsistence in the Western Desert." *Human Ecology* 15:391–434.

Cashdan, E.
  1984 "G//ana Territorial Organization." *Human Ecology* 12:443–463.

Cohen, M. N.
  1981 "Pacific Coast Foragers: Affluent or Overcrowded?" in *Affluent Foragers*, S. Koyama and D. H. Thomas, eds., pp. 275–295. Senri Ethnological Studies 9. National Museum of Ethnology, Osaka, Japan.

Goddard, P.
  1916 *The Beaver Indians*. Anthropological Papers of the American Museum of Natural History 10. New York.

Gould, R. A.
  1982 "To Have and Have Not: The Ecology of Food Sharing Among Hunter-Gatherers," in *Resource Managers: North American and Australia Hunter-Gatherers*, N. M. Williams and E. S. Hunn, eds., pp. 69–91. American Association for the Advancement of Science Selected Symposium 67. Westview Press, Boulder, Colorado.

Gragson, T.
 1993 "Human Foraging in Lowland South America: Pattern and Process of Resource Procurement." *Research in Economic Anthropology* 14:107–138.

Hawkes, K.
 1993 "Why HunterGatherers Work: An Ancient Version of the Problem with Public Goods." *Current Anthropology* 34:341–362.

Honigmann, J. J.
 1949 *Culture and Ethos of Kaska Society*. Yale University Publications in Anthropology 40. New Haven, Connecticut.

Jones, K. T., and D. B. Madsen
 1989 "Calculating the Cost of Resource Transportation: A Great Basin Example." *Current Anthropology* 30:529–534.

Keeley, L. H.
 1988 "Hunter-Gatherer Economic Complexity and 'Population Pressure': A Cross-Cultural Analysis." *Journal of Anthropological Archaeology* 7:373–411.

Kelly, R. L.
 1990 "Marshes and Mobility in the Western Great Basin," in *Wetlands Adaptations in the Great Basin*, J. C. Janetski and D. B. Madsen, eds., pp. 259–276. Museum of Peoples and Cultures Occasional Papers 1. Brigham Young University, Provo, Utah.
 1991 "Sedentism, Sociopolitical Inequality, and Resource Fluctuations," in *Between Bands and States*, S. A. Gregg, ed., pp. 135–158. Center for Archaeological Investigations Occasional Paper 9. Southern Illinois University Press, Carbondale, Illinois.
 1992 "Mobility/Sedentism: Concepts, Archaeological Measures, and Effects." *Annual Review of Anthropology* 21:43–66.
 1995 *The Foraging Spectrum: Diversity in Hunter-Gatherer Lifeways*. Smithsonian Institution Press, Washington, D.C.

Leacock, E.
 1954 *The Montagnais Hunting Territory and the Fur Trade*. American Anthropological Association Memoir 78. Menasha, Wisconsin.

Lindström, S.
 1996 "Great Basin Fisherfolk: Optimal Diet Breadth Modeling of the Truckee River Subsistence Aboriginal Fishery," in *Hunter-Gatherer Fishing Strategies*, M. G. Plew, ed., pp. 114-179. Boise State University Press, Boise, Idaho.

McClellan, C.
 1975 *My Old People Say: An Ethnographic Survey of Southern Yukon Territory*. National Museum of Man Publications in Ethnology 6. Ottawa, Canada.

Meehan, B.
 1982 *Shell Bed to Shell Midden*. Australian Institute of Aboriginal Studies, Canberra.

Price, T. D., and J. A. Brown
 1985 "Aspects of Hunter-Gatherer Complexity," in *Prehistoric Hunter-Gatherers: The Emergence of Cultural Complexity*, T. D. Price and J. A. Brown, eds., pp. 3–20. Academic Press, New York.

Rai, N.
 1990 *Living in a Lean-To: Philippine Negrito Foragers in Transition*. Anthropological Papers 80. Museum of Anthropology, University of Michigan, Ann Arbor.

Renouf, M.
 1987 "Sedentary Coastal Hunter-Fishers: An Example from the Younger Stone Age of Northern Norway," in *Archaeology of Prehistoric Coastlines*, G. Bailey and J. Parkington, eds., pp. 102–115. Cambridge University Press, Cambridge.

Rhode, D.
 1990 "On Transportation Costs of Great Basin Resources: An Assessment of the Jones-Madsen Model." *Current Anthropology* 31:413–419.

Rowley-Conwy, P., and M. Zvelebil
 1989 "Saving it for Later: Storage by Prehistoric Hunter-Gatherers in Europe," in *Bad Year Economics*, P. Halstead and J. O'Shea, eds., pp. 40–56. Cambridge University Press, Cambridge.

Sahlins, M. D.
 1972 *Stone Age Economics*. Aldine, Chicago.

Savishinsky, J.
 1974 *The Trail of the Hare*. Gordon and Breach Science Publishers, New York.

Simms, S. R.
 1987 *Behavioral Ecology and Hunter-Gatherer Foraging: An Example from the Great Basin*. British Archaeological Reports, International Series 381. Oxford.

Smith, E. A.
 1991 *Inujjuamiut Foraging Strategies*. Aldine de Gruyter, Hawthorne, New York.

Tanaka, J.
1980 *The San Hunter-Gatherers of the Kalahari: A Study in Ecological Anthropology.* University of Tokyo Press, Tokyo.

Wiessner, P.
1982 "Risk, Reciprocity and Social Influences on !Kung San Economics," in *Politics and History in Band Societies*, E. Leacock and R. Lee, eds., pp. 61–84. Cambridge University Press, Cambridge.

Winterhalder, B., W. Baillageon, F. Cappelletto, I. R. Daniel, Jr., and C. Prescott
1988 "The Population Ecology of Hunter-Gatherers and Their Prey." *Journal of Anthropological Archaeology* 7:289–328.

Woodburn, J.
1968 "An Introduction to Hadza Ecology," in *Man the Hunter*, R. B. Lee and I. DeVore, eds., pp. 49–55. Aldine, Chicago.

# CHAPTER 3

# The Mobile Faunas: Reliable Seasonal Indicators for Archaeozoologists?

*Arturo Morales Muñiz*

*Universidad Autónoma de Madrid*

## Abstract

Species found at a site can be used in seasonality analysis as long as the inferential basis upon which the analysis rests (i.e., the concept of analogues sensu Baird 1989) is assumed to hold. Phenologies, however, tend to be extremely labile phenomena and drastic phenological status shifts in the recent past are well documented. Since most analyses of seasonality are pushed back to the Pleistocene-Holocene transition, one can expect such phenological shifts to have occurred at least as frequently in the more distant past as well. Without a clear phenological status assignment of the taxa from a particular site, the whole inferential building collapses and patterns evidenced by subfossil faunas, no matter how "evident," might be completely misleading. Using birds as seasonal indicators, the paper concludes by discussing one case study from two sites in southern Spain.

## INTRODUCTION

Four kinds of animal remains are taken to provide evidence of seasonal occupation in archaeological sites: (1) seasonally deposited hard tissues, (2) hard tissues that are worn down at known rates, (3) hard tissues undergoing identifiable changes in a particular time of the year, and (4) species (sensu lato) present in a given location in a particular time of the year (Davis 1987:76). In addition, in certain taxa, both sex ratios and demographic parameters can be helpful in this same context.

None of these methods provide accurate "point estimates" and the overall accuracy of the analysis relies upon the use of modern analogues as defined by Baird (Lundelius 1983; Baird 1989). Furthermore, the validity of the application of the analogue concept is determined by the amount and quality of the data we have on the biology of both the animals and the tissues under consideration; at present, these are restricted to very few taxa (Münzel 1983; Baglinière et al. 1992). It should be stressed that this line of argument must precede other considerations when dealing with a particular sample. This requirement applies both to instances when a taphocenosis[1] can be safely organized into taphonomic groups (Gautier 1987) and the different site formation processes, including cultural factors, can be set apart and to those instances when this is not the case. Some further considerations to be taken into account in the case of individual animals include:

(1) The biological "plasticity" of species. In general, the more stenoecious[2] a taxon, the more predictable its association with specific environmental parameters. In the case of seasonal taxa, for example, obligate migrators are more predictable in their phenologies[3] than facultative migrators (Bernis 1966; Baker 1978; Alerstam 1990). Seasonal inference can be enhanced, then, by the adequate selection of target taxa.

(2) The life-cycle stage selected. Juveniles are unequivocal indicators of breeding, as are female birds with medullary bone (Driver 1982) or deer with grown antlers. Their association with specific stages of the year is thus greater than the one exhibited by other cohorts. As in the case of target taxa, one should try to base seasonal analysis on the adequate (target) life stage.

(3) The environment being sampled. As Avery and Underhill (1986:339) have properly stressed, "In higher

latitude regions the marked effect of climatic extremes causes the movements and breeding of many species to be highly predictable." In this situation, the seasons at which animals are exploited can be accurately determined.

These three constraints (target taxa, life stages, and places) are not fixed. Archaeozoologists have to work during temporal periods (Pleistocene and Holocene) when climatic fluctuations have been the rule. On most occasions, one has to determine in advance many complementary parameters in order to make sure that the extrapolation of analogues will produce meaningful results.

The correct assignment of season has a wide range of applications for the study of human evolution. It has also provided some spectacular results ranging from the seasonal dating of burials through fish vertebrae (Casteel 1972) or the determination of the hunting season for aurochs during the Danish Mesolithic (Richter 1982) to the shift to sedentism in Israel as evidenced by the seasonal dating of gazelles' teeth (Davis 1983) and the seasonal cropping of birds along South Africa's coastlines during the Holocene (Avery and Underhill 1986). For these reasons one must not miss the chance to investigate seasonality whenever possible. But this does not automatically guarantee good results.

In the remainder of this paper we explore the theoretical possibilities of seasonal analysis in the case of the Iberian bird fauna and their practical consequences in a couple of Spanish cave sites. These sites have important implications for the evolution of Paleolithic communities in the Mediterranean regions of the peninsula.

## A BRIEF PHENOLOGICAL CONSIDERATION OF THE IBERIAN AVIFAUNA

Though the Iberian peninsula is considered a mild geographical area, its peculiar location and orography ensure not only a varied range of climates but also a strong oceanic-continental gradient, with the inner regions exhibiting rather extreme climatic fluctuation. Compressed within Iberia we find climates which range from those of subtropical Africa to those of Northern Europe. The Pleistocene witnessed widespread mountain glaciation as well as climates close to tropical conditions (Costa et al. 1990). In order to make meaningful statements about faunal samples, archaeozoologists

must beware of the range of past and present climatic situations one might possibly encounter. In particular, one must beware to what extent the degree of seasonality varied during the Pleistocene and Holocene, for without a thorough knowledge of this, the analogue models may be useless.

Systematic phenological data collection for birds did not start in Spain until the late sixties (Bernis 1966). For this reason, the extent and accuracy of these records, though acceptable, is still not comparable to that found in neighboring countries. Some general facts are, nevertheless, evident:

(1) With some 500 bird species, the Iberian avifauna includes many taxa from both migratory (including both facultative [i.e., summer and winter visitors] and obligate [i.e., strict migrants]) and resident species. In many instances, the division between these two categories can be misleading. Many resident species increase their winter populations through an influx of wintering birds (Anatidae being the most dramatic example) thus qualifying in more than one phenological category (Sociedad Española de Ornitologia 1985).

(2) Among wintering birds, special note should be taken of those species that have been breeding in Iberia until very recent times but that no longer do. Cranes (*Grus grus*) bred in Spain for the last time in 1953 (Bernis 1966). Other species that are suspected breeders in the peninsula during this century include the greylag goose (*Anser anser*), but the list would probably be much longer had it not been for our scarcity of phenological records (Bernis 1966).

(3) Since quite a few winter visitors are facultative rather than obligate (Alerstam 1990), their movements tend to be less predictable than in aestival (early summer) breeders.[4] Irruptions, sudden mass displacements of northern species into the peninsula during a cold wave, happen almost every year, filling the territory with such "exotic" birds as waxwings (*Bombycilla garrulus*) or swans (*Cygnus olor*). These phenomena may be illustrative of more regular displacements that occurred in the past (e.g., during glaciation periods) and also give a hint as to what taxa could have been regular components of our past bird communities.

(4) Though most summer visitors are aestival breeders, one should not forget what Bernis (1966) calls "tourists," that is, winter visitors that do not return for breeding to central and northern Europe. The reasons for this phenomenon are still not that clear (i.e., the most affected taxa are slow-developing birds such as some gulls and waders which might not breed for some years) and the causes are probably multiple (e.g., curlews [g. *Numenius*] and godwits [g. *Limosa*] have

lately become abundant on plains artificially flooded for rice cultivation in southwest Spain, so trophic disjunctions might also be involved). But the fact remains clear; as in the previous case, all these species warn us to be ready to make phenological status shifts at any moment and for the same reason, not to be too dogmatic with official records (Bernis 1988a, 1988b).

(5) By far the most elusive category of Iberian avifaunas is that of migratory birds, animals that cross past the peninsula and that, at most, stop for "refueling." Many of these animals are recorded in the official lists as either "vagrant," "occasional," or "obligatory migrants," depending on the frequency of observation, but this is nothing more than an arbitrary division. It is among these taxa that one should expect the most dramatic phenological status changes to have taken place in the past. This is especially so if one takes into account the continental glaciations during the Pleistocene, which completely upset marine currents and available ground for breeding on the European subcontinent (CLIMAP 1976; McIntyre et al. 1976). From this viewpoint, we are more in agreement with Jenkinson and Sutherland's "Pleistocene Inheritance Model" of bird migration (1984) than we are with the "Flandrian Model" discussed by Moreau (1954), Mayr and Meise (1980), and Curry-Lindhal (1981).

## PHENOLOGICAL PATTERNS: SOME FURTHER CONSIDERATIONS

Though the phenological status of many bird taxa can be established in a rather straightforward manner, if phenological data are going to be used to infer the pattern of occupation at a particular site, certain points should be kept in mind:

(1) A phenological status assignment is necessarily a compromise that has been reached through reconciliation of occasionally conflicting data. As such, it is very seldom an indisputable fact. For example, almost all guillemots (*Uria aalge*) found nowadays in the Iberian peninsula are winter visitors. The fact that some isolated pairs still breed in some spots of the northwestern peninsular coasts has granted this species its official "resident" status (de Juana 1991). Much the same applies to Cory's shearwater (*Calonectrix diomedea*), a migratory species that qualifies as a summer visitor in the official record only because it happens to be more frequent at that particular time of the year (fig. 1D). On the other hand, many pelagic birds

recorded as migratory species (de Juana 1991) also qualify as winter visitors, a classification that could be extended to other species such as the Ruddy shelduck (*Tadorna ferruginea*), assigned to the "vagrant" or "occasional" categories due to its very low number of recorded occurrences. Though the list could go on forever, the message should be clear; phenological status assignments are arbitrary and are found to be more so the more we learn about the animals themselves.

(2) Since migratory movements are gradual events dependent on a host of exogenous and endogenous triggers, the occurrence of particular species during specific stages of the annual cycle can change a lot even among close geographical areas. Latitudinal gradients in phenologies are particularly illustrative. Figure 2 records the earliest and latest occurrences of five seasonal species (two swallows, two swifts, and the cuckoo) in three regions of the Iberian Peninsula: (A) Andalucia (southern Spain), (B) Extremadura (central Spain), and (C) the Basque country (northern Spain). Notwithstanding the fact that some of the earliest and latest records might be difficult to observe due to low densities or to the adoption of more seclusive habits by some species (cuckoos, for example, stop singing after breeding), there is a clear pattern emerging with lower latitudes (which yield milder climates) exhibiting a not-so-concentrated presence of each species during the annual cycle. The fact that in more benign environmental circumstances the seasonal character of the bird fauna is relaxed should remind archaeozoologists not to extrapolate data from their own countries, normally of medium-high latitude, to subfossil samples subjected to weaker seasonal fluctuations (Eastham 1988). Any paleoenvironmental data that indicate milder climates should be taken as a signal for caution.

(3) Many migratory species are known to be much more erratic in their movements than previously suspected. Figures 1A, 1B, and 1C depict three successive phenological records for Yelkouan's shearwater in the Bay of Málaga (southern Spain). Despite similar recording effort and homogeneous conditions of analysis, the populational shifts from year to year are very clear (Patterson 1987). As a matter of fact, from the data available, it would be difficult to assign the species to a single, clear-cut phenological group. Even though not all migratory species display such a degree of variation, the lesson for the paleoenvironmental analyst should, once again, be clear.

(4) Phenological status can shift swiftly. Sometimes the causes are well known (e.g., Iberian storks becoming resident birds due to accommodation to feeding in dumpyards during the last decade [Lázaro

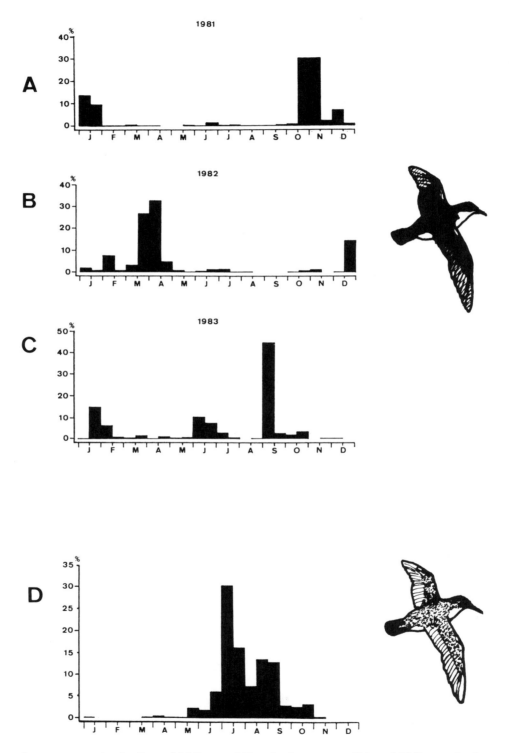

**Figure 1.** Seasonal movements in the Bay of Málaga of Cory's shearwater (D) and Yelkouan's shearwater (A, B, C). The erratic migrations of Yelkouan's shearwater might occur during almost any time of the year, while Cory's shearwater migration, though concentrated during the "summer" (sensu lato) interval of the year, practically covers the whole annual period. For the archaeozoologist's purposes, the low frequency stages might be just as important as the high frequency, for they might hold the key to shifts that might have taken place in the past. Data taken from Patterson (1987), with modifications.

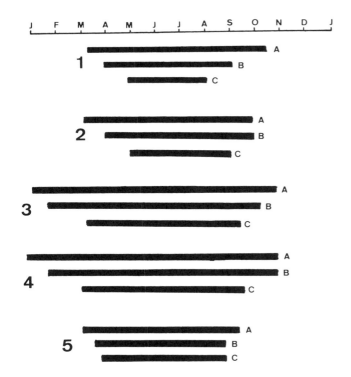

**Figure 2.** Phenological data on five summer visitors (1: *Apus apus*, 2: *Apus melba*, 3: *Hirundo rustica*, 4: *Delichon urbica*, and 5: *Cucculus canorus*) in three latitudes of the Iberian peninsula (A: Andalucia [southern Spain], B: Extremadura [central Spain], and C: Basque country [northern Spain]). A restriction of residential periods as one moves northwards is evident. For the archaeozoologist, however, the important aspect is the opposite one (i.e., the relaxation or disappearance of the seasonal character at lower latitudes for some species) (data taken from Santos and Tellería 1977; Aguilar 1980; de Juana 1982; Finlayson, 1992).

1984]). Sometimes these causes can only be imagined (why did cranes breed in Spain until 1953 and not thereafter?). One way or the other, fast switches in phenological status evidence the weaknesses in the use of analogues in paleoseasonality studies (Bernis 1988a, 1988b; Berthold et al. 1992). If this is the case for extant species, what could one postulate about the phenologies of extinct ones (but see table 2)?

(5) However, by far the greatest dangers the archaeozoologist faces in these types of analysis come from biases distorting the situation recorded in a sam-

ple. One of these biases is taxonomic. Thus it is not only clear that in countries such as Spain there are more summer visitors than wintering birds, but also that summer birds normally responding to endogenous drives are, as a rule, better "quality-indicators" than wintering taxa whose drives are exogenous to a large extent (Baker 1978; Alerstam 1990). Actually, in the Iberian peninsula, a winter community is better characterized by its absences than by its presences (Tellería 1988).

While not denying the above statements, a series of biases favors the presence of winter visitors in archaeozoological samples and these biases, in the long run, may prove more important than those favoring summer visitors. For one thing, except for prey birds, most aestival breeders tend to be small-sized passerines while winter visitors, whether ducks, geese, waders, or marine birds, are on average much larger. Also, most of the latter taxa are easier to identify than the osteologically uniform passerines and, at any rate, their large size ensures higher retrieval probabilities in archaeological sediments even if sieving and flotation techniques are practiced (Grayson 1984). Finally, and this might well be the most important point, many winter visitors constitute important economic resources, even today, not only because of their larger size but also because of their gregarious behavior, which optimizes hunting effort. Summer visitors, except for a few colonial species such as bee-eaters or house martins, tend to be dispersed to a much larger extent due to territorial behavior.

As a corollary of the last point, one should also beware that places such as plains, deltas, lakes, and so on, which favor the concentration of birds, whether strictly migratory or winter residents, and places located along migratory routes (shores, in particular) will have a larger share of seasonal indicators in their samples simply because of chance (Avery and Underhill 1986). For this reason, sites located around these areas will not be strictly comparable with sites where the presence of resident taxa is not so affected by periodic massive influxes of newcomers.

All these limitations are reasons for concern. In fact, at times one might indeed feel overwhelmed by so many potential drawbacks and start questioning the validity of the whole inferential process. But before surrendering, one should at least try once to apply these "theoretical" considerations in the operative framework of a real situation.

## Two Case Studies: Cueva de Nerja and Zafarraya

Cueva de Nerja and Zafarraya are two cave sites from the province of Málaga in southern Spain. At present, Nerja is 1 km from the coast whereas Zafarraya lies some 20 km farther inland (fig. 3). Both sites are located on hilly terrain with abundant cliffs.

Chronologically, Cueva de Nerja has an occupation that ranges from late Pleistocene well into the Holocene (approximately 15,000–1800 B.P.) (Jordá 1986). Culturally, the occupation has two well-defined stages: (a) Magdalenian–Epipaleolithic (GAK 8965: 14,570 ± 540 B.P. & GAK 8976: 11,380 ± 270 B.P.) and (b) Neolithic–Chalcolithic (GAK 8973: 5210 ± 180 B.P. & GAK 8960: 2860 ± 220 B.P. The sequence from Cueva de Nerja is interesting, for it offers the faunal analyst the possibility to follow the economic strategy from a hunter-gatherer situation to a stage with domestication. It further offers the possibility of checking whether these two economic strategies could possibly be correlated with a shift from a seasonal occupation of the cave during Paleolithic times to a more permanent (i.e., sedentary) condition in the Neolithic.

No such possibility exists in Zafarraya. This site, which has been dated with Uranium-Thorium back to Mousterian times (dates ranging from 29,500–25,500 B.P.) has become famous for its Neanderthal remains, apparently the youngest in Europe (Barroso and Medina 1989; Barroso et al. 1993). No faunal reports have been published but the archaeological papers stress the intensive hunting of wild goat, *Capra pyrenaica* (more than 90 percent of the identified remains), and a peculiar assortment of carnivores where the Indian wild dog, *Cuon alpinus*, dominates the assemblage (Barroso, pers. comm.). The birds are at present being studied at our laboratory (Hernández n.d.). Though taphonomic analyses have not been completed, it seems clear that at both sites the large majority of the fauna became incorporated as a result of human activities.

Table 1 presents the preliminary results from Zafarraya, whereas table 2 presents those from the Paleolithic levels of Nerja and table 3 presents those from its Neolithic levels. Tables 2 and 3 will be dealt with as a homogeneous sample since the different analyses will be taken as a single unit (Boessneck and Driesch 1980; Eastham 1986; Hernández 1995).

The first striking thing is the low number of identified remains (NR) in all samples. Since the sediments were sieved and great numbers of small fish remains

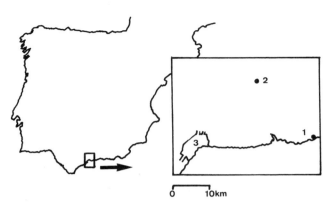

**Figure 3.** Location of Cueva de Nerja (1) and Zafarraya (2). The city of Málaga is number 3.

were found in all samples (Roselló et al. 1995), one must conclude that bird remains were, in fact, infrequent items of the taphocenosis. This pattern agrees with findings of bird remains in other sites and archaeological contexts (Ervynck 1993).[5]

The second general pattern is diversity. The Paleolithic levels of Nerja have the richest avifauna while that from Zafarraya has the poorest. There is an obvious correlation of this parameter with sample size (see bottom lines in tables 1, 2, and 3).

In order to compare the samples for seasonality analysis, the species lists have been turned into "phenolograms" by assigning each species the official phenological status (first column of tables 1, 2, and 3) following de Juana (1991) and then adding their NR into each one of the five phenological categories considered (winter and summer visitors, residents, migratory, and "others"). The results are shown in figures 4 and 5.

A casual look through these graphs is extremely illustrative for it shows two different kinds of patterns. (1) Both Zafarraya and Nerja's Neolithic levels indicate year-round incorporation of birds into the taphocenosis, as evidenced by the dominance of resident taxa (figs. 4A, 5). This pattern could be taken as an argument for a sedentary occupation of the caves on the part of the agents accumulating these remains (in particular, humans). (2) In contrast, the Paleolithic levels of Nerja exhibit a preferential accumulation of wintering birds (fig. 4B), which seems consistent with seasonal occupation of the cave on the part of those accumulating agents.

Obviously, since among other things, year-round availability of the birds need not imply year-round procurement, we are confronted here with two questions:

## TABLE I

### List of bird taxa with number of identified remains from Zafarraya

| SPECIES | ST | NR |
|---|---|---|
| Neophron percnopterus | E | 4 |
| Gypaetus barbatus | R | 5 |
| Gyps fulvus | R | 4 |
| Alectoris rufa | R | 1 |
| Numenius/Limosa | - | 1 |
| Columba livia | R | 1 |
| Columba livia/oenas | - | 11 |
| Athene noctua | R | 1 |
| Apus melba | E | 1 |
| Ptyonoprogne rupestris | R | 1 |
| Pyrrhocorax pyrrhocorax | R | 2 |
| Pyrrhocorax graculus | R | 10 |
| Pyrrhocorax sp | R | 8 |
| **TOTAL** | | **49** |

The phenological status (ST) assignment follows de Juana (1991): E = summer visitor, R = resident, I = winter visitor, P = migratory. No phenological status has been given to nonspecific taxa.

(1) are the patterns real? and (2) what do they mean? An answer to the first question can partly come by answering the second one but, in essence, it is impossible to reach. A historical process so distant in time and suffering such a continuous leakage of information (which in many cases can not be calibrated) can never be faithfully reconstructed. The inferential basis is so restricted that its reliability is seriously compromised. However, one must be reminded that these patterns are coincident in the various faunal reports dealing with different areas of the caves, and, if only from this standpoint, they may reflect more than mere artifacts (tables 1–3). An answer to the second question, on the other hand, is in principle possible, provided one can delimit its main components.

In order to do so, we might start by stating the hypotheses which could explain those particular arrangements: (1) the phenological spectra do evidence a shift in the type of accumulation from a seasonal to a permanent one at Cueva de Nerja, (2) the phenological spectra evidence a shift in the exploitation of avian resources, (3) the phenological spectra evidence a shift in climate, (4) the phenological spectra are misleading for they do not apply to past situations, (5) the phenological spectra indicate a differential retrieval of

remains in the different samples, and (6) the data are palimpsests of remains accumulated by different agents (i.e., humans, owls, hyenas, etc.).

Some of these options are not necessarily exclusive and some are inextricably linked to others.

## DISCUSSION: WHICH OPTION IS RIGHT?

Of the six options previously stated, the one we can most readily discard is the fifth one. From what has been said concerning retrieval methods, it should be clear that there are no grounds for suspecting any type of partial recovery bias that could have caused the differences seen in figures 4 and 5. As stated in the introduction, the last hypothesis can be tentatively dismissed on the grounds that it is addressing issues (i.e., the delimitation of the activities of various process[es]/agent[s]) that should be considered only after the main topic (whether the bird taphocenoses point to seasonal or year-round events of accumulation) has been considered. Obviously, this is not to say that different agents have not had their share influencing the final configuration of the patterns.[6]

The third hypothesis (phenological spectra evidence a climatic shift) and the fourth one (the phenological status of the birds today cannot be extrapolated to the past) are intimately associated and will be explored together. It is true, and much complementary information exists to show, that both Paleolithic samples come from periods of climate colder than the present one (Mourer-Chauviré and Antunès 1991; Mourer-Chauviré 1993; Rodrigo 1994). The Neolithic of the Iberian peninsula, on the other hand, seems to have been climatically similar to present-day conditions (Costa et al. 1990). For this reason, we should expect changes to have occurred in the phenological status of the Paleolithic taxa but to have been far less dramatic in the case of those from Neolithic times.

The impact of such status shifts on the "phenolograms" of figures 4 and 5 can be fully appreciated with one example. If we were to change the status of the gannet (Sula bassana) from winter visitor to resident, the phenologram of Nerja's Paleolithic avifauna would show a similar frequency of these two phenological groups (i.e., residents would rise to 32 percent while winter visitors would come down to 38 percent) thus eliminating its strongly seasonal character. One must stress that this hypothetical scenario is more than mere speculation. Lack of suitable breeding grounds,

TABLE 2

**List of bird taxa with number of identified remains in the four samples retrieved from the Paleolithic levels of Nerja**

| SPECIES | ST | NT82 | NM82 | NT79 | NM79/81 | TOTAL |
|---|---|---|---|---|---|---|
| *Gavia stellata* | I | | | 1 | | 1 |
| *Calonectrix diomedea* | E | 15 | 2 | 16 | | 33 |
| *Puffinus yelkouan* | P | 6 | | 3 | | 9 |
| *Puffinus gravis* | P | | | 2 | | 2 |
| *Puffinus griseus* | P | | | | 1 | 1 |
| *Sula bassana* | I | 28 | | 47 | 5 | 80 |
| *Phalacrocorax carbo* | I | 1 | | | | 1 |
| *Phalacrocorax aristotelis* | R | 4 | | | | 4 |
| *Anser albifrons* | I | | | 1 | | 1 |
| *Anas crecca* | I | | | | 2 | 2 |
| *Anas clypeata* | I | 1 | | | | 1 |
| *Anas platyrhynchos* | R | | | 3 | 11 | 14 |
| *Aythya nyroca* | R | | 1 | | 1 | 2 |
| *A. ferina/fuligula* | - | 1 | | | | 1 |
| *Branta bernicla* | I | 3 | | | | 3 |
| *Melanitta nigra* | I | | | 3 | | 3 |
| *Tadorna ferruginea* | I | 2 | | | | 2 |
| *Tadorna tadorna* | R | | 2 | 6 | | 8 |
| *Milvus milvus* | R | 2 | | 1 | | 3 |
| *Accipiter gentilis* | R | | | 1 | | 1 |
| *Buteo buteo* | R | | 1 | 1 | | 2 |
| *Gypaetus barbatus* | R | | | 1 | | 1 |
| *Circaetus gallicus* | E | | | | 1 | 1 |
| *Falco tinnunculus* | R | | | | 1 | 1 |
| *Alectoris rufa* | R | 5 | | | 3 | 8 |
| *Grus grus* | I | | 1 | | | 1 |
| *Fulica atra* | R | 1 | 1 | 1 | | 3 |
| *Larus cachinnans/fuscus* | R | | | 3 | | 3 |
| *Larus fuscus* | R | | | | 2 | 2 |
| *Larus audouinii* | R | 3 | 1 | | | 4 |
| *Larus marinus* | I | 2 | | 1 | | 3 |
| *Alca torda* | I | 1 | 1 | 1 | | 3 |
| *Uria aalge* | R | 3 | 1 | 1 | 1 | 6 |
| *Pinguinus impennis* | I | | 1 | 2 | 1 | 4 |
| *Columba livia* | R | | | 24 | 4 | 28 |
| *Bubo bubo* | R | | 1 | | | 1 |
| *Alauda arvensis* | R | 1 | | | | 1 |
| *Hirundo rustica* | E | 1 | | | | 1 |
| *Monticola solitarius* | R | | | | 3 | 3 |
| *Turdus sp* | - | 2 | | | | 2 |
| *Lanius excubitor* | R | | | | 2 | 2 |
| *Pyrrhocorax graculus* | R | 1 | | | 1 | 1 |
| *Pyrrhocorax pyrrhocorax* | R | 1 | | 1 | 1 | 3 |
| *Corvus corone* | R | | | 2 | 2 | 4 |
| *Corvus corax* | R | | 1 | 1 | | 2 |
| *Sturnus sp* | R | | | 1 | | 1 |
| *Coccothraustes coccothraustes* | R | | | | 1 | 1 |
| **TOTAL** | | 84(21) | 14(12) | 124(24) | 43(18) | 265(47) |

NT79 taken from Boessneck and Driesch (1980); NM79/81 taken from Eastham (1986). NT82 and NM82 are the two samples being studied by us. For explanation of symbols in the phenological status (ST) column, see table 1. No assignment of status has been made on nonspecific categories except when this is the same for the species involved. Both *Tadorna ferruginea* (an occasional winter visitor) and *Pinguinus impennis* (now extinct) have been assigned to the winter visitor category, but see text for further explanations. Numbers within parentheses in the bottom line specify the number of taxa for that sample.

TABLE 3

List of bird taxa with number of identified remains in the four samples retrieved from the
Neolithic levels of Nerja

| SPECIES | ST | NT82 | NM82 | NT79 | NM79/81 | TOTAL |
|---|---|---|---|---|---|---|
| Calonectrix diomedea | E | | | 1 | | 1 |
| Sula bassana | I | 7 | 2 | 1 | | 10 |
| Phalacrocorax carbo | I | 1 | | | | 1 |
| Phalacrocorax aristotelis | R | 6 | 1 | | | 7 |
| Anas crecca | I | | | | 1 | 1 |
| Buteo buteo | R | | 1 | | | 1 |
| Aquila crysaetos | R | | | 2 | | 2 |
| Haliaetus albicilla | - | 2 | | | | 2 |
| Falco tinnunculus | R | | | | 1 | 1 |
| Alectoris rufa | R | 3 | | 1 | 2 | 6 |
| Coturnix coturnix | E | | | | 2 | 2 |
| Larus marinus | I | | | 1 | | 1 |
| Alca torda | I | | 1 | | | 1 |
| Uria aalge | R | | | | 1 | 1 |
| Pinguinus impennis | I | 1 | | | | 1 |
| Columba livia | R | 13 | | 3 | | 16 |
| Columba palumbus | R | 1 | | | | 1 |
| Cuculus canorus | E | | 1 | | | 1 |
| Bubo bubo | R | | | 1 | | 1 |
| Tyto alba | R | 1 | | 1 | | 2 |
| Athene noctua | R | | | 1 | | 1 |
| Monticola solitarius | R | | | | 3 | 3 |
| Oenanthe leucura | R | | | | 1 | 1 |
| Corvus corone | R | | | | 1 | 1 |
| Corvus corax | R | 2 | | | | 2 |
| TOTAL | | 37(10) | 6(5) | 14(9) | 12(8) | 69 |

Campaign symbols as in table 2; phenological status (ST) symbols as in table 1. Status assignment for *Pinguinus impennis* is debatable. No status has been given to nonspecific taxonomic categories except when this is the same for the species involved. Numbers within parentheses in the bottom line specify the number of taxa for that sample.

due to extensive glaciation and disappearance of shallow seas in northern Europe during Magdalenian times, inevitably led to a latitudinal displacement of marine bird populations southwards. Probably not only the gannets but also many other species of similar biological habits were forced to breed on the rocky shores of southern European seas, such as the ones surrounding Nerja (Hernández 1995). No such changes could have been detected in the supposedly colder environment of Zafarraya for it is too far from the shore (Hernández 1995).

Obviously, one could argue that if the climate was indeed much colder during the Paleolithic stages of Nerja, one could expect the temperature tolerances and trophic requirements of certain species to preclude their appearance in the habitats surrounding the cave and thus from the taphocenoses as well. We are now specifically referring to such birds as the blue rock thrush (*Monticola solitarius*) and the short-toed eagle (*Circaetus gallicus*). But the case is indeed a very weak one. Both occur at present in other areas of Europe (*Circaetus* actually reaches quite high in latitude) and the thrush has an important northern African population to replenish Iberian stocks. Both of them, furthermore, would not mean much in terms of our phenolograms for not only are their NRs low but they also

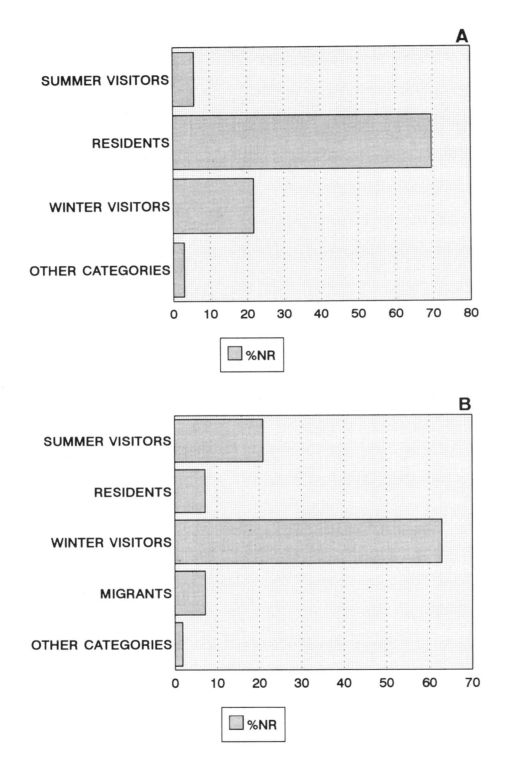

**Figure 4.** Phenological group abundances, expressed as percentages of the number of identified remains (% NR) in the Neolithic (A) and Paleolithic (B) levels of Cueva de Nerja.

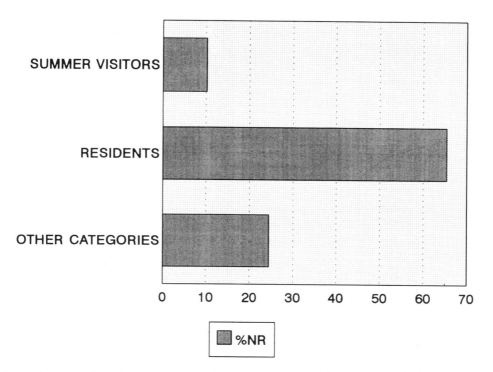

**Figure 5.** Phenological group abundances, expressed as percentages of the number of identified remains (% NR) in the Paleolithic site of Zafarraya.

belong to different phenological categories. The main line of reasoning, however, would not be affected; unsuitable breeding places for marine birds in northern latitudes need not have similar effects at lower latitudes for terrestrial birds. The case for suspecting that the Paleolithic "phenologram" of Nerja is misleading remains strong.

The second hypothesis (that the phenological spectra in Nerja evidence a shift in the exploitation of avian resources) is also linked to the previous ones and is, to a certain extent, a truism. People tend to hunt whatever happens to be more common, the easier the better (notwithstanding some special cases). If we favor this idea, the change in avian taxa that occurs from Paleolithic to Neolithic levels in Nerja need not be associated with a shift in the exploitation of the birds but could most parsimoniously be explained by a shift in the composition of the bird faunas, to which humans obviously responded. In other words, since there are no hints of real "strategic" changes from Paleolithic to Neolithic (i.e., no preferential hunting of juveniles or certain species; no different ways of cutting or chopping bones; and no dissimilar distribution of bones across species, which could point towards ritual uses, processing of carcasses, trade systems, etc.) one can assume that these types of phenomena can safely be incorporated into the "climatic-phenological" model previously discussed (Hernández 1995).

If we assume this to be true, then the first hypothesis (i.e., that the phenological shifts in Paleolithic to Neolithic birds of Nerja reflect a change from seasonal to permanent occupation) might still hold but would not be explained through the bird faunas or, at least, not exclusively by them. As a matter of fact, this is probably the hypothesis that is the most difficult to either prove or disprove. In order to do so we need complementary evidence within the fauna and also of an archaeological and paleoenvironmental nature.

From the standpoint of the fauna, it is true that domestic species appear in the Neolithic layers of Nerja, but this, by itself, does not make the occupation permanent (Boessneck and Driesch 1980; Morales and Martín 1995). During the Paleolithic occupation, Aura and Pérez (1992) state that red deer and wild goat might be indicating autumn-winter hunting, but they say that these data should be taken with care and our unpublished mammal fauna does not come to any definitive conclusion on this point (Morales and Martín 1995). As for Zafarraya, the wild goat exploitation does seem to correlate well with a hunting strategy being carried out preferentially during the spring and summer seasons (Barroso and Medina 1989).

Turning to the birds, one should analyze the species lists in detail rather than group species into any type of categories. When one does so, it is obvious that Nerja's Paleolithic gets its high diversity from the ample presence of "aquatic" birds (i.e., pelagic, shore, freshwater, etc.). It is the disappearance of this sector of the avifauna (for which there are good reasons at Zafarraya but not so in Nerja's Neolithic) that has "impoverished" the other two samples.

A taxonomic similarity analysis demonstrates that both levels of Nerja are more closely related to each other than either one is to Zafarraya. Thus, Nerja's samples share 17 species (68 percent of the total amount of taxa in the Neolithic levels and 36 percent of the Paleolithic levels) while the Paleolithic of Nerja shares five species with Zafarraya (10 percent of Nerja's species but 45 percent of Zafarraya's) and the Neolithic shares three (again, 12 percent of Nerja's species but 27 percent of Zafarraya's) (tables 1–3). This means that Zafarraya is more similar to the Paleolithic levels from Nerja, despite its lack of aquatic birds.

It is clear that Nerja's Paleolithic and Neolithic are more similar to each other than to Zafarraya due to the sharing of aquatic bird taxa. Nerja's Paleolithic high avian diversity, furthermore, is caused by a proportionally higher presence of aquatic taxa, and most of these extra taxa are, at present, nonresident in Iberia. With similar or with different phenological status, most of these latter taxa still show up at present in Iberia during wintertime. Assuming that the Neolithic climate was similar to today's, these taxa could still potentially be hunted, although perhaps in more restricted numbers than during the colder Paleolithic times. The fact that people kept hunting aquatic birds in Nerja during the Neolithic is evident from the faunal lists. Why don't these Paleolithic taxa appear during the Neolithic? Perhaps their absence could be related to their very low frequency at that moment. Since these missing taxa are at present winter visitors, colder climate during the Paleolithic could explain their presence in the Paleolithic samples. If this was indeed the case, the "climatic-phenological" model is reinforced as an explanatory tool and we would have a further reason for not trusting the phenogram of figure 4B. The increase in resi-

dent species during the Neolithic of Nerja could also be most parsimoniously explained as a case of alternative hunting strategy brought about by the drastic reduction of the "traditional" avifaunal resource that vanished as cold-adapted birds became more scarce.

The avifauna from Zafarraya, deprived of aquatic species and diachronic levels, offers no possibility of testing the validity of the "climatic-phenological" model.

## CONCLUSIONS

The emerging patterns appear rather straightforward but we believe there are reasons for not relying too much on them. At the same time, to think that the phenolograms are completely distorted versions of the actual situations is perhaps misleading as well.

Seasonality is a subtle phenomenon to detect and in order to do so one needs to have the appropriate items. We have been addressing the question by analyzing phenological categories and species, but perhaps we have erred. Perhaps these were not adequate items. What could have been adequate items in our case? Well, for one thing, chicks or juveniles or, among adults, animals with medullary bone. Any indication of breeding would be a far more precise indicator of time of the year than the bones from nonbreeding adults. But no remains of juveniles, except for one bone of *Phalacrocorax aristotelis*, were recovered (Hernández 1995). Still this would not have provided the whole answer; the absence of these target items does not preclude breeding and we would still be unable to specify whether a particular species was migratory or a winter visitor or, if breeding was confirmed, whether it was a resident species or a summer visitor. At any rate, we would still need to make an adequate contextualization of the avifauna into taphonomic groups, something for which we currently have no reliable hints (Gautier 1987). But, at the very least, we have stated a series of hypothesis so that in case new data can be incorporated, we can restrict the possibilities further and eventually reach a solution.

Seasonality is indeed a subtle phenomenon to detect. In order to do so when the situation allows for it, one still will need to have ample knowledge about a particular species' biology so as not to take bibliographical and "official" data for what they are not, namely, cookbook recipes!

## Acknowledgments

I am grateful to A. Aguilar (Universidad Autónoma de Madrid) and E. de Juana (Universidad Complutense) for providing useful data and discussions. F. Hernández generously lent the unpublished results of the bird analysis for my own benefit and also provided constructive criticism. E. Roselló typed the manuscript. This paper has benefited from grant nos. PB-94-0186 of the Spanish National Science Foundation (DGICYT) and V/94 from the Institute for the Historical Patrimony of Andalusia (Junta de Andalucía) as well as from two further financial aids from the Patronato de la Cueva de Nerja during 1994 and 1995.

## Notes

1. A taphocenosis is an assemblage of organic materials that are buried together, a death assemblage, a grouping of organisms found together in fossil assemblages.
2. The term "stenoecious" is applied to an organism that can live only in a restricted range of habitats.
3. Phenology is the study of the impact of climate on the seasonal occurrence of flora and fauna.
4. By extension, the term "aestival" encompasses the whole benign stages of the year in temperate latitudes.
5. This low frequency of remains is, incidentally, one additional reason for favoring NR instead of MNI (minimum number of individuals) in comparisons of bird faunas (Grayson 1984)
6. From our own data on species composition, trace analysis, etc., it seems clear that humans were the main accumulating agent at Cueva de Nerja. Meanwhile, the possibility exists that certain taxa (e.g., barn and eagle owls at Nerja and various large carnivores, including hyenas, at Zafarraya) have acted as complementary accumulators of fauna (e.g., certain ungulates, small rodents, passerines) while other taxa (e.g., bats, certain small snails, some birds) constitute intrusive elements. But as often happens in these cases (Payne 1983), this is difficult to either prove or disprove. At any rate, on the basis of the complete taphocenoses' characteristics, the action of these alternative agents seems to have been very restricted indeed.

## BIBLIOGRAPHY

Aguilar, A. L.
1980 "Variación Anual de las Poblaciones de Aves en el Curso Medio del Guadiana Extremeño." Ph.D. diss., Universidad Complutense, Madrid.

Alerstam, T.
1990 *Bird Migration.* Cambridge University Press, Cambridge.

Aura, J. E., and M. Pérez
1992 "Tardiglaciar y Postglaciar en la Región Mediterránea de la Península Ibérica (13.500–8.500 B.P. ): Transformaciones Industriales y Económicas." *Saguntum* 25:25–47.

Avery, G., and L. G. Underhill
1986 "Seasonal Exploitation of Seabirds by Late Holocene Coastal Foragers: Analysis of Modern and Archaeological Data from the Western Cape, South Africa." *Journal of Archaeological Science* 13:339–360.

Baglinière, J. L., J. Castanet, F. Conaud, and F. J. Meunier
1992 *Tissus Durs et Âge Individuel des Vertébrés.* ORSTROM, Paris.

Baird, R. F.
1989 "Fossil Bird Assemblages from Australian Caves: Precise Indicators of Late Quaternary Environments?" *Paleogeography, Paleoclimatology, Paleoecology* 69:241–244.

Baker, R. R.
1978 *The Evolutionary Ecology of Animal Migration.* Hodder & Stoughton, London.

Barroso, C., and F. Medina
1989 "El Último Neanderthal." *Investigación y Ciencia* junio 1989:37–39.

Barroso, C., J. J. Hublin, and F. Medina
1993 "Zafarraya y el Reemplazamiento de los Neandertales por el Hombre Moderno," in *Investigaciones Arqueológicas en Andalucía 1985–1992,* pp. 931–937. Huelva.

Bernis, F.
1966 *Migración en Aves; Tratado Teórico-práctico.* Sociedad Española de Ornitologia, Madrid.
1988a *Los Vencejos.* Universidad Complutense, Madrid.
1988b *Las Aves de los Medios Urbano y Agrícola en las Mesetas Españolas.* Sociedad Española de Ornitologia, Madrid.

Berthold, P., A. J. Helbig, G. Mohr, and U. Querner
1992 "Rapid Microevolution of Migratory Behavior in a Wild Species." *Nature* 360(6405):668–670.

Boessneck, J., and A. von den Driesch
1980 "Tierknochenfunde aus Vier Südspanischen Höhlen." *Studien Über Frühe Tierknochenfunde von der Iberischen Halbinsel* 7:1–83.

Casteel, R. W.
1972 "Some Archaeological Uses of Fish Remains." *American Antiquity* 37:404–419.

CLIMAP
1976 "The Surface of the Ice Age Earth." *Science* 191:1131–1137.

Costa, M., M. García, C. Morla, and H. Sainz
1990 "La Evolución de los Bosques de la Península Ibérica: Una Interpretación Basada en Datos Biogeográficos." *Ecología* 1:31–58.

Curry-Lindhal, K.
1981 *Bird Migration in Africa*. Academic Press, London.

Davis, S. J. M.
1983 "The Age Profiles of Gazelles Predated by Ancient Man in Israel: Possible Evidence for a Shift from Seasonality to Sedentism in the Natufian." *Paléorient* 9:55–62.
1987 *The Archaeology of Animals*. Batsford, London.

Driver, J. C.
1982 "Medullary Bone as an Indicator of Sex in Bird Remains from Archaeological Sites," in *Ageing and Sexing Animal Bones from Archaeological Sites*, B. Wilson, C. Grigson, and S. Payne, eds., pp. 251–254. British Archaeological Reports, British Series 109. Oxford.

Eastham, A.
1986 "The Birds of the Cueva de Nerja," in *La Prehistoria de la Cueva de Nerja*, E. Jordá, ed., pp. 109–131. Patronato de la Cueva de Nerja, Málaga.
1988 "The Season or the Symbol: The Evidence of Swallows in the Paleolithic of Western Europe." *Archaeozoologia* 2(1.2):243–252.

Ervynck, A.
1993 "The Role of Birds in the Economy of Medieval and post-Medieval Flanders: A Diversity of Interpretation." *Archaeofauna* 2:107–119.

Finlayson, J. C.
1992 *The Birds of the Strait of Gibraltar*. T & AD Poyser, Berkhamsted.

Gautier, A.
1987 "Taphonomical Groups: How and Why?" *Archaeozoologia* 1(2):47–52.

Grayson, D. K.
1984 *Quantitative Zooarchaeology*. Academic Press, London.

Hernández, F.
1995 "Cueva de Nerja: Las Aves de las Campañas de 1980 y 1982," in *Fauna de la Cueva de Nerja I*, M. Pellicer, and A. Morales, eds., pp. 219–293. Trabajos sobre la Cueva de Nerja, no. 5. Patronato de la Cueva de Nerja, Nerja.
n.d. "The Birds from the Site of Zafarraya." Manuscript in preparation.

Jenkinson, R. D. S., and A. Sutherland
1984 "Changes in European Geese and Duck Migration Patterns During the Quaternary," in *In the Shadow of Extinction*, R. D. S. Jenkinson and D. D. Gilbertson, eds., pp. 101–109. J. D. Collis, Sheffield.

Jordá, J., ed.
1986 *La Prehistoria de la Cueva de Nerja*. Patronato de la Cueva de Nerja, Málaga.

Juana, E. de
1982 "Selección de Datos Fenológicos para las Aves del Alto Valle del Ebro y Sistema Ibérico Septentrional," in *Miscelánea Conmemorativa*, pp. 1023–1045. Publicaciones de la Universidad Autónoma de Madrid, Madrid.
1991 *List of the Birds of the Iberian Peninsula*. Sociedad Española de Ornitologia, Madrid.

Lázaro, E.
1984 "Contribución al Estudio de la Cigüeña Blanca (*Ciconia ciconia*) en España." Ph.D. diss., Universidad Complutense, Madrid.

Lundelius, E. L., Jr.
1983 "Climatic Implications of Late Pleistocene and Holocene Faunal Associations in Australia." *Alcheringa* 7:125–149.

Mayr, E., and W. Meise
1980 "Theoretische zur Geschichte des Vogelzuges." *Der Vogelzug* 1:149–172.

McIntyre, A., N. G. Kipp, A. Bé, W. H. Crowley, T. Kellog, T. Gardner, J. V. Prell, and W. F. Ruddiman
1976 "Glacial North Atlantic 18,000 Years Ago: A CLIMAP Reconstruction," in *Investigation of Late Quaternary Paleoceanography and Paleoclimatology*, R. Cline and J. Hays, eds., pp. 43–45. Geological Society of America Memoir 145. Boulder, Colorado.

Morales, A., and J. M. Martin
1995 "Los Mamiferos de la Cueva de Nerja," in *Fauna de la Cueva de Nerja I*, M. Pellicer and A. Morales, eds., pp. 57–159. Trabajos sobre la Cueva de Nerja, no. 5. Patronato de la Cueva de Nerja, Nerja.

Moreau, R. E.
1954 "The Main Vicissitudes of the European Avifauna Since the Pliocene." *Ibis* 96:411–431.

Mourer-Chauviré, C.
1993 "The Pleistocene Avifaunas of Europe." *Archaeofauna* 2:53–66.

Mourer-Chauviré, C., and M. T. Antunès
1991 "Presence du Grand Pingouin, *Pinguinus impennis* (Aves, Charadriformes) dans le Pleistocene de Portugal." *Geobios* 24(2):201–205.

Münzel, S. C.
1983 "Seasonal Activities at Umingmak, a Muskox Hunting Site on Banks Island, NWT Canada, with Special Reference to the Bird Remains," in *Animals and Archaeology*. Vol. 1, *Hunters and their Prey*, J. Clutton-Brock and C. Grigson, eds., pp. 249–257. British Archaeological Reports, International Series 163. Oxford.

Patterson, A. M.
1987 "A Study of Seabirds in Málaga Bay, Spain." *Ardeola* 34(2):167–192.

Payne, S.
1983 "Bones from Cave Sites: Who Ate What? Problems and a Case Study," in *Animals and Archaeology*. Vol. 1, *Hunters and Their Prey*, J. Clutton-Brock and C. Grigson, eds., pp. 149–162. British Archaeological Reports, International Series 163. Oxford.

Richter, J.
1982 "Adult and Juvenile Aurochs, *Bos primigenius* Boj. from the Maglemosian Site of Ulkestrup Lyng Yst, Denmark." *Journal of Archaeological Science* 9:247–259.

Rodrigo, M. J.
1994 "Remains of *Melanogrammus aeglefinus* (Linnaeus, 1758) in the Pleistocene-Holocene Passage of the Cave of Nerja, Málaga (Spain)." *Offa* 51:348–351.

Roselló, E., A. Morales, and J. M. Cañas
1995 "Estudio Ictioarqueológico de la Cueva de Nerja," in *Fauna de la Cueva de Nerja I*, M. Pellicer and A. Morales, eds., pp. 161–217. Trabajos sobre la Cueva de Nerja, no. 5. Patronato de la Cueva de Nerja, Nerja.

Santos, T., and J. L. Tellería
1977 *Guión Orientativo Sobre la Fenología de las Aves Estivales Ibéricas.* Sociedad Española de Ornitologia, Madrid.

Sociedad Española de Ornitologia, ed.
1985 *Estudio Sobre la Biología Migratoria del Orden Anseriformes (Aves) en España.* Monografías 39, Instituto de Conservacion de la Naturaleza. Publicaciones Ministerio Agricultura, Madrid.

Tellería, J. L., ed.
1988 *Invernada de Aves en la Península Ibérica.* Sociedad Española de Ornitologia, Madrid.

# CHAPTER 4

# Seasonality of Resource Use and Site Occupation at Badanj, Bosnia-Herzegovina: Subsistence Stress in an Increasingly Seasonal Environment?

*Preston T. Miracle, University of Cambridge*

*Christopher J. O'Brien, USDA Forest Service*

## INTRODUCTION

Increased climatic seasonality around the Pleistocene-Holocene transition has long been proposed by paleontologists as a potential cause of Pleistocene extinctions (see Graham and Lundelius 1984; Grayson 1984a). Increased seasonality has more recently been incorporated into models of cultural evolution (Bonnichsen et al. 1987; Martin and Martin 1987), Paleoindian mobility strategies (Kelly and Todd 1988), nutritional constraints and processing strategies (Speth 1991), and the origins of agriculture (McCorriston and Hole 1991; Moore and Hillman 1992). Excepting the models of agricultural origins in the Near East, these archaeological applications have tended to be highly speculative, but they have served a purpose in making archaeologists consider environmental seasonality as a variable instead of a constant. To move to the next step, we need to make the links between changes in the seasonal distribution of solar insolation, paleoenvironmental histories at the regional level, and human adaptive systems in these prehistoric landscapes. Paleoclimatologists have generated a series of testable hypotheses about past climates that are based on estimates of the previous distribution of solar insolation, and geologists and paleoecologists have been testing these hypotheses at the regional level against pollen spectra, lake levels, ice cores, and other data. To archaeologists lies the task of incorporating these environmental processes into models of past cultural systems and assessing the relevance, if any, of paleoseasonality to the course of human biological and cultural evolution.

This paper has three parts. First, we discuss new data and models of changes in Late Glacial paleoclimates and examine the fit of paleoecological data from the Adriatic Basin to these models. Second, we propose that Paleolithic hunter-gatherers and their prey faced several environmental crises during the Late Glacial. Finally, we present seasonality data based on fetal long bones and tooth-increments in red deer from the Epipaleolithic site of Badanj, Bosnia-Herzegovina (fig. 1) and use these data to examine hypotheses about seasonal mobility in the Adriatic Basin (Bailey et al. 1983), the roles of the Adriatic Plain and its hilly/mountainous hinterland in systems of settlement during the Late Pleistocene (Shackleton et al. 1984; van Andel 1989), and the relationship between redundancy in site use and geographic patterning in settlement on the one hand and environmental stability and predictability on the other (Jochim 1991).

## PALEOENVIRONMENTAL CHANGES AT THE END OF THE PLEISTOCENE

### Environmental Instability, Seasonality, and Global Circulation Models

The dramatic and widespread environmental changes associated with deglaciation at the end of the Pleistocene make this time period especially interesting and appropriate for examining models of subsistence change in hunter-gatherer societies. Recent paleoenvironmental data from ice-cores on Greenland show

**Figure 1.** Map of the Adriatic Basin and Late Glacial sites mentioned in the text.

Pleistocene climates to have been extremely dynamic and unstable. Transitions from full glacial (stadial) to interglacial (also interstadial) regimes take as a little as three to five years to complete and do not occur smoothly, but rather they involve a repeated flip-flopping of mean annual temperatures by up to 7° Celsius and of climates between glacial and interglacial conditions (Johnsen et al. 1992; Alley et al. 1993; Edwards et al. 1993; Taylor et al. 1993). In figure 2 we identify this transition during the Late Glacial as a pulse of "rapid warming." Conditions during interstadials appear to have been much more variable and unpredictable than stadial or interglacial climates (Johnsen et al. 1992; Taylor et al. 1993). We schematically indicate this contrast in climatic variability between interstadial and stadial conditions in figure 2.

Paleoenvironmental analyses and high precision dating of ice cores from Greenland, Antarctica, and Peru show that these Late Glacial climatic fluctuations were worldwide in occurrence (Chappellaz et al. 1993; Bender et al. 1994; Thompson et al. 1995). Furthermore, none of these cores shows a stadial (Older Dryas) between the Bølling and Allerød interstadials. These data suggest, as suspected, that the Older Dryas was a local climatic phenomenon restricted to continental, northwestern Europe; we treat the Bølling and Allerød in southeastern Europe as a single interstadial event. There is close agreement between the pollen-based chronology and the ice cores in the dating of the onset of the Younger Dryas at about 11,000 $^{14}$C yr B.P. and the Pleistocene-Holocene transition at about 10,000 $^{14}$C yr B.P. The onset of the Bølling interstadial, however, occurs about 700 cal yrs earlier in pollen-based chronozones than in ice cores. Given the high precision of the ice core data and our application of these results to an area outside of northwestern Europe, we use the ice cores to date the onset of the Bølling/Allerød interstadial at about 12,500 $^{14}$C yr B.P. (fig. 2; see Miracle 1995).

Intra-annual or seasonal variation in insolation in the Northern Hemisphere is predicted by Milankovitch cycles to have reached a maximum about 10,500 B.P. (Dawson 1992). It is useful at this point to distinguish between seasonality in insolation, temperature, and precipitation. The first depends almost entirely on parameters of the earth's orbit and can be calculated for a given latitude with some accuracy by using Milankovitch's equations. Seasonality in insolation, although an important causal variable, is not the same as seasonality in temperature at the earth's surface. Surface temperature and its seasonality also depends on factors like geography, winds, and the moderating influences of heat/cold reservoirs like oceans and ice sheets. The link between insolation and precipitation is even more indirect. Thus heightened seasonality in solar radiation striking the Northern Hemisphere is likely to have caused increased seasonality in temperature, but not necessarily in precipitation. To the extent that seasonality increased in either of these variables, however, it would have added to environmental unpredictability and instability.

Our interest here, however, is not in the climatic history of Greenland as revealed by the ice cores, but of the Northern Mediterranean region in general and the Adriatic Basin in particular. Furthermore, solar insolation is only one of several variables that drives climatic changes, including the degree of seasonality. The key link between solar radiation and expressed climate lies in the circulation of warm and cold air-masses and the moisture that they carry. Atmospheric circulation also provides the regional tie between different local records of climatic change and thereby provides a powerful bridge between the high-resolution record locked in the ice cores and paleoecological records from other parts of the world. Atmospheric circulation has been successfully modeled for present and past climates using global circulation models (GCMs) and given the boundary conditions of extent and elevation of permanent ice, sea-surface temperatures, continental geography, concentration of greenhouse gasses, and the albedo (reflectivity) of land surfaces (CLIMAP 1976; Kutzbach and Wright 1985; COHMAP 1988; Harrison et al. 1992). These simulations appear to be fairly accurate in predicting temperature, pressure patterns, and wind fields but are less accurate in predicting precipitation and other parameters that depend on a scale of resolution finer than that used in the model (often a grid cell of several degrees in latitude and longitude to each side).

We use a GCM created for Europe (Harrison et al. 1992) to develop predictions for Late Glacial environments and environmental seasonality in the Adriatic Basin. The main expectation of this and other models (Kutzbach and Wright 1985; COHMAP 1988) is a shift of the jet stream at the Last Glacial Maximum (LGM, around 18,000 B.P.) to a west-east track along the main basin of the Mediterranean and a stable high pressure system over the glaciated Alps. In the Adriatic Basin, we predict that there would have been a strong northwest-southeast temperature gradient from the ice sheet margin in the foothills of the Alps to the Adriatic Sea along the trough formed between the Apennines and Dinarides (fig. 1). Mountain glaciation along the peaks of the Apennines and Dinarides would have cre-

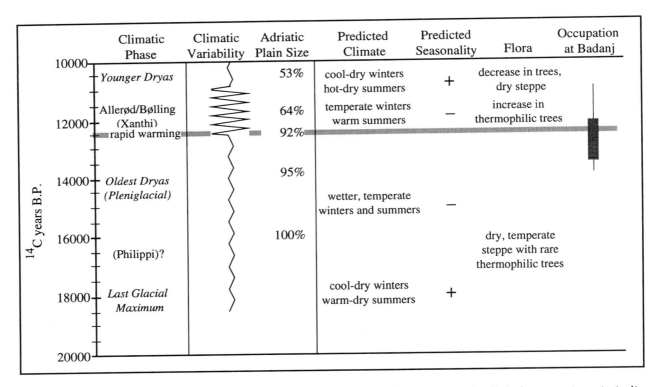

**Figure 2.** Reconstructed Late Glacial environments in the Eastern Adriatic Basin. Stadial phases written in italics, interstadials in Roman script. Climatic variability simplified from Miracle (1995:fig. 4.1). Adriatic Plain size from Miracle (1995:table 4.3). Probable correlations with pollen zones from northeastern Greece (Wijmstra 1969) indicated in parentheses. Predicted climate and seasonality based on Harrison et al. (1992) and Kutzbach and Wright (1985). Increased seasonality (relative to climate today) is indicated with "+," and reduced seasonality is indicated with "−." Reconstructed flora after Culiberg (1991) and Rossignol-Strick et al. (1992). For "occupation at Badanj," thick lines indicate dated deposits (based on ¹⁴C dates ± 2s), thin lines indicate occupation possible but not confirmed.

ated a marked altitudinal zonation in temperatures along the sides of the basin. The position of the jet stream and the storms it carried on the southern edge of the Adriatic Basin would have created a precipitation gradient with the northwest considerably drier than the southeast. The Adriatic's role in moderating climate would have been dramatically diminished since it would have been much cooler (Thiede 1978) and smaller in size than at present (Shackleton et al. 1984).

We summarize the sequence of predicted paleoenvironmental changes in the Adriatic Basin in figure 2. During the Last Glacial Maximum (ca. 18,000 B.P.), winter temperatures would have been 2–5° C cooler and precipitation low, while summers would have been as warm as the present and dry (Harrison et al. 1992:289). By 15,000 B.P., winters were warmer and

there was increased precipitation, while summer temperatures remained the same or even decreased (Harrison et al. 1992:293). The prediction is thus for a reduction in temperature and precipitation seasonality, despite an increasing insolation anomaly. By 12,000 B.P., temperatures around the Mediterranean were similar to those of today, giving a strong temperature gradient to the north. Winter precipitation would have again decreased. During the Younger Dryas (11,000–10,000 B.P.), winter temperatures dropped somewhat in the Mediterranean region, but not as much as in Western Europe. Summer temperatures are predicted to have been warmer than those of today, while precipitation was reduced. Seasonality would have increased in temperature and perhaps also in precipitation. During the early postglacial (9000 B.P.), the jet stream would have moved considerably to the north (latitude of southern Britain) and brought with it increased winter rain and warmer temperatures to the bulk of the European continent (Harrison et al. 1992:292).

This GCM does not directly address the issue of environmental stability and the rapidity of climatic change. If the Greenland ice cores reflect global change in atmospheric circulation, as seems likely, it is probably safe to infer that temperature fluctuations and pulses of rapid warming during the Late Glacial would have simultaneously disrupted environments over very wide areas in south central Europe, although the magnitude of these changes may have been only 2–5° C. Direct evidence of paleoenvironmental seasonality should be forthcoming from ice-coring projects (Alley et al. 1993; Taylor et al. 1993).

## Paleoenvironments in the Adriatic Basin during the Late Glacial

Before we consider paleoecological evidence of environmental change in the Adriatic Basin, it is important to consider dramatic changes that occurred in the landscape itself. The temperature fluctuations of the Late Glacial were coincident with the loss of the productive north Adriatic plain and its rich large ungulate fauna to rising sea levels (Shackleton et al. 1984; van Andel 1989). Late Glacial sea level rises were caused by the rapid thinning and then retreat of continental ice sheets between approximately 12,500 and 9000 B.P., with perhaps a pause between roughly 11,000 and 10,000 B.P. during the Younger Dryas. Reference to global and local sea-level curves places the Adriatic at about −96 meters at 13,000 B.P., −55 meters at 10,000 B.P., and −35 meters at 9000 B.P. (van Andel 1990; Šegota and Filipčič 1991; Miracle 1995). A large Adriatic Plain was still exposed at 13,000 B.P. (fig. 1). Measured relative to its maximum exposure at the Last Glacial Maximum, the Adriatic Plain rapidly reduced in size from 12,500 to 9000 B.P., at which time it had been reduced to a small patch along the western coast of Istria and the Gulf of Trieste covering about 17 percent of its previous area. The exposed northern Adriatic Plain supported sizable ungulate herds of equids, large bovids, and giant deer (Bietti 1990; Miracle 1995). Taxa adapted to open, steppe environments like horse and giant deer declined in abundance and then went extinct as the Adriatic Plain was flooded (Miracle 1995). The sea-level rise would

have displaced both human and animal populations from the plain into the hinterland.

Paleoenvironmental data from the Eastern Adriatic are quite sparse. Here we summarize studies of loess deposits (Brunnacker et al. 1969; Coudé-Gaussen 1990; Cremaschi and van Vliet-Lanoë 1990), land snails (Brunnacker et al. 1969; Poje 1990), mammalian faunas (Cremaschi 1990; Miracle and Sturdy 1991, Miracle 1995), and pollen cores (van Zeist and Bottema 1982; Huntley and Birks 1983; Satta and Renault-Miskovsky 1985; Cremaschi 1990; Culiberg 1991; Rossignol-Strick et al. 1992; Willis 1994).

Loess accumulation at locales both in the north and south of the region indicate dry and windy conditions at the last glacial maximum (Brunnacker et al. 1969; Coudé-Gaussen 1990; Cremaschi and van Vliet-Lanoë 1990). Cold temperatures in the northwest (Po Valley) were not too severe and resulted in only seasonal freezing without permafrost formation (Cremaschi and van Vliet-Lanoë 1990). Land snail assemblages from Istria in the north (Poje 1990) and the Neretva Valley in the south (Brunnacker et al. 1969) contain taxa that prefer mild winters and relatively warm conditions. Arctic and Boreal mammals like arctic fox, wolverine, and reindeer are rare in LGM assemblages from the northern part of the Adriatic Basin and very rare or missing from assemblages from the southern part of the Adriatic Basin (Bietti 1990:139; Miracle 1995). Furthermore, some of the changes in faunal composition that have been interpreted in terms of temperature can better be explained by reference to local factors of geography (Miracle and Sturdy 1991). With the exception of a few faunal assemblages on the edge of the Alpine glaciers in Slovenia, mammalian assemblages give little evidence of particularly cold conditions during the LGM and the Late Glacial.

Pollen spectra from the LGM, summarized in figure 2, are dominated by prairie/steppe taxa from families Gramineae, Artemisia, and Chenopodiaceae but also contain pine pollen and rare pollens of thermophilic species like oak, alder, and ash (Satta and Renault-Miskovsky 1985; Rossignol-Strick et al. 1992; Willis 1994). The floral spectra was enriched by the displacement of many temperate species into "refugia" (di Castri 1981:30-32; Willis 1994), and the high relief around the basin provided diverse microclimates and habitats within a relatively small area. Reconstructions of the Late Glacial vegetation indicate relatively dry, open, and temperate conditions on the Adriatic Plain and up to an elevation of 300–700 meters. Altitudinally this was followed by a more or less forested zone dominated by pine, but also with more thermophilic deciduous species like hazel and beech mixed in. Above approximately 1,000 meters and on up to the snow line (variously placed between 1,300 and 2,000 meters), the landscape was again open, but now covered with alpine/tundra vegetation (Rossignol-Strick et al. 1992). These conditions persisted until around 13,800 B.P. when first pine, birch, and alder begin increasing in abundance. Although arboreal pollen increased in abundance at this time, Rossignol-Strick et al. (1992) consider this change to still be within the Pleniglacial (Older Dryas). They suggest that the Bølling/Allerød interstadials commence with the increase in thermophilic deciduous trees, including hornbeam (indicating mild winters), that peaked in abundance between 12,600 and 11,800 B.P. (Rossignol-Strick et al. 1992). From about 10,900–10,000 B.P., there is a decline in tree taxa of all types (hornbeam disappears) and an increase in Artemisia and Chenopodiaceae. These drier and perhaps cooler conditions probably are the local expression of the Younger Dryas (Rossignol-Strick et al. 1992:417). By about 9400 B.P. trees again increased in abundance with the important addition of Mediterranean taxa like pistachio, olive, and hornbeam.

Each temperature pulse probably led to the rapid expansion of mixed pine and broad leaf trees from their existing refugia in the eastern Adriatic.[1] Although the paleoenvironmental record shows these as smooth transitions from steppe/savanna conditions to wooded steppe or forest, this probably reveals more about the coarse scale of the data than the process of change itself. There may have been significant lags (on the order of several decades) between the decimation and colonization of local plant communities. While annual plants and r-selected species would have probably been selected for during these periods of rapid and dramatic climatic change (McCorriston and Hole 1991), they appear to have been quickly replaced by parkland deciduous forests with relatively few Mediterranean representatives.

These data fit the circulation model fairly well (fig. 2), given several important modifications. The temperature gradient predicted by the GCM appears in the pollen and mammalian data, although land snails do not show a contrast between the south and north. There is no evidence of a precipitation gradient within the Adriatic Basin; relatively arid conditions appear to have prevailed throughout the Late Glacial. The jet stream and the storms it carried may have passed south of the "heel" of Italy along the axis of the Mediterranean proper. The Younger Dryas appears in the pollen spectra as a decrease of arboreal and Mediterranean taxa, and the paleoclimatic interpretation of drier and perhaps cooler conditions fits the predictions of the GCM. These paleoecological records are too coarse to give an indication of environmental stability. Evidence for changes in environmental seasonality are discussed below.

## Evidence of Increased Environmental Seasonality

Indirect evidence of environmental seasonality is available from two sources, floral and faunal composition. McCorriston and Hole (1991:54–55) have recently suggested that a Mediterranean flora is indicative of a highly seasonal distribution of rainfall and climatic or anthropogenic disturbance of landscapes. Mediterranean floras can thus be used as proxies of highly seasonal and unstable climatic conditions in the past (McCorriston and Hole 1991:56). Paleontologists have long suggested that environmentally "mixed" or "disharmonious" faunal assemblages—associations of species that today are allopatric due to contrasting temperature tolerances—indicate more equable climates with cooler summers and warmer winters (Graham and Lundelius 1984:224–225; Grayson 1984a). If an equable Pleistocene climate is the major cause of "disharmonious" communities and assemblages, then the disappearance of such communities in the Holocene as well as at other times would imply a relative increase in environmental seasonality.

Mediterranean-type taxa are present in Pleistocene pollen spectra from the Adriatic region, but frequencies are more suggestive of scattered stands or patches in "refugia" than developed communities, as also appears to have been the case in the Near East (McCorriston and Hole 1991). Species typical of Mediterranean communities expand in the Adriatic Basin only after the transition to the Holocene (Rossignol-Strick et al. 1992), and perhaps as late as after 8000 B.P. (Miracle and Sturdy 1991). If, however, Younger Dryas climates were arid year-round, Mediterranean vegetation would have been limited by a lack of winter precipitation. An increase in seasonal temperature contrasts, as predicted by the GCM, in this case would not be reflected by the indicators discussed above. The pollen data, sparse as they are, do not indicate strongly seasonal rainfall prior to the Holocene. They neither support nor refute a model of increased temperature seasonality during the Younger Dryas.

Others have suggested that steppe vegetation is indicative of an extreme seasonal temperature range (Kelly and Huntley 1991:221). The continual presence of sclerophyllous taxa during the Late Glacial, however, argues against severe winters and extreme temperature seasonality. Furthermore, steppes today and their climatic associations may be poor analogs for these Late Glacial vegetative communities (Kelly and Huntley 1991:221). Even if steppe vegetation is at best an equivocal indication of high temperature seasonality, its predominance during the LGM and Younger Dryas fits the predictions of the GCM of increased seasonality at these times (fig. 2).

Turning to the faunal data, there are several apparently disharmonious faunal assemblages from Late Glacial sites in the northwestern Adriatic Basin. The "disharmonious" nature of these assemblages arises from the presence of boreal/tundra-adapted taxa such as wolverine, arctic fox, and reindeer. Dated assemblages come from the Bølling/Allerød interstadial Šandalja Level B/s at 12,320±100 B.P. [Miracle 1995]; Županov spodmol Level 2D at 12,410±70 B.P. [Brodar and Osole 1979]). If these taxa were in the area during the summer, their presence would indicate summer temperatures depressed relative to the present and a decrease in temperature seasonality. This interpretation fits the predictions of the GCM in figure 2. However, these taxa are all highly mobile and may have been regular seasonal (winter) migrants into the area. Alternatively, they may have come south only during especially cold and severe conditions, in which case they may reflect increased climatic instability during the Bølling/Allerød interstadial as predicted above (Miracle 1995). Whatever the interpretation, similarly dated Late Glacial faunal assemblages in the central and southern portion of the Adriatic Basin lack the boreal/tundra-adapted taxa cited above (Sala 1983; Bietti 1990:112; Miracle and Sturdy 1991; Miracle 1995). Although the lack of these taxa could indicate greater summer extremes in temperature and hence seasonality, it is likely that winter temperatures were also less severe in the southern portion of the basin due to the moderating influence of the Adriatic. Testing the hypothesis of greater seasonality in the southern part of the basin must await further data collection.

## Summary

The sparse data that exist indicate that temperature seasonality may have been greater during the LGM and Younger Dryas and reduced during the Bølling/Allerød interstadial. Interannual climatic instability, however, may still have been greater during the interstadial, and warming pulses may have caused widespread disruptions in the biota, although data still need to be collected to address these issues.

Late Glacial paleoenvironmental changes also would have had a significant impact on the length of the growing season and hence the availability and quality of forage and plant resources for animal and human populations. Both temperature and precipitation determine the length of the growing season. Increased temperature seasonality leads to a shorter growing season and poor forage quality, as well as a longer lean season (Guthrie 1984:268–269). At a given location, an increase in temperature will also tend to decrease the amount of moisture available to living organisms due to increased evaporation. Plants require moisture to grow; hence a decrease in available moisture, whether through decreased precipitation or increased temperatures and/or increased seasonality in moisture availability, will shorten the growing season. The overall result is a decrease in the amount and quality of forage and even more importantly, the length of time for which it is available. The reduction in forage quality and length of growing season would have given animals less time to put on fat reserves, and the longer lean season would have forced them to metabolize more of their reserves (Kelly and Todd 1988; Speth 1991). The quality of animal resources would be more variable, and animals would be less buffered against resource fluctuations. Ungulate populations would have been much more prone to crash in lean years or seasons.

The combination of increased temperature seasonality, particularly due to hot summers, and reduced precipitation would have significantly shortened the growing season during the Younger Dryas. The growing season during the Bølling/Allerød interstadial would have been comparatively longer on average, while it may have been somewhat shorter during the Pleniglacial, although not as short as during the Younger Dryas. Although climates may have been less stable during the Bølling/Allerød, average living conditions should have been better relative to the Pleniglacial and Younger Dryas due to the longer growing season and decreased temperature seasonality.

Late Glacial hunter-gatherers in the Adriatic Basin would thus have faced several environmental crises. The rise in the Adriatic Sea would have displaced populations from the plain into the hinterland, leading to a higher local population density in the hinterland. Loss of the Adriatic Plain also meant loss of its rich ungulate fauna and from the perspective of a prehistoric hunter, resource depletion. Both the Bølling/Allerød interstadial and the Younger Dryas may have presented crises, although these would have been of a different nature. The temperature pulses of the Late Glacial that opened the interstadials were followed by a rapid expansion of forest cover from south to north. This would have disrupted and fragmented existing open and steppe habitats and led to a decrease in the large mammal biomass available to hunters (Kelly 1983). Furthermore, environmental unpredictability would have been greater during the Bølling/Allerød interstadial. The Younger Dryas, on the other hand, had overall harsher conditions with increased temperature seasonality, decreased precipitation, and a shorter growing season. We must turn to the archaeological evidence to determine which, if any, of these climatic variables had a significant impact on the strategies of prehistoric hunter-gatherer groups.

## SEASONAL MOBILITY IN THE EASTERN ADRIATIC AND RESPONSES TO ENVIRONMENTAL UNPREDICTABILITY

We focus our attention on several hypotheses that can be tested with our seasonality data from Badanj. First, we examine hypotheses about seasonal mobility in the Adriatic Basin (Bailey et al. 1983) and the roles of the Adriatic Plain and its hilly/mountainous hinterland in systems of settlement during the Late Pleistocene (Shackleton et al. 1984; van Andel 1989). Then we discuss a model recently proposed by Jochim (1991) that links redundancy in site use and geographic patterning in settlement to environmental stability and predictability. Finally, we propose ways in which hunter-gatherers may have responded to the environmental crises of the Late Glacial and manners in which one might monitor such responses by using seasonality data.

A seasonal transhumance model for Upper Paleolithic hunters in the Adriatic Basin (northwest Greece) was first proposed by Higgs in the early 1960s, and in its original form posited a yearly migration between winter-occupied sites near the coast and summer-occupied sites in the uplands of the hinterland (Bailey et al. 1983). Recent reworkings of this model still stress the importance of seasonal mobility, but the proposed patterns are much more complicated than the simple "winter on the coast, summer in the

mountains." Focus is on the timing and place of population aggregations. A pattern of summer aggregation in the uplands, where resources would have been predictable and abundant, and winter dispersal primarily down to the lowlands is proposed (Bailey et al. 1983:77). More recently still, Bailey and Gamble (1990:164) have suggested that sites in the hinterland were "specialized additions to a system of economic exploitation centered on the coastal lowlands." In terms of seasonality indicators, sites in the hinterland should produce evidence of summer occupation/resource use and inventories indicative of specialized activities, while sites in the lowlands should show winter occupations.

One alternative proposed to the seasonal mobility (transhumance) model is a year-round occupation of the Adriatic Plain (Shackleton et al. 1984). The basis of the hypothesis is the reconstructed richness of the Adriatic Plain, with abundant game and "broad-spectrum" resources and readily available surface water in areas bordered by steep mountains like the Eastern Adriatic (van Andel 1989:737). In this essentially "Garden-of-Eden" model, high environmental productivity made seasonal migrations unnecessary, and van Andel (1989:737) further suggests that the peripheral hinterland would have only been visited sporadically to garner information about fallback resources. Archaeologically, we would expect to find sites on or near the Adriatic Plain with evidence of occupation/resources from all seasons of the year and the full range of residential and productive activities. Sites in the hinterland, in contrast, should show evidence of a more narrow range of activities related to brief, seasonal, logistic trips to monitor environmental conditions. Some specialized resource procurement may have occurred on these trips, or in the event of productive crises, entire bands may have relocated from the coastal area to the hinterland as a fallback strategy.

Both models predict winter occupation at lowland sites near the coast. They differ in the role assigned to the hinterland. In the former model (Bailey and Gamble 1990), sites in the hinterland play a regular, albeit specialized, role in the overall system of settlement. In the latter model, in contrast, use of the hinterland is predicted to have been sporadic. These predictions for hinterland use are not mutually exclusive, and different hinterland areas may have been tied into settlement systems in very different ways.

While it is critically important to consider the geography of settlement and seasonal contrasts in the use of landscapes, the models discussed above are essentially static and lack time depth. If we are to get at the underlying processes that generate or influence the patterns that we observe, we must incorporate time as a dimension and at the same time make our models dynamic. At this point, however, we run into a major problem since the temporal scale of ethnographic observations and modern environmental data used to model behavioral and cultural responses to environmental variability is often much finer than the chronological resolution of the paleoecological and archaeological data.[2] One way to bridge this gap in scale is to look for regularities between the nature and degree of environmental variability and coarser patterns of settlement and subsistence.

Jochim (1991) has suggested that high environmental predictability should lead to regular and redundant patterning in site use, location, and season of occupation. Frequent and unpredictable environmental fluctuations, on the other hand, would select for behavioral flexibility in the spatial and temporal use of the landscape. Archaeologically, this should be visible as a lack of patterning between site location, site use, and season of occupation. Late Paleolithic and Mesolithic data from southwestern Germany may fit these expectations. During the Late Magdalenian, there is a tight association between geography, site use, and the seasonality of occupation, and Jochim (1991) argues that Pleistocene environments would have been relatively predictable. During the ensuing period of increased environmental unpredictability at the end of the Pleistocene, the link between site location, use, and timing of occupation breaks down and there is great intersite diversity in all of these variables. Finally, during the Mesolithic, there is still high variability in site size and faunal composition, but there is also geographical patterning in the seasonality of occupation. Jochim (1991) infers from this more predictable temporal variability with unpredictable spatial variability during the Early Holocene. Before developing expectations from these models for the seasonality of site use and occupation at Badanj, we first consider its position within the landscape.

Badanj is located well within the karstic hinterland of Herzegovina, an area classified as fluviokarstic or merokarstic since river valleys and some surface drainage are important in shaping the landscape (Cvijič 1960; Herak 1972). Although located at a relatively low elevation (about 100 m/sl), the Pleistocene coastline would have been 35–40 km away to the south, and a direct route would have required traversing rugged and treacherous karstic terrain. Likewise, the edge of the Adriatic Plain would have been about 40 km away

to the southwest, with access provided by the lower Neretva Valley (fig. 1). Reconstructions of the local geography (Miracle and Sturdy 1991) and comparisons of Badanj's faunal assemblages to other sites in the region (Miracle 1995) indicate that the site was situated in a "hinterland" rather than "lowland plain" setting. The site's location in the hinterland suggests occupation from the spring to fall, but not in winter. Groups that overwintered on the Adriatic Plain and spent the summer in the highland interior are predicted to have stopped at Badanj as they monitored herd movement and preyed on migrating ungulates moving into the more mountainous interior. This suggests spring/fall site use. The low elevation of the site and its location near potentially marshy areas (see below) argues against summer occupation, since ungulates would have sought relief from biting insects at higher elevations in the interior. Seasonality indicators should show mostly spring/fall kills.

The record of resource use and occupation at Badanj should display a redundant pattern of resource use, activities, and seasonality of occupation at the site during the Pleniglacial. If we put the start of the Bølling at around 12,500 B.P., seasonality indicators from before that time should be from the spring/fall. Increased environmental unpredictability during the Late Glacial should break down the links between spatial location and temporal scheduling of activities. Seasonality indicators are predicted to come from seasons beyond the spring/fall, suggesting a shift in Badanj's role in the larger settlement system and a more diverse assortment of activities performed on site or during its occupation. The regular pattern of seasonal mobility predicted for the Pleniglacial should disintegrate as it becomes too difficult or costly to predict the location and abundance of resources in both space and time.

We have already discussed at length the sequence of paleoenvironmental changes and from this have predicted several environmental crises during the Late Glacial. The flooding of the Adriatic Plain would have disrupted the existing settlement system. Badanj's geographic position may have slid out of the hinterland with the rise in sea level, and the site may have begun to be more regularly used as a winter base camp after around 12,500 B.P. The increased environmental instability of the Bølling/Allerød interstadial, and in particular the warming pulses at the onset of the Bølling (around 12,500 B.P.) and Holocene (around 10,000 B.P.), would have been periods of marked climatic instability that may have witnessed widespread environmental perturbations and resource failure. Groups experiencing subsistence stress at these times, among other responses, may have more regularly taken prey that otherwise would have been considered undesirable, for example, animals in poor nutritional condition. Red deer tend to be at their thinnest during the early spring. Fat levels in males drop after the rut (late fall) and after parturition in females (late spring-early summer) (Clutton-Brock et al. 1982). Animals taken during the early spring will be both thin and lean. Therefore, the number of animals taken during the early spring should increase during the Bølling/Allerød and particularly at the commencement of the interstadial around 12,500 B.P.

## Excavations at Badanj

Badanj was excavated from 1986 to 1987 as part of the joint American-Yugoslavian research project "Paleolithic-Mesolithic Occupation of the Adriatic-Mediterranean Zone of Bosnia-Herzegovina." The site is a south-facing rockshelter located in the 50-meter deep gorge of the Bregava River, a small, seasonally flowing tributary of the Neretva River. The site has ready access to small plateaus to the northwest and southeast, riverine-woodland habitats along the valley floor, and heavily dissected broken limestone terrain ("angry karst") to the south and southwest (Miracle and Sturdy 1991). The snow line may have been as low

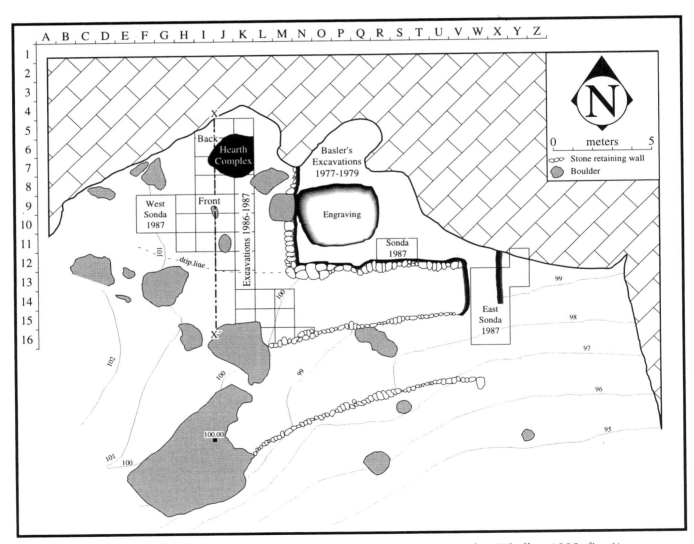

**Figure 3.** Plan of recent excavations at Badanj at the end of the 1986 season (after Whallon 1989; fig. 1).

as 400 m during the Late Glacial (Miracle and Sturdy 1991). If so, most of the area to the northeast of Badanj would have been under snow from the late fall to early spring.

Horizontal excavations covered about 35 square meters on the western side of the site (fig. 3) and comprised a three- to four-meter-wide transect from the back wall of the shelter to the front limit of prehistoric occupation (Whallon 1989). About 20 cultural and natural levels were excavated, along with a deep hearth complex that appears to have been continuously reused during successive occupations (fig. 4). In figure 4 we summarize our interpretation of the site's stratigraphy.[3] The left column lists levels in stratigraphic order from near the back cave wall (northern part of excavation in fig. 3). Some of these levels, particularly 5, 5a, and 11M, showed evidence of mixing. Many of these deposits from the back of the cave appear to reflect trash dumps or middens that were cut into underlying levels. These middens commonly interfingered with the sediments from the large hearth basin. The hearth subdivisions indicated in the central column of figure 4 are arbitrary and do not reflect natural layers or discrete depositional events. The stippling in figure 4 indicates the probable time of hearth use. It is not possible, however, to link periods of hearth use to individual levels from either the back or the front of the rockshelter. The hearth basin appears to have been repeatedly emptied, excavated, and filled with debris. The hearth basin frequently cuts into the "front" levels from the southern portion of the site (right column in fig. 4 excavation levels). Levels from the front of the site are in clear superposition relative to each other and, excepting Levels 1 and 2, give no indications of mixing. Stratigraphic links between the front and back portions of the site are complicated by the interposed hearth basin. Lines between levels indicate superpositional relationships between the front and back parts of the site.[4] The AMS radiocarbon dates are from Levels 6 and 13 (Miracle and Sturdy 1991). Excavations yielded rich Epipaleolithic assemblages that are typologically similar to the final Epigravettian in the southern Adriatic area of Italy (Whallon 1989). Assemblages from levels below Level 6 contain greater percentages of backed bladelets and microgravettes, while assemblages from Level 6 and above contain greater percentages of "thumbnail" flake scrapers and microliths (Whallon 1989).

Red deer is numerically dominant in faunal assemblages from all levels and is relatively constant in fre-

| Excavation Levels | | | $^{14}$C Dates |
|---|---|---|---|
| Back | Hearth | Front | |
| | | Surface | |
| | | 1 | |
| | | 2 | |
| 5 | | | |
| 2a / 2b | | | |
| 5a | Upper Hearth | 3 | |
| 7 | | 4 | |
| | Lower Hearth | 6 | 12,380±110 B.P. (OxA-2197) |
| 7a | | | |
| 11 / 11M | Basal Hearth | 8 | |
| | | 9 | |
| | | 10 | |
| | | 14 | |
| 12 | | | |
| 16 / 17 | | 13 | 13,200±150 B.P. (OxA-2196) |

**Figure 4.** Stratigraphic sequence of excavated levels at Badanj. In figure 3, back levels are in the northern area of the 1986–1987 excavations marked "Back"; hearth levels are in the "Hearth Complex"; front levels are in the area marked "Front."

quency, with the exception of a significant drop in abundance in Levels 8, 9, 10, and 14 (Miracle and Sturdy 1991). It, along with the constant but rare large bovids (most likely *Bos*) and equids (mostly *Equus hydruntinus*), was the most important sources of meat and fat. Hare (*Lepus* sp.) is present in small, yet significant numbers at all levels of the site. Carnivore remains (a large canid—probably wolf, lynx, wild cat, fox, badger) are extremely rare in all levels of the site. The smaller bovids (*Capra* and *Rupicapra*) and roe deer inversely vary in abundance; the former are most abundant in Levels 8, 9, 10, 13, and 14 and decline sharply in frequency above Level 3, while roe deer is very rare or missing from Levels 3 and below. The increase in roe deer in the upper levels is probably related to an expansion of forest cover, but we note that this may well still date within the Bølling/Allerød interstadial and need not mark the Pleistocene-Holocene boundary as previously argued by Miracle and Sturdy (1991:95). This alternative interpretation finds support from evidence of an expansion of forest cover between about 12,500 and 11,000 B.P. in the Adriatic core (Rossignol-Strick et al. 1992). For the time being, we will leave the dating of these upper levels an open question and await further AMS results.

## SEASONALITY INDICATORS IN THE BADANJ FAUNAL REMAINS

### Introduction

We limit our discussion of seasonality indicators from Badanj to fetal bone growth and cementum increments. These data were chosen because sample sizes are relatively large and the precision and accuracy of seasonality estimates based on these techniques are fairly high. Analyses focus on red deer since their remains are the most numerous in all assemblages from Badanj. Seasonality data are available on other species from Badanj, including the presence of migratory birds, tooth eruption in ungulates, and tooth sections from other taxa. These other data are limited by small sample sizes and/or uncertainty over the reliability of results and will be presented at a later date.

Fetal remains can be highly indicative of the season of death of the target species and hence very useful in reconstructing the seasonality of site occupation and the scheduling of subsistence activities. Fetuses from species that bear young only once a year during a fairly restricted time period are strong evidence of winter-spring deaths of pregnant females. With the exception of most rodents and lagomorphs, which often bear several litters a year, most ungulate and carnivore species in mid- to high-latitude environments meet these conditions. Since mammalian fetuses develop and grow very rapidly, fetal size has the potential to give fairly precise estimates of the number of days since conception (fetal age). Fetal ungulate and carnivore remains may allow us not only to identify a kill as "winter" or "spring," but to make finer distinctions within these seasons at a level of months or even weeks.

When appropriately utilized, increment analysis functions as a powerful tool for distinguishing aspects of prey seasonality and demography crucial to understanding the broader patterns of human settlement and subsistence. While the method has been applied archaeologically for two decades (Saxon and Higham 1969; Benn 1974; Kay 1974), it is only within the last five years that advances in the methodology of increment analysis as applied to archaeological dentitions have established the credibility of the technique for determining season and age of death for individuals (Gordon 1988; Lieberman et al. 1990; Pike-Tay 1991). The relatively complete dentitions that are needed to reliably use dental eruption and attrition are extremely rare at Badanj due to the high fragmentation of the bones, making sectioning particularly appropriate for seasonality analysis of the Badanj assemblages.

### Fetal Long Bones

Fetal remains have received surprisingly little attention in the archaeozoological and paleontological literature. Paleontologists and archaeozoologists generally make only passing references to fetal remains in assemblages (e.g., Bouchud 1975). The causes of this research bias against fetal remains are probably the rarity of fetal remains in assemblages, whether due to excavation techniques or poor preservation, and the assumed difficulty of identifying remains to finer taxonomic levels such as genera and species. However, the recent atlas for the identification of fetal remains of domestic animals (Prummel 1987a, 1987b) shows that elements may often be identifiable to genera from older fetuses. The apparent lack of interest by archaeozoologists and archaeologists in fetal remains is difficult to understand given the recognized value of fetal remains for inferring seasonality (e.g., Spiess 1979). The oft-cited review of seasonality studies by Monks (1981) makes no reference to fetal remains, and more recent reviews of seasonality made within the context of French Upper Paleolithic studies (Gordon 1988; Pike-Tay 1991) are similarly silent on the subject.[5] Little has been done by archaeozoologists with fetal remains beyond listing their presence and noting their indication of a winter/spring occupation.

The most detailed study of archaeological fetal remains of which we are aware is Spiess (1979). Spiess regressed hind-foot length on age (days since conception) for four fetal caribou published by Kelsall (1957). He then calculated the percentage of hind-foot length represented by different long bones in six immature *Rangifer* specimens. As Spiess notes, to calculate fetal age from diaphysis length, he must assume that fetal growth is constant and that during this growth the proportions between total hind-foot diaphyseal lengths remain constant (Spiess 1979:94). He suggested that the calculated dates of death are accurate within one month of the actual date of death; this taking into account error in age estimation, variation in date of conception around the peak conception date, and variation in the timing of the peak conception date. In his application of these regressions to archaeological data from the Abri Pataud, Spiess further assumed that conceptions peaked on October 15 and that the fetal remains came from reindeer (Spiess 1979:187). Given these assumptions and regression equations, Spiess suggested that fetal reindeer remains from the Abri Pataud resulted from a winter occupation from December to February, and that this pattern of occupation was repeated over a span of more than 15,000 years (Spiess 1979:188).

## Methods

Estimates for the time of death based on fetal long bone length were calculated using slightly modified regression equations published by Wenham et al. (1986:338–340). The animals used in this study were 17 farm-raised red deer hinds of known age (3 to 14 years, average = 10.29 years) that were kept on controlled diets, mated on known dates, and randomly allocated to slaughter between 72 and 224 days gestation (Wenham et al. 1986:337). Fetuses were radiographed in the lateral position, and measurements were taken from the radiographs with a vernier microscope or gauge. Measurements were taken on skull length and depth, and on the diaphyseal length and breadth at mid-shaft of the humerus, radius, metacarpal, femur, tibia, metatarsal, ilium, and ischium (length only on the latter two). Cross-plots of linear measures against fetal age showed almost linear relationships, and they fitted Gompertz equations to the data to relate body weight to fetal age and skeletal dimensions to weight and age combined. As archaeologists, we are interested in working these relationships in the opposite direction, that is, using skeletal dimensions to calculate fetal age. Therefore, we re-expressed their equations to predict age from skeletal dimensions and dropped body weight from the equations. Body weight figures into the equations as an allometric factor and is only important when fetuses are extremely light or heavy for their age (a difference of 14 percent in body weight affects the age estimate by only two days). The slightly modified equations did quite well in predicting fetal ages from humerus lengths and metatarsal lengths (data read from Wenham et al. 1986:figs. 3–4). These equations for length are as follows (where $t$ is the fetal age and $l$ is the diaphyseal length):

1. humerus: $t = \dfrac{-\ln[3.049 - \ln(l)] + 1.941}{.01}$

2. radius: $t = \dfrac{-\ln[2.999 - \ln(l)] + 1.916}{.011}$

3. metacarpal: $t = \dfrac{-\ln[3.189 - \ln(l)] + 2.091}{.012}$

4. femur: $t = \dfrac{-\ln[3.195 - \ln(l)] + 2.000}{.01}$

5. tibia: $t = \dfrac{-\ln[3.303 - \ln(l)] + 2.000}{.011}$

6. metatarsal: $t = \dfrac{-\ln[3.169 - \ln(l)] + 2.157}{.013}$

7. ilium: $t = \dfrac{-\ln[2.241 - \ln(l)] + 1.883}{.011}$

8. ischium: $t = \dfrac{-\ln[2.071 - \ln(l)] + 2.210}{.014}$

These equations are appropriate for fetuses between the ages of 72 days and 224 days. Fetuses younger than 72 days would have only rudimentary bones with very poor preservation potential. Fetuses older than 224 are almost full-term (gestation length in *Cervus* populations ranges between 223–238 days [Sadleir 1987:131]) and have bones that are indistinguishable from neonatal individuals.

The main limitation of these equations is that they are based on animals raised under artificial conditions. We can be quite certain that hinds in wild populations experience nutritional stress during the winter and hence when they are pregnant. The ability of hinds to buffer this stress depends on the availability of local forage during the winter and the amount of fat put on during the preceding summer and fall. We lack data on the impact of the mother's nutritional status on fetal development, but we may infer on the basis of numerous studies of other mammal species that the mothers in poorer health conditions will bear smaller offspring. The result of using regression equations based on well-fed animals to estimate fetal age in stressed populations will be to underestimate the fetal age in the stressed populations, that is, estimates will systematically be younger than true ages.

## Results

A large number of fetal/neonatal remains were identified from the excavated levels at Badanj (tables 2–3).[6] They have been quantified as number of identified specimens (NISP) and minimum number of individuals (MNI). MNIs were calculated for each excavation level and for the site as a whole. As expected (see Grayson 1984b:27–35), the sum of MNIs from each excavation level (total MNI=23) greatly exceeds the MNI calculated for the site as a whole (MNI=11). We favor the more conservative MNI estimate since excavation levels were not separated by sterile layers, and hence assemblages from adjacent levels may not be independent.

Fetal remains comprise 1.65 percent of the total ungulate NISP. These remains consisted primarily of long bone diaphyses. Identification to element was relatively easy in the case of elements like the ulna and humerus that have distinctive features on the diaphysis. Many fragments of other limb elements could not be

TABLE I

**Counts of fetal remains by excavation level at Badanj**

| Level | Fetal Remains | | | Total NISP | % Total NISP | Weight (gm)/Count Fragments[1] |
|---|---|---|---|---|---|---|
| | NISP | MNI | Basis of MNI | | | |
| 1 / 2 / 5 | 8 | 1 | left humerus | 565 | 1.42 | 1.11 |
| 2a / 2b | 9 | 3 | left humerus | 690 | 1.30 | 1.19 |
| 3 | 5 | 1 | left ulna 516 | 0.97 | 0.71 | |
| 4 | 7 | 1 | left femur | 374 | 1.87 | 0.68 |
| 5a | 7 | 1 | right ischium | 382 | 1.83 | 0.65 |
| 7 | 8 | 2 | left humerus | 638 | 1.25 | 0.48 |
| Lower Hearth (LH) | 3 | 1 | right humerus | 139 | 2.16 | 0.55 |
| 6 | 19 | 2 | right humerus | 523 | 3.63 | 0.48 |
| 7A | 3 | 1 | right femur | 201 | 1.49 | 0.62 |
| 11 / 11M | 5 | 2 | right humerus | 424 | 1.18 | 0.47 |
| 8 | 0 | 0 | | 92 | 0.00 | 0.71 |
| 9 | 0 | 0 | | 197 | 0.00 | 0.33 |
| 10 | 0 | 0 | | 127 | 0.00 | 0.28 |
| 14 | 0 | 0 | | 97 | 0.00 | 0.21 |
| Basal Hearth (BH) | 17 | 3 | left humerus | 554 | 3.07 | 0.41 |
| 12 | 10 | 2 | right humerus | 566 | 1.77 | 0.33 |
| 16 / 17 | 5 | 1 | right ilium | 276 | 1.81 | 0.23 |
| 13 | 8 | 2 | right humerus | 538 | 1.49 | 0.24 |
| **TOTAL** | 114 | 23 | | 6899 | 1.65 | 0.44 |

[1]Unidentified fragments not identified to genus or species.

NISP and MNI are for fetal remains. "Basis of MNI" lists the element used to determine MNI. Total NISP is the total number of identified elements (all species) from each level. % Total NISP is Fetal NISP/Total NISP expressed as a percentage. Excavation levels listed in approximate stratigraphic order, but see figure 4 and accompanying discussion.

identified beyond "long bone fragment," and the number of humeral fragments relative to other limb elements is probably inflated due to the difficulty of making these other identifications. We have not included skull, rib, and vertebral fragments, and those fragments not identifiable to particular long bones due to uncertainties of identification. Remains identifiable to element were also sufficiently distinctive to allow identification to taxonomic order or family. None of the remains were identified as carnivore, equid, or large bovid. Furthermore, most of the more diagnostic remains such as the metapodials showed clear cervid characteristics. Given the predominance of red deer remains in the levels with fetal remains, we can safely assume that most of the fetal remains are also from red deer.

In contrast to the nonfetal red deer assemblages, carpals, tarsals, and phalanges are very poorly represented in the fetal remains (table 2). Several factors might explain this pattern of preservation. First, there may be a recovery bias against these very small elements. Second, these elements may have been preferentially destroyed by a number of taphonomic factors mediated by a common variable such as bone density. Third, variation in the sequence of ossification may lead to a bias for or against early- or late-forming elements.

An excavation or recovery bias against small fetal remains seems unlikely since the three-mm-mesh screens used in excavation recovered equally minute lagomorph and carnivore phalanges. Sediment samples wet screened with nylon stockings did not differ in composition from the rest of the assemblage, except by

TABLE 2

Counts of fetal remains by skeletal element at Badanj,
all levels combined

| Element | NISP | MNI | Basis of MNI |
|---|---|---|---|
| Scapula | 4 | 2 | right |
| Humerus | 25 | 11 | right |
| Radius | 10 | 5 | right |
| Ulna | 5 | 3 | right |
| Metacarpal | 3 | 1 | |
| Ilium | 5 | 3 | right |
| Ischium | 5 | 3 | right |
| Pubis | 1 | 1 | right |
| Femur | 12 | 5 | left |
| Tibia | 6 | 2 | left |
| Calcaneus | 1 | 1 | left |
| Metatarsal | 2 | 1 | |
| Metapodial | 31 | 4 | |
| Phalanx 1 | 2 | 1 | |
| Phalanx 2 | 1 | 1 | |
| Phalanx 3 | 1 | 1 | |
| Total | 114 | 11 | |

the presence of large quantities of bone slivers and fragments that resemble "bone meal." The lack of data on bone density and nutritional content of different fetal elements makes it impossible to directly evaluate hypotheses of differential destruction by physical processes, or carnivore or human preferences. Intuitively, however, it seems unlikely that the compact and nutritionally undesirable carpals and tarsals of adults would be dramatically different relative to the rest of the skeleton in fetuses. In a recent study on skeletal growth in fetal red deer, Wenham et al. (1986) document a significant and systematic variation in the timing of formation of different bones and their corresponding epiphyses. Ossification centers for the diaphyses of all of the major limb bones had already formed by 72 days into term (Wenham et al. 1986:345–364, table VII). Phalanges and the calcaneus showed ossification centers by 90 days into term, while ossification centers for the remaining carpals or tarsals were not present prior to 142 days into term (Wenham et al. 1986:345–364, table VII). Fetuses younger than 90 days of age will have rudimentary long bone diaphyses but will lack carpals, tarsals, and phalanges. Fetuses between 90 and 140 days of age will have well-

developed diaphyses, rudimentary phalanges, and calcanei but will lack other carpals and tarsals. Finally, fetuses older than 140 days progressively form the remaining carpals, tarsals, and epiphyses. We favor the variation in element formation as an explanation for the absence of carpals, tarsals, and phalanges from the Badanj fetal assemblages. We further note that an excavation recovery bias would act more strongly on small elements such as phalanges and calcanei from younger as opposed to older fetuses. Therefore, on the basis of the element composition of the fetal assemblage, we suggest that most fetus-bearing hinds were taken prior to mid-March (about 140 days into term if conception occurred in mid-October).

The fetal age estimates in table 3 were made with the equations given above. We have assumed a date of conception on October 15 and length of gestation is 233 days, giving parturition on June 5. Ovulation dates for red deer range from September to October and conception is highly synchronous; 75 percent of females in one study conceived in 15 days (Sadleir 1987: 128–129). Clutton-Brock and Albon (1989:51–53) report that over 80 percent of conceptions occur within one month, with recorded median dates falling between 6 and 20 October depending upon the population. Mean gestation length in four different populations ranged from 231–236 days, with an overall range of 223–238 days (Sadleir 1987:131). An error estimate of ± one month in fetal age estimates should reflect this variability in the timing of conception and length of pregnancy. We note a further source of error caused by the difficulty in determining if an element was whole or if it was missing a portion of the proximal or distal end. Use of regression formulas on incomplete elements will lead to underestimation of the age-at-death of the fetus, shifting seasonality estimates towards earlier in the year.

Interpretation

The fetal remains provide solid evidence that female animals were being hunted and brought to the site during the winter/spring. Application of the regression equations to complete long bones shows that it is possible to make fairly fine seasonal distinctions within the winter/spring. For example, fetal remains from Levels 6 and 12 indicate two distinct seasons of site use/occupation, winter and late spring, while indicators from the remaining levels can be accounted for by a single late winter/early spring occupation. This might indicate a change in site use during the formation of

TABLE 3

**Fetal seasonality indicators at Badanj**

| Level | Element | Date of Death | Season |
|-------|---------|---------------|--------|
| 2 | Radius, diaphysis | mid-December to mid-February | W |
| 2 | Ischium | mid-January to April | LW–SP |
| 2 | Humerus, diaphysis | February to mid-April | LW/ES |
| LH | Humerus, diaphysis | January-February | W |
| 6 | Humerus, diaphysis | January-February | W |
| 6 | Femur, diaphysis | February to mid-April | LW/ES |
| 6 | Metacarpal, distal epiphysis | April to mid-June | LS |
| 6 | Metapodial, distal epiphysis | April to mid-June | LS |
| 7A | Tibia, diaphysis | mid-December to mid-February | W |
| 7A | Femur, diaphysis | January-February | W |
| 11 | Humerus, diaphysis | February to mid-April | LW/ES |
| 11 | Tibia, proximal epiphysis | April to mid-June | LS |
| 12 | Radius, diaphysis | mid-December to mid-February | W |
| 12 | Radius, diaphysis | mid-December to mid-February | W |
| 12 | Humerus, diaphysis | January-February | W |
| 12 | Humerus, diaphysis | January-February | W |
| 12 | Humerus, diaphysis | January-February | W |
| 12 | Femur, diaphysis | January-February | W |
| 12 | Ilium | mid-March to mid-June | SP |
| BH | Radius, diaphysis | mid-December to mid-February | W |
| BH | Humerus, diaphysis | January-February | W |
| BH | Humerus, diaphysis | January-February | W |
| BH | Humerus, diaphysis | January-February | W |
| BH | Femur, diaphysis | February to mid-April | LW/ES |
| BH | Femur, diaphysis | February to mid-April | LW/ES |
| BH | Humerus, diaphysis | February to mid-April | LW/ES |
| BH | Calcaneus | mid-January to mid-June | LW–SP |

"W" is winter; "LW" is late winter; "ES" is early spring; "LS" is late spring; "SP" is spring.

Levels 6 and 12, either by a more frequent reoccupation at different seasons or single occupations of longer duration, or both. However, the regression equations, in this case, do not add much to what we would know from just scoring the presence and absence of fetal remains, that is, winter-spring resource and site use. Nevertheless, this is an important observation; we can conclude from it that there was considerable stability to the pattern of winter/spring hunting and site use over at least 1,000 years and perhaps even longer.

There is, however, considerable variation by level in the frequency of fetal remains when measured as a percentage of the number of identified specimens. Fetal remains are completely absent from several levels and reach a frequency of over 3.5 percent in others (table 1). In presenting changes in frequency over time, we treat the front and back portions of the site and the hearth complex separately (fig. 5) due to our uncertainty over precisely where the sequences are linked. We have also grouped Levels 1, 2, and 5 together since these levels from the top of the site all showed some evidence of mixing.

The histogram of % NISP of fetal remains (all levels included) is strongly bimodal, with modes at 0 percent and 1.2–1.6 percent (fig. 6). The outliers on the high end of the range may form a third mode. With

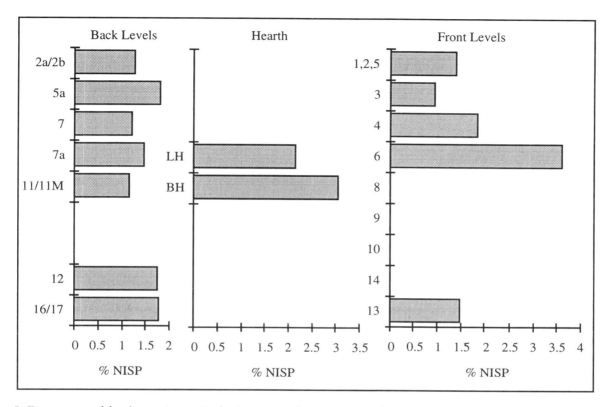

**Figure 5.** Frequency of fetal remains at Badanj measured as % NISP of identified fragments (data from table 1). Within each column, younger levels at the top of the graph. The stratigraphic relationship between the front levels, back levels, and the hearth complex is only approximate (see figure 4).

regards to the frequency of fetal remains, we can divide the excavated levels into three groups: no fetal remains (N=4), some fetal remains (N=11), and abundant fetal remains (N=2). These different levels, however, are not distributed at random within the stratigraphy. Fetal remains are found in all of the back and hearth levels but are absent from four out of ten level groups in the front of the site (figs. 4–5). Levels lacking fetal remains (8, 9, 10, and 14) in the front of the site form a continuous series, and the transition to abundant fetal remains in Level 6 is abrupt. Furthermore, this is not a simple change from lower to upper parts of the stratigraphy, since fetal remains are present in significant quantities in Level 13 at the bottom and in Levels 2a/2b and 1/2/5 at the top of the sequence.

The levels from the back of the site and the hearth complex, with the exception of the Basal Hearth, display a relatively uniform pattern of fetal representation. It is impossible to place the levels like the Basal Hearth and Level 11/11M precisely in the stratigraphy

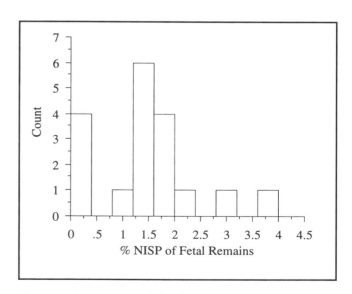

**Figure 6.** Histogram of the frequency of fetal remains (% NISP) in excavation levels at Badanj.

relative to the front levels. For the most part they cut into the underlying levels (8, 9, 10, 12, 14, 16/17) and contain stratigraphically mixed sediments. The Basal Hearth, however, appeared in rare cases to interdigitate with parts of these levels, and pieces of the Basal Hearth may be contemporaneous with Levels 8, 9, 10, or 14. Unfortunately we do not know if the fetal remains from the Basal Hearth were evenly distributed throughout it or were stratigraphically clustered. Thus it is impossible to know if any of these fetal remains are contemporaneous and thus indicate spatial partitioning of the site with regards to the disposal of fetuses as opposed to chronological differences. The stratigraphic situation of Level 11/11M is similar to the Basal Hearth, with the important difference that there are no direct contacts between Level 11/11M and front levels. It seems likely that the fetal remains from the Basal Hearth and Level 11/11M date to a later use and occupation of the site than the Levels 8, 9, 10, and 14.

There are a variety of factors besides past activities at Badanj that might explain these stratigraphic patterns in fetal abundance. First, high frequencies of fetal remains might be a product of large samples. Although there may appear to be a weak, positive relationship between sample size and % NISP fetal remains, this relationship only pertains if one lumps together the two (perhaps three) demonstrably different modes and treats the sample as one population (fig. 7). Variation in the frequency of fetal remains has little to do with effects of sample size.

Second, differences in the frequency of fetal remains might depend on taphonomic processes of bone fragmentation and destruction. As a general rule of thumb, one expects the remains of young individuals to be preferentially destroyed since epiphyseal ends are unfused, spongy, and easily chewed. A patterned bias against juvenile individuals has been widely recognized in paleontological and archaeological assemblages. What goes for juvenile animals is usually thought to apply to fetuses "in spades." Fetal elements lack a hard bone cortex and in general are assumed to be extremely fragile. We note, however, that the only complete adult ungulate bones were small carpals, tarsals, and sesamoids; the only complete ungulate long bones were fetal. This might suggest that the preservation of fetal elements is an all or nothing process; either they are consumed and completely destroyed or they are left untouched. Even so, one expects that destructive processes that more thoroughly fragment an assemblage would also be more likely to destroy fetal elements. It is therefore quite surprising that a measure like the average weight of unidentified fragments (weight/count), which is a good measure of the degree of fragmentation, does not show a relationship with % NISP fetal remains (fig. 8). Differential bone destruction does not appear to account for the variation in frequency of fetal remains at Badanj. Therefore, we interpret the Badanj fetal remains in behavioral terms related to the seasonality of site use and ungulate procurement.

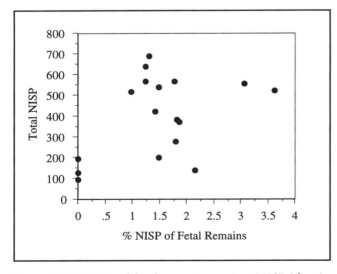

**Figure 7.** % NISP of fetal remains against NISP identified elements.

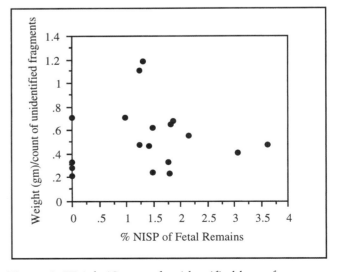

**Figure 8.** Weight/Count of unidentified bone fragments.

We suggest that the fetal remains show three different patterns of procurement/site-use practiced at Badanj. The recurrent pattern appears to have been to take at least a few pregnant females during a winter-spring use of the site. Towards the end of the pleniglacial, during the occupations that produced Levels 8, 9, 10, and 14, the hunting of pregnant females appears to have stopped. As discussed in detail above, most if not all of the fetal remains from Levels 11/11M and Basal Hearth are probably not contemporary but date to a later time period. At sometime near the stadial-interstadial transition (Level 6 at Badanj on the basis of the radiocarbon dates), this pattern dramatically changed and for a probably brief period there was a marked selection for pregnant females. Shortly thereafter, the pattern returned to a more moderate take of pregnant females.

It is difficult to know how to interpret the frequency of fetal remains since detailed comparative data from other sites are rare. For instance, the Abri Pataud, considered to be a "classic" winter occupation (Spiess 1979; Gordon 1988), has fewer than 0.12 percent of reindeer NISP represented by fetal remains, and this estimate is based only on assemblages that contained fetal remains (table 4). This is an order of magnitude less than that found at Badanj. We might speculate that female animals were hunted in relatively greater numbers at Badanj than at the Abri Pataud. Given that female cervids tend to be in relatively better physiological condition than males during the winter (Clutton-Brock et al. 1982:156–157), this might have important implications for the types of subsistence stresses that groups in the two regions were encountering and their responses to them. A number of processes, however, could create this contrast including collecting procedures, bone preservation, and differences in prehistoric behavior.

Spiess (1979:188) suggested that the fetal long bones showed "that over this span of more than 15,000 years . . . the Abri was inhabited during December, January, and February." Again, we point out that the pattern is not constant at the Abri Pataud. Fetal remains are actually missing from a majority of the excavated assemblages. From the remaining assemblages, fetal remains are 10 times more common in the Proto-Magdalenian than in any of the other levels except for the Aurignacian, where the difference is by only a factor of five. On the surface, this does not appear to be a regular pattern of winter habitation over a span of greater than 15,000 years. As discussed above, however, we lack the comparative data needed to make sense of these changes and differences.

## TABLE 4
### Summary of fetal remains from the Abri Pataud

| Level | NISP[1] Reindeer | NISP[2] Fetal | %NISP Fetal |
|---|---|---|---|
| 2 (Proto-Magdalenian) | 823 | 9 | 1.09 |
| 3: Main (Perigordian VI) | 1442 | 1 | 0.07 |
| 3/4 (Eboulis) | 906 | 1 | 0.11 |
| 5 (Perigordian IV) | 9950 | 4 | 0.04 |
| 11 (Aurignacian) | 373 | 1 | 0.27 |
| Total | 13494 | 16 | 0.12 |

[1]From Bouchud 1975:70–71, table 1. Long bone shaft fragments were excluded from the totals.

[2]From Spiess 1979:188, table 6.1. Fetal remains from Eboulis 1/2 and Level 6 were not included due to missing or contradictory NISP counts.

In sum, with the exception of Levels 8, 9, 10, and 14, there is evidence of a repeated late winter-early spring use of Badanj. The available data do not indicate whether the winter and spring indicators found in these levels were the product of more extended occupations or slight variations in the timing of brief stops. The regression age estimates showed that a number of the fetal remains were from fairly early in the term and can best be classified as full "winter."

## Cementum Increments

### Method

Sample Size

A sample of 124 incisiform teeth, representing all seven taxa within the Badanj deposits (Miracle and Sturdy 1991), was made available for increment analysis. However, the final number of teeth sectioned for the analysis was restricted in terms of absolute numbers and taxa represented due to a lack of modern controls and limitations of the sectioning techniques. Appropriate control populations in which the parameters of increment formation are well established are not available for most taxa from Badanj. Currently, increment analysis is a "species-specific" technique in which appropriate application to archaeological samples is predicated upon research establishing the parameters of increment formation for comparative populations existing in ecologically analogous contexts (Lieberman et al. 1990; Pike-Tay 1991). This requirement may become less absolute as the biology of cementum formation is more thoroughly understood (Lieberman and Meadow 1992). Sufficient comparative research is available to justify application of increment analysis for three taxa from Badanj: large bovids (identifiable only to *Bos*) (Coy et al. 1982; Rackham 1986; Sten 1991; Beasley et al. 1992), roe deer (*Capreolus capreolus*) (Szabik 1973; White 1974), and red deer (*Cervus elaphus*).[7] Difficulties in physically manipulating the small roe deer incisors on the available sectioning and grinding equipment, however, precluded their use in this analysis. *Bos* was represented by only two teeth, one of which had no root segment, so none were included in the analysis. Therefore, although the final sample was limited to a total of 67 red deer incisors, we note that red deer dominate the assemblage (Miracle and Sturdy 1991) and comprise 54 percent of the total tooth sample available for sectioning.

*Cervus* Sample

Table 5 lists the *Cervus* incisiform teeth available for analysis by level and tooth type (deciduous incisor, first incisor, second incisor, etc.). Teeth from each level were identified to type and side with the exception of 13 deciduous incisors which could not be confidently assigned to type. The final number of identified specimens (NISP) that were available for increment analysis was 67 teeth.

Minimum number of individuals (MNI) were then derived for the entire sample following the procedure outlined by White (1953) in which the element type and side with the highest frequency was taken as the minimum value. Additional comparative analysis was made to further differentiate individuals on the basis of the degree of wear on the teeth. Table 6 identifies the NISP and MNI values determined by level for the Badanj assemblage. MNIi is the initial number of individuals derived from the tooth with the highest frequency, taking only one side into consideration. MNIa is the adjusted value after considering differences in wear. In most cases, first and second incisors were the only tooth types of sufficient size to confidently differentiate individuals on the basis of wear. Although this method of MNI determination is somewhat subjective, conservative guidelines were followed and only teeth with extreme differences were considered separate individuals. The MNIa results depicted in table 6 are thus considered accurate estimates of the number of individuals represented by tooth elements.

It is important to note that each level was treated as a separate aggregate for determining MNI, and as a result, the total MNI is greater than that calculated for the Badanj assemblage as a whole (Grayson 1984b). However, we feel the degree of interdependence is low for several reasons. First, the upper level (2b, 3, 5a, and 7) sample is stratigraphically separated from the lower level (13, 16, 17, and LH) sample, suggesting that two different populations of red deer individuals are represented. Therefore, we have some temporal separation of independent populations, at least at the scale of the

TABLE 5
**Cervus tooth samples from Badanj**

| Level | dI1 | dI indet | I1 | I2 | I3 | C | Total |
|---|---|---|---|---|---|---|---|
| 2b | 0 | 0 | 0 | 2 | 0 | 1 | 3 |
| 3 | 1 | 4 | 2 | 2 | 1 | 1 | 11 |
| 5a | 0 | 1 | 2 | 0 | 1 | 3 | 7 |
| 7 | 1 | 5 | 4 | 4 | 4 | 5 | 23 |
| BA (LH) | 0 | 0 | 2 | 0 | 1 | 0 | 3 |
| 16 | 0 | 3 | 0 | 0 | 0 | 0 | 3 |
| 17 | 0 | 0 | 0 | 2 | 0 | 0 | 2 |
| 13 | 1 | 0 | 5 | 3 | 6 | 0 | 15 |
| Total | 3 | 13 | 15 | 13 | 13 | 10 | 67 |

"dI1"=deciduous first incisor; "dI indet"=deciduous incisor, position indeterminate; "I1, I2, I3"=permanent first, second, and third incisors; "C"=canine.

TABLE 6
**NISP and MNI values for the Badanj Cervus sample**

| Level | NISP | MNIi | MNIa |
|---|---|---|---|
| 2b | 3 | 2 | 2 |
| 3 | 11 | 2 | 4 |
| 5a | 7 | 1 | 2 |
| 7 | 23 | 3 | 5 |
| BA (LH) | 3 | 1 | 1 |
| 16 | 3 | 1 | 1 |
| 17 | 2 | 1 | 1 |
| 13 | 15 | 4 | 5 |
| Total | 67 | 15 | 21 |

MNIi=initial value derived from element with the highest frequency.
MNIa=value adjusted for differences in wear and size.

site as a whole. Second, tooth samples in adjacent levels were cursorily examined for similarities in tooth type, side, and degree of wear. For the most part, sufficient differences existed to warrant the assumption that interdependence of teeth was reasonably low. This is particularly true for individuals from the lower levels that demonstrated marked interassemblage differences. Finally, we reasoned that the results from the increment analysis would sufficiently separate or link individuals on the basis of age and season of death to test the assumption of low interdependence.

Table 7 compares *Cervus* MNI values from the tooth sample against those for the entire site. MNIsite values are based on the most numerous element and side, considering all available skeletal elements. MNIa values are taken from table 6 above.

The teeth available for increment analysis represent slightly over 25 percent of the total number of *Cervus* individuals recorded from Badanj when levels are treated independently. The sample is drawn from levels near both the top and bottom of the stratigraphy. We conclude that the sample is sufficient to highlight any major changes over time in red deer exploitation at Badanj.

Increment Analysis

Teeth were analyzed following the procedures outlined in Gordon (1988), Pike-Tay (1991), and O'Brien (1994). A low-speed Beuhler Isomet® saw was used to cut longitudinal sections parallel to the sagittal (labial-lingual) axis of the tooth. Cut faces were then polished with 600 grit and 1000 grit alumina oxide powders, washed, dried, and mounted on clean petrographic slides using Epo-Tech® epoxy. The two cut halves were then sectioned away from the slide and the process repeated. The number of slides produced from this process varied from one to six per tooth, with a mean of 3.0 slides/tooth. Sections were ground to appropriate thickness using a large rotary grinder and sometimes polished with fine grinding powders. Although polishing is often recommended to enhance the clarity of the section, in fact, the grit particles frequently become embedded on the surface of the section obscuring the microscopic detail (Beasley et al. 1992; O'Brien 1994).

Section viewing was completed using a polarizing light microscope at magnifications from 40X to 100X. Under polarized light, opaque increments appear dark and translucent increments appear light (Pike-Tay 1991; Lieberman and Meadow 1992). The entire perimeter of a tooth section was examined although

TABLE 7

**Comparison of total site MNI with MNI calculated for the tooth sample**

| Level | MNIsite | MNIa |
|-------|---------|------|
| 1 | 4 | - |
| 2 | 3 | - |
| 5 | 2 | - |
| 2a | 7 | - |
| 2b | 2 | 2 |
| 3 | 6 | 4 |
| 4 | 5 | - |
| 5a | 4 | 2 |
| 7 | 5 | 5 |
| BA (LH) | 4 | 1 |
| 6 | 4 | - |
| 7a | 3 | - |
| 11 / 11M | 5 | - |
| 8 | 2 | - |
| 9 | 1 | - |
| 10 | 2 | - |
| 14 | 2 | - |
| BH | 5 | - |
| 12 | 6 | - |
| 16 / 17 | 4 | 2 |
| 13 | 5 | 5 |
| Total | 81 | 21 |

MNIa values are from Table 6, this study.

the clearest area for increments was found to occur just coronal to the apical "pad" of the root (approximately a third of the distance up the tooth) on the lingual side. This is an area of acellular cementum accretion in which increments appear uniform in width and have been found to correspond with seasonal cycles in the life history of an individual. Analysis of increments in acellular cementum avoids the potential error of determining season of death from increments in the cellular cementum of root apices which are more erratic in appearance and may not consistently correspond to seasonal periods (Lieberman and Meadow 1992).

Sections from each tooth were examined for the number of opaque increments and the type and relative width of the outer increment. Although all slides were examined, they were subjectively ranked on the basis of the increment clarity, and readings from the clearest sections took precedence in determining the final number of increments and the appearance of the outermost increment.

## Results

### Sample Problems

Of the 67 teeth available for sectioning, less than 30 percent (N=19) produced sections with increments that could be reasonably interpreted. There were two reasons for this. First, as with the small roe deer teeth, third incisors, canines, and frequently second incisors were too small or fragmented to properly section. Attempts were made to section several small teeth resulting in the mostly complete destruction of the specimen and no readable sections. Fortunately, as MNI values were derived from the more easily sectioned larger teeth, the number of individuals sampled was not significantly affected as a result of problems associated with sectioning mechanics.

Secondly, most teeth in the sample exhibited large areas of mechanical abrasion that effectively stripped large portions of cementum from the tooth, prohibiting any effective analysis. These areas were easily identified as rough, torn surfaces of the cementum when viewed under high magnification and contrasted markedly with the smooth, even surfaces of cementum unaffected by abrasion. Additional sections were made for abraded teeth in an effort to isolate areas of "clean" cementum.

Table 8 compares the NISP and MNI samples originally available for increment analysis with samples producing sections with "readable" cementum deposits. Of an original NISP of 67 teeth, 19 (28.4 percent) exhibited sections with cementum increments from which age and season of death could be determined. The total MNI of the sample was affected much less by abrasion; an MNI of 18 was identified from sections out of the initial sample of 21 individuals.

### Seasonality Data

Table 9 identifies the seasonality data derived from outer increment type and relative width for each tooth producing interpretable sections. All teeth comprising the original MNIa sample (N=21) are listed regardless of whether or not their cementum deposits could be read. Specimens producing readable sections and coming from separate individuals are assigned an "individual #" under *MNIr*, while readable sections that could not be identified as coming from separate individuals are labeled with a dash.

TABLE 8

**Badanj NISP and MNI samples compared after increment analysis**

| Level | Initial Sample | | Sectioned Sample | |
|---|---|---|---|---|
| | NISP | MNIa | NISPr | MNIr |
| 2b | 3 | 2 | 2 | 2 |
| 3 | 11 | 4 | 3 | 3 |
| 5a | 7 | 2 | 1 | 1 |
| 7 | 23 | 5 | 6 | 5 |
| 13 | 15 | 5 | 7 | 7 |
| 16 | 3 | 1 | 0 | 0 |
| 17 | 2 | 1 | 0 | 0 |
| BA (LH) | 3 | 1 | 0 | 0 |
| **Total** | **67** | **21** | **19** | **18** |

NISP and MNI values under "Initial Sample" are the original sample derived from Table 6; NISPr=number of specimens producing sections with readable cementum. MNIr=number of individuals from the MNIa sample producing sections with readable cementum.

For teeth with readable sections, the outer increment ([O]paque or [T]ranslucent) is identified, as well as the relative width of the increment in relation to previously deposited increments of that type. In cases where both increment types are listed and/or a range of widths is indicated, the sections for that tooth produced the indicated range of readings. Seasonal time frames were assigned using the information on increment formation in red deer compiled by Pike-Tay (1991:64). Seasons were divided into Winter (W), Spring (Sp), Summer (Su), and Fall (F) and frequently subdivided into Early (E), Middle (M), or Late (L).

## Discussion

Sample size is an important, but often neglected, aspect of the proper application of increment analysis to archaeological faunas. Since increment analysis is necessarily measuring the season and age at death of *individuals*, MNI is the preferable measure of sample size (Monks 1981; Pike-Tay 1991), despite the fact that NISP values are often used (Gordon 1988; Olsen 1989). This is particularly important for smaller sample sizes in which the potential interdependence of tooth types is high. Equally important is relating the MNI to be analyzed for increment information to the total MNI for the site, based on additional criteria.

TABLE 9

**Seasonality data for *Cervus* individuals at Badanj**

| MNIr Individual # | Level | Outer Increment Type | Width | Season |
|---|---|---|---|---|
| 1 | 2b | T/O | 1.00/<0.25 | LF/EW |
| 2 | 2b | O/T | 1.00/<0.25 | W/ESp |
| 3 | 3 | T | 0.50-1.00 | Su/F |
| 4 | 3 | T | 0.75 | MF |
| 5 | 3 | T | 0.25-0.50 | Su |
| 6 | 5a | T | 0.25 | LSp |
| 7 | 7 | T | 0.50 | Su |
| 8 | 7 | T | 1.00 | LF |
| 9 | 7 | T/O | 1.00/<0.25 | LF/EW |
| 10 | 7 | T | 1.00 | LF |
| - | 7 | T/O | 1.00/<0.25 | LF/EW |
| 11 | 7 | O | - | W |
| 12 | 13 | O | - | W |
| 13 | 13 | T | 1.00 | LF |
| 14 | 13 | T | 1.00 | LF |
| 15 | 13 | O | - | W |
| 16 | 13 | T | 1.00 | LF |
| 17 | 13 | O/T | 1.00/<0.25 | LW/ESp |
| 18 | 13 | T | 0.75 | MF |

Outer increment is opaque (O), transitional opaque-translucent (O/T), transitional translucent-opaque (T/O), or translucent (T). Increment width is relative to previously deposited increments of the same type. Seasons were divided into winter (W), spring (Sp), summer (Su), and fall (F), with subdivisions of early (E), middle (M), or late (L).

Without this information it is difficult to evaluate the degree to which seasonality determined from dental increments reflects the total range of seasonal behaviors originally contributing to site formation, both in terms of the particular taxon under study as well as other taxa represented (cf. Gordon 1988; White 1990; Pike-Tay 1991). Seasonal uniformity in the timing of death for a small number of individuals should not be assumed as representative of the entire population, particularly if total site MNI is large (see Clottes 1989). Even if hunters pursue the same taxon throughout the year, seasonal differences in the economic value of head parts relative to transport and processing costs (Bunn et al. 1988; Stiner 1990) may differentially affect the introduction of teeth into the assemblage and bias the overall seasonal pattern.

With these issues in mind, we are confident that the *Cervus* teeth sectioned for increment analysis adequately sample the population of red deer introduced to Badanj during the accumulation of the examined levels. Although MNI values were calculated by treating levels independently, the potential interdependence of tooth elements was probably low and the results of the increment analysis would aid in evaluating the extent to which interdependence was a problem. Discriminating individuals on the basis of increment differences is not uncommon and can provide additional MNI information beyond that gained by other means (Kay 1974; Pike-Tay 1991). In fact, increment differences (i.e., total number and outer increment type) warranted the addition of several individuals previously unidentified on the basis of visual characteristics, suggesting that if anything, our initial MNI calculations were underestimates.[8] Despite the loss of some teeth from extensive abrasion and the corresponding reduction in MNI, 60 percent of the red deer population from sampled levels at Badanj provided information on season and age

(MNIr of 18 out of MNIsite of 30, data from tables 8 and 9). We conclude that enough deer were sampled from levels near the top and bottom of the site to tell us something about broad changes in patterns of human subsistence over time.

The Badanj *Cervus* highlight another issue currently being raised with regard to increment analysis: the potential error of determining season and age of death from isolated teeth subject to mechanical or chemical abrasion of the outer cementum surfaces. Lieberman and Meadow (1992) have noted that postdepositional processes are likely to strip or modify outer increments since cementum is much softer than dentine. This is of obvious concern, as interpretation of the outer increment is the basis for determining season of death for the individual and accurate analysis presumes the cementum to be intact. Lieberman and Meadow (1992:68) conclude that "analysis of loose teeth can often lead to a false determination of the age and season of death of specimens," and recommend that only teeth encased in alveolar bone be used for increment studies (cf. Lieberman, this volume [eds.]).

While the potential loss of increments due to postdepositional processes is intuitively sound, Lieberman and Meadow (1992) offer no actual evidence demonstrating significant seasonal or age differences between alveolar-encased and isolated teeth from individuals within the same assemblage. Their warning against using isolated teeth carries the implicit assumption that postdepositional processes will so uniformly eliminate increments along all areas of the tooth as to leave no indication that the cementum was affected. Furthermore, their argument could be taken to suggest a uniformity in the effects of postdepositional processes on isolated teeth and does not consider the extreme variation inherent in the burial history of an individual. While we recognize their arguments as potentially valid, they need to be demonstrated rather than assumed.

We are particularly concerned that a blanket exclusion of isolated teeth from increment analysis will effectively eliminate a significant number of assemblages from consideration for use with a potentially powerful method of determining seasonality. This is particularly true for assemblages with a high degree of fragmentation in which alveolar-encased teeth are unavailable (such as Badanj) or for assemblages from which researchers are hesitant to release complete mandibles or maxillae for sectioning.

We consider it more likely that effects on tooth increments will vary with the specific taphonomic his-

tory of the individual, and will be detectable in most contexts. It is recognized that a wide range of processes (e.g., mechanical weathering [Behrensmeyer 1978; Lyman and Fox 1989], chemical diagenesis of bone mineral [Price et al. 1992], and profile compaction and processing [Klein and Cruz-Uribe 1984; Marean 1991]) differentially affect the preservation of information inherent in skeletal elements, but under most circumstances they can be detected in one fashion or another. We are proceeding with the hypothesis that mechanical abrasion, such as that exhibited by the Badanj teeth, will leave evidence identifying it as such so that adversely affected samples may be avoided. Chemical weathering is another matter, although we note that alveolar-encased teeth are no less subject to the effects of chemical weathering or leaching than isolated teeth.

There can be no doubt that the Badanj teeth suffered a significant degree of mechanical abrasion precluding analysis for a large sample of specimens. However, areas of abrasion could be easily identified and avoided, did not uniformly cover all areas of a specimen, and were not present on all specimens. Multiple sections from teeth aided in providing areas of cementum untouched by abrasive processes. Isolated zebra teeth from Hadza abandoned camps exhibited similar patterns of abrasion but recorded the same seasonal information as alveolar-encased samples (O'Brien 1994). Clearly, the problem of cementum preservation needs to be addressed in a more adequate fashion, but we currently see no reason to be suspicious of the Badanj increment results.

TABLE 10

**Summary of seasonality indicators at Badanj from red deer tooth sections**

| Level | Number of Sections MF–MSp | LSp–EF | Seasonality Interpretation |
|---|---|---|---|
| 2b | 2 | 0 | Winter |
| 3 | 0 | 3 | Summer to Fall |
| 5a | 0 | 1 | Late Spring |
| 7 | 5 | 1 | Late Fall-Winter and Summer |
| 13 | 7 | 0 | Mid-Fall to Early Spring |

Seasonality abbreviations same as those used in Table 9.

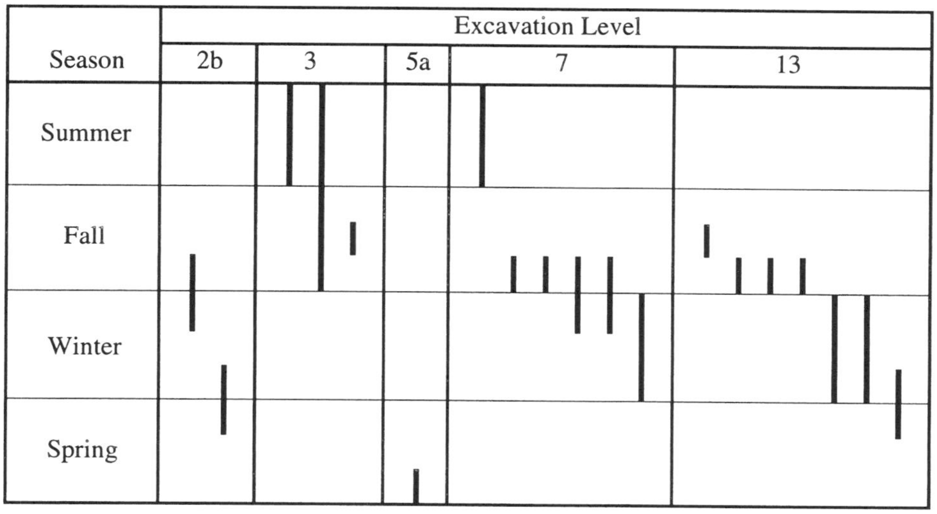

**Figure 9.** Seasonality of death of red deer at Badanj (data from table 9). Each vertical line represents a readable tooth section.

In figure 9 and table 10 we summarize the results of the tooth sectioning and our interpretations of red deer hunting and site use. We stress in this presentation the contrast between what we assume to be warm- season (late spring-early fall) versus cold-season (mid fall-mid spring) indicators. Considering the assemblage as a whole, teeth from cold-season kills outnumber those from warm-season kills by almost three to one. Furthermore, levels rarely contain both cold- and warm-season kills; only Level 7 has a summer kill mixed in with more numerous fall-winter kills. This suggests that the site was used, and/or that red deer were hunted, only seasonally during the time span required for a given occupation level to accumulate. Although sample sizes are regrettably small from the upper three levels, the data show a shift in seasonality from exclusively cold season during Level 13, to predominantly cold season in Level 7, to warm season in Levels 5a and 3, and back to cold season in Level 2b.

Seasonality information provided by the increment analysis reveals an interesting pattern of red deer exploitation over time. Lower stratigraphic levels (L7–L13) are almost uniformly represented by animals killed during the winter period (i.e., late fall through early spring). Upper stratigraphic levels demonstrate a shift in seasons by the addition of animals killed during the summer (i.e., late spring through mid fall).

## Summary of Seasonality Indicators

The fetal remains and tooth increments give contrastive yet complementary indications of seasonality. We are limited in our comparison to the levels that provided readable tooth sections. Unfortunately, none of these levels had complete enough fetal long bones to use the regression equations to estimate fetal age and compare the results to seasonality estimates based on teeth. In table 11 we compare the relative frequency of

TABLE 11

**Comparison of seasonality indicators from Badanj**

| Level | MNIr | %MNI MF–MSp | % Fetal MNI |
|-------|------|-------------|-------------|
| 2b[1] | 2 | 100 | 50 |
| 3 | 3 | 33 | 17 |
| 5a | 1 | 0 | 25 |
| 7 | 5 | 80 | 40 |
| 13 | 7 | 100 | 40 |

[1]Fetal MNI and %Fetal NISP values calculated for only Level 2b to make them comparable to the tooth sectioning data. NISP fetal remains=3; Total NISP=127.

"MNIr" from Table 8. "% MNI MF-MSp" is the MNI of red deer represented by teeth with winter or spring seasonality divided by "MNIr" multiplied by 100. "% fetal MNI" is the MNI of fetuses divided by MNIsite.

red deer (% MNI) killed during the winter (mid-fall to mid-spring) based on cementum increments with the % MNI of fetuses. These measures closely covary, although sample sizes are small. It is satisfying to get similar results from independent measures. This suggests that these measures are sampling from the same population of animals, which in turn implies that winter-hunted animals were commonly pregnant females.

The tooth sections significantly augment seasonality interpretations based only on fetal remains. Fall kills, primarily late fall, are relatively common in both Levels 7 and 13, while other fall indications come from Levels 3 and 2b (the latter LF/EW). On the other hand, remains from fetuses in a relatively advanced stage of development would indicate occupations and/or kills well into the spring, a season poorly represented by the tooth sections.

The MNI of fetuses gives a reasonable estimate of the minimum number of pregnant females, since red deer hinds have a twinning rate around one percent (Sadleir 1987:132). This is a minimum estimate since we cannot control for either the abandonment of fetuses offsite prior to the transport of female carcasses or

for the preferential destruction of fetal bones. As noted previously, however, the frequency of fetal remains is not positively correlated with the intensity of bone fragmentation. We further assume that fetuses were not transported to the site separately from hinds. We can now compare the MNI of pregnant females to the total MNI of red deer from each level (fig. 10). We interpret this as the minimum percentage of kills that must have been made during the winter-spring and the minimum percentage of hinds taken in each assemblage. The latter link is justified since an overwhelming majority of red deer hinds in the reproductive prime (4–13 years of age) are pregnant each year (Clutton-Brock et al. 1982:84–85; Bunnell 1987:149). The pattern of stratigraphic changes is almost identical to that observed in figure 5.

Gathering these observations together, we infer a seasonality of occupation and red deer hunting that extended from the mid- to late fall to the mid- to late spring in Level 13. Regrettably, we presently lack tooth sections from Levels 8, 9, 10, and 14. If the Basal Hearth fetuses are for the most part not contemporary with the deposition of Levels 8, 9, 10, and 14 but are

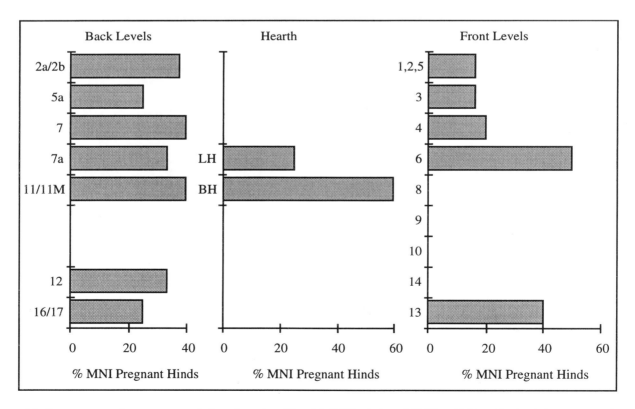

**Figure 10.** Percentage of pregnant red deer females ([fetal MNI/red deer MNI] * 100) at Badanj (percents calculated from tables 2 and 8).

intrusive from above, the absence of fetal remains in Levels 8, 9, 10, and 14 would indicate a shift from hunting red deer hinds during the winter-spring to either using alternative resources during winter-spring visits, targeting only male animals during winter-spring visits, or hunting red deer at other seasons. The concurrent increase in the relative abundance of chamois-ibex in Levels 8, 9, 10, and 14 may indicate that they replaced red deer hinds as prey during winter-spring occupations and that male animals were targeted.

If the Basal Hearth and Levels 8, 9, 10, and 14 are contemporary and we treat them together, the percent total fetal NISP is 1.59. Fetal representation at Badanj now appears relatively constant over time except for the spike in Level 6 when remains are over twice as frequent. During the occupation of Levels 8, 9, 10, and 14, there would have been a significant spatial division within the site, with fetal remains deposited only in the back of the site in the hearth. The behavioral interpretation of this pattern is not immediately evident. It might reflect seasonal contrasts in the use of areas within the site, for example, winter-spring use focused around the hearth and occupation during other seasons focused in the front part of the site. Another possibility would be a deliberate collection of fetal remains, perhaps along with waste from carcass dismemberment, in the front of the site and their disposal in the hearth or down the talus slope. In either event, the representation of fetal remains in the hearth would appear inflated relative to the front of the site. Whatever the interpretation, chronological or spatial, this alternative strategy was used between about 13,200 and 12,400 B.P.

During the occupation of Level 6, the strategy shifted back to taking pregnant hinds. The hunting of pregnant females was a particularly important part of the overall site use at this time. At some time after 12,400 B.P., we have the first evidence of a summer use of the site in Level 7. In the overlying Levels 5a and 3 there are as many or more indicators for late spring-summer-fall use as there are for winter-early spring use. We interpret this as a significant shift in red deer procurement and site use, from a late fall-winter-early spring focus in the lower levels, to a much more even mix of summer and winter indicators. In Level 2b again we have exclusively late fall-early spring indicators in the teeth, while fetal remains from Levels 2a/2b combined suggest a relatively high percentage of pregnant hinds in the assemblage (37.5 percent). We are hesitant to place too much emphasis on this apparent return to a cold-season focus in resource procurement and occupation since the majority of red deer individuals from Levels 2a/2b were not available for incremental analysis.

## Discussion

Interpretation of these seasonality indicators from Badanj with regard to the model predictions developed above depends to a large extent on how we place the site in the landscape. Our expectations for Badanj are dramatically different if we consider it to be a "lowland" site that would have been regularly incorporated in the systems of procurement on the Adriatic Plain or if we push it into the "hinterland." In this case, we regard the low altitude of Badanj (about 100 m) to be deceptive. While the site has access to local pockets of good grazing, it is relatively far-removed from large and productive winter grazing areas on the Adriatic Plain and the summer ranges on the gentle Neogene poljes further inland (Miracle and Sturdy 1991). We thus place Badanj within the "hinterland," and will evaluate the models accordingly. The apparent abandonment of Badanj at the LGM (Whallon 1989) has led others to place the site in the hinterland (Bailey and Gamble 1990:151).

With seasonality data from only one site, it is difficult to test between alternative models of hunter-gatherer settlement. Nonetheless, the available evidence from Badanj does not support the model of year-round occupation of the plain (Shackleton et al. 1984; van Andel 1989). This model posits that territories were located on the plains and that although the hinterland may have been part of the range used by a group, its use was sporadic and limited to periods of shortfall on the plains. In contrast, Badanj appears to have been regularly used on a seasonal basis. Furthermore, it seems unlikely that the fall season, which is well represented in tooth sections from Levels 13 and 7, would have been a period of subsistence stress in the area. In fact, the early fall is the season when one expects red deer of both sexes to be in relatively good condition (Clutton-Brock et al. 1982:75, 124). The second model predicts winter use of the plains and regular use, perhaps mostly during the summer, of specialized sites in the hinterland (Bailey and Gamble 1990). Badanj, despite its location in the hinterland, appears to have been most regularly and consistently used during the winter. We hesitate, however, to take the next step and categorize the site's place in the settlement system, whether as a field or base camp or both.

We find more evidence in support of Jochim's hypothesis of a more diverse and a less structured and less redundant use of the landscape in response to environmental unpredictability. The site was consistently used during the cold season at the end of the pleniglacial (see fig. 2, before 12,500 B.P., Levels 13, 16, 17, and probably Level 12). Around the time of the jump to the interstadial conditions of the Bølling/Allerød (between 13,000–12,500 B.P.), fetal evidence of winter occupation disappears (Levels 8, 9, 10, and 14) and after 12,400 B.P., we find late spring and summer tooth sections in levels in addition to evidence of winter use provided by tooth sections and fetal remains.

The seasonality data for the Badanj red deer show a redundant pattern of winter use to hunt female herds. A targeting of female animals is supported by the relative rarity of red deer antler in the deposits from all levels, since female red deer do not carry antlers. From our late-twentieth century environmental-management perspective, a strategy that targets females appears "wasteful" and detrimental to the viability of local game populations. Differences by sex in the seasonal cycle of red deer physiological condition, however, reveal a logic to such a strategy.

Male red deer spend all of the fat reserves accumulated over the summer in reproductive display and competition with other males (Clutton-Brock et al. 1982:123–124). Males may lose up to 20 percent of their body weight and more significantly, almost completely expend their fat reserves by the end of October. They remain in poor physical condition throughout the winter and spring until May when they start putting on rump and kidney fat. The condition of females during the winter is highly dependent on whether or not they carried a calf the previous year, as their fecundity is also. Milk hinds, those with calf from the previous year, are very lean as measured by the weight of kidney and rump fat and remain lean throughout the year (Clutton-Brock et al. 1982:75, 85). Yeld hinds, those without calf from the previous year, are heavier and much fatter than milk hinds, although their nutritional condition steadily deteriorates, and their weight drops throughout the winter until they are almost as lean as milk hinds by April or May (Clutton-Brock et al. 1982:74–75). Yeld hinds, however, are more likely to conceive (fecundity of 90 percent) than milk hinds (fecundity of 74 percent) the following year (Clutton-Brock et al. 1982:84–85). Therefore, one can be certain that stags taken in the winter will be in poor physical condition and will carry very little body fat. If one targets female groups during the winter, however, one will take at least some yeld hinds that will be in relatively good physical condition and will carry at least some body fat.

The seasonal dynamics of red deer herd organization make it likely that winter hunts would target single-sex groups and suggest advantages to hunting herds of females. First, with the exception of very young stags, males and females remain segregated throughout most of the year and especially during the winter (Clutton-Brock et al. 1982; Pike-Tay 1991). Second, although median party size decreases for both sexes during the winter, hinds are found in slightly larger groups than stags (Clutton-Brock et al. 1982:178). Finally, there are significant differences in group cohesiveness between males and females. Stags form groups that fluctuate greatly in size and composition, while hinds form very stable groups of related individuals (Clutton-Brock et al. 1982). These observations suggest that hunters would encounter sexually segregated herds during the winter and that hind groups would be more stable in composition and generally larger than the male herds.

We suggest that female herds would have been the preferred prey of bands with few dietary sources of fat or carbohydrates during the winter. We offer the hypothesis that Badanj was used as a special productive camp to hunt and process relatively fat-rich, female red deer. The products would have then been transported to residential camps located on or closer to the plains. The secondary species, first the caprids, later roe deer, and at all time hare, would have been procured for the immediate consumption of the hunters. We thus predict that seasonality indicators in these secondary species should be similar to those found in red deer. Major deviations from this pattern occurred around the stadial-interstadial transition. Pregnant females were no longer processed in the front of the site at the time of deposition of Levels 8, 9, 10, and 14, and depending on the stratigraphic interpretation of Level 11/11M and the Basal Hearth, pregnant females may be missing from throughout the site at this time. If the site was still being used in the winter, we might infer that more males were being taken, and given their poor physical condition in the winter, this would indicate a degradation of the diet and perhaps some subsistence stress. On the other hand, if the seasonality of occupation also changed to summer and/or fall, we would have evidence of a major repositioning of Badanj within the larger settlement system.

## CONCLUSIONS

In summary, we suggest the following scenario for the occupation of Badanj and the Late Pleistocene use of the region. Prior to the Late Glacial, here defined as beginning with the Bølling at about 12,500 B.P., occupation would have been focused on the productive Adriatic Plain. During the Late Glacial, the hinterland was increasingly used to procure resources. This procurement may have been carried out by specialized subgroups of the larger band or by movement of the entire foraging group. As the Adriatic Plain contracted from 12,500–9000 B.P., groups were pushed out of their lowland ranges. The role of the hinterland hence shifted from being peripheral or marginal range relative to core territory on the plains, to becoming central to the settlement system.

The repeated and regular use of Badanj in the hinterland of the Adriatic Basin suggests that the plains were not inhabited year-round, although they may have been the focus of subsistence-settlement systems. As discussed above, we think that Badanj may have been used as a special activity camp. The solid evidence of use during the winter, however, comes as somewhat of a surprise. Our null hypothesis, derived from the Paleolithic studies in Epirus (Bailey et al. 1983), was for a fall-spring use of Badanj to intercept red deer seasonally migrating from the plains (winter range) to the larger poljes and uplands of the interior. One site does not a settlement system make; forthcoming studies of seasonality at the sites of Šandalja II and Kopacina, both located near the edge of the Adriatic Plain, will help resolve the role of the Adriatic Plain relative to its hinterland in Pleistocene settlement systems.

The addition of summer season occupations in some of the upper levels fits Jochim's hypothesis of increasing environmental instability/unpredictability causing a more diverse and less regularly patterned use of the landscape. Analysis of seasonal changes in red deer herd structure and nutritional composition indicates that female herds would have provided a more reliable supply of fat during the winter than males. This pattern remained relatively constant with the exception of the period around the stadial-interstadial transition. If the switch at this time was to the hunting of males during the winter, then this might be some evidence of subsistence stress as predicted. These data are few and open to other interpretations (for example, nonwinter hunting) and neither support nor refute our hypothesis of subsistence stress from environmental instability.

We hope that this paper will generate some grist for our theoretical mills. The degree and nature of environmental seasonality has been dramatically different in the past, and its reconstruction and modeling is far more complicated than the calculation of insolation constants. Just as we now recognize, with a few exceptions (e.g., Gordon 1988), that we cannot dress Upper Paleolithic bands in "Nunamiut," "Cree," or "Barrenland" seasonal rounds, we must also address the fact that these groups may not have lived in highly seasonal Boreal or temperate environments. We have summarized current evidence for the frequency, magnitude, and rate of paleoenvironmental changes during the Late Pleistocene, and we have suggested a way of generating testable hypotheses for our paleoecological data (see also Miracle 1995). Our study of seasonality in red deer procurement and site use at Badanj was significantly enriched by the combination and comparison of results from analyses of both fetal remains and tooth increments. Fetal remains have been oft neglected in zooarchaeological reports, and we hope that our detailed examination will spur others to reexamine existing remains and pay more attention to their analysis and interpretation. Tooth increments were particularly important to our analyses of seasonality due to the extreme fragmentation of the remains. We are optimistic about the further application of this technique in the future. Problems of sample size and preservation remain, but analysis of the Badanj assemblages has shown that a careful and informed application of the technique can yield good results. Although our paleoecological and archaeological data, particularly in the Adriatic Basin, continue to lag far behind our theoretical constructs, we firmly maintain that it is only through attempts to refute existing hypotheses that we will collect appropriate data and develop more innovative and creative methods and models.

## Acknowledgments

We would like to thank Robert Whallon, Renato Kipnis, Lynn Fisher, John Speth, and Tom Rocek for constructively critical comments on earlier drafts. We alone, however, stand behind the final product. This is publication no. 3 from the project "Paleolithic-Mesolithic Occupation of the Adriatic-Mediterranean Zone of Bosnia-Herzegovina."

## Notes

1. Only some pollen cores in southern and southeastern Europe show these Late Glacial fluctuations (Willis 1994).

2. Notable exceptions would be contexts like the American Southwest where dendrochronology can provide both a measure of paleoenvironmental variability and enough chronological precision to measure cultural responses.

3. This is a preliminary "working" stratigraphy prepared by Whallon and Miracle. A final stratigraphy will be presented in a monograph in preparation.

4. While Level 6 was in clear superposition relative to Level 7a, its relationship to Level 11/11M was less clear, and thus a dashed line is used.

5. In all fairness, the latter two studies specifically focused on dentitions and incremental structures in teeth.

6. All excavated levels are included in the analysis except for the Surface, Upper Hearth, and mixed Upper/Lower Hearth. Faunal assemblages from the Surface and Upper Hearth are extremely small (NISP 10 and 3 respectively) and did not contain any fetal remains. The undifferentiated Upper/Lower Hearth assemblage (identified as "Hearth" in the field) still awaits coding and analysis.

7. See Pike-Tay (1991) for a comprehensive review of the research on dental increments in red deer.

8. Teeth were considered to be from different individuals following the conservative criteria outlined by Pike-Tay (1991) in which variation must exceed 1 year in age (i.e., one increment difference) and/or one-third season (e.g., early versus mid Fall).

## BIBLIOGRAPHY

Alley, R. B., D. A. Messe, C. A. Shuman, A. J. Gow, K. C. Taylor, P. M. Grootes, J. W. C. White, M. Ram, E. D. Waddington, P. A. Mayewski, and G. A. Zielinski
    1993 "Abrupt Increase in Greenland Snow Accumulation at the End of the Younger Dryas Event." *Nature* 362:527–529.

Bailey, G., and C. Gamble
    1990 "The Balkans at 18,000 B.P.: The View from Epirus," in *The World at 18,000 B.P.* Vol. 1, *High Latitudes*, O. Soffer and C. Gamble, eds., pp. 148–167. Unwin Hyman, London.

Bailey, G., P. Carter, C. Gamble, and H. Higgs
    1983 "Epirus Revisited: Seasonality and Inter-Site Variation in the Upper Paleolithic of North-West Greece," in *Hunter-Gatherer Economy in Prehistoric Europe*, G. N. Bailey, ed., pp. 64–78. Cambridge University Press, Cambridge.

Beasley, M. J., W. A. B. Brown, and A. J. Legge
    1992 "Incremental Banding in Dental Cementum: Methods of Preparation for Teeth from Archaeological Sites and for Modern Comparative Specimens." *International Journal of Osteoarchaeology* 2:37–50.

Behrensmeyer, A. K.
    1978 "Taphonomic and Ecologic Information from Bone Weathering." *Paleobiology* 4:150–162.

Bender, M., T. Sowers, M.-L. Dickson, J. Orchardo, P. Grootes, P. A. Mayewski, and D. A. Meese
    1994 "Climate Correlations Between Greenland and Antarctica During the Past 100,000 Years." *Nature* 372:663–666.

Benn, D. W.
    1974 "Annuli in the Dental Cementum of White-Tailed Deer from Archaeological Contexts." *Wisconsin Archaeologist* 55:90–98.

Bietti, A.
    1990 "The Late Upper Paleolithic in Italy: An Overview." *Journal of World Prehistory* 4(1):95–155.

Bonnichsen, R., D. Stanford, and J. L. Fastook
    1987 "Environmental Change and Developmental History of Human Adaptive Patterns; The Paleoindian Case," in *North America and Adjacent Oceans During the Last Deglaciation*, W. F. Ruddiman and H. E. Wright, Jr., eds., pp. 403–424. Geological Society of America, Boulder.

Bouchud, J.
    1975 "Étude de la Faune de l'Abri Pataud," in *Excavation of the Abri Pataud, les Eyzies (Dordogne)*, H. L. Movius, ed., pp. 69–153. American School of Prehistoric Research, Bulletin 30. Peabody Museum of Archaeology and Ethnology, Harvard University, Cambridge, Massachusetts.

Brodar, M., and F. Osole
    1979 "Nalazista Paleolitskog i Mezolitskog Doba u Sloveniji," in *Praistorija Jugoslavenskih Zemalja I*, D. Basler, ed., pp. 135–157. Svjetlost, Sarajevo.

Brunnacker, K., Dj. Basler, V. Lozek, H.-J. Beug, and H.-J. Altemüller
1969 "Zur Kenntnis der Lösse im Neretva-Tal." *Neues Jahrbuch für Geologie und Paläontologie. Abhandlungen* 132(2):127–154.

Bunn, H. T., L. E. Bartram, and E. M. Kroll
1988 "Variability in Bone Assemblage Formation from Hadza Hunting, Scavenging, and Carcass Processing." *Journal of Anthropological Archaeology* 7:412–457.

Bunnell, F. L.
1987 "Reproductive Tactics of Cervidae and Their Relationships to Habitat," in *Biology and Management of the Cervidae*, C. M. Wemmer, ed., pp. 145–167. Smithsonian Institution Press, Washington, D.C.

Chappellaz, J., T. Blunler, D. Raynaud, J. M. Barnola, J. Schwander, and B. Stauffer
1993 "Synchronous Changes in Atmospheric $CH_4$ and Greenland Climate Between 40 and 8 Kyr B.P." *Nature* 366:443–445.

CLIMAP Project Members
1976 "The Surface of the Ice-Age Earth." *Science* 191:1131–1137.

Clottes, J.
1989 "Reply to White." *Current Anthropology* 30(5):620–621.

Clutton-Brock, T. H., and S. D. Albon
1989 *Red Deer in the Highlands*. BSP Professional Books, Oxford.

Clutton-Brock, T. H., F. E. Guinness, and S. D. Albon
1982 *Red Deer: Behavior and Ecology of Two Sexes*. University of Chicago Press, Chicago.

COHMAP Members
1988 "Climatic Changes of the Last 18,000 Years: Observations and Model Simulations." *Science* 241:1043–1052.

Coudé-Gaussen, G.
1990 "The Loess and Loess-Like Deposits Along the Sides of the Western Mediterranean Sea: Genetic and Palaeoclimatic Significance." *Quaternary International* 5:1–8.

Coy, J. P., R. T. Jones, and K. A. Turner
1982 "Absolute Ageing of Cattle from Tooth Sections and its Relevance to Archaeology," in *Ageing and Sexing Animal Bones from Archaeological Sites*, B. Wilson, C. Grigson, and S. Payne, eds., pp.127–140. British Archaeological Reports, British Series 109. Oxford.

Cremaschi, M.
1990 "Depositional and Post-Depositional Processes in Rock Shelters of Northern Italy during the Late Pleistocene: Their Paleoclimatic and Paleoenvironmental Significance." *Quaternaire* 1:51–64.

Cremaschi, M., and B. van Vliet-Lanoë
1990 "Traces of Frost Activity and Ice Segregation in Pleistocene Loess Deposits and Till of Northern Italy: Deep Seasonal Freezing or Permafrost?" *Quaternary International* 5:39–48.

Culiberg, M.
1991 "Late Glacial Vegetation in Slovenia." *Dela IV Razred za Naravoslovne Vede* 29:1–52.

Cvijič, J.
1960 *La Geographie des Terrains Calcaires*. Monographies de Academie Serbe des Sciences et des Arts, Classe des Sciences Mathematiques et Naturalles, T. 341, no. 26. Naucno Delo, Beograd.

Dawson, A. G.
1992 *Ice Age Earth: Late Quaternary Geology and Climate*. Routledge, London.

di Castri, F.
1981 "Mediterranean-Type Shrublands of the World," in *Mediterranean-Type Shrublands*, F. di Castri, D. W. Goodall, and R. L. Specht, eds., pp. 1–52. Elsevier, Amsterdam.

Edwards, R. L., J. W. Beck, G. S. Burr, D. J. Donahue, J. M. A. Chappell, A. L. Bloom, E. R. M. Druffel, and F. W. Taylor
1993 "A Large Drop in Atmospheric $^{14}C/^{12}C$ and Reduced Melting in the Younger Dryas, Documented with $^{230}Th$ Ages of Corals." *Science* 260:962–968.

Gordon, B.
1988 *Of Men and Reindeer Herds in French Magdalenian Prehistory*. British Archaeological Reports, International Series 390. Oxford.

Graham, R. W., and E. L. Lundelius, Jr.
1984 "Coevolutionary Disequilibrium and Pleistocene Extinctions," in *Quaternary Extinctions*, P. S. Martin and R. G. Klein, eds., pp. 223–249. University of Arizona Press, Tuscon.

Grayson, D. K.
1984a "Nineteenth-Century Explanations of Pleistocene Extinctions: A Review and Analysis," in *Quaternary Extinctions*, P. S. Martin and R. G. Klein, eds., pp. 5–39. University of Arizona Press, Tucson.
1984b *Quantitative Zooarchaeology*. Academic Press, New York.

Guthrie, R. D.
1984 "Mosaics, Allelochemics, and Nutrients: An Ecological Theory of Late Pleistocene Megafaunal Extinctions," in *Quaternary Extinctions*, P. S. Martin and R. G. Klein, eds., pp. 259–298. University of Arizona Press, Tucson.

Harrison, S. P., I. C. Prentice, and P. J. Bartlein
1992 "Influence of Insolation and Glaciation on Atmospheric Circulation in the North Atlantic Sector: Implications of General Circulation Model Experiments for the Late Quaternary Climatology of Europe." *Quaternary Science Reviews* 11:283–299.

Herak, M.
1972 "Karst of Yugoslavia," in *Karst, Important Karst Regions Of The Northern Hemisphere*, M. Herak and V. T. Stringfield, eds., pp. 25–83. Elsevier, Amsterdam and New York,

Huntley, B., and H. J. B. Birks
1983 *Atlas of Past and Present Pollen Maps.* Cambridge University Press, Cambridge.

Jochim, M. A.
1991 "Archeology as Long-Term Ethnography." *American Anthropologist* 93(2):308–321.

Johnsen, S. J., H. B. Clausen, W. Dansgaard, K. Fuhrer, N. Gundestrup, C. U. Hammer, P. Iversen, J. Jouzel, B. Stauffer, and J. P. Steffensen
1992 "Irregular Glacial Interstadials Recorded in a New Greenland Ice Core." *Nature* 359:274–275.

Kay, M.
1974 "Dental Annuli Age Determination on White-Tailed Deer from Archaeological Sites." *Plains Anthropologist* 19(65):224–227.

Kelly, M. G., and B. Huntley
1991 "An 11,000-Year Record of Vegetation and Environment from Lago di Martignano, Latiu, Italy." *Journal of Quaternary Science* 6(3):209–224.

Kelly, R. L.
1983 "Hunter-Gatherer Mobility Strategies." *Journal of Anthropological Research* 39:277–306.

Kelly, R. L, and L. C. Todd
1988 "Coming into the Country: Early Paleoindian Hunting and Mobility." *American Antiquity* 53(2):231–244.

Kelsall, J. P.
1957 *Continued Barren-Ground Caribou Studies.* Canada Department of Northern Affairs and Natural Resources, Wildlife Management Bulletin Series 1, no. 12. Ottawa.

Klein, R. G., and K. Cruz-Uribe
1984 *The Analysis of Animal Bones from Archeological Sites.* University of Chicago Press, Chicago.

Kutzbach, J. E., and H. E. Wright, Jr.
1985 "Simulation of the Climate of 18,000 Years B.P.: Results for the North American/North Atlantic/European Sector and Comparison with the Geologic Record of North America." *Quaternary Science Reviews* 4:147–187.

Lieberman, D. E., and R. H. Meadow
1992 "The Biology of Cementum Increments (With an Archaeological Application)." *Mammal Review* 22(2):57–77.

Lieberman, D. E., T. W. Deacon, and R. H. Meadow
1990 "Computer Image Enhancement and Analysis of Cementum Increments as Applied to Teeth of *Gazaella gazella*." *Journal of Archaeological Science* 17:519–533.

Lyman, R. L., and G. L. Fox
1989 "A Critical Evaluation of Bone Weathering as an Indication of Bone Assemblage Formation." *Journal of Archaeological Science* 16:293–317.

Marean, C. W.
1991 "Measuring the Postdepositional Destruction of Bone in Archaeological Assemblages." *Journal of Archaeological Science* 18:677–694.

Martin, L. D., and J. B. Martin
1987 "Equability in the Late Pleistocene," in *Quaternary Environments of Kansas*, W. C. Johnson, ed., pp. 123–127. Kansas Geological Survey, Lawrence.

McCorriston, J., and F. Hole
1991 "The Ecology of Seasonal Stress and the Origins of Agriculture in the Near East." *American Anthropologist* 93:46–69.

Miracle, P. T.
1995 "Broad-Spectrum Adaptations Re-Examined: Hunter-Gatherer Responses to Late-Glacial Environmental Changes in the Eastern Adriatic." Ph.D. diss., University of Michigan.

Miracle, P. T., and D. A. Sturdy
1991 "Chamois and the Karst of Herzegovina." *Journal of Archaeological Science* 18:89–108.

Monks, G. G.
1981 "Seasonality Studies," in *Advances in Archaeological Method and Theory*, vol. 4, M. Schiffer, ed., pp. 177–240. Academic Press, New York.

Moore, A. M. T., and G. C. Hillman
1992 "The Pleistocene to Holocene Transition and Human Economy in Southwest Asia: The Impact of the Younger Dryas." *American Antiquity* 57(3): 482–494.

O'Brien, C. J.
1994 "Determining Seasonality and Age in East African Archaeological Faunas: An Ethnoarchaeological Application of Cementum Increment Analysis." Ph.D. diss., University of Wisconsin, Madison.

Olsen, S. L.
1989 "Solutré: A Theoretical Approach to the Reconstruction of Upper Paleolithic Hunting Strategies." *Journal of Human Evolution* 18:295–327.

Pike-Tay, A.
1991 *Red Deer Hunting in the Upper Paleolithic of South-West France: A Study in Seasonality*. British Archaeological Reports, International Series 569. Oxford.

Poje, M.
1990 "Gornjopleistocenks Fauna Mekušaca Šandalja II kod Pule (Istra)." *RAD Jugoslavenske Akademije Znanosti i Umjetnosti* 449:97–112.

Price, T. D., J. Blitz, J. Burton, and J. A. Ezzo
1992 "Diagenesis in Prehistoric Bone: Problems and Solutions." *Journal of Archaeological Science* 19:513–529.

Prummel, W.
1987a "Atlas for the Identification of Foetal Skeletal Elements of Cattle, Horse, Sheep and Pig, Part 1." *Archaeozoologia* 1(1):23–30.
1987b "Atlas for Identification of Foetal Skeletal Elements of Cattle, Horse, Sheep and Pig, Part 2." *Archaeozoologia* 1(2):11–42.

Rackham, D. J.
1986 "A Comparison of Methods of Age Determination from the Mandibular Dentition of an Archaeological Sample of Cattle," in *Teeth and Anthropology*, E. Cruwys and R. A. Foley, eds., pp. 149–168. British Archaeological Reports, International Series 291. Oxford.

Rossignol-Strick, M., N. Planchais, M. Paterne, and D. Duzer
1992 "Vegetation Dynamics and Climate During the Deglaciation in the South Adriatic Basin from a Marine Record." *Quaternary Science Reviews* 11:415–423.

Sadleir, R. M. F. S.
1987 "Reproduction of Female Cervids," in *Biology and Management of the Cervidae*, C. M. Wemmer, ed., pp. 123–144. Smithsonian Institution Press, Washington, D.C.

Sala, B.
1983 "Variations Climatiques et Séquences Chronologiques sur la Base des Variations des Associations Fauniques à Grands Mammifères." *Rivista di Scienze Preistoriche* 38:161–180.

Satta, S., and J. Renault-Miskovsky
1985 "Le Paléoenvironnement et la Paléoclimatologie des Pouilles (Sud de l'Italie): Études Pollinique Préliminaire des Niveaux Épigravettiens de la Grotte Paglicci." *Bulletin de l'Association Française pour l'Etude de Quaternaire* 4:219–227.

Saxon, A., and C. F. W. Higham
1969 "A New Research Method for Economic Prehistorians." *American Antiquity* 34(3):303–311.

Šegota, T., and A. Filipčič
1991 "Arheološki i Geološki Pokazatelji Holocenskog Položaja Razine Mora na Istočnoj Obali Jadranskog Mora." *RAD Hrvatske Akademije Znanosti i Umjetnosti* 458:149–172.

Shackleton, J. C., T. H. van Andel, and C. N. Runnels
1984 "Coastal Paleogeography of the Central and Western Mediterranean During the Last 125,000 Years and Its Archaeological Implications." *Journal of Field Archaeology* 11:307–315.

Speth, J. D.
1991 "Nutritional Constraints and Late Glacial Adaptive Transformations: The Importance of Non-Protein Energy Sources," in *The Late Glacial in North-West Europe: Human Adaptation and Environmental Change at the End of the Pleistocene*, N. Barton, A. J. Roberts, and D. A. Roe, eds., pp. 169–178. Council for British Archaeology Research Report 77. London.

Spiess, A. E.
1979 *Reindeer and Caribou Hunters*. Academic Press, New York.

Sten, S. A.
  1991 "A Method of Age Determination on Archaeological and Modern Cattle (*Bos taurus*) by Counting of Tooth Annuli in Cementum." *Laborativ Arkeologi* 5:195–199.

Stiner, M. C.
  1990 "The Use of Mortality Patterns in Archaeological Studies of Hominid Predatory Adaptations." *Journal of Anthropological Archaeology* 9:305–351.

Szabik, E.
  1973 "Age Estimation of Roe-Deer from Different Hunting Grounds of South-Eastern Poland." *Acta Therioliga* 18:223–236.

Taylor, K. C., G. W. Lamorey, G. A. Doyle, R. B. Alley, P. M. Grootes, P. A. Mayewski, J. W. C. White, and L. K. Barlow
  1993 "The 'Flickering Switch' of Late Pleistocene Climate Change." *Nature* 361:432–436.

Thiede, J.
  1978 "A Glacial Mediterranean." *Nature* 276:680–683.

Thompson, L. G., E. Mosley-Thompson, M. E. Davis, P.-N. Lin, K. A. Henderson, J. Cole-Dai, J. F. Bolzan, and K.-B. Liu
  1995 "Late Glacial Stage and Holocene Tropical Ice Core Records from Huascarán, Peru." *Science* 269:46–50.

van Andel, T. H.
  1989 "Late Quaternary Sea-Level Changes and Archaeology." *Antiquity* 63:733–745.
  1990 "Addendum to 'Late Quaternary Sea-Level Changes and Archaeology.'" *Antiquity* 64:151–152.

van Zeist, W., and S. Bottema
  1982 "Vegetational History of the Eastern Mediterranean and the Near East During the Last 20,000 Years," in *Palaeoclimates, Palaeoenvironments and Human Communities in the Eastern Mediterranean Region in Later Prehistory*, J. L. Bintliff and W. Van Zeist, eds., pp. 277–321. British Archaeological Reports, International Series 133(1). Oxford.

Wenham, G., C. L. Adam, and C. E. Moir
  1986 "A Radiographic Study of Skeletal Growth and Development in Fetal Red Deer." *British Veterinary Journal* 142:336–349.

Whallon, R.
  1989 "The Paleolithic Site of Badanj: Recent Excavations and Results of Analysis." *Glasnik Zemaljskog Muzeja Bosne i Hercegovine, Arheologija* 44:7–20.

White, G.
  1974 "Age Determination of Roe Deer (*Capreolus capreolus*) from Annual Growth Layers in the Dental Cementum." *Journal of Zoology* 174:511–516.

White, R.
  1990 "Reply." *Current Anthropology* 31(1):70–71.

White, T. E.
  1953 "A Method of Calculating the Dietary Percentages of Various Food Animals Utilized by Aboriginal Peoples." *American Antiquity* 18:396–398.

Wijmstra, T. A.
  1969 "Palynology of the First 30 Metres of a 120 M Deep Section in Northern Greece." *Acta Botanica Neerlandica* 18:511–527.

Willis, K. J.
  1994 "The Vegetational History of the Balkans." *Quaternary Science Reviews* 13:769–788.

CHAPTER 5

# Natufian "Sedentism" and the Importance of Biological Data for Estimating Reduced Mobility

*Daniel E. Lieberman*

*Rutgers University*

## INTRODUCTION

Sedentism[1]—a strategy of reduced mobility in which most of a population lives in one site continuously throughout the year—is an elusive, if not tenuous, concept that has recently captured the attention of many archaeologists. Reduced mobility strategies (of which sedentism is the extreme) are interesting among hunter-gatherers for several reasons. First, sedentism may represent an anomalous strategy for non-food producers since most anthropologists agree that hunter-gatherers tend to be highly mobile (Lee and DeVore 1968). Second, sedentary hunter-gatherers tend to be culturally more complex than mobile ones (Testart 1982; Cohen 1985; Price and Brown 1985). Hunter-gatherers that live in permanent villages often have larger group sizes, higher fertility rates, more exchange and storage, and tend to be more socially hierarchical than mobile foragers. And third, sedentism is closely linked with theories concerning the origins of agriculture. Sedentism may be an important precursor to the development of farming because it favors social structures typical of agriculturalists (Bender 1978), because it may lead to population growth (Cohen 1977; Henry 1989), or because it results in localized environmental deterioration that provides a potential stimulus for the adoption of food production (Bar-Yosef and Belfer-Cohen 1989; Lieberman 1993a, 1993c).

The issue of whether or not the Natufians were sedentary merits special attention because they were probably the first humans to invent agriculture. Natufi-

an hunter-gatherers, who occupied the southern Levant at the end of the Pleistocene and the beginning of the Holocene, have been the subject of intense debate since they were first identified by Garrod (1932) and Neuville (1934). The Natufians are associated with major and sudden changes in the archaeological record of the southern Levant. In contrast to previous cultural phases, Natufian sites are larger, denser, more complex, and contain a much greater variety of stone tools as well as numerous burials, houses, and even domesticated dogs (summarized in Bar-Yosef and Valla 1991). Garrod (1957) and Neuville (1934) both believed that the Natufians were the first farmers because of the enormous numbers of sickle blades and the stone structures that were found in Natufian sites. Later archaeologists rejected the claim that the Natufians practiced agriculture, but they still assumed that the Natufians were sedentary on the basis of the evidence for relatively permanent structures which suggest that Early Natufian sites were the first villages (Perrot 1966; Binford 1968). Recent researchers have argued that the Natufians were sedentary because they are characterized by many of the hallmarks of complex hunter-gatherers associated with sedentism in the ethnographic record (Bar-Yosef 1983; Henry 1985).

In the absence of a priori data on whether or not the Natufians were sedentary, circular logic often hampers discussions of the relationship between cultural complexity and the origins of agriculture in the southern Levant. On the one hand, Natufian sedentism is inferred from the evidence for their cultural complexity; on the other hand, aspects of Natufian cultural complexity that may have led to the origins of agriculture are inferred from the assumption that they were sedentary. The resolution of these issues—which are central to questions about the origins of food production in the Levant and elsewhere—requires data on Natufian seasonality and mobility patterns that are independent of other archaeological remains.

In this paper I argue that biological evidence for the season of death of hunted animals is, so far, the best indication that many Natufian sites were occupied *during all seasons of the year*. While the size, density, and complexity of Natufian sites may be linked to sedentism, the most reliable data for estimating the season of occupation of archaeological sites are biological traces of seasonality derived from fauna because they preserve evidence for seasonal behaviors that are formed independently of the context in which the material was deposited or excavated. Natufian reduced mobility can be inferred from seasonal bands in the cementum of teeth of gazelle hunted by Natufians and is also supported by previously published data from migratory birds (Pichon 1991), human commensals (Tchernov 1991a), and the mortality profiles of hunted gazelle (Davis 1983). Estimating site seasonality from fauna does not eliminate the problem of how to interpret the *context* of such data. However, it does avoid the problematic middle-range associations between particular complex behaviors (such as sedentism) and their archaeological residues that often lead to circular reasoning.

## "ARCHAEOLOGICAL" EVIDENCE FOR NATUFIAN SEDENTISM

The Natufian is dated to between 12,800 and 10,300 b.p. (Belfer-Cohen 1991; Weinstein-Evron 1991), immediately following the Geometric Kebaran Cultural Complex, and immediately preceding the Pre-Pottery Neolithic A (Bar-Yosef and Belfer-Cohen 1989; Henry 1989). The Natufian culture is primarily defined on the basis of the techno-typological aspects of its lithic industry, which is characterized primarily by lunates as well as by numerous sickle blades, backed bladelets, burins, scrapers, and denticulated pieces (Garrod 1957; Bar-Yosef 1970); Natufian assemblages are also rich in ground stone and bone tools (Campana 1991; Wright 1991) and art objects (Belfer-Cohen 1991). Natufian sites, which are restricted primarily to the Mediterranean phytogeographic zone, range from 15 m² to over 1,000 m² (Bar-Yosef 1983). In contrast to sites from the preceding Kebaran and Geometric Kebaran

periods, Natufian sites usually contain the foundations of circular stone houses (Valla 1991). Many of the above indications of occupational intensity have been used to argue that the Natufians were sedentary (discussed below).

The distinctive Natufian economy, which was based on the intensive exploitation of mostly gazelle and wild cereals, may be related to a strategy of reduced mobility (Lieberman 1993c). Gazelle remains comprise up to 90 percent of the bones in many Natufian sites (Bar-Yosef 1981; Davis 1982; Henry 1989; Cope 1991; Tchernov 1991a), and cereal harvesting and processing is evidenced by the remains of cereals in several sites, the abundance of sickle blades with polish (Anderson 1991; Unger-Hamilton 1991), numerous grinding stones, mortars, and pestles (Wright 1991), and the high percentages of caries in Natufian teeth (Smith 1991). The Natufian economy, however, was also broad-based. Natufian sites contain an enormous range of small animals such as hares, tortoises, and birds (Pichon 1989; Edwards 1990; Tchernov 1991a).

In the absence of a priori data on seasonality, most researchers have tried to estimate whether the Natufians lived in permanent villages from archaeological traces of their occupational intensity. Theoretically, long-term habitation of a site is characterized by investment in the site, especially architecture (Rafferty 1985). Remnants of stone foundations have been found in a few pre-Natufian sites from northern Israel, including Ein-Gev I and III (Bar-Yosef 1970; Martin 1978) and Haon (Bar-Yosef 1975), but these are insignificant in comparison with the size, number, and complexity of Natufian structures. Natufian houses, which are well documented at sites such as Ain Mallaha (Perrot 1966; Valla 1991) and Hayonim Cave (Belfer-Cohen 1988; Bar-Yosef 1991), tend to be semisubterranean with stone foundations, post holes, earth floors, and hearths. These structures vary in diameter between three and seven m, and in some sites were built on top of the remains of previous houses (Valla 1991).

Natufian houses required a considerable investment of effort and time to build and maintain, especially considering the energetic cost of transporting the stones for the foundations. Accordingly, many archaeologists (e.g., Perrot 1966) have suggested that these houses provide evidence that Natufian sites were permanent villages. As noted by Rafferty (1985:129–130), the ethnographic record demonstrates that sedentary people are more likely to build substantial houses than highly mobile people. Edwards (1989), however, challenges the assumption that sedentism can be inferred from the presence of houses, noting that many mobile peoples (including the Bedouin) also build relatively substantial structures, particularly if they are likely to return to the same location year after year on a seasonal basis. Flannery (1972) suggested that rectilinear houses tend to be indicative of permanent occupations while nomadic peoples tend to build circular houses.

Archaeologists also suggest that the Natufians were sedentary on the basis of the large size of the sites and from the density and diversity of artifacts. As sites are occupied for increasingly long periods of time, it is expected that they will grow in size and that the density of artifacts will increase (Rafferty 1985). Moreover, sites that are occupied throughout the year should have a much greater variety of artifact types than seasonal camps, reflecting the range of maintenance and extractive activities that take place in permanent settlements. These criteria for sedentism, however, are equivocal. Natufian sites, which are generally larger than many preceding Epipalaeolithic sites, fall into three size categories: small (15–100 m²), medium (400–500 m²), and large (> 1,000 m²). Many small Natufian sites (such as Hayonim Cave) reflect their location in caves that restrict site size. Large, open-air Natufian sites have lithic densities that range between 500 and 2,000 tools/m³, far higher than in sites from earlier cultural complexes (Bar-Yosef 1983). The diversity of tool types in some sites may be the result of long-term and multiseasonal habitations but may also reflect other site formation processes or differences in the environmental context of sites. For example, Byrd (1989) identified three clusters of sites on the basis of the diversity of ground stone and chipped stone artifacts, suggesting that sites in the Mediterranean phytogeographic zone typically have more diverse assemblages than sites in the arid peripheries of the Levant.

The presence of ceremonial structures and graveyards often correlates with sedentism (Stark 1981; Rafferty 1985). While Natufian sites lack any obvious ceremonial structures, the large cemeteries from Hayonim (Belfer-Cohen 1988), el-Wad (Garrod and Bate 1937), Kebara (Turville-Petre 1932), Hatoula (Ronen and Lechevallier 1991), and Ain Mallaha (Eynan) (Perrot 1989) contain the remains of dozens of individuals,[2] and numerous graves are present at smaller sites such as Azraq 18 (Garrard et al. 1988), Wadi Hammeh 27 (Edwards et al. 1988; Edwards 1991), Rakefet (Belfer-Cohen et al. 1991), and Erq el-Ahmar (Neuville 1951). Natufian burials are diverse with variation in skeletal position, the number of individuals per grave, and the presence and nature of associated grave goods (Bar-Yosef 1983; Perrot 1989). Edwards (1989) points out that many mobile peoples prefer to use certain sites for

important ritual activities, such as the burial of the dead, but the paucity of secondary burials suggests that these large cemeteries reflect the interment of Natufians from or near the sites in which they were buried.

A number of researchers associate storage structures with sedentism (Perrot 1966; Redman 1978; Testart 1982), but such structures are by no means characteristic of only sedentary peoples. Moreover, many storage technologies, such as skins or unlined pits, are difficult to document in the archaeological record. Nevertheless, a number of possible storage facilities have been found at Natufian sites. In particular, shallow oval or circular pits were excavated at Ain Mallaha (Valla 1984) and Jericho (Kenyon 1981); stone-lined pits were uncovered at Hayonim (Bar-Yosef 1991) and Wadi Hammeh 27 (Edwards 1989, 1991); and Garrod and Bate (1937) documented several rock-cut pits at el-Wad. It is not clear, however, whether all these structures were used for storage and whether they were intrusive from higher levels.

## BIOLOGICAL SOURCES OF EVIDENCE FOR SEDENTISM

Natufian sites were in general larger, denser, more diverse, and contained more storage structures, graves, and houses than are found in any site from previous cultural complexes. These data demonstrate that Natufian sites were intensively occupied but do not constitute good proof that the Natufians were sedentary. Such occupational intensity could result from numerous site formation processes, including frequent seasonal reoccupation of the same sites year after year. However, a handful of studies using biological indicators of seasonality have also suggested that Natufian sites were occupied for multiple seasons and were therefore probably relatively permanent habitations. Data on site seasonality have been extrapolated primarily from plant remains, the presence of migratory birds, and the age profiles of hunted animals. New data (presented below) are now available from seasonal bands in the cementum of animal teeth.

Plant remains are a particularly important source of data on the seasonal use of resources because plants were most likely the primary constituents of hunter-gatherer diets. Unfortunately, pollen and seed analyses of Natufian sites are rare because Levantine soil conditions are not generally favorable for the preservation of flora and many Natufian sites were excavated before

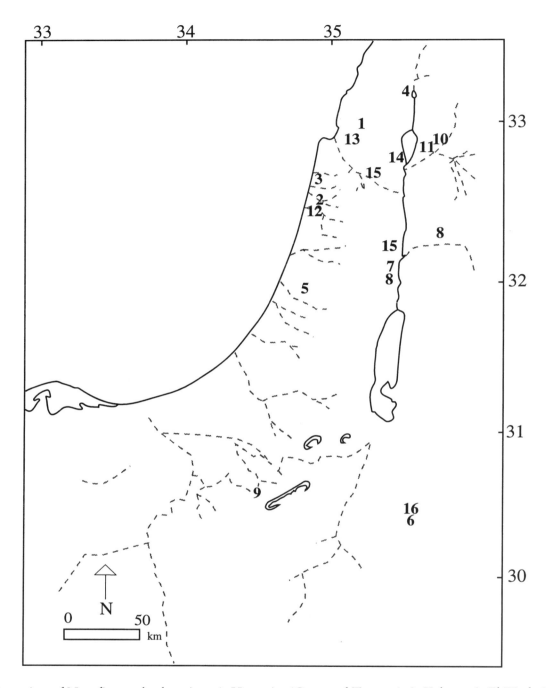

**Figure 1.** Location of Natufian and other sites: 1. Hayonim (Cave and Terrace), 2. Kebara, 3. El Wad, 4. Ain Mallaha (Eynan), 5. Hatoula, 6. Wadi Judayid, 7. Fazael VI and VII, 8. Salibiya I, 9. Rosh Horesha, 10. Nahal Ein Gev I, 11. Ein Gev I, 12. Nahal Hadera V, 13. Neve David, 14. Ohalo II, 15. Urkan e Rub IIa, 16. Tor Hamar.

archaeologists regularly recovered plant remains (Colledge 1991). Only a few Natufian sites provide evidence for hunter-gatherer plant use in the southern Levant, including Hayonim Cave (Hopf and Bar-Yosef 1987), Hayonim Terrace (Valla et al. 1989), and Wadi Hammeh 27 (Colledge 1991; Edwards 1991). All these sites demonstrate that Natufian hunter-gatherers commonly gathered a wide range of plants during several seasons, including annuals that are available in the spring and summer such as barley (*Hordeum spontaneum*), chick peas (*Cicer* spp.), field peas (*Pisum* spp.), lentils (*Lens* spp.), and lupins (*Lupinus* spp.), and nuts that are harvestable in the fall such as acorns (*Quercus* spp.) and almonds (*Amygdalus* spp.). The Late Natufian site of Tel Abu Hureyra I in the northern Levant yielded the most spectacular range of plant remains that clearly indicate long-term, multiseasonal use of the site (Hillman et al. 1989).

Because of their preservation, faunal remains have more potential for resolving the extent to which Natufian sites were permanently occupied. One of the most compelling sources of evidence for seasonal resource use is Pichon's (1987, 1989, 1991) analysis of the migratory birds from Hayonim Cave and Ain Mallaha (Eynan). A diverse range of avian fauna migrate seasonally through the southern Levant, because it forms the only land bridge between Africa and Eurasia. While the absence of evidence for the capture of migratory birds from a particular season does not mean that the site was then unoccupied, Pichon's data suggest that the occupants of Ain Mallaha and Hayonim hunted both winter and summer birds, accounting for at least ten months out of the year (September through July).

Further evidence for Natufian sedentism was proposed by Davis (1982, 1983), who estimated the season of occupation of Hayonim Cave, Hayonim Terrace, and Ain Mallaha using the age profiles of hunted mountain gazelle (*Gazella gazella*). Davis compared the proportion of juveniles from these sites (by estimating their age at death from dental eruption patterns and molar crown heights) with the proportion of juvenile gazelle from known wild populations. The relatively high proportion of juveniles at these Natufian sites, which reflects the average seasonal age structure of wild gazelle populations, suggests that the sites were inhabited throughout the year. In contrast, sites from earlier periods tend to have age profiles that reflect hunting during just one season. Similar studies at Tel Abu Hureyra (Legge and Rowley-Conwy 1987) suggest that Persian gazelle (*Gazella subgutterosa*) were hunted seasonally in more arid regions of the Levant during the Late Natufian.[3]

The presence of human commensals is the most controversial source of data used to gauge the relative permanence of Natufian occupations. Tchernov (1984, 1991a) has suggested that the relatively higher proportions of human commensals such as *Mus musculus*, *Rattus rattus*, and *Passer domesticus* at Ain Mallaha and Hayonim Cave in comparison with sites from earlier cultural complexes indicate that these animals evolved to take advantage of the new niche created by relatively permanent human occupation. Sedentary camps provide constant sources of food (refuse) as well as reduce the risk of predation. Edwards (1989) and Tangri and Wyncoll (1989) criticized Tchernov's hypothesis, pointing out that such species are found in Levantine sites dating back to the Middle Palaeolithic. However, their presence relative to other rodents and other small animal species dramatically rises during the Natufian at these sites (Tchernov 1991a, 1991b).

Unfortunately, most of the above faunal analyses have focused on only two recent excavations, Hayonim Cave and Ain Mallaha (Eynan). While it is encouraging that the different estimates of seasonality from both Hayonim and Ain Mallaha all point to multiseasonal occupation of these sites, more data from more sites are needed to understand Natufian mobility patterns. Similar analyses have not been widely employed because complete faunal remains were not saved from many sites (e.g., Kebara and el-Wad) but are necessary to estimate the age profiles of animals from a site. In addition, many Natufian sites were excavated before sieving was frequently used so that there are few bones of small animals or birds necessary for the analysis of commensals or migratory birds.

## CEMENTUM INCREMENT ANALYSIS

Seasonal bands in dental cementum are an alternative source of information on site seasonality that can provide plentiful, accurate, and reliable estimates of the season of death of hunted animals. Cementum is a tissue that surrounds the roots of teeth in concentric bands—similar to the rings on trees—whose function is to mineralize collagen fiber bundles (Sharpey's fibers) from the gum (periodontal ligament) onto the tooth root, thus holding the tooth into the mandible or maxilla. Because of this important function, cementum grows slowly and constantly throughout the life of an animal. When thin-sectioned and viewed under a transmitted polarized light microscope, cementum appears in alternating translucent and opaque bands (fig. 2). Numerous studies have demonstrated that the number of cementum bands is correlated with the age of the tooth at the time of an animal's death and that the nature of the outermost band is correlated with its season of death (Klevezal and Kleinenberg 1967; Grue and Jensen 1979; Lieberman and Meadow 1992). Translucent bands tend to accrue during periods of growth (e.g., spring, summer), and opaque bands are laid down during periods of reduced growth (e.g., winter).

The optical differences between cementum bands are the result of predictable changes in seasonal growth patterns and diets. Controlled experiments of cementum growth in laboratory goats and rats demonstrate that cementum bands in most mammals can be attributed to two separate phenomena: (1) variations in mineral density that result from changes in the growth rate of the tissue and (2) variations in collagen orientation that result from differences in the mechanical force necessary to chew different diets (Lieberman 1993a, 1993b, 1994a). In most animals these two phenomena covary seasonally (illustrated in fig. 3).

Variations in the *mineral density* of cementum bands reflect seasonal growth rates because of the unique nature of cementogenesis. Unlike most types of bone, cementum deposits from a single mineralizing front along the margin of the periodontal ligament. Extrinsic collagen fiber bundles (termed Sharpey's fibers) are produced by fibroblasts in the periodontal ligament and intrinsic collagen fibers are produced by cementoblasts in a radiating fashion around the Sharpey's fibers (Lieberman 1993b). This collagen matrix is then mineralized by cementoblasts, which precipitate calcium phosphate into lattice spaces in the collagen (see Lowenstam and Weiner 1989). The rate of cementum mineralization proceeds constantly and independently of collagen matrix production, so animals whose tooth roots grow more slowly deposit more mineral per unit volume of cementum than animals whose tooth roots grow more rapidly. Therefore periods of reduced tissue growth, which usually correspond to winter in most species in most habitats, result in hypermineralized bands relative to periods of rapid tissue growth. These bands are best viewed in microradiographs but can also be seen in thin sections in transmitted light.

Cementum bands can also result from variations in collagen fiber orientation mineralized during different seasons. As mentioned above, Sharpey's fiber bundles are the sole means of attachment of a tooth root to the rest of the chewing apparatus and are slowly mineralized by cementoblasts in between the periodontal lig-

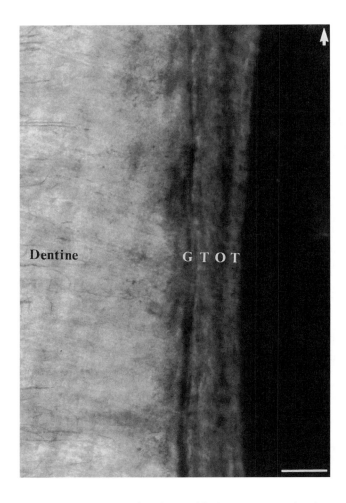

**Figure 2.** Transmitted polarized light micrograph of cross section through a goat $M_1$, showing the cementum bands. This individual has three cementum bands, the outermost of which is translucent. G=granular layer of tomes (the dentine cementum border); T=translucent band; O=opaque band. Arrow points toward crown. Scale bar = 50 µm.

ament and the tooth root. Experiments in which animals were given food of different hardness (Lieberman 1993a, 1993b, 1994a) demonstrate that the orientation of Sharpey's fibers can be influenced by the frequency and/or magnitude of forces generated from chewing diets of different quality. Sharpey's fibers mineralized during periods in which an animal was fed harder food are oriented more vertically relative to the border of the tooth than Sharpey's fibers mineralized during periods of softer food. In most species, seasons of reduced food availability cause animals to chew

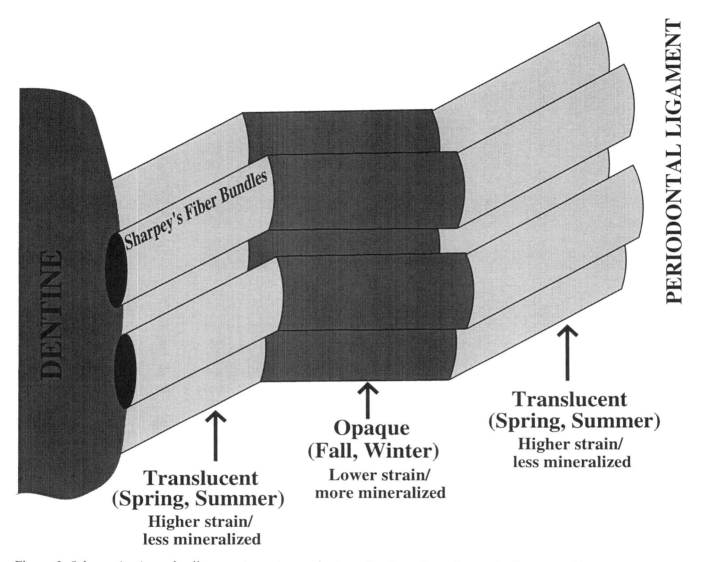

**Figure 3.** Schematic view of collagen orientation and mineralization of gazelle tooth. Sharpey's fibers mineralized during the spring and summer are more vertically oriented (relative to the dentine-cementum border) and are less mineralized than Sharpey's fibers during the fall and winter. These differences result in the optical phenomenon of cementum banding that enable estimation of season of death (see text for explanation).

harder food that is lower in nutritional quality than during high-growth seasons. The differences in Sharpey's fiber orientation in cementum bands deposited during these seasons are manifested as alternating opaque and translucent bands under transmitted polarized light because of the high birefringence of collagen (light passed through cementum bands with different collagen orientations is refracted in different directions that must be aligned with the polarizer to be visible).

In most species, opaque cementum bands are both hypermineralized relative to translucent bands and have more vertically oriented Sharpey's fibers. Periods of reduced tissue growth result from seasonal variations in diet quality. Animals tend to eat lower-quality foods that are tougher and lower in nutrition during the winter in temperate environments and during the dry season in many tropical environments. Reduced nutritional intakes result in hypermineralization, and higher frequencies and magnitudes of strain result in changes in cementum collagen orientation. Therefore, archaeologists interested in estimating the season of death of animals can do so by determining the nature of the outermost band of cementum, given a knowledge of the seasonal diets of the animal. Such correlations should be tested on a comparative sample of modern individuals from similar environments and with similar seasonal diets (see Lieberman 1994a).

Fortunately, mountain gazelle (*Gazella gazella*), which are the most common animal in southern Levantine Epipalaeolithic sites, have very seasonal diets that result in clear cementum bands. Gazelle are primarily browsers during the long, dry summer but switch to being grazers during the winter rainy season. Their summer diet, which is primarily comprised of *Zizyphus lotus* (jujube), is tougher but nutritionally superior to their winter diet, which is comprised of mostly grasses and forbs (Baharav 1981). Consequently, cementum which is deposited between April and September is less mineralized but has more vertically aligned collagen than cementum which is deposited between October and February. Rainy season opaque bands grow relatively slowly at an average rate of 2.66 μm/month, and dry season translucent bands grow relatively rapidly at a rate of 4.55 μm/month (details in Lieberman 1994a). Translucent and opaque acellular cementum bands in mountain gazelle are clearly visible under polarized transmitted light and can be used to estimate the season of death of animals with reasonable accuracy and precision (Lieberman et al. 1990; Lieberman 1993a, 1994a).

## CEMENTUM INCREMENT ANALYSES OF LEVANTINE ARCHAEOLOGICAL SAMPLES

Mountain gazelle teeth from ten Natufian sites (shown in fig. 1) were analyzed to estimate their season of death. For comparison, I also include analyses of gazelle teeth from 15 other Epipalaeolithic and Palaeolithic sites. I concentrated on mountain gazelle for several reasons. Mountain gazelle not only have very clear seasonal banding patterns (discussed above), but they are the predominant animal in almost every Palaeolithic and Epipalaeolithic site, particularly in the Natufian. In addition, mountain gazelle are territorial, nonmigratory, easy to hunt, breed rapidly, and inhabit a large variety of forest, woodland, and steppic habitats in the southern Levant (Grau and Walther 1976;

Baharav 1981, 1983). Late Pleistocene hunter-gatherers, therefore, had constant access to gazelle. Given the evidence that gazelle were hunted throughout the year by Late Pleistocene hunter-gatherers (Lieberman 1994a), the absence of gazelle from a particular season at a site is a potential indicator that the site was not then occupied. However, it must be kept in mind that estimates of season of occupation based on absence of evidence are problematic because they can be explained by other hypotheses. For example, gazelle may have been avoided during seasons when their fat content was low. Estimates of season of occupation derived from cementum increment analyses, therefore, need to be considered *minimal* estimates of seasonal activity and need to be examined in the context of other seasonality data.

Table 1 and figure 4 summarize the results of the analyses. Table 1 includes sample sizes of gazelle, the mean and mode of their estimated season of death, the range of such estimates, and an index of seasonality ($I_s$), which summarizes the diversity of seasonal kills from each site. $I_s$ (calculated as the ratio of fall-winter kills minus spring-summer kills divided by the total number of kills) is thus −1.0 for sites in which animals were killed solely in the spring-summer, 1.0 for sites in which animals were killed solely in the fall-winter, and 0.0 for sites in which animal deaths are distributed equally throughout the year. The techniques for preparing and analyzing the samples are described elsewhere (Lieberman et al. 1990; Lieberman and Meadow 1992; Lieberman 1994a). I analyzed only teeth from anthropogenic contexts; in addition, I restricted the analysis to teeth that were still encased in maxillary or mandibular bone because loose teeth can potentially yield false estimates of season of death from loss of the outermost cementum layer(s) that can exfoliate through postdepositional processes (cf. Miracle and O'Brien, this volume [eds.]). Each sample was analyzed without knowledge of the site from which it came, and an estimate of its season of death was made with the aid of computer image analysis and enhancement (Lieberman et al. 1990).

It is important to stress that these estimates from cementum increment analysis, like all indicators of seasonality, can only provide a *minimal* indication of the seasonal occupation of a site that must be considered in the context of other biological and nonbiological data. In addition, estimates of seasonality from faunal data presented here are hampered by small sample sizes (see below) and by the potential that the season of death of animals hunted close in time to the transition period between seasons may be estimated incorrectly. In spite

TABLE I

Cementum increment analysis results from sites discussed in text along with the other faunal seasonality data and indication of other archaeological correlates of occupational intensity

| Site | Age (ka) | N | Mean | Range | Mode | $I_s$ | Estimate | Size | Arch. | Burials | Storage | Primary Sources |
|---|---|---|---|---|---|---|---|---|---|---|---|---|
| | | | | | SEASONALITY | | | | | | | |
| *Natufian Cultural Complex* | | | | | | | | | | | | |
| Hayonim B | 12 | 11(15) | 3.4 | 1–6 | spring | 0.09 | Multiseasonal | S | Yes | 48 | | Bar-Yosef, 1991; Belfer-Cohen 1988 |
| Hayonim Ter. | 11.9 | 6(13) | 4.2 | 2–6 | fall/winter | 0.00 | Multiseasonal | L | Yes | 9 | Yes | Henry et al., 1981; Valla et al., 1991 |
| Kebara B | 12 | 12(12) | 3.3 | 2–7 | fall/winter | -0.17 | Multiseasonal | M | Yes | 31 | | Turville-Petre, 1932 |
| El Wad B | 10–12 | 10(15) | 3.7 | 1–6 | winter | 0.20 | Multiseasonal | M | Yes | 96 | Yes | Garrod and Bate, 1937 |
| Ain Mallaha | 12 | 17(20) | 3.9 | 1–7 | winter/spring | 0.06 | Multiseasonal | L | Yes | 105 | Yes | Perrot, 1966; Valla, 1991 |
| Hatoula | 11 | 12(17) | 3.1 | 1–7 | fall | 0.38 | Multiseasonal | M-L | ? | 3 | | Ronen and Lechevallier, 1991 |
| W. Judayid | 12–12.8 | 10(16) | 4.6 | 2–7 | spring | -0.60 | Multiseasonal | M | ? | 0 | | Henry et al., 1985 |
| Fazael VI | 11–12 | 3(3) | 6.3 | 6–7 | sp/summer | -1.00 | Spring | S | No | 0 | | Bar-Yosef et al., 1974 |
| Salibiya I | 11.5 | 5(6) | 5.4 | 5–6 | spring | -1.00 | Spring | M | No | 0 | | Crabtree et al., 1991 |
| Rosh Horesha | 10.5–11 | 11(15) | 2.1 | 1–5 | fall/winter | 0.82 | Fall/Winter | L | Yes? | 0 | | Marks and Larson, 1977 |
| *Kebaran and Geometric Kebaran* | | | | | | | | | | | | |
| Hayonim C | 14–17 | 8(8) | 2.6 | 2–3 | winter | 1.00 | Fall/Winter | S | No | 0 | | Bar-Yosef, 1991 |
| Kebara C | ? | 12(12) | 2.5 | 1–5 | fall | 0.67 | Fall/Winter | S | No | 0 | | Turville-Petre, 1932 |
| Ein Gev I | 16 | 9(14) | 2.7 | 2–3 | winter | 0.78 | Fall/Winter | S | Yes | 1 | | Bar-Yosef, 1970 |
| N. Hadera V | 14–17 | 3(6) | 5.3 | 5–6 | spring | -1.00 | Spring | S | No | 0 | | Saxon et al, 1978 |
| Neve David | 13 | 11(16) | 2.5 | 1–5 | fall/winter | 0.64 | Fall/Winter | L? | Yes? | 2? | | Kaufman, 1986 |
| Ohalo II | 19 | 10(18) | 2.8 | 1–5 | fall/winter | 0.50 | Fall/Winter | M | No | 2 | | Nadel and Hershkovitz, 1991 |
| Urkan e Rub | 15 | 4(5) | 5 | 5–6 | sp/summer | -1.00 | Spring | S | No | 0 | | Hovers et al., 1988 |
| Tor Hamar | 12.7 | 8(9) | 1.9 | 1–3 | fall/winter | 0.75 | Fall/Winter | S | No | 0 | | Henry and Garrard, 1980 |
| *Upper Palaeolithic* | | | | | | | | | | | | |
| Kebara UP | 44–54 | 15(21) | 5.2 | 5–7 | spring | -0.86 | Sp/Summer | S | No | 0 | | Bar-Yosef et al., 1992 |
| Hayonim D | 27–29 | 10(12) | 1.9 | 1–3 | fall/winter | 1.00 | Fall/Winter | S | No | 0 | | Belfer-Cohen and Bar-Yosef, 1981 |
| El Wad C | 20–25 | 10(15) | 5.2 | 5–6 | spring | -1.00 | Sp/Summer | S | No | 0 | | Garrod and Bate, 1937 |
| El Wad D | 27–33 | 11(12) | 2 | 1–3 | fall | 0.82 | Fall/Winter | S | No | 0 | | Garrod and Bate, 1937 |
| N. Ein Gev I | 20–25 | 8(9) | 2.3 | 1–5 | fall/winter | 1.00 | Fall/Winter | S | No | 1 | | Bar-Yosef, 1973 |

Numbers in parentheses are the total number of samples studied (not all samples yielded results). For seasonality, teeth from animals that died in the fall or winter were scored as 1 and 3, respectively, and animals who died in either season are scored as 2. Similarly, animals that died in the spring or summer were scored as 5 and 7, respectively, and animals who died in either season are scored as 6. No teeth were scored as 4 because there is no observable transition between opaque (winter) and translucent (spring) increments. Seasonal estimates are presented as the mean, mode, and range of season of death estimates,

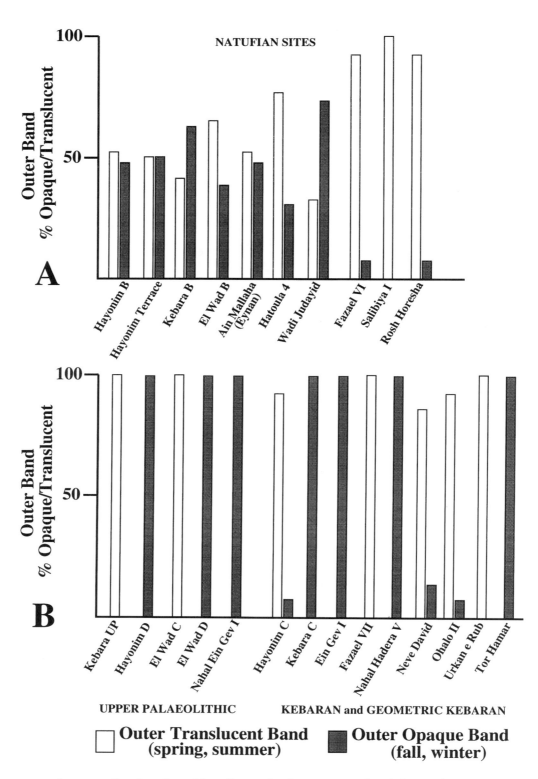

**Figure 4.** Summary of seasonality data from Natufian and other Upper Palaeolithic and Epipalaeolithic sites from the southern Levant (see table 1). Results are plotted in terms of the relative percentage of gazelle teeth with an outer translucent band (spring/summer death) and with an outer opaque band (fall/winter death).

of these problems, the data from Early Natufian sites appear to reflect a sudden change from previous periods in terms of the seasonal hunting of gazelle. With the exception of one site[4] (Fazael VI), all the Early Natufian sites analyzed in the study have evidence for gazelle hunting during most seasons of the year, which suggests that they were probably occupied on a multi-seasonal basis. This is demonstrated by the high range of the estimated seasons of death, the relatively equal percentages of animals killed in the dry season and wet season, and the significantly lower mean $I_s$ of Natufian sites (0.43 ±0.3) compared with those of non-Natufian sites (0.85 ±0.17) (p < 0.05 in an unpaired student's T-test). In addition, the high coefficient of variation for the season of death of gazelle at these sites indicates that the sites were unlikely to have been occupied solely during the transitional period between seasons. Note that these data cannot confirm the hypothesis of year-round habitation but instead show some seasonal tendencies in several instances. Wadi Judayid, for example, has a significant predominance of gazelle hunted during the spring/summer, and Hatoula 4 has a predominance of gazelle hunted during the winter (Lieberman 1994b, 1995). Although few Late Natufian sites are available for analysis (Bar-Yosef and Valla 1991), the pattern of multiseasonal gazelle hunting appears to persist throughout the Natufian.

The Natufian pattern nevertheless contrasts with the evidence for single-season hunting of gazelle at every site in the southern Levant dating to the earlier phases of the Epipalaeolithic and Upper Palaeolithic. A single factor analysis of variance (ANOVA) indicates that the absolute value of the $I_s$ differs significantly (p < 0.05) between Natufian and non-Natufian sites (but not between Kebaran and Upper Palaeolithic sites). All Upper Palaeolithic, Kebaran, and Geometric Kebaran sites (table 1, fig. 4) appear to have gazelle that were hunted during just a single season. These data suggest that Late Pleistocene hunter-gatherers prior to the Natufian probably migrated seasonally from the highlands to lowlands on a seasonal basis. Lowland sites were generally occupied during the winter and spring, and highland sites were almost always occupied during the summer and fall. Such a strategy of frequent seasonal mobility from highlands to lowlands makes sense because it corresponds with the seasonal and geographic distribution of resources that were attractive to hunter-gatherers (Lieberman 1993c).

It is important to note, however, that the gazelle hunting data presented above imply that not all sites classified as Natufian may have been occupied for more than one season per year. A few small sites in the Jordan Valley (Fazael VI and Salibiya I) and one Late Natufian site from the Negev (Rosh Horesha) contain mandibles from gazelle that appear to have been killed during only one season, suggesting that the sites were occupied during a single season. These sites also highlight some of the problems with the sample sizes used to estimate site seasonality. In particular, the faunal sample from Fazael VI is too small to be sure that the site was only occupied during the spring. Although the estimated size of the site is fairly large, 400 to 500 m[2] according to Bar-Yosef et al. (1974) and Goring-Morris (1980), it either could be a palimpsest resulting from a number of seasonal occupations at the same location or could represent a more substantial long-term occupation that is not evident because of the small area excavated. More fauna and micromorphological analyses are needed from the site to provide additional information about the site formation processes. Additional data are also needed to confirm the seasonality estimate of Salibiya I, although the results reported here do support the hypothesis of the excavators (Crabtree et al. 1991) that the site was occupied only in the spring for special purpose activities.

Two potential problems with these analyses merit special discussion. Most importantly, limited samples sizes are a serious issue. An ANOVA reveals that the sites with evidence for gazelle hunting during multiple seasons have signficantly larger total samples sizes (p=0.056) than sites with evidence for gazelle hunting during just one season. Not all the sites with large samples are multiseasonal, however, so that an ANOVA fails to demonstrate any significant difference in seasonal gazelle hunting among those sites with sample sizes greater than eight (p > 0.24). These results suggest that sites with less than ten mandibles have inadequate sample sizes for resolving issues of differences in seasonal gazelle hunting and site occupation. An additional issue of some concern is the potential that gazelle killed at sites just before and after the transitional period between the wet and dry seasons will reflect multi-seasonal hunting patterns even though they could result from a short-term occupation that spanned the transition from season to season. Such occurrences are identifiable by the presence of outer cementum increment widths solely at the extremes in two possible combinations: very thin opaque and very thick translucent or very thick opaque and very thin translucent. These distributions do not occur, however, in the data presented above.

## DISCUSSION

The above data on the seasonal hunting of gazelle constitute a strong body of evidence in support of the hypothesis that Natufian sites were occupied for more than one season. These occupations are important because they differ from earlier Epipalaeolithic and Palaeolithic cultural complexes in the southern Levant, in which sites were inhabited during just a single season. Moreover, these data agree with previously published estimates of the season of death of fauna from a few Natufian sites (discussed above) and with estimates of Middle Palaeolithic, Upper Palaeolithic, and Kebaran seasonal occupations (Lieberman 1991). However, the resolution of the data are not sufficient to distinguish between complete sedentism,[5] in which a site is permanently occupied for twelve months out of the year, and some less intense pattern of sedentism, in which a site is occupied for the majority of the year (as defined above). Whether or not the Natufians were completely sedentary or relatively sedentary is a moot point because occupation of a site for ten or twelve months out of the year is likely to have the same cultural and environmental effects. What is important is that some form of sedentism occurred during the Early Natufian.

Given these conclusions based on biological sources of evidence for seasonal activities, it is reasonable to ask whether there is any relationship between cultural complexity and reduced mobility in the Natufian. Every Natufian site with significant architecture, large numbers of burials, numerous art objects, high artifact densities, and possible storage structures has faunal evidence for multiseasonal occupation. These sites may have been occupied by mobile hunter-gatherers for several different seasons during the year, but it seems more likely that they were relatively permanently occupied given the confluence of evidence discussed above. The presence of architectural remains, art objects, burials, and other indicators of occupational intensity are not independent of reduced Natufian mobility patterns. Although Edwards (1989) suggests that Natufian architecture is not correlated with sedentism, his argument is based the fact that the highly mobile Bedouin build huts with foundations similar to those found in the Natufian. Such an ethnographic analogy, however, may be inappropriate for hunter-gatherers. For example, the presence of PPNB stone structures in the Sinai probably results from a seasonal pattern similar to that of the Bedouin (Bar-Yosef 1984). Nevertheless, while architectural features seem

to accompany relatively permanent year-round site occupation in the Natufian, they should not be used as a priori indicators of either sedentism or mobility. Hatoula layer 4 was interpreted by Ronen and Lechavallier (1991) to be a repeatedly occupied seasonal camp because of the lack of architecture found in the 30 m² area excavated. Cementum increment analysis data suggest, however, that Hatoula was inhabited for longer periods of time during the Late Natufian and that architecture may exist elsewhere in the site (Lieberman 1995). In addition, no architecture was found in the two m² excavated at Wadi Judayid, which also appears to have been relatively permanently occupied during the Early Natufian (Henry et al. 1985).

Of course, not all Natufian sites have architectural remains, burials, art objects, or even evidence for multiseasonal occupation, and there is no good reason to assume that all Natufians were sedentary. It would be surprising if all Natufian sites were large, multiseasonal base camps. Natufians living in the arid regions of the southern Levant outside the Mediterranean vegetational zone were probably not able to live year-round in any sites because of the much lower and more seasonally marked availability of food in steppic habitats. Furthermore, even the most sedentary hunter-gatherers employ logistical camps that are used for acquiring special resources. Ainu hunter-gatherers in Japan, for example, lived in permanently occupied villages from which men went on trips in the fall and the spring to hunt deer and bear, whose meat was stored for later consumption (Watanabe 1972). Most large and relatively permanently occupied Northwest Coast Native American villages were connected to smaller, specialized salmon collecting sites (Renouf 1984). Single-season encampments in the Jordan Valley such as Salibiya or Fazael may have been logistical sites where cereals were gathered and gazelle were hunted for later consumption at larger base camps.

## CONCLUSION

Reduced seasonal mobility, agriculture, and the emergence of cultural complexity are obviously interrelated in complex ways. It appears that sedentism (or at least long-term, multiseasonal site occupation) first occurred at some time during the Early Natufian and thus preceded agriculture in the southern Levant by at least 2,000 years. But there is not yet enough evidence to understand how sedentism and cultural complexity are related to each other (Price and Brown 1985). Perhaps hunter-gatherer sedentism and hunter gatherer complexity developed in tandem. Woodburn (1980) and Testart (1982), for example, both argue that non-nomadic hunter-gatherers who rely on storage and delayed consumption require more hierarchical social structures to organize and control shared resources. Such theories can only be tested in the archaeological record diachronically, by relating estimates of site seasonality with the archaeological correlates of cultural complexity.

The limited data summarized above suggest that the early Natufian was a period of rapid social, economic, and technological innovation that represents a punctuated burst of change at the beginning of the Holocene. But it is possible that the roots of the Natufian "revolution" can be traced back to the earlier Geometric Kebaran. According to Kaufman (1986), the Geometric Kebaran was a transitional phase between the Kebaran and the Natufian, as evidenced by several Geometric Kebaran sites, Hefzibah and Neve David, that are larger than 1,000 m² and contain cereal processing tools and a variety of other artifacts. While the limited data on Geometric Kebaran seasonality from Neve David (table 1) do not support Kaufman's hypothesis, they do not refute it either. More information is needed on the seasonality and subsistence strategies of hunter-gatherers immediately preceding the Natufian.

As further information on seasonality becomes available from both the southern Levant and elsewhere, archaeologists will be able to test and refine hypotheses about the sequence of events that ultimately led to the emergence of agriculture. But such inferences need to be grounded on a priori data that is independent of the possible behavioral residues of seasonal activities in the archaeological record. Of the various sources of evidence on seasonality that can be gleaned from archaeological sites, cementum increment analysis and other biological indicators of season of death of animals have a crucial role in contributing to our understanding of the origins and implications of sedentism.

## Acknowledgments

This research was supported by grants to the author from the National Science Foundation, the Irene Levi-Sala CARE Foundation, the Wenner-Gren Foundation, and the L. S. B. Leakey Foundation. I would like to thank O. Bar-Yosef, T. Rocek, and R. Meadow, as well as the many researchers who allowed me to analyze samples from their excavations and/or collections: P. Crabtree, D. Henry, E. Hovers, D. Kaufman, M. Lechevallier, A. Marks, J. Perrot, A. Ronen, E. Tchernov, and The Natural History Museum (London).

## Notes

1. Definitions of sedentism abound, however, to a large extent because archaeologists use the term to address a wide variety of questions about mobility (see Preucel 1990).
2. Forty-five individuals were recovered from Shukbah, but little is known about the site and the archaeological context of the burials.
3. The Persian gazelle (*Gazella subgutterosa*), however, is probably a migratory species unlike the mountain gazelle (*Gazella gazella*), which is territorial and nonmigratory (Baharav 1983).
4. Salibiya I may also be a single seasonal occupation but is Late Natufian. Moreover, it should be noted that the seasonality estimates for both these sites suffer from sample sizes that are too small to be reliable.
5. As defined by Higgs and Vita-Finzi (1972).

## BIBLIOGRAPHY

Anderson, P.
1991 "Harvesting of Wild Cereals During the Natufian as Seen from the Experimental Cultivation and Harvest of Wild Einkorn Wheat and Microwear Analysis of Stone Tools," in *The Natufian Culture in the Levant*, O. Bar-Yosef and F. R. Valla, eds., pp. 521–556. International Monographs in Prehistory, Archaeology Series 1. Ann Arbor.

Baharav, D.
1981 "Food Habits of the Mountain Gazelle in Semi-Arid Habitats of Eastern Lower Galilee, Israel." *Journal of Arid Environments* 4:63–69.
1983 "Observation on the Ecology of the Mountain Gazelle in the Upper Galilee, Israel." *Mammalia* 47:59–69.

Bar-Yosef, O.
1970 "The Epipalaeolithic Cultures of Israel." Ph.D. diss., Hebrew University, Jerusalem.
1973 "Nahal Ein Gev I, Preliminary Report." *Mitekufat Haeven* 11:1–7.

1975 "Les Gisements 'Geometriques Kébarien A' d'Haon, Vallée du Jourdain, Israël." *Bulletin de la Société Préhistorique Française* 72:10–14.

1981 "The Epipalaeolithic Complexes in the Southern Levant." *Colloques Internationaux du C.N.R.S.* 598:389–408.

1983 "The Natufian in the Southern Levant," in *The Hilly Flanks and Beyond*, T. C. Young, P. E. L. Smith, and P. Mortensen, eds., pp. 11–42. Oriental Institute Studies in Ancient Oriental Civilization, no. 36. Oriental Institute of the University of Chicago, Chicago.

1984 "Seasonality among Neolithic Hunter-Gatherers in the Southern Sinai," in *Animals and Archaeology*. Vol. 3, *Early Herders and their Flocks*, J. Clutton-Brock and C. Grigson, eds., pp. 145–160. British Archaeological Reports, International Series 202. Oxford.

1991 "The Archaeology of the Natufian Layer at Hayonim Cave," in *The Natufian Culture in the Levant*, O. Bar-Yosef and F. R. Valla, eds., pp. 81–92. International Monographs in Prehistory, Archaeology Series 1. Ann Arbor.

Bar-Yosef, O., and A. Belfer-Cohen
1989 "The Origins of Sedentism and Farming Communities in the Levant." *Journal of World Prehistory* 4:447–498.

Bar-Yosef, O., and F. R. Valla
1991 "The Natufian Culture—An Introduction," in *The Natufian Culture in the Levant*, O. Bar-Yosef and F. R. Valla, eds., pp. 1–10. International Monographs in Prehistory, Archaeology Series 1. Ann Arbor.

Bar-Yosef, O., P. Goldberg, and T. Leveson
1974 "Late Quaternary Stratigraphy and Prehistory in Wadi Fazael, Lower Jordan Valley, a Preliminary Report." *Paléorient* 2:415–428.

Bar-Yosef, O., B. Vandermeersch, B. Arensburg, A. Belfer-Cohen, P. Goldberg, H. Laville, L. Meignen, Y. Rak, J. D. Speth, E. Tchernov, A. M. Tillier, and S. Weiner
1992 "The Excavations at Kebara Cave, Mt. Carmel." *Current Anthropology* 33:497–550.

Belfer-Cohen, A.
1988 "The Natufian Settlement at Hayonim Cave." Ph.D. diss., Hebrew University, Jerusalem.

1991 "The Natufian in the Levant." *Annual Review of Anthropology* 20:167–186.

Belfer-Cohen, A., and O. Bar-Yosef
1981 "The Aurignacian at Hayonim Cave." *Paléorient* 7:19–42.

Belfer-Cohen, A., L. A. Schepartz, and B. Arensburg
1991 "New Biological Data for the Natufian Populations in Israel," in *The Natufian Culture in the Levant*, O. Bar-Yosef and F. R. Valla, eds., pp. 411–424. International Monographs in Prehistory, Archaeology Series 1. Ann Arbor.

Bender, B.
1978 "Gatherer-Hunter to Farmer: A Social Perspective." *World Archaeology* 10:204–237.

Binford, L. R.
1968 "Post Pleistocene Adaptations," in *New Perspectives in Archaeology*, S. R. Binford and L. R. Binford, eds., pp. 313–341. Aldine, Chicago.

Byrd, B.
1989 "The Natufian: Settlement Variability and Economic Adaptations in the Levant at the End of the Pleistocene." *Journal of World Prehistory* 3:159–197.

Campana, D. V.
1991 "Bone Implements from Hayonim Cave: Some Relevant Issues," in *The Natufian Culture in the Levant*, O. Bar-Yosef and F. R. Valla, eds., pp. 459–466. International Monographs in Prehistory, Archaeology Series 1. Ann Arbor.

Cohen, M. N.
1977 *The Food Crisis in Prehistory: Overpopulation and the Origins of Agriculture*. Yale University Press, New Haven.

1985 "Prehistoric Hunter-Gatherers: The Meaning of Social Complexity," in *Prehistoric Hunter-Gatherers: The Emergence of Cultural Complexity*, T. D. Price and J. A. Brown, eds., pp. 99–122. Academic Press, New York.

Colledge, S.
1991 "Investigations of Plant Remains Preserved in Epipalaeolithic Sites in the Near East," in *The Natufian Culture in the Levant*, O. Bar-Yosef and F. R. Valla, eds., pp. 391–398. International Monographs in Prehistory, Archaeology Series 1. Ann Arbor.

Cope, C.
1991 "Gazelle Hunting Strategies in the Southern Levant," in *The Natufian Culture in the Levant*, O. Bar-Yosef and F. R. Valla, eds., pp. 341–358. International Monographs in Prehistory, Archaeology Series 1. Ann Arbor.

Crabtree, P. J., D. V. Campana, A. Belfer-Cohen, and D. E. Bar-Yosef
1991 "First Results of the Excavations of Salibiya I, Lower Jordan Valley," in *The Natufian Culture in the Levant*, O. Bar-Yosef and F. R. Valla, eds., pp. 161–172. International Monographs in Prehistory, Archaeology Series 1. Ann Arbor.

Davis, S. J. M.
1982 "Climatic Change and the Advent of Domestication: The Successions of Ruminant Artiodactyls in the Late Pleistocene-Holocene in the Israeli Region." *Paléorient* 8:5–15.
1983 "The Age Profiles of Gazelles Predated by Ancient Man in Israel: Possible Evidence for a Shift from Seasonality to Sedentism in the Natufian." *Paléorient* 9:55–62.

Edwards, P. C.
1989 "Problems of Recognizing the Earliest Sedentism: the Natufian Example." *Journal of Mediterranean Archaeology* 2:5–48.
1990 "Revising the Broad Spectrum Revolution and Its Role in the Origins of Southwest Asian Food Production." Antiquity 63:225–246.
1991 "Wadi Hammeh 27: An Early Natufian Site at Pella, Jordan," in *The Natufian Culture in the Levant*, O. Bar-Yosef and F. R. Valla, eds., pp. 123–148. International Monographs in Prehistory, Archaeology Series 1. Ann Arbor.

Edwards, P. C., S. J. Bourke, S. M. Colledge, J. Head, and P. G. Macumber
1988 "Late Pleistocene Prehistory in the Wadi al-Hammeh, Jordan Valley," in *The Prehistory of Jordan*, A. N. Garrard and H. G. Gebel, eds., pp. 525–565. British Archaeological Reports, International Series 396. Oxford.

Flannery, K.
1972 "The Origins of the Village As a Settlement Type in Mesoamerica and the Near East: A Comparative Study," in *Man, Settlement and Urbanism*, P. J. Ucko, R. Tringham, and G. W. Dimbleby, eds., pp. 23–53. Duckworth, London.

Garrard, A. N., A. V. B. Betts, B. Byrd, and C. Hunt
1988 "Summary of Palaeoenvironmental and Prehistoric Investigations in the Azraq Basin," in *The Prehistory of Jordan*, A. N. Garrard and H. G. Gebel, eds., pp. 311–337. British Archaeological Reports, International Series 396. Oxford.

Garrod, D. A. E.
1932 "A New Mesolithic Industry: The Natufian of Palestine." *Journal of the Royal Anthropological Society* 62:257–269.

1957 "The Natufian Culture: The Life and Economy of a Mesolithic People in the Near East." *Proceedings of the British Academy* 43:211–237.

Garrod, D. A. E., and D. M. A. Bate
1937 *The Stone Age of Mount Carmel*, vol. 1. Clarendon Press, Oxford.

Goring-Morris, A. N.
1980 "Late Quaternary Sites in the Wadi Fazael, Lower Jordan Valley." Master's thesis, Hebrew University, Jerusalem.

Grau, G. A., and F. Walther
1976 "Mountain Gazelle Agonistic Behavior." *Animal Behavior* 24:215–267.

Grue, H., and B. Jensen
1979 "Review of the Formation of Incremental Lines in Tooth Cementum of Terrestrial Mammals." *Danish Review of Game Biology* 11:1–48.

Henry, D. O.
1985 "Preagricultural Sedentism: The Natufian Example," in *Prehistoric Hunter-Gatherers: The Emergence of Cultural Complexity*, T. D. Price and J. A. Brown, eds., pp. 365–381. Academic Press, New York.
1989 *From Foraging to Agriculture: The Levant at the End of the Ice Age*. University of Pennsylvania Press, Philadelphia.

Henry, D. O., and A. N. Garrard
1988 "Tor Hamar: An Epipalaeolithic Rockshelter in Southern Jordan." *Palestine Exploration Quarterly* 120:1–25.

Henry, D. O., A. Leroi-Gourhan, and S. Davis
1981 "Hayonim Terrace: Late Pleistocene Changes in Environment and Economy." *Journal of Archaeological Science* 8:33–58.

Henry, D. O., P. Turnbull, A. Emery-Barbier, and A. Leroi-Gourhan
1985 "Archaeological and Faunal Remains from Natufian and Timnian Sites in Southern Jordan." *Bulletin of the American Schools of Oriental Research* 257:45–64.

Higgs, E. S., and C. Vita-Finzi
1972 "Prehistoric Economies: A Territorial Approach," in *Papers in Economic Prehistory*, E. S. Higgs, ed., pp. 27–36. Cambridge University Press, Cambridge.

Hillman, G. C., S. M. Colledge, and D. R. Harris
    1989 "Plant-Food Economy During the Epipaleolithic Period at Tell Abu Hureyra, Syria: Dietary Diversity, Seasonality, and Modes of Exploitation," in *Foraging and Farming: The Evolution of Plant Exploitation*, D. R. Harris and G. C. Hillman, eds., pp. 240–268. Unwin Hyman, London.

Hopf, M., and O. Bar-Yosef
    1987 "Plant Remains from Hayonim Cave, Western Galilee." *Paléorient* 13:117–120.

Hovers, E., L. K. Horwitz, D. E. Bar-Yosef, and C. Cope-Miyashiro
    1988 "The Site of Urkan-E-Rub IIa: A Case Study of Subsistence and Mobility Patterns in the Kebaran Period in the Lower Jordan Valley." *Mitekufat Haeven* 21:20–48.

Kaufman, D.
    1986 "A Re-Consideration of Adaptive Change in the Levantine Epipalaeolithic," in *The End of the Palaeolithic Old World*, L. G. Straus, ed., pp. 117–128. British Archaeological Reports, International Series 238. Oxford.

Kenyon, K. M.
    1981 *Excavations at Jericho*. Vol. 3, *The Architecture and Stratigraphy of the Tell*. British School of Archaeology in Jerusalem, London.

Klevezal, G. A., and S. E. Kleinenberg
    1967 *Age Determination of Mammals by Layered Structure in Teeth and Bone*. Nauk, Moscow. Translations Series, no. 1024, Foreign Languages Division, Department of the Secretary of State of Canada. Fisheries Research Board of Canada, Ste. Anne de Bellevue, Quebec.

Lee, R. B., and I. DeVore, eds.
    1968 *Man the Hunter*. Aldine, Chicago.

Legge, A. J., and P. A. Rowley-Conwy
    1987 "Gazelle Killing in Stone Age Syria." *Scientific American* 257(2):88–95.

Lieberman, D. E.
    1991 "Seasonality and Gazelle Hunting at Hayonim Cave: New Evidence For 'Sedentism' During the Natufian." *Paléorient* 17(1):47–57.
    1993a "The Biology of Cementogenesis and its Application to the Evolution of Hunter-Gatherer Seasonal Mobility during the Late Quaternary in the Southern Levant." Ph.D. diss., Harvard University.
    1993b "Life History Variables Preserved in Dental Cementum Microstructure." *Science* 261:1162–1164.

    1993c "The Rise and Fall of Hunter-Gatherer Seasonal Mobility: The Case of the Southern Levant." *Current Anthropology* 34:599–631.
    1994a "The Biological Basis for Seasonal Increments in Dental Cementum and their Application to Archaeological Research." *Journal of Archaeological Science* 21:525–539.
    1994b "Seasonality Estimates from Hatoula," in *Le Gisement de Hatoula en Judée Occidentale, Israël*, M. Lechevallier and A. Ronen, eds., pp. 125–128. Mémoires et Travaux du Centre de Recherche Français de Jerusalem, no. 8. Paris.
    1995 "Cementum Increment Analyses of Teeth from Wadi Hisma: Estimates of Site Seasonality," in *Prehistoric Cultural Ecology and Evolution: Insights from Jordan*, D. O. Henry, ed., pp. 391–398. Plenum, New York.

Lieberman, D. E., and R. H. Meadow
    1992 "The Biology of Cementum Increments (An Archaeological Perspective)." *Mammal Review* 22:57–77.

Lieberman, D. E., T. W. Deacon, and R. H. Meadow
    1990 "Computer Image Enhancement and Analysis of Cementum Increments as Applied to Teeth of *Gazella gazella*." *Journal of Archaeological Science* 17:519–533.

Lowenstam, H. A., and S. Weiner
    1989 *On Biomineralization*. Oxford University Press, Oxford.

Marks, A. E., and P. A. Larson
    1977 "Test Excavations at the Natufian Site of Rosh Horesha," in *Prehistory and Paleoenvironments in the Central Negev, Israel*, vol. 2, A. E. Marks, ed., pp. 173–189. Southern Methodist University Press, Dallas.

Martin, G.
    1978 "Ein Gev III." *Israel Exploration Journal* 28:262–263.

Nadel, D., and I. Hershkovitz
    1991 "New Subsistence Data and Human Remains from the Earliest Levantine Epipalaeolithic." *Current Anthropology* 32:631–635.

Neuville, R.
    1934 "Le Préhistoire du Palestine." *Revue Biblique* 43:237–259.
    1951 *Le Paléolithique et le Mésolithique du Désert de Judée*. Archives de L'Institut de Paléontologie Humaine, Memoire no. 24. Paris.

Perrot, J.
1966 "Le Gisement Natoufien de Mallaha (Eynan), Israel." *L'Anthropologie* 70:437–484.
1989 "Les Variations du Mode de la Sepulture dans le Gisement Natoufien de Mallaha (Eynan), Israel," in *Investigations in South Levantine Prehistory*, O. Bar-Yosef and B. Vandermeersch, eds., pp. 287–295. British Archaeological Reports, International Series 497. Oxford.

Pichon, J.
1987 "L'Avifaune." *Mémoires et Travaux du Centre de Recherche de Jérusalem* 4:115–150.
1989 "L'Environnement du Natoufien en Israel," in *Investigations in South Levantine Prehistory*, O. Bar-Yosef and B. Vandermeersch, eds., pp. 61–69. British Archaeological Reports, International Series 497. Oxford.
1991 "Les Oiseaux en Natoufien, Avifaune et Sédentarité," in *The Natufian Culture in the Levant*, O. Bar-Yosef and F. R. Valla, eds., pp. 371–380. International Monographs in Prehistory, Archaeology Series 1. Ann Arbor.

Preucel, R.
1990 *Seasonal Circulation and Dual Residence in the Pueblo Southwest: A Prehistoric Example from the Pajarito Plateau, New Mexico*. Garland, New York.

Price, T. D., and J. A. Brown
1985 "Aspects of Hunter-Gatherer Complexity," in *Prehistoric Hunter-Gatherers: The Emergence of Cultural Complexity*, T. D. Price and J. A. Brown, eds., pp. 3–20. Academic Press, New York.

Rafferty, J. E.
1985 "The Archaeological Record on Sedentariness: Recognition, Development, and Implications." *Advances in Archaeological Method and Theory* 8:113–156.

Redman, C. L.
1978 *The Rise of Civilization*. W. H. Freeman, San Francisco.

Renouf, M. A. R.
1984 "Northern Coast Fishers: An Archaeological Model." *World Archaeology* 16:18–27.

Ronen, A., and M. Lechevallier
1991 "The Natufian of Hatula," in *The Natufian Culture in the Levant*, O. Bar-Yosef and F. R. Valla, eds., pp. 149–160. International Monographs in Prehistory, Archaeology Series 1. Ann Arbor.

Saxon, E. C., G. Martin, and O. Bar-Yosef
1978 "Nahal Hadera V: An Open-Air Site on the Israeli Littoral." *Paléorient* 4:253–265.

Smith, P.
1991 "The Dental Evidence for Nutritional Status in the Natufians," in *The Natufian Culture in the Levant*, O. Bar-Yosef and F. R. Valla, eds., pp. 425–432. International Monographs in Prehistory, Archaeology Series 1. Ann Arbor.

Stark, B. L.
1981 "The Rise of Sedentary Life," in *Supplement to the Handbook of Middle American Indians*. Vol. 1, *Archaeology*, J. A. Sabloff, ed., pp. 345–372. University of Texas Press, Austin.

Tangri, D., and G. Wyncoll
1989 "Of Mice and Men: Is the Presence of Commensal Animals in Archaeological Sites a Positive Correlate of Sedentism?" *Paléorient* 15:85–94.

Tchernov, E.
1984 "Commensal Animals and Human Sedentism in the Middle East," in *Animals and Archaeology*. Vol. 3, *Early Herders and Their Flocks*, J. Clutton-Brock and C. Grigson, eds., pp. 91–115. British Archaeological Reports, International Series 202. Oxford.
1991a "Biological Evidence for Human Sedentism in Southwest Asia During the Natufian," in *The Natufian Culture in the Levant*, O. Bar-Yosef and F. R. Valla, eds., pp. 315–340. International Monographs in Prehistory, Archaeology Series 1. Ann Arbor.
1991b "Of Mice and Men. Biological Markers For Long-Term Sedentism; A Reply." *Paléorient* 17:153–160.

Testart, A.
1982 "The Significance of Food Storage Among Hunter-Gatherers: Residence Patterns, Population Densities, and Social Inequalities." *Current Anthropology* 23:523–537.

Turville-Petre, F.
1932 "Excavations in the Mugharet el-Kebarah." *Journal of the Royal Anthropological Institute of Great Britain and Ireland* 62:271–276.

Unger-Hamilton, R.
1991 "Natufian Plant Husbandry in the Southern Levant and Comparison with that of Neolithic Periods: The Lithic Perspective," in *The Natufian Culture in the Levant*, O. Bar-Yosef and F. R. Valla, eds., pp. 483–520. International Monographs in Prehistory, Archaeology Series 1. Ann Arbor.

Valla, F. R.
  1984 *Les Industries de Silex de Mallaha (Eynan) et du Natoufien dans le Levant*. Mémoires et Travaux du Centre Français de Jerusalem, no. 3. Association Paléorient, Paris.
  1991 "Les Natoufiens de Mallaha et l'Espace," in *The Natufian Culture in the Levant*, O. Bar-Yosef and F. R. Valla, eds., pp. 111–122. International Monographs in Prehistory, Archaeology Series 1. Ann Arbor.

Valla, F. R., H. Plisson, and R. Buxo i Capdevila
  1989 "Notes Préliminaires sur les Fouilles en Cours sur la Terrasse d'Hayonim." *Paléorient* 15:245–257.

Valla, F. R., F. Le Mort, and H. Plisson
  1991 "Les Fouilles en Cours sur la Terrasse d'Hayonim," in *The Natufian Culture in the Levant*, O. Bar-Yosef and F. R. Valla, eds., pp. 95–110. International Monographics in Prehistory, Series 1. Ann Arbor.

Watanabe, H.
  1972 "The Ainu," in *Hunters and Gatherers Today*, M. G. Bicchieri, ed., pp. 448–484. Waveland Press, Prospect Heights, Illinois.

Weinstein-Evron, M.
  1991 "New Radiocarbon Dates for the Early Natufian of el-Wad Cave, Mt. Carmel, Israel." *Paléorient* 17:95–98.

Woodburn, J.
  1980 "Hunters and Gatherers Today and Reconstruction of the Past," in *Soviet and Western Anthropology*, E. Gellner, ed., pp. 95–117. Columbia University Press, New York.

Wright, K.
  1991 "The Origins and Development of Ground Stone Assemblages in Late Pleistocene Southwest Asia." *Paléorient* 17:19–45.

CHAPTER 6

# Natufian Seasonality:
# A Guess

*François R. Valla*

The Natufian culture in the Levant, which lasted from 12,500 to 10,250 B.P. (12,700–9800 cal B.C.), occupied an area spanning from the Mediterranean coast to the middle Euphrates Valley and to the Edom mountains in southern Jordan. The landscape of this region demonstrates extreme contrasts: while the mountains in Lebanon reach 3,083 m above sea level, those north of Aqaba reach only 1,754 m, and the Dead Sea is measured at 396 m below the level of the Mediterranean. Diverse soils and climates strongly influence the region's flora and fauna. Four broad types of vegetation zones—the Mediterranean, Irano-Turanian, Saharo-Arabian, and Sudanese—are belts that stretch more or less parallel to the coast. In all probability, such a variety of environments could not have sustained a uniform system of seasonal exploitation by humans over a period of more than two thousand years. Given the varied environmental conditions and the limited nature of the archaeological observations, I hesitate before making any strong assertions. In fact, does a true understanding of Natufian seasonality lie beyond our grasp, serving only as an "illegitimate question," in the Kantian sense?

Either implicitly or explicitly, this question underlies some of the main debates raised in attempts to understand the Natufian culture. As early as 1932, Dorothy Garrod argued, based on the finding of a few flint blades displaying sickle gloss, that the Natufians practiced agriculture (Garrod 1932). Her suggestion implied that communities that were thought to have been partially mobile, due to the needs of hunting, were actually affected by a set of seasonal agricultural activities (clearing, sowing, harvesting). Subsequently, Jean Perrot proposed that the Natufian people, rather

than having been agriculturists, were foragers engaged in intensive collection of naturally growing cereals. Managing these seasonal resources, particularly through storage practices, could have minimized the necessity for seasonal mobility (Perrot 1966, 1968). Recently, Perlès and Phillips (1991) linked the very definition of the Natufian culture and its geographical extension to a system of seasonality. To their understanding, the only "true" Natufian is that found in the large sites of Mt. Carmel and the Galilee area (see also Belfer-Cohen 1991). Using the term "Natufian" beyond the limits of this area would be legitimate only if the so-called Natufian sites were established by people coming from the Natufian homeland on a seasonal basis. Otherwise, people living there would have been "foreign" to the Natufian sphere and therefore dependent upon another way of life.

Although it lies at the crux of so many archaeological problems, the Natufian system of seasonality has rarely been examined thoroughly because of both a lack of reliable data on this period and conflicting interpretations of the existing data. We must, therefore, be aware of the uncertainty of any hypotheses put forward at this stage. This lack of relevant, specific information also requires that we make explicit the general reasons that strengthen the interpretation of Natufian seasonality. A preliminary model will be established below using the available data and bearing in mind their limitations. This model will then be evaluated in terms of the diverse geographical contexts in the Near East, and the resulting constructs will be incorporated into a chronological perspective on the Natufian phenomenon.

## NATUFIAN SEASONALITY?
## SOME GENERAL REASONS BEHIND
## A HYPOTHESIS

Today's Mediterranean climate is characterized by distinct extremes: wet winters from November to April and dry, hot summers from May to October. The existence of such a sharp pattern provides a strong basis for the modeling of social activities in accordance with the shifts in annual climatic conditions. Furthermore, it is generally accepted that alternating seasons have a major impact on both the animal and plant resources upon which human life relies. Questions arise, however, concerning the exact origins of this climatic pattern. Could this climate and the associated flora, mainly the park-forest of oak and pistachio and the accompanying annuals (including the Gramineaes), have been established through a rapid shift at the end of the Natufian around 11,000 B.P. (Wright 1977)? A detailed discussion of climatic changes in the Levant over the last 15,000 years is not appropriate in this context. In fact, the topic has been much debated in recent years by climate specialists. The growing recognition of the Younger Dryas as a worldwide event and the use of calibration of ${}^{14}$C dates will allow a much better understanding in the future of the situation in the Levant at the transition from the Pleistocene to the Holocene (see Baruch and Bottema 1991; papers in Bar-Yosef and Kra 1994; a synthesis can be found in Sanlaville 1996).

It is sufficient to note here that the climate during the Natufian was, on the average, colder than today's climate, becoming even colder during the Younger Dryas, with some warming towards the very end of the period. Interestingly, the available evidence on the flora indicates that vegetation was not radically different than it is today. For example, as early as 19,000 B.P., the plant community at Ohalo II on Lake Kinneret appears very similar to its modern counterpart (Kislev et al. 1992). Annuals, including wheat and barley, are found there. The examination of the rich samples of carbonized plant remains collected in the Epipalaeolithic layers of the Euphrates Valley yielded a similar conclusion (Hillman et al. 1989). One minor deviation is that einkorn (*Triticum beoticum*), found at Abu Hureyra and Mureybet, and pistachio trees, found at Abu Hureyra, no longer grow near these sites. Their presence in the Natufian strata probably indicates more moisture at that time (Hillman et al. 1989:255; van Zeist and Bakker-Herres 1984:194). This accords well with trees, presently surviving as relics, found in

the Negev and the Edom mountains (Horowitz 1977; Henry et al. 1985). If these indications are correct, then it seems that a Mediterranean-type vegetation covered large areas in the Levant at the end of the Pleistocene. Moreover, it appears that this vegetation, and probably the climatic regime upon which it depended, was prevalent in places where it has since been replaced by a steppic cover.

Demonstrating that the Natufian people followed a seasonal cycle requires evidence that they depended on seasonally accessible resources on a regular basis. Although finding this evidence is, in a few instances, a relatively straightforward task, the necessary data are lacking in general. At present, the idea of Natufian seasonality remains only a probable interpretation, drawn from both natural conditions and a few conclusive observations.

It is clear that the Natufians were feeding on mammals such as gazelle, ox, wild boar, and goat. However, because these animals were sedentary, determining the season in which they were killed is difficult and requires sophisticated methods (Simmons and Ilany 1975–1977; Bokonyi 1972). According to Lieberman (1991, 1992, 1993), gazelles were caught both in winter and summer at Hayonim, Mallaha, and Hatoula, but only during spring/summer at Salibiyah I and Fazael VI, and in fall/winter at Rosh Horesha. The study of birds provides better information on seasonal hunting. Seasonal patterns are evident in an examination of migratory birds that fly across the Levant each year and, in many cases (ducks, teals, and so on), stay there as winter visitors. At Mallaha, where such birds were attracted by the Hula Lake, and at Mureybet, where they took advantage of the Euphrates River, Pichon has been able to demonstrate that they were hunted as winter game. At both sites, birds were probably hunted year-round and were hunted in increasing numbers when resident communities were expanded by migratory visitors (Pichon 1984).

Fruits and seeds, the majority of which are highly seasonal, are another important source of information, but unfortunately carbonized plant remains are scarce in most of the sites investigated thus far. Moreover, discoveries of small numbers of seeds are not useful in this discussion, because these could be derived from casual, rather than systematic, gathering. Nevertheless, this criticism does not affect all existing observations. The thousands of seeds identified at Abu Hureyra belong to some 150 species, and most of these are edible (Hillman et al. 1989). Many of these seeds were undoubtedly gathered on a systematic basis for the duration of the human occupation of this site. Cereals and clovers (Trifoliae) illustrate this point, as they are available for only a short period from April to June. According to Hillman and his associates, humans were present at the site at least from spring to the beginning of summer and again during autumn when seasonal gathering is beyond doubt. In fact, they were probably there year-round (Hillman et al. 1989:261–264).

At the site of Mureybet (Phases IA and IB), approximately 800 seeds and fruits are known (van Zeist and Bakker-Herres 1984). However, this sample is too small to demonstrate systematic collection of a particular species. Both cereals (a dozen examples) and legumes are rare. Among the plants that are relatively abundant, *Polygonum* (available from June to November) and *Astragalus* (present from April to June) are those most probably eaten by people. Samples obtained from other sites are either still under study (Wadi Hammeh 27, Tabaqa) or are not large enough (Mallaha, Hayonim Cave and Terrace) (Edwards et al. 1988; Byrd and Colledge 1991; Hopf and Bar-Yosef 1987; Valla et al. 1989).

A third avenue for exploring seasonal activities among the Natufians is the study of fish remains. This approach appears paradoxical given that freshwater fish, at the latitudes considered here, is repeatedly given as an example of a resource available year-round (Cauvin 1977; Nadel and Hershkovitz 1991). Nevertheless, it is the social dimension of the fishing practices that relates to our discussion of seasonality. Fish bones are found on many Natufian sites, including sites such as Hatoula, where sea fish were brought from the coast some 30 km away (Lernau 1985; Davis et al. 1994). They were also abundant at Mureybet, on the Euphrates River, as well as at Mallaha, where thousands of fish vertebrae were collected. Indeed, a sample isolated in a large pit, and as such archaeologically homogeneous, was studied by Desse (1987). He demonstrated that although fishing took place year-round, it was practiced in accordance with a seasonal pattern; people fished during winter, more so in the spring, continued through the summer, but then fished much less in autumn (fig. 1). In other words, it is not enough for a resource to be known and technically available for it to be used. The group's own choice intervenes as another key factor in determining the practice, and it seems that in the Natufian, the group favored a seasonal cycle.

This evidence leads to a second set of factors, specifically, characteristics of the human social domain, which supports the idea of seasonality among the Natufians. Human societies, it seems, are usually structured by opposing tendencies to both aggregate

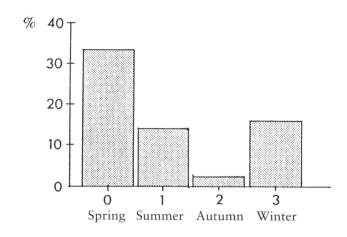

Figure 1. Seasonal pattern of fishing of Cyprins at Mallaha (Late Natufian). N=173. After Desse 1987.

and fission periodically during the annual cycle. This tendency determines their social structure. Marcel Mauss first recognized this phenomenon: "Social life does not maintain the same level at different times of the year. On the contrary, it undergoes regular and successive phases of increasing and decreasing intensity, rest and activity, expenditure and recovery. It is indeed as if it were imposing on the system and mind of individual people a force which they can only stand for a while, after which they have to reduce it and partly escape. This would explain the rhythm of dispersal and grouping, individual life and collective life, examples of which have been observed. One wonders whether seasonal influences proper are more than occasional causes which simply indicate the most convenient part of the year for each phase to take place, rather than being compulsory and determinant causes of the all mechanism" (Mauss and Beuchat 1978 [1904–1905]:473). By looking beyond seasonal changes that resulted from constrained access to resources and even allowing that some environments did provide subsistence for year-round occupation, we become aware of another influence on the pattern of seasonality. Though the practice of some alternation between aggregation and dispersal periods might have been influenced by natural rhythms, ultimately it was dictated by purely social needs.

Mauss lists the following among the main features of aggregation periods: intense communal life, feasts and religious ceremonies, active intellectual life, and a high level of sexual activity. In contrast, dispersal periods are marked by the opposite characteristics, such as the restriction of social life to the nuclear family, diminishment or absence of religious and intellectual activities, and so on. Do the archaeological data support such an annual schedule among the Natufians?

Natufian sedentism is seen by many researchers as one of the most distinctive features of this culture (Perrot 1968; Bar-Yosef 1983; Valla 1988; Henry 1989; Bar-Yosef and Belfer-Cohen 1989). Attempts to identify seasonal activities among the Natufians along the threads outlined above have produced evidence for cyclical occupation as well as the possibility of more permanent occupation at places such as Mallaha, Abu Hureyra, and Mureybet. Additional relevant observations favoring a year-round human presence at sites are the systematic rebuilding of houses on the same spot as at Mallaha (Valla 1981, 1991), the multiplicity of graves as evidenced at Mallaha, Hayonim, el-Wad, and Nahal Oren (Perrot et al. 1988; Belfer-Cohen 1988; Garrod and Bate 1937; Noy 1989), and the sudden increase in human commensals: mice, sparrows and dogs (Tchernov 1991; Davis and Valla 1978; Valla et al. 1991; Tchernov and Valla 1997).

A possible interpretation of these conflicting observations, namely, sedentism versus seasonal dispersal, is offered by a remark from Mauss, who noted that Western societies live according to some degree of seasonal patterning. One only has to stay in a large city during the summer, when it is generally deserted by its vacationing inhabitants, to recognize the validity of his observation (Mauss and Beuchat 1978 [1904–1905]: 472). Although such a comparison is not an explanation, it is possible that the Natufian people practiced a form of sedentarism that also involved a temporary dispersal of the group during a certain season. The decrease in fishing activity by the Mallaha inhabitants during autumn provides an argument for a temporary dispersal in the Galilee. Some families from Mallaha may have spent a few weeks on their own in the mountains of Galilee, in the Lebanese Beqaa, in the Golan, or on the Hauran basaltic plateau. This suggestion is enhanced by the idea that empty-handed hunters there could have taken advantage of the fruits of pistachio, almond, and oak trees at this time.

## A GEOGRAPHICAL READING

Earl Saxon (1974) put forward a model of this kind in which he suggested that the inhabitants of Kebara could have dispersed in the Negev for some time each year. However, this assertion contradicts an observation made by several researchers. Family similarity links groups in the Galilee, the Judean desert, the Negev, the Transjordan, and the middle Euphrates Valley to the same cultural area. And yet, key differences, some more obvious than others, distinguish each site and each region from its neighbors. These differences are visible in the style and technical features of the flint industries (Valla 1984; Olszewski 1986), as well as the style and quantitative characteristics of the bone tool assemblages (Stordeur 1991, 1992). Regardless of their exact nature, some of these specifics should not be interpreted merely as functional variability, but rather as technical habits or "coup de main," by which people at the group and province levels expressed their individuality.

The study of the basalt and limestone industries would most likely add more data to these observed differences and would support the identification of four distinct areas of Natufian settlement. These consist of a "center," the Mt. Carmel and Galilee area, and three provinces, namely central Palestine, the Negev and Edom mountains, and the middle Euphrates. These latter provinces become more and more peripheral with distance from the center. The suggested regional division is supported by the existence of the Harifian industry, which can be considered as a variant of the Final Natufian in the north but is limited to the Negev and Northern Sinai areas (Scott 1977; Goring-Morris 1987:316). It is also important to note that large areas of land outside of these recognized entities remain virtually unknown at this time. Finally, it should be emphasized that the connotations of the terms "center" and "periphery" as used here have to do with some kind of restricted diffusionism.

According to our present knowledge, the geographical distribution of sites varies greatly among the different regions. Within the Mt. Carmel and Galilee "center," no site appears higher than 250 m above sea level, with Hayonim Cave found at this altitude. Most sites seem to have been settled for long periods of time, as evidenced by the thick, widely spread, and densely packed material deposits, which sometimes comprise artistic objects. A different situation is encountered in Central Palestine, where sites are found in plains and valleys (Shukba, Hatoula, Fazael, Salibiya) as well as in mountains (Judean desert, edge of the Negev). With the exception of Shukba, settlements are smaller than they are in the "center," and they contain much thinner deposits. Some sites at higher altitudes are quite small but still present artistic manifestations. In the Edom and Negev region, a handful of relatively large sites are found in the highlands. Some of these are quite rich in material remains but contain few traces of artistic activities (e.g., Wadi Judayid, Rosh Zin, Rosh Horesha, Saflulim, Beidha). This region also contains some small or very small lowland findspots. The Natufian of the middle Euphrates region is known mainly through two large tells in the valley, Abu Hureyra and Mureybet. In Lebanon, lowland (Les Sables de Beyrouth, Jiita) and high altitude stations (Saaide II) seemingly coexisted (Copeland 1991; Schroeder 1991). Eastern Jordan contains a series of small sites, some with stone constructions, as described by Betts (1991; see also Garrard et al. 1996).

Keeping in mind our earlier perspective, these observations raise two questions. First, are there traces of a seasonal system of activities within each region that is congruent with that region's specific distribution of sites? Secondly, are there indications for a seasonal system of activities that allowed contact among groups from different areas?

Each of the large sites in the "center" can be seen as an aggregation place for a particular group, but there is no clear evidence for their possible locations during the dispersal period. An obvious hypothesis would be that families isolated themselves in the mountains. However, there is no doubt that exchange between the groups was vital for their survival, even from a purely biological standpoint. A few observations may indicate contacts outside the area in question. A type of flint tool known as the Dhour Choueir bladelet, belonging to an older, mainly Lebanese, tradition, is found at Mallaha (Valla 1984). Does this indicate links and exchanges in this direction? At Hayonim Terrace, a few special isoceles triangles have been recovered. These are not part of the local tradition but are reminiscent of earlier artifacts known from Syria and east of the Jordan River (Valla 1984:fig. 87, no. 17). Similarly, does the early use of the microburin technique at el-Wad mean contact eastwards or possibly towards the south, in the Negev, where the use of this technique is older and systematic? For the moment, it is possible to state only that if groups in the Mt. Carmel-Galilee "center" obeyed a tendency to disperse for a few weeks each year, then there is little evidence for this within the region itself. Similarly, the faint indications for contact outside the region do not support the hypothesis for seasonal movement.

The situation in Central Palestine could allow for the construction of a model in which people aggregated successively in lowland and highland sites. Groups could have stayed in the plains and valleys during winter, as suggested by the hunting of winter migratory birds at Hatoula (Pichon 1985) and by winter catches of gazelles at the same site (Lieberman 1992, 1993). Then, during spring (and summer?), people could have visited the mountains. Evidence for these mountain stays may be found in the reaping knives from Oumm ez-Zoueitina as well as in the relatively large number of flints with gloss from Tor Abou Sif, if indeed these tools can be related to cereal gathering (Neuville 1951). However, this interpretation does not allow for the hypothesis that people need alternating periods of communal and isolated life. Moreover, the pattern of use of the microburin technique, seen generally in the highlands, strongly suggests distinct traditions and does not support such an assertion.

The evidence indicates that most known Central Palestine sites, both in the highlands and lowlands, are aggregation sites for different groups. External influences are clearer here than in the Mt. Carmel and Galilee area, pointing in both the northern and southern directions. The repeated finding of a particular tool, such as the case of the barbed point in the Judean Desert, indicates links with the large coastal sites in the "center," such as Kebara, el-Wad, and Hayonim (Turville-Petre 1932; Garrod and Bate 1937; Henry and Leroi-Gourhan 1976). On the other hand, the relative frequency of geometric microliths over nongeometric ones at Hatoula and Fazael IV is a southern characteristic (Lechevallier and Ronen 1985, 1994; Bar-Yosef et al. 1974; Valla 1984:177). Provisionally, I suggest that Natufian groups in Central Palestine practiced seasonal systems involving periods of dispersal that were longer than those practiced by groups in the Mt. Carmel-Galilee Center. It seems that these systems were not based on the successive exploitation of both mountain and lowland areas, but rather on the specialized use of each of these ecological zones (strictly speaking, there are three such zones, since conditions in the lower Jordan Valley are not the same as those in the coastal plain, even though they may have been more similar in the past). Finally, while it seems clear that the Mt. Carmel-Galilee area functioned as a link between the northern and southern regions, what remains unclear is the seasonal basis of the relations implicit in this role.

The Negev sites are distributed topographically in a manner opposite to those of the Galilee: the main aggregation sites are in the highlands whereas the dispersal occurred towards the lowlands. Interpretation of the seasonal rhythm depends upon the way in which the pattern of seasonal exploitation of resources is reconstructed. A pattern built around the gathering of ripe autumn fruits, such as pistachio, would imply that autumn and winter would be the time for aggregation. However, a pattern based upon the exploitation of annuals (cereals, etc.) would suggest aggregating during spring and summer. Goring-Morris (1987:437ff.) believes that both systems prevailed successively, one during the Late Natufian, the other during the Harifian. Indeed, Lieberman asserts that a Natufian presence took place at Rosh Horesha during winter.

In terms of contact with adjacent regions, and in accordance with the view adopted here, a northern influence pervades the whole area and indicates the "membership" of groups in the Natufian culture. If a particular object could symbolize this influence, then perhaps the grooved stones from Rosh Zin could be suggested (Henry 1976). But, once again, the possibly seasonal pattern of the "flow" eludes us. The relatively extreme climate of the Negev may have prevented the lengthening of aggregation periods in the manner characteristic of the Mt. Carmel-Galilee "center." Sites indicating those periods are, nonetheless, well preserved. The possibility of contact with other regions, mainly northwards, is suggested by a large number of cultural traits. From a biological standpoint, it is doubtful that the population of the Negev at that time could be conceived of as an isolated entity.

After looking at the organization of presently known Natufian sites region by region, I must modify the earlier hypothesis regarding the seasonal system of their inhabitants. From examination of the Mt. Carmel and Galilee sites on the one hand and the Euphrates sites on the other, I initially envisioned a system based on a long period of aggregation followed by a short dispersal episode, possibly during autumn. It was then argued that in the Mt. Carmel and Galilee, this dispersal period could have been spent in the mountain areas. Clearly, this scheme cannot be transferred without modification to either Central Palestine or the Negev.

In Central Palestine, aggregation places are located in both mountains and lowlands. Their smaller size, compared to the "villages" in the "center," may result from a combination of shorter aggregation periods and shorter-term use of sites. I suggest that even limited periods of aggregation may have resulted in food shortages in poor environments. Yet these sites can be attributed to aggregated people, rather than to dispersed families, as based on observations of the positively identifiable aggregations sites. When it is possible to guess the number of families that grouped together during these periods, in both the north and south, the figure never exceeds a dozen. If this estimate is correct, it seems unlikely that groups could split into units any larger than a nuclear family during dispersal periods. Because the sites in Central Palestine do not correspond to such small units, they should be aggregation places. Unfortunately, our information is too sparse to allow further interpretation.

In the Negev, the situation is again different. Here, the system of seasonal mobility takes advantage of the topography particular to that area, and groups meet in the highlands. However, the details in this region are not as clear as in Central Palestine.

## A CHRONOLOGICAL SCALE

The introduction of the time factor will enable a more comprehensive view of the whole Natufian complex. It will then become possible to gain a better understanding of the powerful attraction of the Mt. Carmel-Galilee "center," the development of its influence in adjacent regions, and its subsequent decline.

Chronological subdivisions of the Natufian have been established on the basis of three lines of evidence: stratigraphic observations (when available), flint tool characteristics (mainly the frequency of Helwan retouch on lunates and the mean length of those microliths), and radiocarbon. It is not necessary to repeat those details here (Valla 1984, 1987). However, bearing in mind that only broad trends can be identified through archaeological seriation, three stages have been defined within the Natufian. These are an Early Natufian phase, from 12,500 to 11,250 B.P. (ca. 12,700 to 11,250 cal B.C.); a Late Natufian, from 11,250 to 10,500 B.P. (11,250 to 10,000 cal B.C.); and a Final Natufian, ending about 10,250 B.P. (9800 cal B.C.). These dates, obviously approximate, do not preclude discrepancies between the different regions where the Natufian culture is found.

Most of the large sites (five out of six) in the Mt. Carmel and Galilee area were settled by the Early Natufian (fig. 2). There is a return to the caves (Bar-Yosef and Martin 1981), which were occupied by groups in their aggregated state. Where no cave existed at a favorable location, people built semisubterranean curvilinear dwellings (Mallaha, Wadi Hammeh 27, but also Hayonim cave) (Perrot 1966; Edwards 1991; Bar-Yosef 1991). The Natufian model is established: long aggregation periods involving intense collective life, short seasons of dispersal, and return to and resettlement of the same place. Stone and bone working display unprecedented developments, art objects are relatively frequent, and some people are buried with personal adornments.

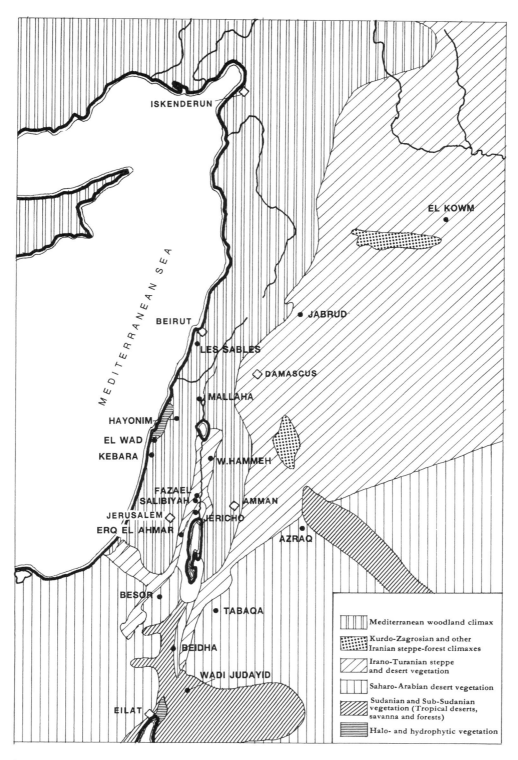

**Figure 2.** Map of main Early Natufian sites plotted on the modern vegetation distribution as recorded by M. Zohary (1973).

This model clearly does not diffuse randomly, given that not a single Early Natufian site is known in the coastal plain south of Kebara or on the western slopes of the Samarian and Judean ridges. On the other hand, at least three sites in the Lower Jordan Valley—Fazael VI, Salibiyah XII, and Jericho—have been assigned to this phase (Bar-Yosef et al. 1974; Schuldenrein and Goldberg 1981; Kenyon 1981). Aggregation sites towards the south, such as Erq el-Ahmar, Tabaqa, Beidha and Wadi Judayid, (Neuville 1951; Byrd and Colledge 1991; Byrd 1989; Henry et al. 1985; Henry 1995) are found at higher altitudes, usually in the Rift watershed. It is possible, therefore, that the Jordan Valley acted as a favored route for the southward diffusion of Natufian characteristics. Nevertheless, it seems that this diffusion encountered some obstacles. The group that settled at Erq el-Ahmar returned there for only a limited number of years, and the occupation at Beidha was never very large, with the exception of Upper Besor 6 (Goring-Morris, pers. comm.). The Early Natufian Negev sites are very small and may have accommodated nuclear families rather than aggregated groups. Was the natural environment in the south so harsh that it prevented people from gathering either for lengthy periods or repeatedly at the same location? Or were people reluctant to gather in this manner? Data are very sparse towards the northern part of the Levant. Les Sables de Beyrouth was perhaps a large aggregation site near the coast. The use of Yabrud rockshelter (Rust 1950) is reminiscent of the use of Erq el-Ahmar. All of these points indicate that the earliest phase of the Natufian can be understood as a period of relatively minimal diffusion.

The Natufian culture reaches its largest extension during the second, so-called late phase (fig. 3). The number of settlements remains stable in the Mt. Carmel-Galilee area. Kebara Cave and Wadi Hammeh 27 are deserted, but a new village is founded at Nahal Oren (Stekelis and Yisraeli 1963; Noy et al. 1973). There is perhaps also a trend to abandon the caves. The size of houses (becoming smaller at Mallaha) and their grouping at Hayonim Terrace (less dense than earlier in the cave) may indicate a lesser degree of intensity of social life. A reduction in art objects at Hayonim and el-Wad may express the same change. Natufian influence is now present in the coastal plain of Central Palestine (Poleg 18M, Shukba, Hatoula) (Bar-Yosef 1970; Garrod and Bate 1942; Lechevallier and Ronen 1985). It is maintained in the Lower Jordan Valley at Salibiyah.

The influence of the Natufian becomes more important in the Judean mountains, where a complicat-

ed situation develops. It is not impossible that the former influence of the Mt. Carmel-Galilee "center," still visible at Oumm ez-Zoueitina, was superseded by that of the Negev. El-Khiam and Tor Abou Sif, where people made no use of the Helwan retouch but practiced the microburin technique, may bear witness to this assertion. In fact, the Natufian model is now widespread in the Negev, where it is adapted and modified to fit both local traditions and the constraints imposed by the marginal conditions of the Negev. It may be useful to compare developments there with those in the nearby Edom mountains, but all that can be said about the latter area at this time is that some settlements did exist there as part of the Natufian sphere (Gebel et al. 1988; Henry et al. 1981; Henry 1995).

Some of the most striking progress initiated by the Natufian influence can be seen in northern Jordan and southern Syria, where no Early Natufian sites are known. By the Late Natufian, the highlands are inhabited as far as Jawa, at sites such as Azraq 18, Ain Rahub, and Taibe (Garrard 1991; Muheisen et al. 1988; Cauvin 1974). Desert conditions in this area allowed Betts to identify what seem to be both aggregation and dispersal sites (Betts 1991). Only a few isolated sites have been recorded farther north at this point. Like the Negev, the middle Euphrates area produces a tradition that appears to be even more unique given the lack of intermediary sites between this area and the Mt. Carmel-Galilee "center." As opposed to the southern situation, where the seasonal mobility pattern of the "center" is modified by a lengthening of the dispersal period, the alternating aggregation and dispersal periods in the Euphrates area maintain the traditional rhythm, emphasizing aggregation (Hillman et al. 1989; Moore 1991). Broadly speaking, it appears that the model elaborated in the Mt. Carmel and Galilee area during the Early Natufian was successfully transferred to neighboring provinces during the Late Natufian, with some adaptations and modifications.

Separating the late and final phases of the Natufian is not easy because of the poor documentation available for the latter. It appears that the Mt. Carmel-Galilee area undergoes a general decline and indeed loses its role as "center." Hayonim is abandoned. At Mallaha, less work is invested in house building, perhaps indicating that aggregation periods were shortened. It is possible that the former seasonal system was better preserved at Nahal Oren and el-Wad, but there is no satisfactory plan available for Nahal Oren, and the corresponding layer at el-Wad is heavily mixed (Valla et al. 1986). A seasonal system similar to that which formerly prevailed in the south may have

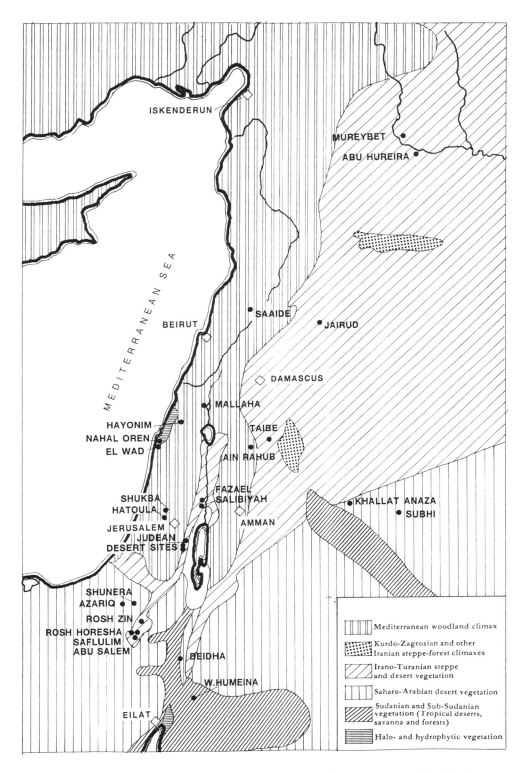

**Figure 3.** Map of main Late–Final Natufian sites plotted on the modern vegetation distribution as recorded by M. Zohary (1973).

become the preference there. In Central Palestine, Fazael IV seems to maintain the earlier system, but on a more restricted scale. The Negev situation is different, where the weakening of influence from the "center" gives way to a new cultural entity, the Harifian. Although this culture preserves strong Natufian affinities, the system of alternating between gathering in the highlands and dispersal in the lowlands seems to degenerate. Aggregation sites are found in the piedmont, whereas some small ephemeral findspots exist together with sites built on the plateau (Goring-Morris 1991). A new mode of resource exploitation may have been adopted, but this remains unclear (fig. 4). The new orientation of the Harifian vis-à-vis the Natufian is indicated in a number of ways. A definite expansion in the northern Sinai and the replacement of Mediterranean decorative shells with shells from the Red Sea are among the most significant.

Final Natufian data are seemingly missing for the eastern side of the Jordan Valley and for most of Syria (but see Wadi Humeima in Henry 1995), and the nearest site is in the middle Euphrates Valley, at Mureybet (J. Cauvin 1977; M. C. Cauvin 1991), though this is unfortunately an isolated example. In many ways, Mureybet keeps the tradition seen at Abu Hureyra, particularly the seasonal system, which is maintained unmodified. Permanence of residency occurs at both

sites, although it is based upon the exploitation of different resources. In this way, the Euphrates area follows a trend separate from that of the Galilee. As such, the area remains more "Natufian," in a way, than the Negev, although the direct influence from the "center" weakens there as well. Even so, the three regions are still part of the same interaction sphere, as visible in a general reduction in size of lunates and even more clearly through the communal adoption of notched arrowheads from Judea and the Edom mountains to Iraq. By this point, however, the old prestige of the Mt. Carmel-Galilee "center" has vanished. The Natufian culture is over.

The study of the Early Natufian raises the question of how the Natufian ideology and way of life, as expressed in the large sites in the Mt. Carmel and Galilee area, could be transferred to regions with less favorable environmental conditions. This way of life, marked by its long aggregation and short dispersal periods, seems to have been difficult to implement in the south. It is even uncertain if any transfers succeeded. Natufian features appear superimposed on the local way of life, adapted to local conditions, and possibly maintaining long dispersal periods. By the Late Natufian, however, the model from the Mt. Carmel-Galilee "center" predominates, and aggregation periods become longer, perhaps even in remote peripheries. A

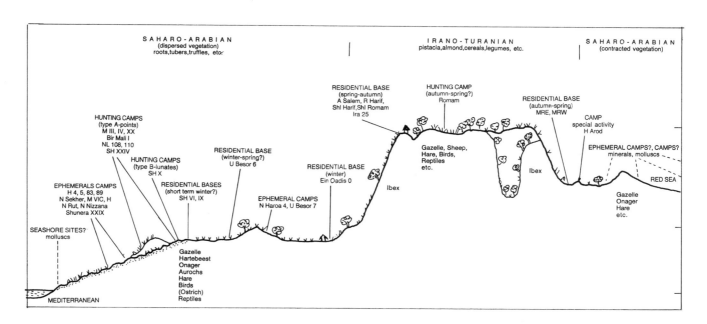

**Figure 4.** Seasonal exploitation of the Negev by the Harifians according to N. Goring-Morris (1991).

kind of equilibrium seems to have been achieved. The trend for annual grouping at the same place—perhaps a consequence of the renewed utilization of caves at the beginning of the Early Natufian—is noted everywhere. Due to natural conditions, the socioeconomic mode of the Natufian proves more successful in the middle Euphrates than in the south. During the Final Natufian, this mode tends to vanish from the Mt. Carmel-Galilee area. Those regions that had been influenced by it and adapted it in the former period now follow their own trajectories of cultural development. It is best preserved in the middle Euphrates area, despite the cultural particulars inherent there.

## SUMMARY AND CONCLUSIONS

Little solid data are available to help reconstruct a potential seasonal system for the Natufian. This paper attempts to put together the available data and to make explicit the general factors that support the argument that such a system existed. It has been necessary to reconcile these factors with the observations that led several researchers to claim that a sedentary way of life was practiced by the Natufians. An initial outline for a seasonal pattern was presented and was then elaborated upon by examining both how it could be incorporated into the geographical diversity of the Natufian world and the changes that took place during the two thousand years of its existence. At the very least, the variety of views reached in this process has the benefit of guarding against any temptation to treat the Natufian as a single unit, at least where patterns of seasonality are concerned. The main weakness of these views, however, aside from their necessarily hypothetical nature, could be a disregard of local peculiarities.

The Natufian system of seasonality that is presented here is rather simple, consisting of two phases: an aggregation period and a dispersal period. The unique nature of this system is the lengthening of the aggregation period and the habit of systematically gathering in the same place year after year. These characteristics may explain the possible choice made by the less mobile members of the group not to move for the few weeks of dispersal. This decision, in turn, could account for the data pointing to year-round occupation at those particular sites. This would have resulted in an unprecedented richness in social life as evidenced by the rise of art and adornment, the adoption of new or previously rare tool types (e.g., grooved stones, barbed

points), the domestication of the dog, and so on. This Early Natufian system, typical in the Mt. Carmel-Galilee area by the Early Natufian, would have proved attractive to people in the surrounding regions. Yet, nevertheless, it turned out to be difficult to implement it elsewhere without adaptation.

During the Late Natufian, a balance was achieved and the system reached its broadest extension. This equilibrium may have resulted from the adjustment of both human and ecological factors, amongst which group size, length of aggregation period, the desire to return to the same place and its accessible resources, and the renewable nature of these resources, may have been the most important. It is possible that the more limited the resources at a site, the stronger the constraints on group size and length of aggregation period until a time when gathering there was no longer feasible. Finally, the system would have exerted too much pressure on the environment (even in the area of its origin), as indicated by a certain degeneration in the number of gazelles (Cope 1991). This would explain why the system lost its efficiency by the Final Natufian and subsequently vanished. However, the possible role of human choices in this disappearance should also be considered. Whatever the case, the system continued to work in the middle Euphrates, and it is well established that this area was to play a key role in future developments (Cauvin 1978).

The Natufian system of seasonality can be understood as a kind of preadaptation to the sedentary way of life subsequently practiced in the villages of food producers. Nevertheless, there is only a minimum of continuity from one to the other in the southern Levant. The only place where no obvious hiatus can be determined between the Natufian culture and what follows is in Central Palestine. It is certainly not by chance that this area produced some of the best Early Neolithic sites (Kenyon 1981; Bar-Yosef et al. 1991). Nevertheless, the Natufian system of seasonality did not develop fully in this area, thus very small groups of people experienced it. This may be demonstrated by the return to caves, which offered only limited space to gathered families. Even in open-air sites, when exposed buildings offer an idea of group size, it always appears that small numbers of people lived and worked there. The fallacious notion of large groups comes from excavators' interpretations made from the accumulation of generations of rubbish in the same spot (Neuville 1951:128; Marks and Friedel 1977:149; Bar-Yosef 1983). In all probability, most sites, including those of medium or small size (according to our criteria), were aggregation sites. If the hypothesis that groups split at the nuclear family level holds, then the chances of dispersal sites surviving are practically zero. Unlike aggregation sites, dispersed encampments were apparently not returned to systematically. Some small caves, such as Ain Sakhri and Nahal Hilazon, are possible exceptions. Elsewhere, only rare conditions of preservation, as is the case in desert environments, allow access to the remains of sites of this kind.

In this paper, I have used the term "center" to designate the Mt. Carmel-Galilee area. It is appropriate to question the validity of the use of this term. A "center" is defined by means of its opposition to "peripheries," that is, "differences in potential" among the different areas involved in the system. Using these terms, I intend, along with Braudel (1979), to pose some disparities that create a flux, a source of change that may entail some kind of "domination." I do not wish to use the word "domination" in the strong sense. In this context, it refers only to a relative and mitigated superiority congruent to the means of the group involved. This superiority can be expressed at the political level, when one group takes control of another, at the economic level, when a better system of exploitation is installed, or at the prestige level, when an attractive social organization is developed. While nothing is known about the political level in the Natufian, the former analyses do not contradict the hypothesis according to which, at the economic and prestige levels, the system prevailing in the Mt. Carmel and Galilee area during the first half of the thirteenth millennium B.P. was considered an attractive model by groups in neighboring areas.

## ACKNOWLEDGMENTS

I wish to thank Ofer Bar-Yosef and Thomas R. Rocek, who invited me to participate in their symposium on "Seasonality and Sedentism, Combining New and Old World Perspectives," and A. Belfer-Cohen, O. Bar-Yosef, R. Rocek, and J. Speth for comments on an earlier draft. I also wish to thank Brian Boyd for translating the French version and N. Ornstein for editorial modifications.

## BIBLIOGRAPHY

Baruch, U., and S. Bottema
1991 "Palynological Evidence for Climatic Changes in the Levant ca. 17.000–9.000 B.P.," in *The Natufian Culture in the Levant*, O. Bar-Yosef and F. R. Valla, eds., pp. 11–20. International Monographs in Prehistory, Archaeological Series 1. Ann Arbor, Michigan.

Bar-Yosef, O.
1970 "The Epi-Paleolithic Cultures of Palestine." Ph.D. diss., Hebrew University, Jerusalem.
1983 "The Natufian in the Southern Levant," in *The Hilly Flanks and Beyond*, T. Young, P. Smith, and P. Mortensen, eds., pp. 11–42. Studies in Ancient Oriental Civilizations 36. University of Chicago Press, Chicago.
1991 "The Archaeology of the Natufian Layer at Hayonim Cave," in *The Natufian Culture in the Levant*, O. Bar-Yosef and F. R. Valla, eds., pp. 81–92. International Monographs in Prehistory, Archaeological Series 1. Ann Arbor, Michigan.

Bar-Yosef, O., and A. Belfer-Cohen
1989 "The Origins of Sedentism and Farming Communities in the Southern Levant." *Journal of World Prehistory* 3(4):447–489.

Bar-Yosef, O., and R. S. Kra
1994 *Late Quaternary Chronology and Paleoclimates of the Eastern Mediterranean*. Radiocarbon, Tucson.

Bar-Yosef, O., and G. Martin
1981 "Le problème de la "sortie des grottes" au Natoufien, repartition et localisation des gisements epi-paleolithiques du Levant mediterranéen." *Bulletin de la Société Préhistorique Française* 78(6): 187–192.

Bar-Yosef, O., P. Goldberg, and T. Leveson
1974 "Late Quaternary and Stratigraphy in Wadi Fazael, Jordan Valley: A Preliminary Report." *Paleoriént* 2(2):415–427.

Bar-Yosef, O., A. Gopher, E. Tchernov, and M. Kislev
1991 "Netiv Hagdud: An Early Neolithic Village Site in the Jordan Valley." *Journal of Field Archaeology* 18:405–424.

Belfer-Cohen, A.
1989 "The Natufian Graveyard in Hayonim Cave," in *Préhistoire du Levant*, O. Aurenche, M. C. Cauvin and P. Sanlaville, eds., pp. 297–308. Editions du C.N.R.S., Paris.

1991 "The Natufian in the Levant." *Annual Review of Anthropology* 20:167–186.

Betts, A.
1991 "The Late Epipaleolithic in the Black Desert, Eastern Jordan," in *The Natufian Culture in the Levant*, O. Bar-Yosef and F. R. Valla, eds., pp. 217–234. International Monographs in Prehistory, Archaeological Series 1. Ann Arbor, Michigan.

Bokonyi, S.
1972 "Zoological Evidence for Seasonal or Permanent Occupation of Prehistoric Settlements," in *Man, Settlement and Urbanism*, P. J. Ucko, R. Tringham, and G. W. Dimbleby, eds., pp. 121–126. Duckworth, London.

Braudel, F.
1979 *Civilisation matérielle, économie et capitalisme, XVe–XVIIe siècle, 3 Le temps du monde*. Armand Colin, Paris.

Byrd, B. F.
1989 *The Natufian Encampment at Beidha: Late Pleistocene Adaptation in the Southern Levant*. Jutland Archaeological Society Publications, vol. 23. Aarhus, Denmark.

Byrd, B. F., and S. M. Colledge
1991 "Early Natufian Occupation along the Edge of the Southern Jordanian Steppe," in *The Natufian Culture in the Levant*, O. Bar-Yosef and F. R. Valla, eds., pp. 265–276. International Monographs in Prehistory, Archaeological Series 1. Ann Arbor, Michigan.

Cauvin, J.
1977 "Les Fouilles de Mureybet (1971–1974) et leur Signification pour les Origines de la Sedentarisation au Proche-Orient." *Annual of the American School of Oriental Research* 44:19–48.
1978 *Les premiers villages de Syrie-Palestine du IXeme au Viie millenaire avant J.C.* Collection de la Maison de l'Orient Ancien 4. Maison de l'Orient, Lyon.

Cauvin, M. C.
1974 "L'industrie Natoufienne de Taibe dans le Hauran." *Bulletin de la Société Préhistorique Française, Etudes et Travaux* 71(2):469–478.
1991 "Du Natoufien au Levant Nord? Jayroud et Mureybet, Syrie," in *The Natufian Culture in the Levant*, O. Bar-Yosef and F. R. Valla, eds., pp. 295–314. International Monographs in Prehistory, Archaeological Series 1. Ann Arbor, Michigan.

Cope, C.
1991 "Gazelle Hunting Strategies in the Natufian," in *The Natufian Culture in the Levant*, O. Bar-Yosef and F. R. Valla, eds., pp. 341–358. International Monographs in Prehistory, Archaeological Series 1. Ann Arbor, Michigan.

Copeland, L.
1991 "Natufian Sites in Lebanon," in *The Natufian Culture in the Levant*, O. Bar-Yosef and F. R. Valla, eds., pp. 27–42. International Monographs in Prehistory, Archaeological Series 1. Ann Arbor, Michigan.

Davis, S. J. M., and F. R. Valla
1978 "Evidence for the Domestication of the Dog 12,000 Years Ago in the Natufian of Israel." *Nature* 276:608–610.

Davis, S. J. M., D. Lernau, and J. Pichon
1994 "The Animal Remains: New Light on the Origin of Animal Husbandry," in *Le Gisement de Hatoula en Judée Occidentale, Israël*, M. Lechevallier and A. Ronen, eds., pp. 83–100. Mémoires et Travaux du Centre de Recherche Français de Jérusalem, 8. Association Paléorient, Paris.

Desse, J.
1987 "L'ichtyofaune," in *La faune du Gisement Natoufien de Mallaha (Eynan), Israël*, J. Bouchud, ed., pp. 151–156. Mémoires et Travaux du Centre de Recherche Français de Jérusalem 4. Association Paléorient, Paris.

Edwards, P.
1991 "Wadi Hammeh 27: An Early Natufian Site at Pella, Jordan," in *The Natufian Culture in the Levant*, O. Bar-Yosef and F. R. Valla, eds., pp. 123–148. International Monographs in Prehistory, Archaeological Series 1. Ann Arbor, Michigan.

Edwards, P., S. Bourke, S. Colledge, J. Head, and P. Macumber
1988 "Late Pleistocene Prehistory in the Wadi al-Hammeh, Jordan Valley," in *The Prehistory of Jordan*, A. Garrard and H. G. Gebel, eds., pp. 525–565. British Archaeological Reports, International Series 396. Oxford.

Garrard, A. N.
1991 "Natufian Settlement in the Azraq Basin, Eastern Jordan," in *The Natufian Culture in the Levant*, O. Bar-Yosef and F. R. Valla, eds., pp. 234–244. International Monographs in Prehistory, Archaeological Series 1. Ann Arbor, Michigan.

Garrard, A. N., S. Colledge, and L. Martin
1996 "The Emergence of Crop Cultivation and Caprine Herding in the 'Marginal Zone' of the Southern Levant," in *The Origins and Spread of Agriculture and Pastoralism in Eurasia*, D. Harris, ed., pp. 204–226. UCL Press, London.

Garrod, D. A. E.
1932 "A New Mesolithic Industry: The Natufian of Palestine." *Journal of the Royal Anthropological Institute* 62:257–266.

Garrod, D. A. E., and D. M. A. Bate
1937 *The Stone Age of Mount Carmel.* The Clarendon Press, Oxford.
1942 "Excavations at the Cave of Shoukbah, Palestine, 1928." *Proceedings of the Prehistoric Society* 8:1–20.

Gebel, H. G., M. S. Muheisen, and H. J. Nissen
1988 "Preliminary Report on the First Season of Excavation at Basta," in *The Prehistory of Jordan*, A. N. Garrard and H. G. Gebel, eds., pp. 101–133. British Archaeological Reports, International Series 396(i). Oxford.

Goring-Morris, A. N.
1987 *At the Edge. Terminal Pleistocene Hunter-Gatherers in the Negev and Sinai.* British Archaeological Reports, International Series 361. Oxford.
1991 "The Harifian of the Southern Levant," in *The Natufian Culture in the Levant*, O. Bar-Yosef and F. R. Valla, eds., pp. 173–216. International Monographs in Prehistory, Archaeological Series 1. Ann Arbor, Michigan.

Henry, D. O.
1976 "Rosh Zin: A Natufian Settlement near Ein Avdat," in *Prehistory and Palaeoenvironments in the Central Negev.* Vol. 1, *The Avdat-Aqev Area, Part 1*, A. E. Marks, ed., pp. 311–347. Southern Methodist University Press, Dallas.
1989 *From Foraging to Agriculture: The Levant at the End of the Ice Age.* University of Pennsylvania Press, Philadelphia.
1995 *Prehistoric Cultural Ecology and Evolution, Insight from Southern Jordan.* Plenum Press, New York.

Henry, D. O., and A. Leroi-Gourhan
1976 "The Excavation of Hayonim Terrace: An Interim Report." *Journal of Field Archaeology* 3:391–406.

Henry, D. O., A. Leroi-Gourhan, and S. Davis
1981 "The Excavation of Hayonim Terrace: An Examination of Terminal Pleistocene Climatic and Adaptive Changes." *Journal of Archaeological Science* 8:33–58.

Henry, D. O., P. Turnbull, A. Emery-Barbier, and A. Leroi-Gourhan
1985 "Archaeological and Faunal Remains from Natufian and Timnian Sites in Southern Jordan." *Bulletin of the American School of Oriental Research* 257:45–64.

Hillman, G. C., S. M. Colledge, and D. R. Harris
1989 "Plant Food Economy During the Epipaleolithic at Tell Abu Hureyra, Syria: Dietary Diversity, Seasonality and Modes of Exploitation," in *Foraging and Farming: The Evolution of Plant Exploitation*, D. R. Harris and G. C. Hillman, eds., pp. 240–268. Unwin Hyman, London.

Hopf, M., and O. Bar-Yosef
1987 "Plant Remains from Hayonim Cave, Western Galilee." *Paléorient* 13(1):117–120.

Horowitz, A.
1977 "Pollen Spectra from Two Early Holocene Prehistoric Sites in the Har Hart (West Central Negev)," in *Prehistory and Paleoenvironments in the Central Negev, Israel.* Vol. 2, *The Avdat-Aqev Area, Part 2 and the Har Harif*, A. E. Marks, ed., pp. 323–326. Southern Methodist University Press, Dallas.

Kenyon, K.
1981 *Excavations at Jericho.* Vol. 3, *The Architecture and Stratigraphy of the Tell.* British School of Archaeology in Jerusalem, London.

Kislev, M. E., D. Nadel, and I. Carmi
1992 "Epipaleolithic (19,000 B.P.) Cereal and Fruit Diet at Ohalo II, Sea of Galilee, Israel." *Review of Palaeobotany and Palynology* 73:161–166.

Lechevallier, M., and A. Ronen
1985 *Le Site Natoufien-Khiamian de Hatoula, près de Latroun, Israel. Fouilles 1980–1982.* Cahier du Centre de Recherche Français de Jérusalem 1. Jerusalem.
1994 *Le Gisement de Hatoula en Judée Occidentale, Israël.* Mémoires et Travaux du Centre de Recherche Francais de Jérusalem 8. Association Paléorient, Paris.

Lernau, H.
1985 "Fish Remains from Hatoula," in *Le Site Natoufien-Khiamian de Hatoula, près de Latroun, Israel. Fouilles 1980–1982*, M. Lechevallier and A. Ronen, eds., p. 102. Cahier du Centre de Recherche Français de Jérusalem 1. Jerusalem.

Lieberman, D. E.
1991 "Seasonality and Gazelle Hunting at Hayonim Cave: New Evidence for 'Sedentism' during the Natufian." *Paléorient* 17(1):47–57.
1992 "Were the Natufian 'Sedentary'?" Paper presented at the 57th Annual Meeting of the Society for American Archaeology, Pittsburgh, Pennsylvania. (See Lieberman's paper in this volume.)
1993 "The Rise and Fall of Seasonal Mobility Among Hunter-Gatherers." *Current Anthropology* 34(5): 599–631.

Marks, A. E., and D. A. Friedel
1977 "Prehistoric Settlement Patterns in the Avdat-Aqev Area," in *Prehistory and Paleoenvironments in the Central Negev, Israel*. Vol. 2, *The Avdat-Aqev Area, Part 2, and the Har Harif*, A. E. Marks, ed., pp. 131–158. Southern Methodist University Press, Dallas.

Mauss, M., and H. Beuchat
1978 "Essai sur les Variations Saisonières des Sociétés Eskimos (1904–1905)." Etude de morphologie sociale. L'Annee Sociologique IX Repris in Sociologie et Anthropologie, pp. 389–477. Presses Universitaires de France, Paris.

Moore, A. M. T.
1991 "Abu Hureyra I and the Antecedents of Agriculture on the Middle Euphrates," in *The Natufian Culture in the Levant*, O. Bar-Yosef and F. R. Valla, eds., pp. 277–294. International Monographs in Prehistory, Archaeological Series 1. Ann Arbor, Michigan.

Muheisen, M., H. Gebel, C. Hannss, and R. Neef
1988 "'Ain Rahub, a Final Natufian and Yarmukian Site near Irbid," in *The Prehistory of Jordan*, A. Garrard and H. Gebel, eds., pp. 472–502. British Archaeological Reports, International Series 396. Oxford.

Nadel, D., and I. Hershkovitz
1991 "New Subsistence Data and Human Remains from the Earliest Levantine Epipaleolithic." *Current Anthropology* 32:631–635.

Neuville, R.
1951 *Le Paleolithique et le Mesolithique du Desert de Judée*. Archives de l'Institut de Paléontologie Humaine, Mémoire 24. Masson, Paris.

Noy, T.
1989 "Some Aspects of Natufian Mortuary Behaviour at Nahal Oren," in *People and Culture in Change*, I. Hershkovitz, ed., pp. 53–57. British Archaeological Reports, International Series 508. Oxford.

Noy, T., A. J. Legge, and E. Higgs
1973 "Recent Excavations at Nahal Oren, Israel." *Proceedings of the Prehistoric Society* 39:75–99.

Olszeswki, D. I.
1986 *The North Syrian Epipaleolithic. The Earliest Occupation at Tell Abu Hureyra in the Context of the Levantine Late Epipaleolithic*. British Archaeological Reports, International Series 309. Oxford.

Perlès, C., and J. Phillips
1991 "The Natufian Conference—Discussion," in *The Natufian Culture in the Levant*, O. Bar-Yosef and F. R. Valla, eds., pp. 637–644. International Monographs in Prehistory, Archaeological Series 1. Ann Arbor, Michigan.

Perrot, J.
1966 "Le Gisement Natoufien de Mallaha (Eynan), Israel." *L'Anthropologie* 70(5–6):437–483.
1968 "La Prehistoire Palestinienne," in *Supplement au Dictionnaire de la Bible*, L. Pirot, ed., vol. 8, col. 286–446. Letouzy and Ané, Paris.

Perrot, J., D. Ladiray, and O. Soliveres-Massei
1988 *Les hommes de Mallaha (Eynan). Israël*. Mémoires et travaux du Centre de Recherche Français de Jérusalem 7. Association Paléorient, Paris.

Pichon, J.
1984 "L'avifaune Natoufienne du Levant." Ph.D. diss., Université de Paris VI. Paris.
1985 "Etude préliminaire de l'avifaune de Hatoula," in *Le Site Natoufien-Khiamian de Hatoula, près de Latroun, Israel. Fouilles 1980–1982*, M. Lechevallier and A. Ronen, eds., pp. 99–101. Cahier du Centre de Recherche Français de Jérusalem 1, Jerusalem.

Rust, A.
1950 *Die Hohlenfunde von Jabrud*. K. Wachholtz, Neumunster.

Sanlaville, P.
1996 "Changements Climatiques dans la Région Levantine à la Fin du Pléistocène Supérieur et au début de l'Holocène. Leurs Relations avec l'évolution des Sociétés Humaines." *Paléorient* 22:7–30.

Saxon, E. C.
1974 "The Mobile Herding Economy of Kebarah Cave, Mount Carmel: An Economic Analysis of the Faunal Remains." *Journal of Archaeological Science* 1:27–45.

Schroeder, B.
1991 "Natufian in the Central Beqaa Valley, Lebanon," in *The Natufian Culture in the Levant*, O. Bar-Yosef and F. R. Valla, eds., pp. 43–80. International Monographs in Prehistory, Archaeological Series 1. Ann Arbor, Michigan.

Schuldenrein, J., and P. Goldberg
1981 "Late Quaternary Palaeoenvironments and Prehistoric Site Distributions in the Lower Jordan Valley: A Preliminary Report." *Paléorient* 7(1):57–71.

Scott, T. R.
1977 "The Harifian of the Central Negev," in *Prehistory and Paleoenvironments in the Central Negev*. Vol. 2, *The Avdat-Aqev Area, Part 2 and the Har Harif*, A. E. Marks, ed., pp. 271–322. Southern Methodist University Press, Dallas.

Simmons, A. H., and G. Ilany
1975–1977 "What Mean These Bones?" *Paléorient* 3:269–274.

Stekelis, M., and T. Yisraeli
1963 "Excavations at Nahal Oren." *Israel Exploration Journal* 13:1–12.

Stordeur, D.
1991 "Le Natoufien et son Evolution à travers les Artefacts en Os," in *The Natufian Culture in the Levant*, O. Bar-Yosef and F. R. Valla, eds., pp. 457–482. International Monographs in Prehistory, Archaeological Series 1. Ann Arbor, Michigan.
1992 "Change and Cultural Inertia: From the Analysis of Data to the Creation of a Model," in *Representations in Archaeology*, J. C. Gardin and C. S. Peebles, eds., pp. 205–222. Indian University Press, Bloomington.

Tchernov, E.
1991 "Biological Evidence for Human Sedentism in Southwest Asia during the Natufian," in *The Natufian Culture in the Levant*, O. Bar-Yosef and F. R. Valla, pp. 315–340. International Monographs in Prehistory, International Series 1. Ann Arbor, Michigan.

Tchernov, E., and F. R. Valla
1997 "Two New Dogs, and Other Natufian Dogs from the Southern Levant." *Journal of Archaeological Science* 24:65–95.

Turville-Petre, F.
1932 "Excavations at the Mugharet el-Kebarah." *Journal of the Royal Anthropological Institute* 62:271–276.

Valla, F. R.
1981 "Les Etablissements Natoufiens dans le Nord d'Israël," in *Préhistoire du Levant*, J. Cauvin and P. Sanlaville, eds., pp. 409–419. Editions du C.N.R.S., Paris.
1984 *Les Industries de silex de Mallaha (Eynan) et du Natoufien dans le Levant*. Mémoires et travaux du Centre de Recherche Français de Jérusalem 3. Association Paléorient, Paris.
1987 "Chronologie Relative et Chronologie Absolue dans le Natoufien," in *Chronologies in the Near East*, in O. Aurenche, J. Evin, and F. Hours, eds., pp. 267–294. British Archaeological Reports, International Series 379. Oxford.
1988 "Les Premiers Sédentaires de Palestine." *La Recherche* 19:578–585.
1991 "Les Natoufiens de Mallaha et l'espace," in *The Natufian Culture in the Levant*, O. Bar-Yosef and F. R. Valla, eds., pp. 111–122. International Monographs in Prehistory, Archaeological Series 1. Ann Arbor, Michigan.

Valla, F. R., F. Le Mort, and H. Plisson
1991 "Les Fouilles en Cours sur la Terrasse d'Hayonim," in *The Natufian Culture in the Levant*, O. Bar-Yosef and F. R. Valla, eds., pp. 95–110. International Monographs in Prehistory, Archaeological Series 1. Ann Arbor, Michigan.

Valla, F. R., H. Plisson, I. Buxo, and R. Capdevila
1989 "Notes Préliminaires sur les Fouilles en Cours sur la Terrasse d'Hayonim." *Paléorient* 15(1):245–257.

Valla, F. R., O. Bar-Yosef, P. Smith, E. Tchernov, and J. Desse
1986 "Un Nouveau Sondage sur la Terrasse d'el-Ouad, Israël (1980–1981). *Paléorient* 12(1):21–38.

van Zeist, W., and J. A. H. Bakker-Herres
1984 "Archaeobotanical Studies in the Levant 3. Late Paleolithic Mureybet." *Palaeohistoria* 26:171–199.

Wright, H. E., Jr.
1977 "Environmental Change and the Origin of Agriculture in the Old and New World," in *Origins of Agriculture*, C. A. Reed, ed., pp. 281–318. Mouton, The Hague-Paris.

Zohary, M.
1973 *Geobotanical Foundations of the Middle East*, 2 vols. Gustav Fisher Verlag, Stuttgart-Amsterdam.

CHAPTER 7

# Scheduling and Sedentism in the Prehistory of Northern Japan

*Gary W. Crawford, University of Toronto*

*Peter Bleed, University of Nebraska*

Since 1974 we have been working on a series of case studies in northeastern Japan ranging in time from the Initial Jomon to the protohistoric ancestors of the Ainu, known as the Satsumon or Ezo-Haji (Crawford and Takamiya 1990). These include research programs on the Oshima Peninsula of southwestern Hokkaido (the Yagi, Hamanasuno, Usujiri B, and Hakodate Airport localities), in the Ishikari Plain (the Zoku-Jomon K135 localities and Mochiyazawa site and the Ezo-Haji Sakushu-Kotoni-Gawa, Botanical Gardens, and Kashiwagi-Gawa sites), and in Aomori (the Kazahari and Tominosawa sites) (Hurley 1974; Crawford et al. 1978; Bleed et al. 1979; Crawford 1983, 1987, 1992b; Crawford and Yoshizaki 1987; Crawford and Takamiya 1990; D'Andrea 1992, 1995a) (table 1 and fig. 1).

The sites we have been researching in northeastern Japan represent a range from hunting and gathering through mixed foraging and farming economies. We group the case studies into three categories with a strong potential for differences in scheduling to be visible in the archaeological record. The first is the Early through Late Jomon, which had large village communities but only minimal evidence for some form of gardening. This phase corresponds to Transition 1 in a model proposed by one of us for the development of agriculture in Japan (Crawford 1992b). Next is the Zoku-Jomon, which has evidence for greater mobility and an ecofactual database both of which indicate clear differences between it and the preceding Jomon periods on the one hand, and the Hokkaido Ezo-Haji, the third category, on the other (see table 1). The Ezo-Haji was the first group in Hokkaido to have substantial farming. The Zoku-Jomon and Hokkaido Ezo-Haji corre-

spond with Transitions 2 and 4 respectively in Crawford (1992b). That is, Transition 2 is the development of the Zoku-Jomon, as well as Tohoku Yayoi cultures, while Transition 4 is the consolidation of agriculture in Hokkaido by the Ezo-Haji.[1] Although the Zoku-Jomon is distinct from the Tohoku Yayoi with which it was contemporaneous, the two cultures interacted and the Zoku-Jomon can be considered part of Transition 2. For the sake of simplicity and continuity with this earlier work (Crawford 1992b), the Transition 1, 2, and 4 terminology is used here.

Addressing the issue of scheduling and sedentism in Japanese prehistory, or any broad issue for that matter, is a daunting task if only because the pace of Japanese archeological research is so great that most summary statements about the era are quickly outdated (Tanaka 1984). New sites are continually being reported and Japanese researchers are exploring virtually every known avenue of archeological insight. Furthermore, the available research has revealed great complexity within the Japanese past so that summary generalizations are hard to support. Even within the Jomon era, cultures from different periods and parts of the Japanese archipelago clearly had very different lifestyles and utilized a diverse range of resources. After all, the Jomon lasted over ten millennia from Okinawa to Sakhalin. Thus, although clear patterns within Jomon technology and society have been related to seasonality and other ecological issues (Akazawa 1986), the Jomon era was not a time of cultural uniformity or simple ecological adjustments. On the contrary, the richness of the record convinces us that it is best to consider the Jomon era in terms of specific regional variations and expressions.

In this paper, we take the view that the Jomon is not "monolithic" and that an approach that examines the details of a limited area of Japan is better than one that makes sweeping generalizations about cultural periods or some Japan-wide pattern. We emphasize the contributions our own research have generated in the context of the investigations of others who are working primarily to the southwest of the region we have been examining. We explore the similarities and differences in seasonality, scheduling, and sedentism among the three categories of occupations (Transitions 1, 2, and 4). In particular, we examine the so-called "Jomon Calendar," which is taken to be the orthodox position in Japanese archaeology. We also examine the view that a conflict in scheduling was a factor that hindered the move of agriculture into northeastern Japan. In addressing this issue, we explore the particulars of a number of data sets that have been collected with the purpose of exploring human-environmental interaction. We do so by developing a comparison among three contrasting phases in the prehistory of northeastern Japan. Ethnographic data regarding the Ainu of northeastern Japan are brought to bear on the analysis as well. This comparative approach brings to light at least three different prehistoric systems in a relatively small geographic area.

## SEASONALITY IN JOMON RESEARCH

The specific issue of seasonality during the Jomon era presents special problems. First, the richness and regional diversity of Jomon cultures has made solving cultural-historical problems the primary focus of Jomon research (Ikawa-Smith 1980). Japanese researchers have tended to emphasize artifact description and typology. The quality of this research has made it possible to describe very fine chronological subdivisions of the Jomon era, but it has also meant that consideration of other aspects of the era has languished.

In recent years, large salvage excavations have exposed several nearly complete Jomon settlements. This work has led Japanese researchers to consider the social aspects of Jomon culture, but the consideration of ecofactual remains is still uncommon. In part, this situation can be linked to the generally poor preservation of animal remains and the perceived lack of plant remains in Jomon sites. The volcanic soils that make up virtually all of Japan simply do not preserve faunal remains in anything other than caves (Serizawa 1979) and shell middens. Plant remains can, of course, be regularly recovered from Jomon sites, but only recently and only in a few areas has the archaeological commu-

TABLE I

**Site chronology in northeastern Japan**

| Site Name | Initial Jomon | Early Jomon | Middle Jomon | Late Jomon | Final Jomon | Tohoku Yayoi | Zoku-Jomon | Hokkaido Ezo-Haji |
|---|---|---|---|---|---|---|---|---|
| Sakushu-Kotoni-Gawa | | | | | | | | X |
| Botanical Gardens | | | | | | | | X |
| Kashiwagi-Gawa | | | | | | | | X |
| Mochiyazawa | | | | | | | X | |
| K135 | | | | | | | X | |
| Kazahari | | | | X | | X | | |
| Tominosawa | | | X | | | | | |
| Usujiri B | | | X | | | | | |
| Hamanasuno | | X | | | | | | |
| Yagi | X | X | | | | | | |
| Nakano B | X | | | | | | | |

**Figure 1.** Location of sites in northeastern Japan.

nity in Japan made any commitment to recover them using flotation. The paucity of faunal materials and the presumed lack of plant remains caused Japanese interests to be focused in other directions. As a result, priorities in Japanese archaeology such as the dominance of CRM work reflect the local situation. Few Japanese archeologists take the ecofunctional approach of anthropologically oriented archeologists in North America and Europe, so that consideration of ecofactual remains has not been a theoretical imperative.

Added to these problems, the issue of Jomon seasonality has not presented itself to Japanese archeologists as a problem that needs solution. The clear evidence for the rapid appearance of rice agriculture in Japan during the Yayoi era encouraged the view that the Jomon were hunters and gatherers. That is, agriculture was synonymous with rice production, and if the Yayoi were the initiators of rice production in Japan, then their predecessors were not people who grew crops. If further interpretation was necessary, many Japanese archeologists have suggested that modern Japanese culinary emphasis on seasonal produce and the cycle of fresh fruits and vegetables can be extended back to Jomon cultures.

Dissatisfaction with such implicit interpretations of Jomon seasonality lead Tatsuo Kobayashi to develop a model that summarizes the available information on Middle Jomon seasonal economy (1986). The so-called "Jomon Calendar" graphically suggests much about the operating conditions of Jomon culture and, as such, has been widely cited. It recently appeared in an American textbook on world prehistory (Price and Feinman 1993). The model indicates two peaks in plant food gathering, one in the spring and one in the fall. Land mammal hunting is depicted as having been primarily a winter activity. Summer and fall were the primary fishing seasons while shellfish collecting took place mainly during the spring and summer. Middle Jomon people hunted sea mammals during the winter through late spring. Unfortunately, the elegance and power of Kobayashi's model has had the undesirable effect of making it the orthodox view, despite the lack of empirical data upon which to base such a model. It has tended to limit investigations by presenting Jomon seasonality as a "solved problem" and forced thinking on the issue into normative terms. The power of the Jomon Calendar has discouraged Japanese researchers from looking for contradictory information or diversity within Jomon economic patterns. One need only look at the ethnohistoric Ainu data to find areas of poor fit between reality and the model. We will return to these points later in this paper.

The Jomon era is among the world's most thoroughly studied archeological expressions of so-called "specialized hunters and gatherers" (Aikens 1981; Akazawa and Aikens 1986; Hayden 1990). As such, the Jomon offers excellent opportunities to examine how such economies come about, stabilize, and change. Realizing this opportunity requires solving a number of problems. This is not the place to outline, much less solve, all these problems, but as a background for the specific discussions that follow, we outline the challenges to Jomon seasonality/scheduling research.

As a starting point, we accept a distinction made long ago between seasonality and scheduling (Flannery 1968). The former refers to cycles in which resources present themselves. The latter describes human accommodations to those patterns and specifically how groups adapt to and make use of resources in their environment. Flannery used this distinction to emphasize mobility and site function. In the Jomon case, the distinction reminds us that both the ecological setting of specific sites and the residues of economic activities must be considered in addressing questions of Jomon economy.

## ISSUES IN JOMON SEASONALITY

Japanese researchers have assembled a great deal of useful information about the Jomon environment (Kotani 1969; Yasuda 1975, 1978; Tsukada et al. 1986). The link between specific sites and their environmental settings has also been addressed by some Japanese researchers (Suzuki 1978, 1985; Yamada et al. 1980; Yamada 1986; Koike 1986; Koike and Ohtaishi 1987) although contextual study of Jomon sites is a research strategy that could be developed further. The paucity of ecofactual remains in Jomon sites is a serious block to seasonality research, although our work strongly indicates that Jomon sites preserve more interpretable ecofactual materials than has been suspected. As systematic recovery of these kinds of materials is becoming an increasingly common part of Jomon research (see Matsui 1992), our understanding of seasonal patterns should improve.

Systematic recovery is at best a partial solution. The scarcity of Jomon ecofactual materials, especially faunal remains, is a reality that will not disappear, and researchers will have to find other ways of addressing Jomon seasonality. Investigating the functional relationships between seasonality, settlement patterns, and technological organization presents one obvious accommodation that has only begun to be explored (Akazawa 1986).

Mounting evidence indicates some gardening took place by 2000–1800 B.C. (uncalibrated), which is the end of the Middle Jomon in southwestern Hokkaido. Gardening seems to have involved growing barnyard millet (*Echinochloa utilis*), foxtail millet (*Setaria italica* ssp. *italica*), and possibly buckwheat (*Fagopyrum esculentum*) (Crawford et al. 1978; Crawford 1983, 1992b, 1997; Crawford and Takamiya 1990). Two of these cultigens, foxtail millet and buckwheat, were domesticated elsewhere in East Asia. Barnyard millet domestication is poorly known, but one center of domestication appears to have been northeastern Japan (Crawford 1983, 1992b, 1997; Yabuno 1987). The trend may not have been limited to Hokkaido, since evidence for plant husbandry has been found at many Jomon sites. This is not the place to evaluate these data; that has been done elsewhere (Crawford 1992a). By the Late Jomon in Aomori Prefecture, Tohoku, rice, foxtail millet, broomcorn millet, and possibly buckwheat were part of the local economy (D'Andrea et al. 1995). The possibility that plant husbandry began in the northeast as early as the Early Jomon should remain open (Crawford 1983). To date, models of Jomon seasonality and scheduling do not entertain the possibility that gardening and/or the use of crops played a role in Jomon subsistence economies.

## The Sites

Ecological relationships and seasonal economic activities are the specific foci of research conducted at a series of sites in southern Hokkaido and northern Aomori Prefecture. Upon review, this work illustrates the problems of research on Jomon economic patterns and shows the kinds of seasonal patterns that marked the Jomon era in northeastern Japan. In particular, the Yagi site project, coupled with research at the nearby Hamanasuno and Usujiri B sites, and research on later periods in Tohoku provide a view of Jomon subsistence economy from a relatively limited area with closely related people belonging to the Ento, Daigi, and Fukurashima traditions (Hurley 1974; Crawford 1983; Crawford and Takamiya 1990; D'Andrea 1992, 1995a) (fig. 1).

Not far to the north in central Hokkaido are three Zoku- or Epi-Jomon occupations. Excavations at the K135-4 and K135-5 sites at the Sapporo Railway Station on the Ishikari Plain and at the Mochiyazawa site

on the Japan Sea coast (fig. 1) have brought to light large collections of plant and animal remains that contrast in many ways with those from the preceding Jomon periods (Sapporo-shi Kyoiku Iinkai 1987; Crawford and Takamiya 1990; Otaru-shi Kyoiku Iinkai 1990; Crawford 1992b; D'Andrea 1995b).

## Environment and Ethnohistory

The climate of northeastern Japan is affected by a number of influences. Regional contrasts result from cold ocean currents moving along the north and east coasts of Hokkaido bringing foggy weather and unstable conditions in the summer (Maekawa 1974:7). The western coast of Hokkaido, in contrast, is warmed by the northward-flowing Tsushima current that also branches through the Tsugaru Strait between Honshu and Hokkaido. Vegetation is affected by snowfall, which is much deeper on the Sea of Japan coast (Shidei 1974:21). Southwestern Hokkaido and Aomori are in a temperate zone with relatively cold winters and mild summers. The average July temperature in Sapporo, for example, is about 22 degrees Celsius while in January it is about -5 degrees. Northeastern Hokkaido is subarctic, in general, while the southwest is cool-temperate. The late spring-early summer monsoon, or *tsuyu*, reaches its northern limit between Hokkaido and Aomori. Most of Hokkaido does not experience the monsoon. The Temperate Mixed Forest, or Cool-Temperate Forest of southwestern Hokkaido is comprised mainly of beech (*Fagus crenata*). In the areas of concern to this paper, beech may be associated with maple, and on valley bottoms *Pterocarya-Aesculus* forests are found. In the Hachinohe area of Aomori, which provides some comparative data for this paper, the forests are dominated by oak (*Quercus*).

Ethnohistoric evidence provides an important perspective, particularly on northern seasonality. Northeastern Japan, consisting of Tohoku and Hokkaido, is the homeland of peoples known variously as the Ainu, Utari, Emishi, and Ezo, to name some of the most common attributions. They provide one example of how people interacted with the local environment. The Ainu are usually thought to be descendants, both culturally and biologically, of the northeastern Jomon (Watanabe 1986). As a result, their resource utilization and community location preferences are usually informed by the assumption that they were strictly hunters and gatherers, albeit hunters and gatherers who maintained year-round resident populations at their settlements (Watanabe 1972). This interpretation, however, is fraught with problems as one of us has explored in detail elsewhere (Crawford and Takamiya 1990; Crawford 1992a). A long history of agriculture has been documented for Ainu ancestors and the interpretation of the Ainu as nonagriculturalists is partly based on what Ainu identity is perceived to be in the context of Japanese society (Peng and Geiser 1977; Crawford 1992b; Howell 1994). More to the point, the Ainu are best conceptualized as descendants of the Tohoku Yayoi who were mixed forager-farmers (Crawford and Takamiya 1990). Nonetheless, revisiting Watanabe's (1972) analysis of seasonality and scheduling of the Tokachi Ainu is instructive, in part because he includes agriculture in his discussion, despite the assumption that the Ainu were exclusively hunter-gatherers. No matter the degree of dependence on agriculture by the Ainu, their economy was mixed and never excluded hunting, fishing, and collecting.

During the winter period, where base snow was extensive such as in the Tokachi area, the Ainu depended largely on stored salmon, venison, and plant food. As the base snow disappeared, fishing, hunting, and collecting began. Collecting was intensive from this time through autumn. Fishing did not intensify until the summer arrival of cherry salmon. Spring hunting focused on bear and deer. Deer were hunted as they migrated into lowland fields. Bear, on the other hand, were hunted in their dens. In the summer months, hunting tapered off because meat was less greasy and furs were sparse. By July, cherry salmon was in abundance and was mostly eaten fresh. By September, dog salmon had replaced cherry salmon as the fish of choice. The main focus of summer collecting was the roots of the *uba-yuri* lily, *Lilium cordatum* var. *glehnii* (or *Cardiocrinum glehnii*). The more a local population depended upon farming, the less they collected this lily root. In October when animal fur was thickening and base snow covered vegetation, field hunting intensified. Nuts, berries, and other fruit were collected at the same time. Most of these resources were prepared for storage over the winter. Fall was also the time for collecting raw materials for clothing and other technological purposes. Dog salmon fishing continued through December or January. Hunting continued in the foothills in winter yarding areas until the snow prevented it. As the bear retreated in the late fall to their dens for the winter, they, too, were hunted.

Although this example is limited to one small area of northeastern Hokkaido, it is instructive. The Ainu were logistically flexible. Although they built permanent villages or hamlets, unmarried men would take up residence at sources of rivers for bear hunting or along river tributaries for fishing. Farming was scheduled by taking effort away from wild plant resource collecting. Because collecting versus hunting and fishing were marked by a sexual division of labor, the balance of attention to farming and collecting was decided by women. Snowfall appears to have been the main factor in scheduling the beginning and ending of the hunting season. Other factors included the quality of meat and fur. This is likely but one variant of a diverse set of Ainu scheduling strategies. Because of the relevance of snowfall to scheduling their activities, Ainu living in parts of northeastern Japan with less snow or earlier or later snowfalls than in Tokachi would likely have made somewhat different scheduling decisions than the ones described here. Unfortunately, the kind of examination that Watanabe made of the Tokachi Ainu has not been made elsewhere. We do not mean to imply that northeastern Jomon scheduling followed this Ainu pattern, but at least it exemplifies one pattern in our area.

## The Northeastern Japan Jomon

The Yagi Project was an international investigation of a large Early Jomon period (Transition 1) community—the Yagi site—in southwestern Hokkaido. Excavations were conducted during the summers of 1978, 1979, and 1980 (Crawford et al. 1978; Bleed et al. 1979; Crawford 1983). A primary goal of the Project was to describe the subsistence economy of the Yagi community. The Yagi site is located on the Pacific coast of the Oshima Peninsula, which forms the curved tail at the southwestern corner of the island of Hokkaido (fig. 1). This portion of the coast faces the rich coastal waters of Uchiura Bay (fig. 2).

Topographically, this portion of the Oshima coast is rugged and broken. Yagi sits on one of the few areas of level ground in the area. It overlooks the mouth of the Yagi River on a terrace that is about 45 m above sea level. The Yagi site is, thus, surrounded by low mountains, the Pacific Ocean, and small rivers.

Since plant foods in southern Hokkaido have a limited seasonal availability, plant remains may yield information about the seasonal activities of the community, but they clearly cannot reflect the entire annual round. For example, most seeds and fruits that account for the majority of relevant remains at these sites mature in the fall and would have been harvested at that time. Buds and green, leafy foods can be collected as early as late winter to early spring, but rarely, if ever, do we recover their remains. Since we expected that faunal materials would be entirely absent from the

**Figure 2.** A Yagi site pit house.

site, seasonal patterns of wild resource utilization by the people of Yagi were approached theoretically. Fortunately, some animal remains were recovered and they help test the theoretical interpretation.

Animal resources and the environments of the immediate Yagi catchment offer a range of wild fish, seals, migratory birds, and land mammals, including deer (Bleed et al. 1989). As important as the array of animal resources available to the hunters of Yagi was the fact that game was presented to the community in a series of seasonal peaks that rarely conflicted. Each season of the year offered a readily available and relatively abundant animal source.

Furthermore, an empirically determined two-hour catchment around the site encompassed essentially all the major habitats present anywhere in southern Hokkaido. In other words, any plants or animals

found in the region were likely to have been available to the Yagi community. Even a good source of flakeable stone was located near the site. Thus, as long as resources were not depleted, the people of Yagi could engage in a complete round of markedly seasonal activities without leaving the immediate vicinity of their home community. A graphical model describes how the theoretically optimal seasonal hunting patterns of the community were developed (Bleed et al. 1989) (summarized in fig. 3). All habitats in the Yagi vicinity have excellent animal resources. Deer would have been available all year, but more available during the fall rutting season and hunted more during the winter when other prey were absent. Hares and rabbits would have been available all year; bear during the winter while hibernating; foxes and other fur bearing animals in the winter due to their winter pelage; migratory fish and birds in the spring and fall; invertebrates during the summer; ocean fish in the summer; anadromous salmon and trout during the spring and fall; ducks, geese, and other waterfowl in the spring and late fall; and seals during late fall and winter. The extent to which snowfall restricted winter hunting as it did in the Tokachi Ainu example is difficult to determine, but some limitation should be anticipated. Like all entirely theoretical models, however, the Yagi seasonal reconstruction begs for empirical substantiation. Two independent lines of support have been developed.

First, during the second and third field seasons at the site, an assemblage of 36,000 small, calcinced animal bone fragments was recovered. Since this included only entirely burned pieces and fewer than 850 individual elements, it must be considered incomplete (table 2). Despite the condition of the assemblage, some of it was identifiable due to the presence of articular sur-

faces or other diagnostic features on some elements (Bleed et al. 1989). Specific seasonal markers are not preserved, but the faunal assemblage is entirely consistent with the predictions of the model. Essentially all of the kinds of game predicted as targets by the theoretical model were taken. Furthermore, the representation of body parts indicates that whole carcasses of deer and sea mammals were brought back to the site for butchering, suggesting that major processing was done at the Yagi site, another prediction of the model. Faunal evidence, thus, does not contradict the model.

The composition of the Yagi stone tool assemblage offers the second line of support for the model of Yagi scheduling. As explained elsewhere (Bleed 1992), the chipped-stone tool assemblage recovered from Yagi is markedly diverse in statistical terms. That is, it includes large numbers of many different kinds of stone tools. Interpreted in light of ideas developed by

TABLE 2

**Animal remains from the Yagi site**

| Common Name | Scientific Name | Number of Elements |
|---|---|---|
| Sika deer | *Cervus nippon* | 847 |
| Seal/sea lion/walrus | pinniped | 93 |
| northern fur seal | *Callorhinus ursinus* | several |
| Whale/dolphin/porpose | Delphinidae | |
| dolphin or porpose | | 3 |
| Fur-bearing carnivores | | 14 |
| red fox/raccoon dog | *Vulpes vulpes/Nycetereutes procyonoides* | 5 |
| wolf | *Canis lupus* | 1 |
| Bird | | 8 |
| hazel grouse | *Tetastes bonasia* | 1 |
| cormorant c.f. | Phalacrocoracidae—c.f. | 3 |
| pelagic or Temmink's | *Phalacrocorax pelagicus* or *P. capillatus* | |
| albatross | Diomedeidae | 1 |
| auk c.f. common murre | *Uria aalge* | 1 |
| small duck/grebe | | 1 |
| Fish | | 54 |
| bony fish | Osteichthyes | 31 |
| salmon | *Oncorhynchus* sp. | 5 |
| tuna | *Thunnus* sp. | 2 |
| greenling? | *Hexagrammidae* | 1 |
| flounder | Pleuronectidae | 1 |
| Invertebrate | | |
| sea urchin | Echinoidea | 1 |

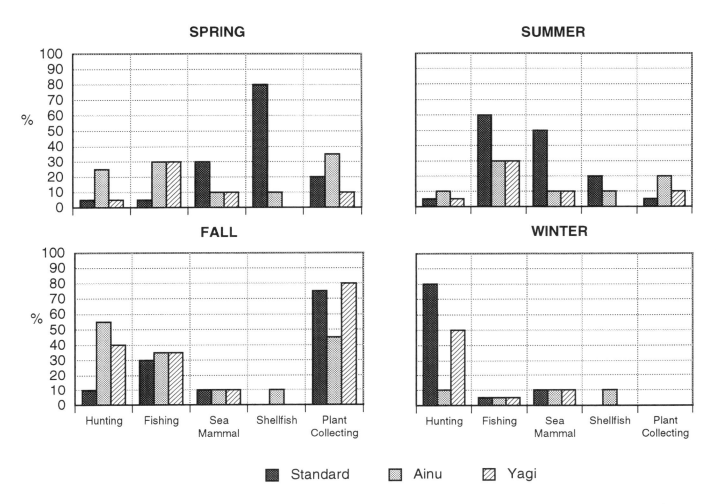

**Figure 3.** A comparison of the standard Jomon Calendar (Kobayashi 1986) with the Early Jomon Yagi site and Ainu scheduling interpretations.

Binford (1980) and refined by others (Kelly 1983; Shott 1986, 1989), the stone tool assemblage appears to reflect the activities of a group that undertook a wide range of activities within the Yagi community. This is the technological adaptation predicted by the theoretical model of Yagi seasonality (Bleed 1992).

Integral to the Yagi Project subsistence research program is a third line of evidence, paleoethnobotanical data. Flotation samples were collected from as many context types as possible including a variety of in-house contexts such as fill layers, floors, and pits; pits outside houses; and sheet middens. About 7,700 liters of soil from Yagi were processed using a froth flotation machine. The Yagi subsistence research program was part of a more extensive program started in

1974 at the Hamanasuno site, a few kilometers from Yagi. Between 1974 and 1982 additional sites sampled include Usujiri B, Nakano B, and Locality 4 of the Hakodate Airport site. All in all, nine temporal components of the Initial through Middle Jomon of southwest Hokkaido, spanning between 4,000 and 5,000 years, have been extensively examined.

Throughout this period, plant remains assemblages are made up of mainly weedy grains and greens producers such as grasses (Poaceae) and knotweeds (Polygonaceae). Fleshy fruits and other seed remains such as sumac (*Rhus*) are next in rank order of density and relative (percent) abundance. Few nut remains are in the samples, with the exception of those from Initial and early Early Jomon contexts from Nakano B and

Yagi. A trend to less reliance on nuts and greater reliance on weedy annuals and perennials is apparent through the end of the sequence we have examined (end of the Middle Jomon or about 1800 B.C.). Furthermore, this quantitative, rather than qualitative, change is largely due to anthropogenesis (Crawford 1983, 1997). An aspect of this anthropogenic process is the probable domestication and husbandry of barnyard grass (*Echinochloa crusgalli*) (Crawford 1983). By the end of the Middle Jomon at Usujiri B, some caryopses of this grass are morphologically indistinguishable from barnyard millet (*E. utilis*) (Crawford 1983, 1992a, 1997).

The bulk of the plant remains at Yagi and the closely related Hamanasuno site represent seeds and fruits available in the fall, just as we anticipated (table 3). Some fruits, however, are available as early as summer. The only evidence for spring or more substantial summer collecting is secondary. Greens of many of the identified plants are readily available in the spring but are not preserved in the archaeological record (table 3). Most of the identified plant foods are storable over the winter. The scheduling evidence from the plant remains, or lack thereof, is similar at each of the Early through Late Jomon sites we have studied. The Ainu plant collecting schedule is not inconsistent with the results of this research. Spring collecting is only indirectly represented, but the interest in harvesting berries, nuts, and other plant foods is substantiated. Missing from the archaeological record, so far at least, is any evidence for collecting *uba-yuri*.

The details of the plant remains from all the Jomon sites we have studied so far are quite similar. This includes the material from the Middle Jomon Usujiri B and Tominosawa sites and the Late Jomon component at Kazahari (Crawford 1983; D'Andrea 1992). One possible significant developmental change from the Early Jomon through Late Jomon is the appearance of cultigens in the record. The data are sketchy and involve buckwheat, millets, and rice. The first southern crop, rice associated with foxtail (*Setaria italica* ssp. *italica*) and broomcorn millet (*Panicum miliaceum*), is in northeastern Japan at the Kazahari site, Aomori at about 1000 cal. B.C. (D'Andrea et al. 1995). One of us has made a case for the domestication of barnyard grass (*Echinochloa crusgalli*) at the Usujiri B site on the Kameda Peninsula just 150 km north of the Kazahari site. Buckwheat, too, may have been grown in Jomon period Hokkaido, but the evidence is still minimal (Crawford et al. 1978; Crawford 1983, 1997). We are unclear, at the moment, whether the commitment to crops increased over this period or

whether crops were grown to a very limited extent throughout the period in question.

Another important issue is the extent to which elaboration of the sociocultural system through time involved elites and changes in redistribution patterns that could have impacted scheduling decisions. At least, both the animal remains and archaeobotanical record are indicative of a complex scheduling system. Its details are not resolvable presently, but the faunal and floral data are consistent with year-round habitation and a community of immobile collectors who were engaged in many different kinds of work that are unusual for foragers (Bleed et al. 1989).

The standard model proposed by Kobayashi differs in a number of details from our reconstruction of Early and Middle Jomon scheduling in northeastern Japan. More hunting likely took place during the fall, fishing occurred throughout the year but with much less taking place during the winter, marine invertebrates were likely harvested all year with more collected during the summer, and spring plant collecting is less in evidence than the standard calendar proposes, although we suspect that much more plant collecting was going on during the spring than our data indicate (fig. 3).

## The Central Hokkaido Zoku-Jomon

The K135-4 and K135-5 excavations were part of mitigation programs linked to the expansion of the Sapporo Railway Station. Excavations took place in 1984 and 1985 (Crawford 1987; Sapporo-shi Kyoiku Iinkai 1987). At the same time, Crawford was researching the Transition 4 Ezo-Haji (early Satsumon) period in Hokkaido with special regard to northern systems of food production (Crawford and Yoshizaki 1987; Crawford and Takamiya 1990; Crawford 1992a, 1992b). The K135-4 and K135-5 sites are Transition 2 Zoku-Jomon occupations, immediately predating the seventh- to eighth-century-A.D. Ezo-Haji expansion in Hokkaido, and therefore are examples of the last Jomon settlements in Japan.

Situated in the Ishikari Plain, the largest lowland in Hokkaido, the sites are some 250 to 500 meters from the now infilled Sakushu-Kotoni River, a tributary of the Toyohira River located about 4.5 km to the northeast. There is little topographic relief in the area, but three to four kilometers to the southwest, highlands rise abruptly to about 200 m. K135 is 16–17 meters above sea level. The Yagi and K135 occupations are both in a temperate forest zone, but their situations

TABLE 3

**Identified plant taxa and their season of availability at Jomon sites in Hokkaido and Aomori, Japan**

| Common Name | Scientific Name | Season Available | Early Jomon | | Middle Jomon | | Late Jomon | Zoku-Jomon | | |
|---|---|---|---|---|---|---|---|---|---|---|
| | | | Yagi | Hamanasuno | Usujiri B | Tominosawa | Kazahari | K-4 | 135-5 | Mochiyazawa |
| **Grains/Greens** | | | | | | | | | | |
| Grasses | gramineae | | | | | | | | | |
| barnyard grass | *Echinochloa crusgalli* | Sept.–Nov. | XX | XX | XX | X | XX | | | X |
| barnyard grass (rice mimic) | *E. crusgalli* var. *oryzicola* | Sept.–Nov. | | | | | | | | XX |
| foxtail grass | *Setaria* c.f. *S. viridis* | fall | X | | X | X | | | | |
| rye/wheat grass | *Elymus/Agropyron* | Aug.–Oct. | XX | | | | | | | |
| panic grass? | *Panicum* c.f. *P. bisculatum* | fall | X | X | | | | | | |
| panicoid grass | Paniceae | various–mainly fall | | XX | | X | XX | | | |
| unknown type | ? | | | | | XX | | | | |
| wall barley | *Hordeum murinum* | late summer–fall | | | | | | X | - | |
| knotweeds | *Polygonum* sp. | greens from early summer | X | X | XX | X | X | X | X | X |
| dock-leaved | *P. lapathifolium* | fall | X | XX | XX | X | | | | |
| great | *P. sachalinense* | fall | X | XX | XX | | | X | X | |
| Japanese | *P. cuspidatum?* | fall | XX | X | | | | X | XX | |
| | *P. foliosum/persicaria?* | fall | X | XX | XX | | | | | |
| | *P. longisetum?* | fall | | X | | | | | | |
| | *P. densiflorum* | fall | | | | X | | | | X |
| chenopod | *Chenopodium* c.f. *C. ficifolium/C. album* | late summer–fall | X | X | XX | | X | | | XX |
| dock | *Rumex* sp. | late summer–fall | XX | | XX | | | | | XX |
| amaranth | *Amaranthus retroflexus* | late summer–fall | | | | | | | | |
| **Fleshy Fruits** | | | | | | | | | | |
| Amur corktree | *Phellodendron amurense* | late summer–fall | XX | X | X | | | X | X | X |
| bramble | *Rubus* sp. | late summer | X | X | X | | X | | X | X |
| crowberry | *Empetrum nigrum* | summer–fall | | | | | | X | - | X |
| dogwood | *Cornus* sp. | summer | X | | | | | X | XX | |
| elderberry | *Sambucus sieboldiana* | fall | X | X | X | X | X | X | XX | X |

X:   present
XX: clusters present

*Table 3 continued on next page*

TABLE 3 CONTINUED

**Identified plant taxa and their season of availability at Jomon sites in Hokkaido and Aomori, Japan**

| Common Name | Scientific Name | Season Available | Early Jomon | | Middle Jomon | | Late Jomon | Zoku-Jomon | | |
|---|---|---|---|---|---|---|---|---|---|---|
| | | | Yagi | Hamanasuno | Usujiri B | Tominosawa | Kazahari | K-4 | 135-5 | Mochiyazawa |
| grape | *Vitis* sp. c.f. *V. coignaetiae* | summer–early fall | X | X | X | | X | XX | XX | X |
| mountain ash | *Sorbus* sp. | summer–early fall | | | | | | | | X |
| nightshade | Solanaceae | | | | | | | | X | |
| black nightshade | *Solanum nigrum* | fall | | | | | | | X | |
| | *Physaliastrum japonicum* | fall | | | | | | | X | |
| silvervine | *Actinidia* c.f. *A. arguta* | late summer–fall | XX | X | X | | X | X | X | X |
| udo | *Aralia cordata* | greens (shoots)– May, fruit-fall | XX | X | XX | | | - | X | |
| tara-no-ki | *A. elata* | greens (buds)– May, fruit-fall | | | | | | | | X |
| **Other** | | | | | | | | | | |
| asada | *Ostrya japonica* | late summer–fall | | X | XX | | X | | | XX |
| bean family | Fabaceae | various, mainly fall | X | X | | | | | | |
| bulrush | *Scirpus* sp. | fall | | X | | | | | | |
| cleavers | *Galium* sp. | late summer–fall | X | X | X | | | | | |
| leek, wild onion | *Allium monanthum* | spring | | | | | | X | - | |
| prickley ash | *Zanthoxylum* sp. | summer | X | | | | | | | |
| sedge | *Carex* sp. | various | X | | | | | | | |
| sedge 2 F | *imbristylus subspicata* | fall | X | X | | | | | | |
| sumac | *Rhus* sp. | fall | X | XX | X | X | | XX | - | X |
| **Nuts** | | | | | | | | | | |
| acorn | *Quercus* sp. | early fall (periodic) | | | | | XX | X | X | XX |
| chestnut | *Castanea* sp. | Oct. (periodic) | | | | | | XX | | |
| walnut | *Juglans ailanthifolia* | Oct.–Nov. (periodic) | | X | | | XX | X | X | XX |
| **Cultigens** | | | | | | | | | | |

X: present
XX: clusters present

contrast in several ways. First of all, they are on opposites sides of the Kuromatsunai Line (fig. 1). This line marks the northern limit of beech, *sawagurumi*, grape (*Vitis flexulosa*), and *asunaru* (*Thujopsis dolobrata*). Northeast of this line grows mainly oak (*Quercus crispula*, *Q. dentata*), elm (*Ulmus davidiana*, *U. laciniata*), basswood (*Tilia maximowicziana*), maple (*Acer mono*), and *Kalopanax septemlobus*. The contrast is largely due the difference in winter low temperatures (Shidei 1974:97).

The fundamental difference between the Zoku-Jomon record and that of the preceding periods is the dominance of nuts in particular contexts. At the K135 localities, individual species of nuts are concentrated in five to ten meter square areas indicating specific processing events (Crawford 1987; Crawford and Takamiya 1990). This is the case at Mochiyazawa as well where specific pits and areas have very high densities of walnut remains, while other pits and areas do not (D'Andrea 1995b) (fig. 4). Concentrations of nuts, particularly single species, are likely a good indication

of a short-term event such as nut processing, perhaps the eating of a portion of a harvest in the fall before storing the remainder over the winter. The Ainu collected walnut, chestnut, and acorns in a narrow time frame (shorter than a week), quickly processing and storing them. The nut distributions at K135 and Mochiyazawa are particularly striking when they are compared with those from Jomon sites in northeastern Japan, where flotation has recovered some nutshell (D'Andrea 1995b). In general at Transition 1 sites, nut remains are not common. The only sites from which any quantities at all have been recovered are from the Early Jomon Yagi site where nut remains come from only one concentration and from the Late Jomon occupation and Transition 2 Tohoku Yayoi component of the Kazahari site where small amounts of walnut have been retrieved from a variety of contexts.

We might also expect to see evidence of short-term events related to the gathering of other plants that could have been harvested during the late fall in the vicinity of K135. Concentrations of one species of

**Figure 4.** The Mochiyazawa site setting.

knotweed, *Polygonum cuspidatum*, occur in K135-5 units A and B only. Elsewhere at K135, this knotweed is only sporadically represented by a few achenes each in the samples in which it occurs. The only other plant remains found in substantial concentrations in particular contexts are a few fleshy fruits: grape (*Vitis*), elderberry (*Sambucus*), silvervine (*Actinidia*), and dogwood (*Cornus*). Including the knotweed, these are all available around the time nuts would be harvested and support our contention of a series of short-term, special purpose occupations at K135.

The animal remains are concentrated by species in certain deposits as well at K135. The K135 localities are stratified. Flood deposits separate occupations of nearly the same time period. The earlier levels have primarily salmon bones while later ones have deer. Fur-

thermore, the Zoku-Jomon occupations do not show the same investment in dwelling construction (no pit houses). Instead, the sites consist of burned soil lenses (hearths?), small pits, and other pits usually interpreted as burials (fig. 5). The K135 localities appear to have been used at certain times for specific purposes. They are not year-round habitations. Thus scheduling by Zoku-Jomon peoples is of a different sort than that of the preceding Jomon.

During this period evidence for the products of farming is found—barley, rice, and related weeds such as the rice field weed, *Echinochloa oryzicola*, a type of barnyard grass that mimics rice in many phenotypic traits. It is at this time that the first potential spring product is recognized in the archaeobotanical record in our area: *Allium monanthum*, or wild onion/leek bulbs

**Figure 5.** A probable Zoku-Jomon burial pit at the Mochiyazawa site.

(*himenira*) found at K135-4. This species is not native to Japan and may have been an agricultural weed (Kasahara 1974). Its distribution at K135-4 is limited to two concentrations in level VIIc of units D7 and E7 (Crawford 1987) totaling twelve bulbs. Quantities of carbonized chestnut and other evidence of fall resources have also been recovered. If we accept that *himenira* was collected in the spring, it is the only evidence possibly inconsistent with a strictly fall occupation at K135-4. A brief spring occupation may have occurred, or the bulbs may have been stored until they were carbonized and eventually incorporated into the archaeological record.

The Zoku-Jomon situation contrasts with the preceding Jomon periods in that settlements seem to be more transitory in the former. These hypothesized short-term, combination living and burial sites of the Zoku-Jomon are not represented in the Early through Final Jomon. That is, earlier occupations are substantial pit-house communities with a wide array of activities represented on them (Bleed 1992). This is not to say that special purpose sites are not known for the Early through Late Jomon. Quarries, for example, are well known. Notable special-purpose sites during the Middle through Final Jomon are cemeteries and associated stone and earthen constructions, but they are not the same as the Zoku-Jomon sites we have studied. The Middle through Final Jomon sites indicate substantial construction efforts, not as transitory as we see at Zoku-Jomon sites, and unlike the latter, they are not associated with food preparation/collecting and living areas. Although in order to fit our model the Zoku-Jomon sites would have been reused over a few centuries, it is the absence of other dwelling sites in the region during the Zoku-Jomon that is conspicuous.

## Mixed Economy Ezo-Haji and Tohoku Yayoi

Not until the Transition 2 Tohoku Yayoi, a contemporary of the Zoku-Jomon to the north, do more substantial quantities of cultigens show up on archaeological sites in the northeast. By A.D 700, the move to a greater investment in agriculture corresponds with the development of the Ezo-Haji from the Tohoku Yayoi across Tohoku and Hokkaido. Sites of this period are comprised of compact villages of rectangular pit houses (fig. 6). This Transition 4 culture is, in our view, the direct ancestor of the Ainu (Crawford and Takamiya 1990). Although crops appear to have been used to some extent earlier than this in the northeast, we feel that substantial scheduling changes should be recognizable in the archaeological record. For example, as we

noted earlier, the Ainu took time away from collecting in order to invest in farming.

The significant difference between the Transition 4 Ezo-Haji and Transitions 1 and 2 cultures discussed here is the high density of cultigens in the former (Crawford 1987; Crawford and Takamiya 1990). Nonetheless, wild plant remains are also present, indicating both the presence of weeds in fields and an economy that still included wild resources, most of which are represented at the earlier sites. Late summer and fall are represented by ten types of fleshy fruits and a few nut remains (table 3). Wild onion/leek (*himenira*) remains may indicate spring collecting. In terms of types of plants in the archaeological record, we do not see much difference among the collections. Relative quantities are, of course, different. Nuts, although present, are found in extremely low densities in contrast to the preceding Zoku-Jomon. Given the likely presence of at least a core resident population of the Ezo-Haji at their hamlets much as in the Ainu model, the contrasts between the Zoku-Jomon and other cultures provide an even stronger indication of the different scheduling decisions that would be inherent during the Zoku-Jomon.

The degree of investment of time and energy into agriculture-related activities at Ezo-Haji sites appears to be very high. This was a major commitment that demanded a great deal of effort during periods that the Zoku-Jomon and earlier groups invested in collecting. Foraging did not disappear and the subsistence economy of the Ezo-Haji can best be described as mixed hunting-fishing-collecting-agriculture. At the Sakushu-Kotoni-Gawa site is a fish weir, and other fish weirs dating to this period are known on Hokkaido. Hunting tools are rare, however. The stone technology of earlier periods is virtually absent. Yet this does not exclude hunting from the range of Ezo-Haji subsistence activities. Data from the Tokyo Bay area indicate that there, too, the shift to food production was largely additive rather than substitutive (Aikens and Akazawa 1992). A mixed economy persisted there well into historic times. With the increased ecological disruption caused by agricultural activities, the productivity of many of the plants whose remains we recover increases due to their preference for sunny forest edges and disturbed open ground (Crawford 1997). As a result, an added benefit of a greater emphasis on agriculture would have been a concomitant increase in the numbers and productivity of weedy plants closer to settlements. This would ameliorate some of the effects of committing more time and energy to agriculture. Thus we do not see the exclusion of many wild resources from the record at sites where agriculture is a major activity.

**Figure 6.** Ezo-Haji rectangular pit houses.

## DISCUSSION

The three patterns outlined in this chapter, the Early through Late Jomon (Transition 1), Zoku-Jomon (Transition 2), and Ezo-Haji (Transition 4), indicate that a variety of strategies met with success in northeastern Japan. The Ainu in the Tokachi region represent a fourth pattern, which is distinctive in that the emphasis on agriculture seems to have been less than that of the Ezo-Haji a millennium earlier in the Ishikari Plain and Oshima Peninsula.

In Transition 1, hunting, collecting, fishing, and a variety of other tasks evidence a complex of activities to be scheduled by resident, year-round populations. An optimal model for the Early Jomon Yagi site indicates a significant degree of correspondence to the archaeological record. Kobayashi's orthodox view, although a good starting point, does not adequately represent what we have found to be the case in northeastern Japan during the earlier Jomon periods. Ours is not the only view that offers evidence contradictory to Kobayashi's model. Shell remains from the Kidosaku site in southwestern Japan show that shells were collected year-round, but early spring and summer dominate (Koike 1986:44). About 60 percent of the shellfish were collected in these seasons because tidal flats are exposed longer then. The drop in late spring is thought to occur during the rainy season (Koike 1986:82).

The Zoku-Jomon is not the continuing Jomon that the name suggests (*zoku* means "continuing" in Japanese). The name actually refers to the continued use of cord-marking on pottery along with stone technology and to the fact that this culture is not the rice-based Yayoi. The period represents a major break in subsistence and mobility patterns from what we see earlier in the archaeological record of Hokkaido and Aomori Prefecture. The ecofactual material from the two K135 localities in Sapporo and from Mochiyazawa are consistent with the intensive collection of a few plant resources, mainly nuts, over short periods of time. Subsequently, the Zoku-Jomon territory became the territory of the ancestral Ainu Ezo-Haji peoples who had made a significant commitment to agriculture. While the archaeobotanical record at these sites is dominated for the most part by cultigens, the evidence for wild resource use is strong. These resources are much the same as those that were used throughout the Holocene in northeastern Japan.

Finally, hypothetical scheduling conflicts have been invoked to explain why agriculture was not readily adopted by populations in northeastern Japan (Akazawa 1982; Aikens and Akazawa 1992). The suggestion is based on a commendable research program that is a rare attempt to broadly interpret important events in Japan's prehistory from an environmental perspective. Our data have not played a role in this model, however. The model compares data from the Tokyo Bay area and regions to the southwest and northeast. The Tokyo area sites are thought to have been occupied by marine/animal oriented peoples. To the southwest, people are thought to have been much more plant oriented. Wet sites such as Torihama have extensive plant remains supporting this view. Fishing was central to people on the northeast coast based on analysis of the Miura Caves artifacts and related collections. A rapid change to agriculture in the southwest occurred, according to Aikens and Akazawa (1992:79) because of local Jomon experience with plants and therefore, because it entailed minimal scheduling conflicts. Conflicts between the rice planting and weeding seasons and the fishing and shellfishing season in the northeast, however, supposedly mitigated against the quick adoption of crops in the northeast (Aikens and Akazawa 1992:79).

Our data, however, evidence a complex and flexible scheduling capability in the northeast. None of the sites we are working on show the predominance of fishing and shellfish collecting that Tokyo Bays sites do. Plants were, indeed, a significant part of northeastern lifeways, at least in our research area. The evidence indicates gardening has likely existed in the northeast from the middle Holocene and that rice appeared as far north as Aomori Prefecture by 900 cal. B.C. In fact, we cast serious doubt on the slowness with which agriculture was incorporated into northeastern lifeways (Crawford 1992b; Barnes 1993). All indications are for an adoption of agriculture not much slower than in southwestern Japan. If anything, scheduling capabilities of northeastern peoples did not stand in the way of the intensification of agriculture. In fact, the variety of data we have outlined for northeastern Japan provides insights as to why the northeastern populations committed to food production so rapidly. Nevertheless, these issues are important and we encourage more extensive research.

## Acknowledgments

Our research in Japan has been supported by the Social Sciences and Humanities Research Council of Canada, the National Science Foundation, National Geographic Society, and Earthwatch. In addition we would like to thank Prof. Masakazu Yoshizaki for facilitating this research. We also express our gratitude to the Boards of Education of Hokkaido, Sapporo, Otaru, Minamikayabe, Hakodate, Hachinohe, and the Hokkaido and Aomori Prefectural Salvage Archaeology Centers.

## Note

1. Transition 2 refers to the consolidation of agriculture throughout Honshu and also includes the southwestern Japan classic Yayoi. Transition 3 is the development of Ezo-Haji agriculture in Tohoku. Neither the classic Yayoi nor Transition 3 are discussed here.

## BIBLIOGRAPHY

Aikens, C. M.
1981 "The Last 10,000 Years in Japan and Eastern North America: Parallels in Environment, Economic Adaptations, Growth of Societal Complexity and the Adoption of Agriculture," in *Affluent Foragers*, S. Koyama and D. H. Thomas, eds., pp. 261–273. Senri Ethnological Studies 9. National Museum of Ethnology, Osaka.

Aikens, C. M., and T. Akazawa
1992 "Fishing and Farming in Early Japan: Jomon Littoral Tradition Carried into Yayoi Times at the Miura Caves on Tokyo Bay," in *Pacific Northeast Asia in Prehistory: Hunter-Fisher-Gatherers, Farmers, and Sociopolitical Elites*, C. M. Aikens and S. N. Rhee, eds., pp. 75–82. Washington State University Press, Pullman, Washington.

Akazawa, T.
1982 "Cultural Change in Prehistoric Japan: Receptivity to Rice Agriculture in the Japanese Archipelago," in *Advances in World Archaeology*, vol. 1, F. Wendorf and A. E. Close, eds., pp. 151–211. Academic Press, New York.
1986 "Hunter-Gatherer Adaptations and the Transition to Food Production in Japan," in *Hunters in Transition*, M. Zvelebil, ed., pp. 151–165. Cambridge University Press, Cambridge.

Akazawa, T., and C. M. Aikens
1986 *Prehistoric Hunter-Gatherers in Japan: New Research Methods.* Bulletin 27. The University Museum, University of Tokyo, Tokyo.

Barnes, G.
1993 *The Miwa Project: Survey, Coring, and Excavation at the Miwa Site*, Nara, Japan. British Archaeological Reports, International Series 582. Oxford.

Binford, L.
1980 "Willow Smoke and Dog Tails: Hunter-Gatherer Settlement Systems and Archaeological Site Formation." *American Antiquity* 45:4–20.

Bleed, P.
1992 "Ready for Anything: Technological Adaptations to Ecological Diversity at Yagi, an Early Jomon Community in Southwestern Hokkaido, Japan," in *Pacific Northeast Asia in Prehistory: Hunter-Fisher-Gatherers, Farmers, and Sociopolitical Elites*, C. M. Aikens and S. N. Rhee, eds., pp. 47–52. Washington State University Press, Pullman, Washington.

Bleed, P., C. Falk, A. Bleed, and A. Matsui
1989 "Between the Mountains and the Sea; Optimal Hunting Patterns and Faunal Remains at Yagi, an Early Jomon Community in Southwestern Hokkaido." *Arctic Anthropology* 26(2):107–126.

Bleed, P., M. Yoshizaki, M. Hurley, and J. Weymouth
1979 *The Yagi Site*. Technical Report, no. 80–14. Division of Archaeological Research, Department of Anthropology, University of Nebraska, Lincoln.

Crawford, G. W.
1983 *Palaeoethnobotany of the Kameda Peninsula Jomon.* Anthropological Papers 73. Museum of Anthropology, University of Michigan, Ann Arbor.
1987 "K135 Iseki kara Shutsu Sareta Shokubutsu Shushi ni Tsuite (K135 Site Plant Remains)," in *K135 Site*, Sapporo-shi Bunkazai Chosa Hokokusho XXX, pp. 565–581. Sapporo-shi Kyoiku Iinkai, Sapporo-shi.

1992a "Prehistoric Plant Domestication in East Asia," in *The Origins of Plant Domestication in World Perspective*, P. J. Watson and C. W. Cowan, eds., pp. 7–38. Smithsonian Institution Press, Washington, D.C.
1992b "The Transitions to Agriculture in Japan," in *Transitions to Agriculture in Prehistory*, A. B. Gebauer and T. D. Price, eds., pp. 117–132. Monographs in World Archaeology 4. Prehistory Press, Madison.
1997 "Anthropogenesis in Prehistoric Northeastern Japan," in *Cultural and Ecological Dynamics of Human-Plant Interaction: Anthropological Investigations*, K. Gremillion, ed., pp. 86–103. University of Alabama Press, Tuscaloosa.

Crawford, G. W., and H. Takamiya
1990 "The Origins and Implications of Late Prehistoric Plant Husbandry in Northern Japan." *Journal of Archaeological Science* 64(245):889–911.

Crawford, G. W., and M. Yoshizaki
1987 "Ainu Ancestors and Early Asian Agriculture." *Journal of Archaeological Science* 14:201–213.

Crawford, G. W., W. M. Hurley, and M. Yoshizaki
1978 "Implications of Plant Remains from the Early Jomon, Hamanasuno Site." *Asian Perspectives* 19(1):145–148.

D'Andrea, A. C.
1992 "Paleoethnobotany of Later Jomon and Early Yayoi Cultures in Northeastern Japan: Northeastern Aomori and Southwestern Hokkaido." Ph.D. diss., University of Toronto.
1995a "Later Jomon Subsistence in Northeastern Japan: New Evidence from Palaeoethnobotanical Studies." *Asian Perspectives* 34:195–227.
1995b "Archaeobotanical Evidence for Zoku-Jomon Subsistence at the Mochiyazawa Site, Hokkaido, Japan." *Journal of Archaeological Science* 22:583–595.

D'Andrea, A. C., G. W. Crawford, M. Yoshizaki, and T. Kudo
1995 "Late Jomon Cultigens in Northeastern Japan." *Antiquity* 69:146–152.

Flannery, K. V.
1968 "Archaeological Systems Theory and Early Mesoamerica," in *Anthropological Archaeology in the Americas*, B. J. Meggers, ed., pp. 67–87. Anthropological Society of Washington, Washington, D.C.

Hayden, B.
1990 "Nimrods, Piscators, Pluckers, and Planters: The Emergence of Food Production." *Journal of Anthropological Archaeology* 9:31–69.

Howell, D.
1994 "Ainu Ethnicity and the Boundaries of the Early Modern Japanese State." *Past and Present* 142:69–93.

Hurley, W. M.
1974 "The Hamanasuno Project." *Arctic Anthropology* 11 (suppl.):171–176.

Ikawa-Smith, F.
1980 "Current Issues in Japanese Archaeology." *American Scientist* 68(2):134–145.

Kasahara, Y.
1974 *Nihon Zasso Zusetsu*. Yokendo, Tokyo.

Kelly, R.
1983 "Hunter-Gatherer Mobility Strategies." *Journal of Anthropological Research* 39:277–307.

Kobayashi , T.
1986 "Trends in Administrative Salvage Archaeology," in *Windows on the Japanese Past: Studies in Archaeology and Prehistory*, R. Pearson, ed., pp. 491–496. Center for Japanese Studies, University of Michigan, Ann Arbor.

Koike, H.
1986 "Prehistoric Hunting Pressure and Paleobiomass: An Environmental Reconstruction and Archaeozoological Analysis of a Jomon Shellmound Area," in *Prehistoric Hunter-Gatherers in Japan: New Research Methods*, T. Akazawa and C. M. Aikens, eds., pp. 27–53. University of Tokyo Press, Tokyo.

Koike, H., and N. Ohtaishi
1987 "Estimation of Prehistoric Hunting Rates Based on the Age Composition of Sika Deer." *Journal of Archaeological Science* 14:251–269.

Kotani, Y.
1969 "Upper Pleistocene and Early Holocene Environmental Conditions in Japan." *Arctic Anthropology* 14(2):251–267.

Maekawa, F.
1974 "Geographical Background to Japan's Flora and Vegetation: General Geography of Japan and Its Relationship to the Flora," in *The Flora and Vegetation of Japan*, M. Numata, ed., pp. 2–20. Kodansha Ltd., Tokyo.

Matsui, A.
1992 "Wetland Sites in Japan," in *The Wetland Revolution in Prehistory*, B. Colces, ed., pp. 5–15. WARP Occasional Paper 6. The Prehistoric Society, University of Exeter, Exeter, United Kingdom.

Otaru-shi Kyoiku Iinkai, ed.
1990 *Ranshima Mochiyazawa Iseki (The Ranshima Mochiyazawa Site)*. Otaru-shi Maizo Bunkazai Chosa Hokokusho 2. Otaru-shi Kyoiku Iinkai, Otaru-shi.

Peng, F. C. C., and P. Geiser
1977 *The Ainu: The Past in the Present*. Bunka Hyoron Publishing Company, Hiroshima.

Price, T. D., and G. Feinman
1993 *Images of the Past*. Mayfield, New York and Toronto.

Sapporo-shi Kyoiku Iinkai
1987 *K135 Iseki (The K135 Site)*. Sapporo-shi Bunkazai Chosa Hokokusho 30. Sapporo-shi Kyoiku Iinkai, Sapporo-shi.

Serizawa, C.
1979 "Cave Site in Japan." *World Archaeology* 10:340–349.

Shidei, T.
1974 "Geographical Background to Japan's Flora and Vegetation: Climate and the Distribution of Vegetation Zones," in *The Flora and Vegetation of Japan*, M. Numata, ed., pp. 20–27. Kodansha Ltd., Tokyo.

Shott, M.
1986 "Settlement Mobility and Technological Organization: An Ethnographic Examination." *Journal of Anthropological Research* 42:15–51.
1989 "Diversity, Organization, and Behavior in the Material Record: Ethnographic and Archaeological Examples." *Current Anthropology* 30:283–315.

Suzuki, K.
1978 "Aomori-ken Kaijo-mura Shutsudo no Dobutsukei Doki (Animal Representations on Pottery from Kaijo-mura, Aomori Prefecture)." *Kokogaku Janaru* 145:18–19.
1985 "Jomon Shakai no Shuukyo to Seigyo (Religion and Occupations in Jomon Society)." *Kokogaku Janaru* 256:49–54.

Tanaka, M.
1984 "The Archaeological Heritage of Japan," in *Approaches to Archaeological Heritage*, H. Cleere, ed., pp. 82–88. Cambridge University Press, Cambridge.

Tsukada, M., S. Sugita, and Y. Tsukada
1986 "Oldest Primitive Agriculture and Vegetational Environments in Japan." *Nature* 322:632–634.

Watanabe, H.
1972 *The Ainu Ecosystem: Environment and Group Structure.* University of Washington Press, Seattle.
1986 "Community Habitation and Food Gathering in Prehistoric Japan: An Ethnographic Interpretation of the Archaeological Evidence," in *Windows on the Japanese Past: Studies in Archaeology and Prehistory*, R. Pearson, ed., pp. 229–254. Center for Japanese Studies, University of Michigan, Ann Arbor.

Yabuno, T.
1987 "Japanese Barnyard Millet (*Echinochloa utilis*, Poaceae) in Japan." *Economic Botany* 41:484–493.

Yamada, G.
1986 "Hokkaido ni Okeru Senshi Jidai no Shokubutsu-sei Shokuryo ni Tsuite (Prehistoric Vegetable Foods in Hokkaido)." *Hokkaido Kokogaku* 22:87–106.

Yamada, G., N. Mino, M. Yano, S. Segawa, H. Onoe, and H. Kusaka
1980 "On the Plant Macrofossils from Quaternary Deposits in Oshima Peninsula, Hokkaido IV." *Hokkaido Kaitakukinenkan Kenkyu Nenpo* 8:37–49.

Yasuda, Y.
1975 "Jomon Bunka Seiriki no Shizen Kankyo (The Natural Environment of the Jomon Formative Period)." *Kokogaku Kenkyu* 21(4):20–33.
1978 "Vegetational History and Paleogeography of the Kawachi Plain For the Last 13,000 Years." *The Quaternary Research* 16(4):211–229.

CHAPTER 8

# Archaeobotanical Indicators of Seasonality: Examples from Arid Southwestern United States

*Karen R. Adams*

*Crow Canyon Archaeological Center*

*Vorsila L. Bohrer*

*Southwest Ethnobotanical Enterprises*

## Abstract

Archaeobotanical remains in arid Southwestern United States sites can indicate short-term, multiseason, and year-round uses of an ancient site or area. Evidence in features or human coprolites of single-season activities can be combined with ecological insights to assess calendrical periods of vegetative growth, flowering, and fruiting. The ability of humans to mute or enhance evidence of plant seasonality are discussed, along with natural forces that also affect the record. Cases for multiseason presence are built upon a suite of single-season indicators plus any insights available from insect degradation of stored plants, agricultural scheduling requirements, and the amount of inferred local environmental disturbance during site habitation. Year-round occupation can be suggested when reproductive or vegetative parts known to remain available during cold or dry dormant seasons are well represented among resources recovered.

## INTRODUCTION

Establishing whether prehistoric groups lived in sites intermittently or year-round enhances our understanding of local and regional population mobility. To determine seasonality, archaeologists assess settlement patterns, the presence or absence of storage features, inferences from lithic and ceramic assemblages regarding potential food processing or storage activities, repeated superpositioning of structures or features,

dense or sparse nature of trash middens, and a variety of other measures (Elson 1992). They also examine bioarchaeological indicators present in teeth, bone, antler, fish parts (Monks 1981), and parasites (Reinhard 1992:237). This paper discusses seasonality as suggested by botanical remains in arid areas of the American Southwest, primarily from the states of New Mexico, Arizona, and Colorado, and to a lesser extent from Nevada, Utah, Texas, and California. Mesic environments would likely provide an alternative set of botanical indicators.

To an ecologist, the term "seasonality" refers to "phenology," or "the branch of science concerned with the relations between climate and periodic biological phenomena, such as the flowering and fruiting of plants."[1] The climatic controls of seasonality interest archaeologists less than the timing and predictability of plant growth, flowering, and fruiting. Archaeologists hope that seasonality information on plants formerly of interest to prehistoric groups will help place them on a landscape during a particular portion of the year. To complicate the issue, people seldom gather a copious harvest without saving some for the future. Thus the problem of determining seasonality of occupation is inextricably linked to aspects of both plant and human behavior.

## SEASONALITY AND PLANT BEHAVIOR

One begins by gathering ecological information about those plant resources the archaeobotanical record indicates were of interest to prehistoric groups. This includes, for example, acquiring data on predictability of fruit maturation and documenting the length of time various resources can be harvested. Length of availability of certain vegetative parts (e.g., flexible new shoots for basketry) might also be of interest.

## Predictability

By establishing the predictability of fruit or grain maturation, one hopes to pinpoint just when humans occupied certain landscapes. Unfortunately, one cannot always rely on statements about reproductive events reported in regional floras representing large and diverse ranges of a taxon. Published flowering and fruiting dates may encompass a gradient of genetic adaptation to various latitudes or altitudes or omit critical ecological details of reproductive strategy.

Local observations provide accurate data on both the earliest maturation date and the length of time reproductive parts can be acquired, especially if these observations include multiple years displaying diversity in rainfall. Even microgeographic differences in maturation have important implications for resource scheduling, acquisition, and sharing. For example, in the immediate area around two major Pueblo III communities approximately 6.5 km apart in southwestern Colorado, the same key native plants ripen up to two weeks earlier near one community than the other (Adams 1993a). Such differences in timing may have resulted in intergroup harvest negotiations.

Many southwestern plant resources fall into three functional categories based on predictability (Bohrer 1975a): truly seasonal ones, those of qualified seasonality, and those with shifting seasonality. For truly seasonal resources such as saguaro or prickly pear cacti, the timing of blossoming or seed maturation is little altered by the vagaries of weather, since flowering may be primarily under photoperiodic control. Plant resources of qualified seasonality depend on environmental conditions reaching a necessary threshold for the crop to develop and mature. In the lower Mojave desert, an inch or more of late fall moisture initiates flower bud formation in many perennial herbs and winter annuals (Beatley 1974). For pinyon pine (*Pinus edulis*),[2] successful maturation of a pinyon nut crop requires two full growing seasons after the female cones become visible, during which there are several stages vulnerable to climate extremes (Little 1938; Lanner 1981). Plant resources of shifting seasonality confine their reproduction to a period when temperatures

are conducive to growth and when moisture arriving within that time period is primarily responsible for triggering development. Examples include perennials like alkali sacaton grass (*Sporobolus airoides*), thornapple (*Datura wrightii*), peyote cactus (*Lophophora williamsii*), or annuals like goosefoot (*Chenopodium* spp.) and sunflower (*Helianthus* spp.). Aseasonal vegetative resources such as tree bark, roots, and cactus pads offer humans foods that are reliable and always available, but generally poor in nutritional qualities.

## Length of Availability

The length of time resources can be harvested varies among taxa. If timing of maturation is predictable, those resources available for only a short while are potentially useful in determining seasonality. For example, in southeastern Arizona, panic grass (*Panicum*) grains offer a relatively short (four to six week) harvest (Adams 1988:347–348). On the other hand, in the same area, three species of oak (*Quercus*) have overlapping periods of acorn maturation that ensure acorns can be gathered for a full five months (Adams 1988:437). The broader window of opportunity for acquiring acorns, added to the difficulties in identifying acorn species from shell fragments, reduces their utility for determining seasonality.

The longer a fruit is retained on a plant, the less helpful the resource is in expressing seasonality. Not all plants release their fruit immediately upon maturity. Fruits that cling to a plant offer convenient and sometimes indefinite "on the plant" storage (Bohrer 1981a). The American Southwest has a goodly supply of sclerophyllous plants with thickened, hardened foliage resistant to water loss. Common also in Mediterranean climates (Lamont et al. 1991), such plants can retain mature fruit for weeks, occasionally months, after ripening. In the Southwest some examples include sotol (*Dasylirion*), juniper (*Juniperus*), cacti, four-wing saltbush (*Atriplex canescens*), and wild gourds (*Cucurbita* spp.).

The "on-the-plant" storage system described for fruits also exists for vegetative plant parts, at least as far as human usage is concerned. The inner bark of trees, succulent stems (e.g., prickly pear pads), succulent leaves like *Agave*, or certain roots or tubers are frequently available when other portions of the plant remain dormant.

Animal behavior can diminish both the length of plant harvest and the quantity of resources accessible to humans. For example, packrats, mice, jays, and domestic turkeys all compete with humans for native foods (e.g., pinyon nuts, acorns, juniper berries, and mesquite pods), effectively shortening the time when humans can harvest them directly.

## SEASONALITY AND HUMAN BEHAVIOR

Season of gathering frequently differs from season of use. Humans can mute the evidence for plant seasonality by storing foodstuffs for varying periods prior to use or until some burning event occurs. If an abandoned residence overgrown by early successional weeds should burn, the carbonized plant parts may contaminate the archaeobotanical record left by the former inhabitants (Minnis 1981). Similarly, when contemporary field stubble and weeds are burned, carbonized seed may infiltrate the archaeological site below (Miksicek 1987:233). In each case, mixing of charred prehistoric and postoccupational intrusive materials can confound interpretation.

Humans can mute seasonality evidence in ways other than storage. For example, they can lengthen season of resource availability by raiding animals nests for stored food. The Navajo in Arizona have gathered pinyon nuts from packrat nests (Vestal 1952:13), while the Seri of northwest Mexico raided packrat nests for mesquite pods (Felger and Moser 1985:338). Great Basin groups looked for rice grass (*Stipa hymenoides*) caches in meadow mouse and other rodent burrows (Fowler 1976:3). Humans have also been known to increase their available food supply by recycling foodstuffs that have already been through the human digestive track. Groups in Baja, California glean organpipe (*Stenocereus*) cactus seeds in this way (Nabhan 1985:84), and the Seri acquire cardon (*Pachycereus*) cactus seeds in a similar manner (Felger and Moser 1985:253).

## SEASONALITY: EXAMPLES FROM ARID SITES

The full range of human behavior regarding seasonal "rounds" in arid areas is probably quite variable. Looking at seasonality among historic nomadic groups in arid Northern Australia, one author wrote:

It will be apparent that an onlooker, seeing these people at different seasons of the year, would find them engaged in occupations so diverse, and with weapons and utensils differing so much in character, that if he were unaware of the seasonal influence on food supply, and consequently upon occupation, he would be led to conclude that they were different groups.

Within the bounds even of a single clan territory a people may spend several months of the year as nomadic. . . . A few months later the same people may be found established on the sea coast in camps that have all the appearance of permanence or at least semi-permanence (Thomson 1939:209).

In the arid Southwest, areas of more erratic rainfall promote the type of seasonal forays that vary widely in location from year to year. The presence of single-use pinyon nut gathering camps might be quite difficult to recognize archaeologically. On the other hand, where rainfall is more predictable, stable and repetitive seasonal rounds would be favored. The more refuse left behind, the better the chances of recovering a portion. The last-used features of a room or site would retain debris suggestive of abandonment season.

All that is known about the archaeobotanical record at a site must be assessed for determining seasonality. While some features will reveal certain season-specific activities, the homogenized midden debris will tell a more complete story of multiseason presence in an area. As with faunal and nonbiological data, the better supported interpretations are based on more than one indicator (Monks 1981). Even with all the evidence clearly laid out, the distinction between a site occupied year-round and one visited intermittently, but in each and every season, might be difficult. To provide contrast, we have therefore organized examples into indicators of short-term, multiseason, and year-round expressions of seasonality.

In considering the examples that follow, one must remember three points. First, the interpretive foundation rests on certain assumptions (table 1) that, if untrue, could nullify our efforts. Second, lack of sufficient plant preservation may lead to false conclusions. For single-season occupation of a site, several indicators including nonbotanical ones should be utilized to reinforce an understanding of seasonality. Third, both multiseason and year-round interpretations are built, like a pyramid, from varied units of single-season indicators. The nature of the basic units determines the ultimate reliability of the final interpretation.

Table i

**Assumptions concerning archaeobotanical remains and seasonality**

SHORT-TERM EXPRESSIONS OF SEASONALITY

*Pollen*

IF pollen/flowers are not routinely stored after gathering, and *if* pollen is not trapped in large amounts in standing water or on vegetative or reproductive parts, *then* high percentages, concentrations, or presence of clumps suggest season of gathering and use of flowers.

*Seeds/Fruit*

IF fleshy fruit is consumed shortly after gathering, *then* concentrations of seeds in coprolites imply season of use.

IF seeds/nuts are prepared for use/storage by parching or roasting shortly after harvest, *then* swollen reproductive parts suggest season of gathering coincides with season of preparation. By the same token, if the charred, durable waste products of food processing (rachis joint, spikelet fragments, etc.) have been preserved, chances are good they burned during processing, which routinely accompanies harvesting.

IF immature fruit is charred shortly after harvest (or it would have decomposed leaving no trace), *then* recovery of charred immature fruit reflects season of both gathering and burning.

IF assemblages of plant parts recovered together are all available in a particular season, *then* the simplest explanation is that they represent a harvest from that season. If they appear to be some of the last materials deposited, they suggest season of "last use." The same explanation applies to single-resource harvests as well.

*Vegetative Parts*

IF the morphology/anatomy of plant parts in relation to an annual cycle of development is understood for a region, *then* this evidence can be used to suggest seasonality of prehistoric activities.

MULTISEASON EXPRESSIONS OF SEASONALITY

*Range of Resources Harvested*

IF resources representing both cool (spring, fall) and warm seasons are recovered, *then* humans must have been present in an area for more than one season.

IF domesticated resources (in the American Southwest, Zea mays, Cucurbita, Phaseolus, Gossypium, and Lagenaria) are present in site deposits, *then* people had to have occupied the site at least during spring planting and fall harvesting.

IF domesticated evidence includes both flowering parts and mature reproductive parts, *then* people were present in both early summer and later during the fall.

*Proportions of Weed Species to Climax Species*

IF greater numbers of people and/or longer periods of time in residence alter local proportions of weed species to climax species, *then* the archaeobotanical record can be used to assess relative degrees of sedentism and how they might have changed over time. The higher the proportion of weedy contributors, the more likely long-term, multiseason occupation is being expressed.

*Plant-insect Interactions*

IF long-term storage increases chances of damage to resources, *then* plant parts with evidence of insect damage have been in storage for some period of time following harvest.

IF humans take advantage of certain insect-plant relationships to help prepare resources for their use, *then* knowledge of these relationships may shed light on seasonality of resource acquisition.

YEAR-ROUND EXPRESSIONS OF SEASONALITY

IF food stress is operating in the late winter and early spring months due to reduced food stores and availability or during a period of summer drought dormancy, *then* a deterioration in human diets might be reflected in human coprolites composed of "aseasonal" resources such as leaves, roots, or bark.

IF people conveniently let some of their resources remain stored "on the plant," *then* resources that remain harvestable through winter months and that show up together in an archaeological deposit can suggest winter occupation.

# SHORT-TERM OR SINGLE-HARVEST EVENTS

Various examples in which plant parts express short-term or single-season harvests are available in the literature on arid sites. Short-term interpretations of seasonality are easier to support for plants of "true" or "qualified" seasonality, whose periods of availability are predictable, than for plants of "shifting" seasonality, whose timing of availability can vary broadly, or for "aseasonal" resources that can be acquired year-round. Table 1 contains some of the key assumptions that underlie single-season interpretations.

## Pollen in Sites

Insights into seasonality from pollen data rely on arguments for its cultural transport. If one can assume that repeated processing or use of a plant in a given location enhanced pollen concentrations until abnormally high (Bohrer 1972), then higher than normal percentages of a given pollen type suggest human usage. The evidence can be presented in the form of spectral distortions or departures from natural "pollen rain," assuming that the modern "pollen rain" is similar to that of past natural or anthropogenic environments and that appropriate prehistoric soil is available (Bohrer 1972, 1981b, 1986). Methods used to recognize cultural activity from entomophilous (insect-carried) pollen in archaeological sites include assessment of morphological, experimental, ethnographic, ecological, and archaeological evidence (Bohrer 1981b). This broad approach can help rule out natural modes of pollen entry, such as moths attracted to the light of a hearth at night, social insects inhabiting roof rafters or wall niches after abandonment, or ground-nesting bees depositing pollen clumps in archaeological sites (Davis and Buchmann 1992).

Once a case for cultural transport of pollen is built, features that have seasonally restricted pollen types can be assigned a calendrical period of use. One must assume that pollen or flowers of most plants were not routinely stored after acquisition. However, this supposition is weakened by knowing that the Pima pick and dry cholla (*Opuntia*) flower buds (Greenhouse et al. 1981; Curtin 1984 [1949]:58–59), other groups dry squash (*Cucurbita*) blossoms and incorporate them into medicines (summarized in Bohrer 1986:202–203), and some have gathered and stored cattail (*Typha*) pollen as well (summarized in Adams 1988).

Assuming that mallow (*Sphaeralcea*) flowers were picked when needed, the recovery of 45 percent mallow (*Sphaeralcea*) pollen from soil beneath an infant burial at Broken K Pueblo in east-central Arizona suggested that the plant or its pollen was used in some form of mortuary ritual during mallow-growing season (Hill and Hevly 1968:207–208). Most insect-pollinated plant percentages are considered "high" at five percent, so one of 45 percent is quite extraordinary. In northeastern Arizona, Gish provided support for Hill and Hevly's initial interpretation by remarking, "Sufficiently consistent evidence exists from several sites to suggest that ritual inclusions of mallow flowers, as indicated by aggregates, are real attributes of burials" (1982:205). Gish also found high frequencies of *Portulaca* pollen (seven percent) and aggregates of up to ten grains each beneath a metate on a floor, in conjunction with over 800 *Portulaca* seeds from the same context secured by flotation (Gish 1982:183).

Human transport of anemophilous (wind-carried) pollen into prehistoric contexts is usually recognized by spectral distortions (Bohrer 1971, 1981b, 1986), the presence of pollen aggregates (clumps) not easily dispersed far from the parent plant (Bohrer 1981b; Gish 1982, 1991), and an assessment of pollen concentrations (Bohrer 1981b; Reinhard et al. 1991). Interpreting prehistoric use of wind-pollinated plants is difficult because of the ubiquity of airborne pollen grains. This is especially true when weedy plants once grew near occupied dwellings and unintentionally increased pollen production.

Unfortunately, diverse plant parts trap a variety of unrelated, wind-carried pollen. For example, Adams (1988:634) found high amounts of oak (*Quercus*) pollen on insect-pollinated manzanita (*Arctostaphylos*), barberry (*Berberis*), and currant (*Ribes*). Human harvests of such fruit might unwittingly introduce additional concentrations of oak pollen into a site or feature. The constant, unintended introductions of such pollen over the life-span of the home (20 years?), together with natural wind deposition, must be weighed against the steady habitual introduction of pollen from harvested plants with an indeterminate collective blossom (plants that bear mature seeds or fruits below while flowers are blooming above, such as alkali sacaton grass or goosefoot). Such plants, whose seed heads are commonly beaten over a basket, are especially likely to release pollen and immature aggregates of pollen along with seed into the container. Clearly, both the botany of the potentially harvested species and aspects of human behavior need thoughtful consideration in any seasonality interpretation.

Interpretations from several prehistoric sites exemplify the role anemophilous pollen types play in seasonality. At the Hay Hollow site in Arizona, high concentrations of Mormon tea (*Ephedra*) pollen in a fire pit and storage pit suggested these features were in use during the spring pollinating season, while high percentages of cheno-am (Chenopodiaceae/*Amaranthus*) pollen from cooking pits and grinding stones, supported by seed evidence, implied use during the summer growing season (Bohrer 1972). Outdoor work surfaces in central Arizona (Bohrer 1984:216) and a locale on the plaza of Arroyo Hondo Pueblo in New Mexico (Bohrer 1986:201) also bore sufficiently elevated percentages of cheno-am pollen to suggest seed utilization.

## Pollen in Human Coprolites

Pollen in human coprolites can provide strong evidence of season of food ingestion, especially if coupled with seed and plant cuticle analysis. Certain open, arid sites such as sand dunes (Wilke 1978) and interior rooms of pueblos (Bohrer 1980:140) preserve coprolites. More mesic environments rarely preserve coprolites. Again, assuming that pollen or flowers were not stored, high concentrations of insect-transported pollen in human coprolites suggest season of consumption. However, wind-transported pollen can enter the digestive system in drinking water or via vegetative parts sought for different reasons. For example, during the spring, any flexible *Salix/Populus* twigs split with the teeth for basketry might carry ample amounts of willow or cottonwood pollen into the digestive track.

Season of ingestion has been suggested by a number of pollen studies. Cattail (*Typha*) pollen appears to have been eaten in some quantity in spring by inhabitants of Lake Cahuilla in southern California (Wilke 1978:74) and at Lovelock Cave, Nevada (Napton and Kelso 1969). Prehistoric inhabitants of Glen Canyon in southern Utah and Antelope House in Canyon de Chelly, Arizona, ate cottonwood (*Populus* sp.) pollen (Martin and Sharrock 1964:174; Williams-Dean and Bryant 1975:108), an early spring resource still utilized in the form of cottonwood catkins among modern Navajos (Elmore 1944:38) and pueblos (Castetter 1935:43). The high percentage of entomophilous yucca (*Yucca*) pollen in a Texas coprolite suggests someone ate yucca flowers, available in early summer (Bryant 1969).

## Seeds and Fruit in Coprolites

Seeds of fleshy fruit can express short-term or single-season seasonality. Assuming consumption accompanies gathering, season of ingestion is strongly indicated when seeds of fleshy fruit are recovered in human coprolites. At Antelope House in Arizona, prickly pear cactus fruits or tunas were assumed to have been consumed fresh in summer due to the high percentages of seeds in four coprolites (Williams-Dean and Bryant 1975:109). Not all fleshy fruit is eaten shortly following harvest, however, and processing can lengthen period of availability and mute seasonality. In Arizona the sweet, fleshy fruit of the saguaro (*Carnegiea gigantea*) cactus provides a dependable and predictable harvest that is routinely processed and stored for later use (Crosswhite 1980).

## Condition as an Indicator of Seasonality

The condition of reproductive parts can reveal something about timing of acquisition. There are examples in the ethnographic record that seeds or nuts are prepared for use or storage by parching or roasting shortly after being picked (Castetter and Underhill 1935:24; Castetter and Bell 1942:181). Recovery of swollen and distorted charred seeds suggests they burned when high in moisture content, probably not long after gathering.

Burned, durable waste products (e.g., rachis joints, spikelet fragments, acorn caps) can offer seasonality clues, assuming that such parts have become charred during processing closely linked in time to harvesting. A number of sites from the Ash Creek area of central Arizona contained few barley (*Hordeum pusillum*) waste products, leading to speculation that people occupied the sites during March or April, when barley can be harvested and processed (Kwiatkowski 1992:63).

Season of harvest is also implied by the presence of charred unripe fruit that would likely have degraded had it not burned shortly after harvest. Charred immature *Yucca* fruit that had not yet split open suggested a late summer harvest at Ancestral Puebloan sites in southwest Colorado (Brandt 1991a, 1991b). Two similar sites in New Mexico preserved burned cholla (*Opuntia*) flower buds, probably picked between May and July (Bohrer 1980:308; Brandt 1991c). Since oven roasting or boiling, followed by drying, are common methods of preparing cholla buds for storage (Greenhouse et al. 1981), the morphologies of fresh (plump, larger) vs. processed (wrinkled, smaller) may be helpful in determining whether cholla buds burned when fresh or in storage.

## Associations that Suggest Seasonality of Last Use

When assemblages of plant parts recovered together are all available in a particular season, the simplest explanation is that they represent harvest from that season. If they appear to be the last materials deposited, the season of last use may be inferred. Contexts such as thermal features (hearths, firepits, roasting pits, ashpits) and catastrophically burned structures can contain residue of final seasonally specific events. In a Pueblo I hamlet in southwestern Colorado, the association of a number of late summer/early fall resources, coupled with evidence of sagebrush (*Artemisia tridentata*) flowering heads in a stage of maturity known to occur in September, suggested that abandonment of some structures occurred in early fall (Adams 1993b). In a central New Mexican early Ancestral Puebloan site swept by fire, the recovery of stacked corn (*Zea mays*) ears on a pithouse floor, along with an abundance of pinyon (*Pinus edulis*) type nutshells and a generally low presence of weedy summer annuals, implied that the last use of the site occurred in late October or early November (Brandt 1991d).

Interpretations of single-season events can also be based on limited resource harvests. Plant remains from three Archaic age dune-related sites along the lower Chaco River in northwestern New Mexico suggested short-term occupation at intervals throughout the growing season (Toll 1983:338–340; Toll and Cully 1983). Food products at a given site or use area consistently represented a single segment of the summer growing cycle, either early (ricegrass) or late (goosefoot, dropseed). This picture of intermittent occupation by mobile bands was corroborated by the absence of structures, storage facilities, well-used prepared hearths, or any readily exploitable perennial crops (Toll and Cully 1983).

## Seasonality Expressed by Photosynthetic Pathway

Charred grass (Gramineae) grains identified to genus or species level can be utilized to suggest sea-

son(s) of food acquisition, roof thatching, or other uses. Grains of taxa that follow the C3 photosynthetic pathway are more likely to represent cool season (spring and/or fall) resources, while those following the C4 pathway represent warm season grasses that mature in the summer (Waller and Lewis 1979). Identification of southwestern prehistoric grasses of economic importance reveals a predominance of cool season species (Bohrer 1975b, 1987; Crane 1977; Wilke 1978:75). However, no presumptions should be made of the seasonal affiliation of the numerous references to "unidentified" grasses extant in many archaeobotanical reports, since ethnographic accounts report consumption of a variety of warm season grasses (Doebley 1984) rare or unrecognized archaeologically.

## Seasonality Expressed by Vegetative Parts

Seasonality interpretations can be based on vegetative parts, provided one knows the timing of plant part development. In arid areas, natural clues abound. For example, failure of the final outer tree ring to complete growth can help pinpoint season of tree cutting. Numerous structural timbers from Long House and Mug House in Mesa Verde were cut either in spring or early summer during their period of rapid growth, as indicated by the presence of incomplete outer rings (Graham 1965:173). The habit of cutting or burning back lemonade-berry bushes (*Rhus aromatica*) in the fall to induce spring growth of long and flexible "sucker" shoots for basketry documents two seasons of human presence where these sucker shoots have been used for basketry or for other needs (Bohrer 1983). At Arroyo Hondo, a child burial included a broken branch of Douglas fir (*Pseudotsuga*), complete with needles and exhibiting swollen terminal leaf buds indicative of a spring cutting (Lang 1986:260).

## MULTISEASON EXPRESSIONS

Multiseason use of an area or presence at a site is suggested when a number of single-season indicators are recovered that represent both cool and warm seasons. As with single-season scenarios, certain assumptions underlie these interpretations (table 1). At two large pueblos in New Mexico, the diversity of taxa and parts in the archaeobotanical records suggested spring through fall occupation (Doebley 1976; Adams 1987), as they did at Homol'ovi III in northern Arizona (Adams 1992).

For southwestern agricultural groups that raised warm-season crops introduced from Mexico, recovery of corn (*Zea mays*), cucurbits (*Cucurbita*), beans (*Phaseolus*), gourds (*Lagenaria*), or cotton (*Gossypium*) implies presence minimally during both late spring planting and fall harvest seasons. If flowering parts are found, midsummer activities are also suggested. At Mesa Verde National Park, recovery of unopened staminate florets (tassels) *and* mature stalks and cobs of corn (*Zea mays*) revealed human activities some weeks apart during the growing season (Cutler and Meyer 1965).

## Proportions of Weed Species to Climax Species

Mobile groups following a broad seasonal round of economic activities would be expected to leave different weed species to climax species records than semisedentary or sedentary groups in more permanent multiseason residences. Perhaps sedentism could be inferred from the amount of disturbance a given environmental setting sustained while people lived there, assuming higher disturbance levels imply higher numbers of people and/or longer periods of residence. Field houses adjacent to large agricultural plots might also be expected to contain evidence of disturbed ground species that flourish in fields. Complicating this issue, some Great Basin prehistoric groups intentionally sought resources in early successional habitats, for example by harvesting pickleweed seeds (*Allenrolfea*) around lake edges (Madsen and Berry 1975:403). In the Southwest, disturbed environments probably existed at Chaco Canyon, New Mexico, where both the pollen record in coprolites (Clary 1984:270) and the macrobotanical record (Toll 1984:244) indicate that the main dietary components were cultivars and weeds. Elsewhere, the human coprolite record at Clyde's Cavern in Utah revealed that disturbed ground species were gradually added to the diet (Winter and Wylie 1974), suggesting that humans had access to an increasingly disturbed environment, some of it likely due to their own activities.

## Plant-insect Interactions

Multiseason occupation can also be recognized via insect damage to stored resources. The longer mesquite pods are kept after harvest, the more bruchid (*Bruchus*)

beetle holes they acquire (Bell and Castetter 1937:24). The first author has observed cycles of hatching and reinfestation over more than 12 months in stored mesquite pods, and with each cycle the pods acquire additional holes. Charred pods with beetle holes in an ancient site would suggest some period of storage prior to burning (Bohrer 1973; Swenson 1984). In another example, prehistoric Ancestral Puebloans in the Mesa Verde area of southwestern Colorado apparently capitalized on the ability of bark beetles and phloem wood borers to help loosen bark from conifer trees cut in late spring or early summer. However, humans finished debarking the trees prior to late July or early August, preventing the insects from burrowing into the wood itself (Graham 1965).

# YEAR-ROUND OCCUPATION

Periods of dormancy, whether due to winter cold or summer drought, rarely offer unique resources. One such resource in the Mojave desert of southern California is a member of the sunflower family known as gray sandplant (*Dicoria canescens*). It grows after late summer rains on open sands, bearing abundant seed in December and January. The achenes (fruit) of this plant were recovered in human coprolites covered by dunes (Wilke 1978:77) and proved critical in establishing dune occupation in winter. Few cases are as clear-cut as this however.

For any site with storage facilities that preserves a range of cool and warm season plant resources, the likelihood increases for occupation through the winter or during a period of drought-induced dormancy (table 1). Coprolites might independently reveal a deterioration in quality of human diets as foodstuffs become scarce. At Salmon Ruin in northwestern New Mexico, yucca (*Yucca*) leaves and juniper (*Juniperus*) bark in human coprolites suggested a period of food stress (Bohrer 1980). Both these resources are nutritionally deficient "aseasonal" foods. In another example, some plants (e.g., cacti, *Juniperus*, *Atriplex canescens*, and *Cucurbita foetidissima*) that retain their reproductive parts for long periods following maturity can provide "on the plant" storage (Bohrer 1981a). If recovered together in an archaeological deposit, such an assemblage of parts might reflect occupation during a period of plant dormancy. The authors know of no way to use pollen in a similar manner.

TABLE 2

**Summary of some arid Southwestern United States archaeobotanical indicators of seasonality**

| | SHORT-TERM | MULTIPLE SEASONS | YEAR-ROUND |
|---|---|---|---|
| **Wild Plants** | | | |
| Pollen | Single season represented in features or coprolite population | Cool and warm seasons in features or coprolite population | |
| Seeds/Fruit | Perishable fruit of single season in coprolite population | Perishable fruit of more than one season in coprolite population | Fruit stored "on the plant" *may* be sought in winter or during drought dormancy |
| | Parched seeds of a single season swollen with moisture from a recent harvest | Parched seeds of more than one season swollen with moisture | |
| | Species of short-term availability (known from the local ecology) present | Species of long-term or overlapping periods of availability present; species with "shifting" seasonality present | |
| Grains | Cool *or* warm season grass grains present | Cool *and* warm season grass grains present | |
| Vegetative Parts | Spring evidence for cutting of shrub shoots; immature carbonized plant parts reveal presence in a period of restricted availability | | Reduction in quality of diet may occur in winter of during drought when "aseasonal" parts eaten |
| Cultivated Plants | None | Agricultural products imply multiseason (planting, harvesting) presence required of crop growers | |
| | | Presence of both flowering parts and mature parts of a single crop reveals multiseason activities | |
| Plant-insect Interactions | None | Insect damage to stored resources; a seasonal cycle of insect damge to trees interrupted by humans | |
| Ecology Insights | Many climax species utilized | Higher proportion of disturbed ground species signals multiple-season presence | |

# DISCUSSION

Archaeobotanical remains in arid Southwestern United States sites can contribute information about the seasonal nature of certain prehistoric activities, as summarized in table 2. The prehistoric plant record offers insights that range from single-season events to year-round occupation of an area. However, the data are best used in conjunction with all the architecture, material culture, and additional biological information the site has to offer. The archaeobotanical record should be accompanied by observations of the timing of maturation of local resources and of how long following ripening the resources can be harvested. The complete archaeobotanical record of cool and warm season resources at a site, often preserved in midden and other secondary deposits, is more likely to reveal multiseason presence in an area. Specific contexts with debris representing original use, such as thermal features, burned storerooms, or abandoned floor assemblages, are most likely to suggest season of last use and/or site abandonment. A look at the proportions of disturbed ground to climax species can suggest levels of prehistoric environmental disturbance reflecting length of occupation, increases in population, or both. Such information may help distinguish sedentary from mobile groups.

## Acknowledgments

Many of the archaeobotanical seasonality examples presented in this paper were assembled by V. L. Bohrer for a 1971 School of American Research Seminar on "Seasonal Economic Patterns in Prehistory," chaired by Dr. Cynthia Irwin-Williams. Adams thanks Crow Canyon Archaeological Center in Cortez, Colorado for research support. The authors both acknowledge the help of Dr. Joe D. Stewart, Suzanne K. Fish, and Joe Keleher for helpful perspective on text clarity and content.

## Notes

1. *Webster's Third New International Dictionary Unabridged*, s.v. "phenology."
2. Native plant terminology conforms primarily to *A Utah Flora* (Welsh et al. 1987), except for a small number of Sonoran desert taxa cited in *Arizona Flora* (Kearney and Peebles 1960).

# BIBLIOGRAPHY

Adams, K. R.
1987 "Domesticated and Native Plants Recovered from Robinson Pueblo and other Regional Sites in the Capitan, New Mexico Area." University of Calgary, Alberta, Canada. Unpublished manuscript.
1988 "The Ethnobotany and Phenology of Plants in and Adjacent to Two Riparian Habitats in Southeastern Arizona." Ph.D. diss., University of Arizona, Tucson.
1992 "Charred Plant Remains from HP-36 (AZ:J:14:36) and Homol'ovi III (AZ:J:14:14) in North-central Arizona." Arizona State Museum, Tucson. Unpublished manuscript.
1993a "Phenology (Seasonality) Studies of Native Plants in the Sand Canyon Locality Considered Important Prehistoric Resources." Crow Canyon Archaeological Center, Cortez, Colorado. Unpublished manuscript.
1993b "Carbonized Plant Remains," in *The Duckfoot Site*. Vol. 1, *Descriptive Archaeology*, R. R. Lightfoot and M. C. Etzkorn, eds., pp. 195–220. Crow Canyon Archaeological Center Occasional Paper 3. Cortez, Colorado.

Beatley, J. C.
1974 "Phenological Events and Their Environmental Triggers in Mojave Desert Ecosystems." *Ecology* 55:856–863.

Bell, W. H., and E. F. Castetter
1937 *Ethnobiological Studies in the American Southwest, V. The Utilization of Mesquite and Screwbean by the Aborigines in the American Southwest.* University of New Mexico Bulletin 314, Biological Series 5:2. Albuquerque.

Bohrer, V. L.
1971 "The Paleoecologic Evidence for Seasonal Patterns in Prehistory." Paper presented at an Advanced Seminar on Seasonal Economic Patterns in Prehistory, School of American Research, Santa Fe.
1972 "Paleoecology of the Hay Hollow Site, Arizona." *Fieldiana, Anthropology* 63(1):1–30.
1973 "Ethnobotany of Point of Pines Ruin, Arizona W:10:50." *Economic Botany* 27(4):423–437.
1975a "The Role of Seasonality in the Annual Harvest of Native Food Plants in the Puerco Valley, Northwest of Albuquerque, New Mexico." *New Mexico Academy of Science Bulletin* 15(2):3.
1975b "The Prehistoric and Historic Role of the Cool Season Grasses in the Southwest." *Economic Botany* 29(3):199–207.

1980 "Dietary Components in Fecal Remains," in *Investigations at the Salmon Site: The Structure of Chacoan Society in the Northern Southwest III*, C. I. Williams and P. H. Shelley, eds., pp. 319–322. Eastern New Mexico University Print Services, Portales.

1981a "Former Dietary Patterns of People as Determined from Archaic-Age Plant Remains from Fresnal Shelter, Southcentral New Mexico." *The Artifact* 19(3–4):41–50.

1981b "Methods of Recognizing Cultural Activity from Pollen in Archaeological Sites." *The Kiva* 46:135–142.

1983 "New Life from Ashes: The Tale of the Burnt Bush (*Rhus trilobata*)." *Desert Plants* 5(3):122–124.

1984 "Domesticated and Wild Crops in the CAEP Study Area," in *Prehistoric Cultural Development in Central Arizona: Archaeology of the Upper New River Region*, P. M. Spoerl and G. J. Gumerman, eds., pp. 183–259. Center for Archaeological Investigations Occasional Paper 5. Southern Illinois University, Carbondale.

1986 "Ethnobotanical Pollen," in *Arroyo Hondo Archaeological Series*, vol. 6, W. Wetterstrom, ed., pp. 187–250. School of American Research, Santa Fe, New Mexico.

1987 "The Plant Remains from La Ciudad, A Hohokam Site in Phoenix," in *Specialized Studies in the Economy, Environment and Culture of La Ciudad*, J. E. Kisselburg, G. E. Rice, and B. L. Shears, eds., pp. 67–237. Anthropological Field Studies 20, pt. III. Office of Cultural Resource Management, Arizona State University, Tempe.

Brandt, C. B.
1991a *Early Agriculture in Montezuma Valley: Analysis of Archaeobotanical Remains from the Towaoc Canal Reach II Project*. Zuni Archaeology Program Ethnobiological Technical Series, no. 91-1. Zuni, New Mexico.

1991b *Macrobotanical Remains from Hanson Pueblo, Site 5MT3876, Southwestern Colorado*. Zuni Archaeology Program Ethnobiological Technical Series, no. 91-13. Zuni, New Mexico.

1991c *The River's Edge Archaeobotanical Analysis: Patterns in Plant Refuse*. Zuni Archaeology Program Ethnobiological Technical Series, no. 91-2. Zuni, New Mexico.

1991d *The River's Edge Archaeobotanical Analysis: Phase II Data Recovery*. Zuni Archaeology Program Ethnobiological Technical Series, no. 91-14. Zuni, New Mexico.

Bryant, V.
1969 "Late Full-glacial and Postglacial Pollen Analysis of Texas Sediments." Ph.D. diss., University of Texas, Austin.

Castetter, E. F.
1935 *I. Uncultivated Native Plants Used as Sources of Food. Ethnobiological Studies in the American Southwest*. University of New Mexico Bulletin 266, Biological Series 4(1). Albuquerque.

Castetter, E. F., and W. H. Bell
1942 *Pima and Papago Indian Agriculture*. Inter-American Studies 1. University of New Mexico Press, Albuquerque.

Castetter, E. F., and R. Underhill
1935 *Ethnobiological Studies in the American Southwest II. The Ethnobiology of the Papago Indians*. University of New Mexico Bulletin 275, Biological Series 4(8). Albuquerque.

Clary, K. H.
1984 "Anasazi Diet and Subsistence as Revealed by Coprolites from Chaco Canyon," in *Recent Research on Chaco Prehistory*, W. J. Judge and J. D. Schelberg, eds., pp. 265–279. Reports of the Chaco Center 8. Division of Cultural Research, U.S. Dept. of Interior, National Park Service, Albuquerque.

Crane, C. J.
1977 "A Comparison of Archaeological Sites on the Uncompahgre Plateau and Adjacent Areas." Master's thesis, Eastern New Mexico University, Portales.

Crosswhite, F. S.
1980 "The Annual Saguaro Harvest and Crop Cycle of the Papago, with Reference to Ecology and Symbolism." *Desert Plants* 2(1):2–62.

Curtin, L. S. M.
1984 *By the Prophet of the Earth. Ethnobotany of the Pima* (1949). Reprint, University of Arizona Press, Tucson.

Cutler, H. C., and W. Meyer
1965 "Corn and Cucurbits from Wetherill Mesa." *American Antiquity* 31(2, pt. 2):136–152.

Davis, O. K., and S. L. Buchmann
1992 "Ground-Nesting Bees in Southwestern U.S.A.: A Potential Source of Pollen Clumps in Archeological Sites." University of Arizona, Tucson. Unpublished manuscript.

Doebley, J. F.
1976 "A Preliminary Study of Wild Plant Remains Recovered by Flotation at Salmon Ruin, New Mexico." Master's thesis, Eastern New Mexico University, Portales.

1984 "'Seeds' of Wild Grasses: A Major Food of Southwestern Indians." *Economic Botany* 38(1):52–64.

Elmore, F. H.
1944 *Ethnobotany of the Navajo*. Monographs of the School of American Research 8. Santa Fe, New Mexico.

Elson, M. D.
1992 "A Methodological Approach to the Study of Sedentism," in *The Rye Creek Project. Archaeology in the Upper Tonto Basin*. Vol. 3, *Synthesis and Conclusions*, M. D. Elson and D. B. Craig, eds. pp. 79–105. Center for Desert Archaeology Anthropological Papers 11. Tucson.

Felger, R. S., and M. B. Moser
1985 *Peoples of the Desert and Sea*. University of Arizona Press, Tucson.

Fowler, C. S.
1976 "The Processing of Ricegrass by Great Basin Indians." *Mentzelia* 2:2–4.

Gish, J. W.
1982 "Pollen Results," in *The Coronado Project Archaeological Investigations, Salt River Project. The Specialist's Volume: Biocultural Analysis*, R. E. Gasser, ed., pp. 96–224. Museum of Northern Arizona Coronado Series 4, Museum of Northern Arizona Research Paper 23. Flagstaff.
1991 "Current Perceptions, Recent Discoveries and Future Directions in Hohokam Palynology." *Kiva* 56(3):237–254.

Graham, S. A.
1965 "Entomology: An Aid in Archaeological Studies," in *Contributions of the Wetherill Mesa Archaeological Project*, D. Osborne, ed., pp. 167–174. Society for American Archaeology, Memoir 19. Salt Lake City, Utah.

Greenhouse, R., R. E. Gasser, and J. W. Gish
1981 "Cholla Bud Roasting Pits: An Ethnoarchaeological Example." *The Kiva* 46(4):227–242.

Hill, J. N., and R. H. Hevly
1968 "Pollen at Broken K Pueblo: Some New Interpretations." *American Antiquity* 33(2):200–210.

Kearney, T. H., and R. H. Peebles
1960 *Arizona Flora*. With supplement. University of California Press, Berkeley.

Kwiatkowski, S.
1992 "The Rye Creek Flotation and Macrobotanical Analyses," in *The Rye Creek Project: Archaeology in the Upper Tonto Basin*. Vol. 2, *Artifact and Specific Analyses*, M. D. Elson and D. B. Craig, eds., pp. 325–375. Center for Desert Archaeology Anthropological Papers 11. Tucson.

Lamont, B. B., D. C. Le Maitre, R. M. Cowling, and N. J. Enright
1991 "Canopy Seed Storage in Woody Plants." *The Botanical Review* 57:277–317.

Lang, R. W.
1986 "Artifacts of Woody Materials," in *Arroyo Hondo Archaeological Series*, vol. 6, W. Wetterstrom, ed., pp. 251–276. School of American Research, Santa Fe, New Mexico.

Lanner, R. M.
1981 *The Pinon Pine, A Natural and Cultural History*. University of Nevada Press, Reno.

Little, E. L., Jr.
1938 *Food Analysis of Pinyon Nuts*. USDA Forest Service, Southwest Forest and Range Experiment Station, Research Note 48.

Madsen, D. B., and M. S. Berry
1975 "A Reassessment of Northeastern Great Basin Prehistory." *American Antiquity* 40(4):391–405.

Martin, P. S., and F. W. Sharrock
1964 "Pollen Analysis of Prehistoric Human Feces: A New Approach to Ethnobotany." *American Antiquity* 30(2):168–180.

Miksicek, C. H.
1987 "Formation Processes of the Archaeobotanical Record," in *Advances in Archaeological Method and Theory*, vol. 10, M. B. Schiffer, ed., pp. 211–248. Academic Press, New York.

Minnis, P.
1981 "Seeds in Archaeological Sites: Sources and Some Interpretive Problems." *American Antiquity* 48(1):143–152.

Monks, G. G.
1981 "Seasonality Studies," in *Advances in Archaeological Method and Theory*, vol. 4, M. B. Schiffer, ed., pp. 177–240. Academic Press, New York.

Nabhan, G. P.
1985 *Gathering the Desert*. University of Arizona Press, Tucson.

Napton, L. K., and G. K. Kelso
1969 "Preliminary Palynological Analysis of Human Coprolites from Lovelock Cave, Nevada," in *Archaeological and Paleobiological Investigations in Lovelock Cave, Nevada: Further Analysis of Human Coprolites*, L. K. Napton, ed., pp. 19–27. The Kroeber Anthropological Society Papers, Special Publication 2. Berkeley, California.

Reinhard, K. J.
    1992 "Parasitology as an Interpretive Tool in Archaeol-
        ogy." *American Antiquity* 57(2):231–245.

Reinhard, K. J., D. L. Hamilton, and R. H. Hevly
    1991 "Use of Pollen Concentration in Paleopharmacol-
        ogy: Coprolite Evidence of Medicinal Plants." *Jour-
        nal of Ethnobiology* 11(1):117–132.

Swenson, J. D.
    1984 "A Cache of Mesquite Beans from the Mecca Hills,
        Salton Basin, California." *Journal of California and
        Great Basin Anthropology* 6(2):246–252.

Thomson, D. F.
    1939 "The Seasonal Factor in Human Culture." Pro-
        ceedings of the Prehistoric Society 5(2):209–221.

Toll, M. S.
    1983 "Changing Patterns of Plant Utilization for Food
        and Fuel: Evidence from Flotation and Macrobotan-
        ical Remains," in *Economy and Interaction Along
        the Lower Chaco River: The Navajo Mine Archeo-
        logical Program, Mining Area III, San Juan County,
        New Mexico*, P. Hogan and J. C. Winter, eds., pp.
        331–350. Office of Contract Archaeology and
        Maxwell Museum of Anthropology, New Mexico.
    1984 "Taxonomic Diversity in Flotation and Macrobot-
        anical Assemblages from Chaco Canyon," in *Recent
        Research on Chaco Prehistory*, W. J. Judge and J. D.
        Schelberg, eds., pp. 241–245. Reports of the Chaco
        Center 8. Division of Cultural Research, U.S. Dept.
        of Interior, National Park Service, Albuquerque.

Toll, M. S., and A. C. Cully
    1983 "Archaic Subsistence in the Four Corners Area: Ev-
        idence for a Hypothetical Seasonal Round," in
        *Economy and Interaction Along the Lower Chaco
        River: The Navajo Mine Archeological Program,
        Mining Area III, San Juan County, New Mexico*, P.
        Hogan and J. C. Winter, eds., pp. 385–391. Office
        of Contract Archaeology and Maxwell Museum of
        Anthropology, New Mexico.

Vestal, P. A.
    1952 *Ethnobotany of the Ramah Navajo*. Papers of
        the Peabody Museum of American Archaeology
        and Ethnology, vol. 40(4). Harvard University,
        Cambridge.

Waller, S. S., and J. K. Lewis
    1979 "Occurrence of C3 and C4 Photosynthetic Path-
        ways in North American Grasses." *Journal of
        Range Management* 32(1):12–28.

Welsh, S. L., N. D. Atwood, S. Goodrich, and L. C. Higgins,
eds.
    1987 *A Utah Flora*. Great Basin Naturalist Memoirs 9.
        Brigham Young University, Provo, Utah.

Wilke, P. J.
    1978 *Late Prehistoric Human Ecology at Lake Cahuilla,
        Coachella Valley, California*. Contributions of the
        University of California Archaeological Research
        Facility 38. University of California, Berkeley.

Williams-Dean, G., and V. Bryant, Jr.
    1975 "Pollen Analysis of Human Coprolites from Ante-
        lope House." *The Kiva* 41(1):97–111.

Winter, J. C., and H. G. Wylie
    1974 "Paleoecology and Diet at Clyde's Cavern." *Amer-
        ican Antiquity* 39(2):303–315.

CHAPTER 9 | Measuring Sedentism with Fauna: Archaic Cultures along the Southwest Florida Coast

*Michael Russo*
*National Park Service*

## THE PROBLEM OF MEASURING SEDENTISM

In the southeastern United States, "Archaic" was originally conceived as a developmental stage in cultural prehistory representing a transition between the nomadic hunting cultures of the early Paleoindians 12,000–10,000 years ago and the incipient agricultural societies that marked the later Woodland/Formative periods 2,700–1,000 years ago. As transitional cultures, Archaic societies (10,000 to 2700 B.P.) were viewed as seasonally nomadic people who moved about the landscape in relation to the periodic abundances of local flora and fauna that constituted their subsistence economies. They differed from Paleoindians in their increased reliance on smaller game, fish, and native plants. The extinction of Pleistocene fauna during the Paleoindian period was viewed as one catalyst that forced Archaic hunter-gatherers to become "increasingly familiar with the natural resources." This, in turn, allowed them to stay at resource collection areas for longer, seasonal periods, an intermediate stage in the evolution to full sedentism.

One result of the "recurrent occupation of restricted localities" was larger, more visible archaeological sites, which, in the interior of the continent, took the form of deeper deposits of artifactual material covering more extensive areas. Along some marine coasts and freshwater rivers and lakes, the recurrent occupations were manifest in the form of deep and extensive shell middens of sizes that suggested sedentary villages.

However, most archaeologists assumed that the presence of shell exaggerated the actual size of any single period of occupation, and the absence of large storage pits, pottery, permanent shelters, ceremonial mounds, and domesticated plants (all of which were expressions of later Woodland/Formative sedentary cultures) was viewed as tangible evidence that these Archaic cultures had not yet achieved permanently settled "development" (Griffin 1952:352–356; Willey and Phillips 1958:104–118; Smith 1986).

In the past few years this limited view of the Archaic has been changing. Markers originally used to define post-Archaic stage developments have all been identified at numerous Archaic period sites across the Southeast. Storage pits, pottery, domesticated plants, public architecture in the form of large ceremonial mounds, and mound complexes have all been identified in the Middle to Late Archaic period about 6000 to 4000 B.P. (e.g., Stoltman 1978; Goodyear et al. 1979:111; Smith 1986:24–27; Steponaitis 1986:373; Abrams 1989:56; Russo 1991b, 1994b; Saunders and Allen 1991; Sassaman 1993; Saunders et al. 1994), and a number of archaeologists have argued that permanently settled villages were associated with these sites (Gibson 1973, 1996; DePratter 1979; Trinkley 1980; Russo 1991b, 1994b, 1996a, 1996b; Russo and Ste. Claire 1993). As such, the appropriate placement of Archaic cultures in the Southeastern "sedentism continuum" requires reconsideration. Is the Archaic a period of semisedentary cultural development across the Southeast, or were some Archaic cultures fully sedentary? Without clearly defined archeological markers of sedentism, how do we test for it?

Unfortunately, middle-range theory linking archaeological features to sedentism is not well developed. Because of this, supportive evidence for sedentism such as pottery, substantial structures, and mound construction, when found in Archaic contexts, has not fully satisfied the archaeological community as evidence of a year-round, permanently settled pattern of living. Thus more direct measures of sedentism are required.

It is the goal of this chapter to offer empirical evidence that the people of Archaic period cultures along Florida's southwest coast were sedentary villagers at least 3,000 years before such a pattern of settlement was thought to have evolved in the Southeast. To this end, a discussion of the traditional markers of sedentism (storage pits, shelters, ceremonial mound construction, large village area, and a subsistence economy as dependable and productive as agricultural economies) is presented in limited form. Since these markers in and of themselves, however, are not universally accepted as evidence for fully sedentary societies, the bulk of the chapter will present methods and data to demonstrate that occupations were year-round rather than seasonal. Specifically, empirical methods of determining the seasonality of six of the most common species of shellfish and fish in the subsistence economy of preceramic Archaic peoples from Horr's Island and related sites are presented. These seasonal determinations are, in turn, used to test whether the site was occupied during a single season as originally suggested (McMichael 1982) or on a year-round basis.

## MIDDLE AND LATE ARCHAIC SITES ALONG FLORIDA'S SOUTHWEST COAST

Prior to the identification of Horr's Island (McMichael 1982) and Useppa Island (Milanich et al. 1984) (fig. 1), coastal preceramic Archaic sites in the Southeast were virtually unknown. Preceramic components were often suspected to lie beneath more recent middens in Florida (Goggin 1952:41) or to be drowned offshore (Goggin 1948), but none had been positively identified. The handful of known Archaic sites along the coast of Florida were small and thought to be seasonal encampments of seminomadic peoples from the interior of the Florida Peninsula (Milanich and Fairbanks 1980; Widmer 1988:204, 211). Because of this mind set, even the identification of the larger sites on Horr's and Useppa Islands resulted in initial interpretations of them as such temporary encampments (Milanich et al. 1984), their large size the result of

repeated visits. The mounds situated on top of the deep Archaic deposits at Horr's Island were dismissed as later, protohistoric constructions (McMichael 1982). Once more intensive work was undertaken on Horr's Island, revealing the size of the site as three times that originally thought and the mounds contemporaneous with the Archaic midden deposits, the view of the site as a temporary encampment came under challenge (Russo 1991b).

The Horr's Island Archaic site sits atop a tall (12–15 meter) island sand dune. Horr's Island and adjacent Marco Island represent two of the few habitable (i.e., high and dry) parcels of land in a coast otherwise dominated by tidal mangrove swamps. The extensive shell midden deposits constituting the Archaic village site (8Cr209) on Horr's Island extend for over 1,000 meters and contain large numbers of post molds suggestive of domestic structures. Living floors characterized by numerous hearths, pits, and postmolds are extensive and overlay each other to a depth of four meters, suggesting long-lived occupations. Radiocarbon dates from the village indicate it was occupied between 3,600 and 7,200 years ago, with the primary occupations occurring between 4,400 and 5,200 years ago (Russo 1991b, 1994a, 1996a, 1996b). No sterile horizons are found in the village deposits, indicating continuous occupation. Adjacent to a central living area 300 meters long, mounded middens consisting of shell, bone, and charcoal remains form an encircling ridge up to five meters in depth (fig. 2).

Two large ceremonial mounds were constructed at the time the Archaic village was occupied. Mound D is located 300 meters east of the village and consists of a central sand mound capped with oyster shell. The apex of Mound D (8Cr211) lies 14 meters above the adjacent Gulf waters and reaches a height of four meters above the dune crest on which it sits.

Mound A (8Cr208) lies within the confines of the village and extends six meters above the dune crest. Like Mound D it consists of a central core sand mound but contains more numerous building episodes characterized by alternating layers of shell and sand. The mound was built on top of early village deposits and is abutted by the shell ridge which encircles the village. Nearby, a smaller mound, Mound B, yielded a flexed burial: a male, 40 years old at the time of death and radiocarbon dated to 4030±230 B.P. (Beta Analytic 35347; corrected and calibrated to a mean of 4480 B.P.). These data combined with overlapping radiocarbon dates from mound and village contexts (Russo 1991b, 1996a, 1996b) indicate contemporaneity of mound construction and site occupation.

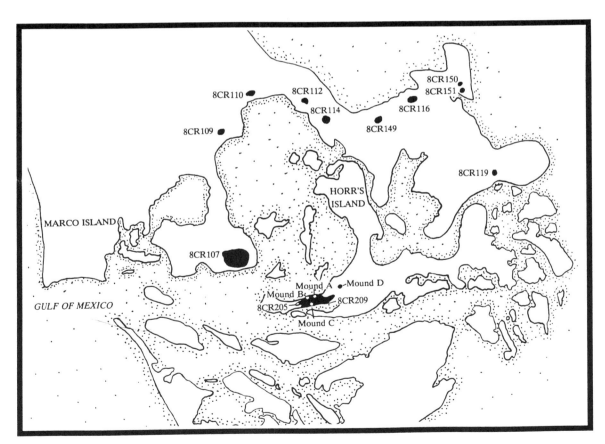

**Figure 1.** Coastal Archaic sites in southwest Florida.

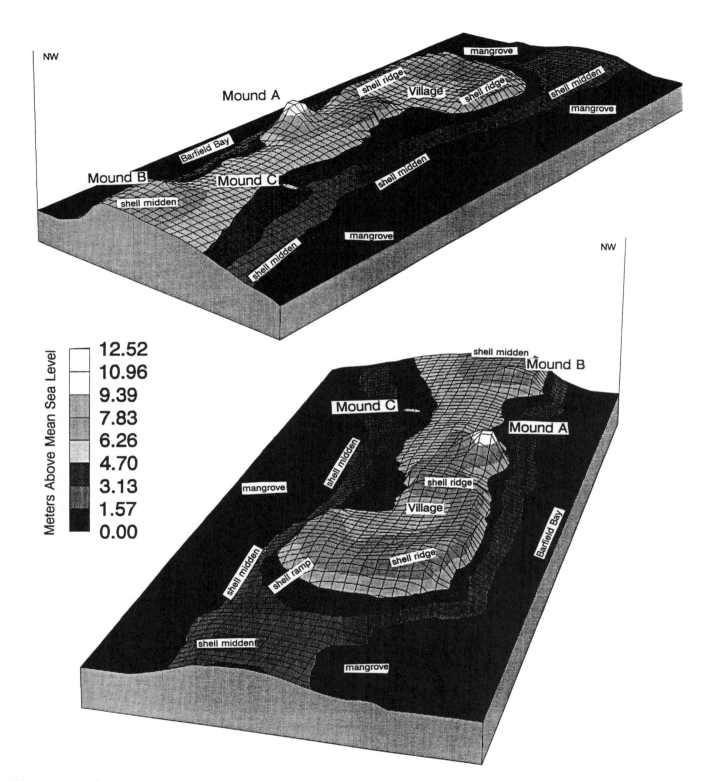

**Figure 2.** Southwestern Horr's Island—Archaic midden and mounds.

A number of Archaic sites have been identified on the adjacent Marco Island. These consist of both extensive and isolated shell middens, most of which lay atop Pleistocene dune ridges. Beyond this, little is known of the sites (Cockrell 1970; Widmer 1974). Nearby on the mainland, the Bayhead Camp Site (8Cr225) and Pelican Bay (8Cr687) have been identified as small scatters of shell midden with Archaic components that lie on or near sand ridges (Estabrook 1989). At one scatter, seasonal analyses revealed that quahog and scallops had been collected during the spring (Russo 1989) and that the site functioned as a seasonal collection station.

Like Horr's Island, Useppa Island sits atop a tall Pleistocene sand dune. It, however, is a much smaller shell midden with no associated mounds. The site was originally interpreted as a shell processing station intermittently used by hunter-gathers from the interior of peninsular Florida (Milanich et al. 1984). More recent work confirms that an extensive shell tool technology had developed during the preceramic Archaic on Useppa Island (Torrence 1992), but the connection of the site with interior groups has been called into question (Russo 1991b). The kinds, numbers, and full range of reductive technologies is similar to those found on Horr's Island, indicating both manufacture and in situ use of the tools on the coast. Seasonality measures have indicated multiseasonal occupation, but the data are preliminary (Torrence 1992) and most data are not yet available for citation.

The sites on Marco, Useppa, and Horr's Islands as well as the two mainland sites represent the only known preceramic Archaic sites on the southwest Florida coast from Charlotte Harbor to the tip of Florida. Their location on top of Pleistocene dunes and low sand ridges supports the long-held view that most Archaic sites have probably been drowned by rising sea levels. The serendipitous location of these few sites above the rising waters combined with their abundant subsistence remains provides the basis for investigations into the pattern of settlement of the little-known coastal Archaic groups.

## MEASURING SEASONALITY TO DETERMINE THE DEGREE OF SEDENTISM

Seasonal occupation of sites is more often assumed than measured. Once a model is developed for a region, sites are fit into the hypothesized seasonal pattern with little or no independent testing of the model's accuracy.

A tautology develops: how does one determine if an upland site with no evidence of shelter or storage pits is a seasonal encampment and not a permanent residence? The fact that there are no household structures or storage pits is one indication. That these features may not have preserved or may not be archaeologically visible is obscured by the model. One way to overcome this tautology is to test the seasonality and hence, the degree of sedentism of a site independent of standard archaeological correlates.

Zooarchaeological and archaeobotanical data have most frequently provided the independent measures of seasonality. Unfortunately, technical problems attend such measures. Plant remains are commonly not preserved at sites, and faunal remains, although more common, may not be associated with any particular season. Seasonality measures are not yet well developed for most faunal species, and interpretations of plant remains that preserve archaeologically are often ambiguous. Although seeds, nuts, and fruits that ripen at certain times of the year have all been used as seasonal indicators of site occupations, the tenuous nature of botanical preservation and the tendency of cultures to store large amounts of these resources beyond their season of harvest frequently renders the use of archaeobotanical remains as seasonal indicators uncertain, unquantifiable, or ambiguous. For example, natural seed fall at a site, if preserved, may yield evidence of seasonality, but there is always the question of what season is being measured, the season of site occupation or the season of seed fall. Bridging arguments are always required to clarify the link of seeds to seasonal patterns of cultural activity (see Adams and Bohrer, this volume [eds.]). Similar problems arise with faunal remains such as deer antlers, which only grow in the winter, but can be collected after they are shed.

## ZOOARCHAEOLOGICAL MEASURES OF SEASONALITY

### Ambiguous Measures of Seasonality: Presence/Absence

In coastal Florida, due to their generally better preservation, zooarchaeological data are more abundant than archaeobotanical data and thus produce larger samples. In determining seasonality at archaeological sites, large samples provide a distinct advantage since they are subject to descriptive and statistical measures of confidence that reduce the ambiguity normally associated with interpretations of seasonality. On this point, I have arbitrarily defined three types of zooarchaeological measures of seasonality and related their potential accuracy to varying levels of confidence. These confidence levels are based in part on the ability of each measure to produce sufficiently large samples for statistical or descriptive tests.

The least persuasive tests are based on mere presence or absence of seasonally occurring species and are considered "ambiguous" because the occurrence or absence of an individual, in and of itself, does not constitute patterned subsistence behavior. For example, the presence of migratory fauna in small numbers (e.g., Neill et al. 1956:394) does not inspire confidence in a prediction of a winter occupation because other archaeological, cultural, or natural processes such as postcultural intrusion, cultural heirlooming, or natural in situ death can account for the isolated presence of an individual bird specimen. Conversely, the absence of a particular species is poor evidence of season of occupation because other factors, the most obvious being small sample size and differential preservation, may account for its absence. Thus the absence of winter migratory waterfowl (as has been encountered among the Horr's Island samples) is insufficient evidence to suggest a warm weather occupation of sites. And obviously the presence of migratory waterfowl, even in significant numbers, is insufficient evidence to suggest an occupation only during winter because the other fauna in an assemblage may have been collected at other times of the year.

Additionally, because presence/absence measures of seasonality treat one species as if it is as important as another, a rarely exploited species from a site is treated as an equally valid measure of site seasonality as the most frequently exploited species (Monks 1981:182). In Florida, the presence of a few bones of deer (traditionally cited as a fall/winter resource because of the peak physical condition of deer at this time of year) in a midden otherwise dominated by coquina shell has been used to suggest a winter occupation of the coast. In these cases the large quantities of shellfish undoubtedly brought the hunter/gatherers to the coast, and determination of the seasonality of the shellfish is more appropriate for determining site occupation. (When actually measured, coquina is most often found to have been collected in the summer [Russo 1993; cf. Miller 1980]).

The presence of certain seasonal growth phenomena in individual animals has also been employed to infer period of capture. For example, the schedule of tooth eruption and epiphysial fusion for the young of several species has been correlated with the stage of tooth and bone development observed in zooarchaeological assemblages to predict season of death.

There are problems with this presence/absence method in coastal middens. Although the time schedules for certain, measurable aspects of growth in animals are rapidly being obtained, most known schedules are for mammals, particularly domesticates. Even these may not have great predictive authority because nutritional and other forms of stress can greatly affect the modal period of epiphysial fusion or tooth eruption (Saxon and Higham 1969:303). However, the primary problem lies in the fact that in coastal Florida, mammal remains are relatively uncommon in zooarchaeological assemblages. Russo (1991b) has shown that it may take up to 1,000 hours to excavate, process, and identify a vertebrate sample of 300 MNI. Of these, typically less than ten percent, or 30 MNI, may be mammals. Of these, one MNI may be deer. Consequently, the chances of obtaining a sufficiently large sample of deer skeletal remains exhibiting physiological conditions pertinent to seasonality are slim. Seasonal measures of more abundant species are required.

## Modal Size Classes as Measures of Seasonality

More accessible and reliable tests of seasonality from abundant species can be obtained through the measure of their population structures. As might be expected from settlements along the southwest Florida coast, fish and shellfish remains provide the most readily available archaeological samples for seasonality measures.

Fish and shellfish have annual cycles of growth and reproduction in which new sets of individuals are produced yearly. In coastal Florida, this is often, but not always, in the spring. These sets, called "young-of-the-year," are usually the most numerous size class in the population for any given species. The adaptive strategy of these fish and shellfish is to produce great numbers of young to compensate for a high predation rate. The consequence is that young-of-the-year age classes are always the most abundant in a species' population. Because the young-of-the-year of certain species grow at known rates throughout the year, those rates can be used to predict the modal size of young-of-the-year. Thus at any given time of the year, the young-of-the-year age class will have the greatest number of individuals of any age class, and their modal size is predictable.

As long as prehistoric human groups were targeting species for the young-of-the-year class or capturing all the size classes of a given species randomly (e.g., using fine mesh nets that prevent the loss of small individuals), the measure of the modal size of the species can be used to determine season of capture. Individuals older than a year (i.e., of a known size too large for young-of-the-year) can be excluded from measure.

Although modal size classes may be used to infer seasons of collection of fish and shellfish, size of individual specimens normally cannot. For most species, individuals of many size classes may be found within a population at a given time. Thus individuals may not be of the seasonal modal size class. That is, any given individual may lie outside the mode, and to appropriately use average sizes of young-of-the-year to measure seasonality, one must assure that the outliers are not what is being measured.

The use of population size classes as predictors of seasonality is intuitively more satisfying, more reliable, and less ambiguous than presence/absence measures. Larger sample sizes allow for the use of descriptive and probability statistics to measure the accuracy of the prediction. That is, the closeness of fit of a zooarchaeological size class distribution curve can be visually or numerically compared with that of a modern curve. With presence/absence data, the degree to which seasonal indicators predict seasonality cannot be measured—the indicator is either there or it is not.

## Incremental Growth Structures as Measures of Seasonality

Potentially the most rigorous measures of seasonality are those of incremental growth, that is, "skeletal" growth structures that form in an annually predictable pattern. Such growth increments are found in the annuli of bivalves, in fish scales, otoliths, vertebra, and other skeletal elements. These structures are most often linked to periodic stress in the environment reflected in the growth of individual animals. Such stresses may include annual changes in temperature, nutrition, or reproductive cycle connected with changes in the season.

Growth increments have been most effectively employed when used as probabilistic measures of population structure. The best known use of incremental growth seasonality from coastal midden data has been applied to the quahogs (*Mercenaria* spp.). These clams deposit measurable, alternating, accretional growth "rings" seasonally throughout the year. As with modal-size-class measures, however, the occurrence of these incremental growths is probabilistic. That is, in any one season an individual quahog may or may not exhibit the increment found in most other quahogs. Therefore, single individuals cannot be used to predict seasonality with any degree of confidence. Rather, a random sample can be measured and known ratios of the growth phases in a seasonal population can be used to retrodict the seasonality of an archaeological assemblage (Quitmyer et al. 1985).

Effectively then, the measure of incremental growth is really a measure of modal-size-class structure. Most individuals are in a particular phase, or size, of annual incremental growth during a particular season as most individual young-of-the-year are of a particular size during a given season. However, there is one practical advantage of modal-incremental-growth-phase measures over size-class measures of young-of-the-year. That is that incremental-growth-phase studies can be used to measure individuals of any age or size, whereas modal-size-class studies are usually limited to young-of-the-year. With incremental growth measures, biases in collection favoring certain size classes will not interfere with seasonal prediction since all size classes will contain these growth increments. Although many practical problems exist for both size-class and incremental-growth seasonality measures (Russo 1991a), they remain the most rigorous zooarchaeological tests of seasonality when used in conjunction with well-studied contemporary analogues.

In southwest Florida nearly all zooarchaeological measures of seasonality, when they have been employed at all, have measured seasonality with the presence/absence method. The goal in this chapter is to offer some reliable and rigorous measures of seasonality based on the population structure and incremental growth of the most abundant species recovered at Horr's Island and associated sites in an effort to develop an empirically derived data base on which to test current models of seasonality and sedentism.

## Seasonal Measures of Southern Quahog

Quahogs are large, hard-shelled clams found in coastal waters from New England to the Gulf of Mexico. They are commonly found in prehistoric coastal middens throughout Florida (Quitmyer et al. 1985; Quitmyer 1990). The species of quahogs that are found in southwest Florida, *Mercenaria campechiensis*, or the southern quahog, grow larger than the northern species and inhabit shallow marine and estuarine waters in a variety of substrates including sand and mud.

The most efficient nontechnological method of collecting quahogs is collection at low tide when water levels expose individuals to the touch of hand or foot. The large, hard clams are readily observed or felt and easily removed from the sand or mud by hand. Extremely low tides characteristic of spring may facilitate collection, although even in deep waters quahogs are easily collected by diving or raking from a small watercraft.

Quahogs have been extensively studied for annual growth increments, which have been used to determine age, growth rate, and season of death (Clark 1979; Quitmyer et al. 1985; Jones et al. 1990). In cross section, valves cut radially exhibit alternating opaque (light) and translucent (dark) bands or phases of growth. In southwest Florida these bands have been strongly correlated with changes in temperature and salinity, which occur throughout the year (Jones et al. 1990:219). During the months of spring, most quahogs exhibit opaque (O) increments of growth. During the rest of the year, a given population is dominated by individuals in the translucent (T) stage of growth (fig. 3).

Quahog shell growth is accretionary. Thus the phase of growth at the time of death can be viewed at the ventral margin. The degree to which growth has progressed into either the light or dark phase can be assessed by comparing the size of the last formed increment of growth (at the shell margin) to the average size of the two preceding increments of the same phase. A convention has been established that divides quahog growth into six phases. If, for example, the size of an ultimate translucent growth band is one-third or less the size of the average of the two previous yearly translucent bands, the clam is in a T1 phase. If it is between one-third and two-thirds, it is in the T2 phase, and if it is more than two-thirds but less than the complete expected mean size, it is in the T3 phase. A similar application is made to the opaque phases of growth (Quitmyer and Jones 1988). From these fine-grained distinctions of growth phases, the relative percentages of phases of growth in a zooarchaeological sample of clams can be graphed for comparison to known seasonal distributions, and season of collection can be predicted.

At Horr's Island, quahogs were the thirdmost commonly exploited shellfish species. Seasonal analysis was conducted on 29 samples of quahogs from village contexts and associated middens. The most common seasons for exploitation of quahogs were spring and summer (fig. 4). Quahogs were collected in the fall and winter less often. In summary, however, they were collected throughout the year.

## Seasonal Measures of Oysters

Along the coast of the southeastern United States, oysters, which are often synonymized with all prehistoric shellfish resources, have been variably described as a resource exploitable throughout the year, a cold weather resource, and a warm weather resource eaten when nothing more nutritional and palatable was available (Milanich and Fairbanks 1980:150; Trinkley 1980; Steinen 1984; Crook 1986:25; Russo 1988:168–169). Empirical tests of oyster seasonality have been few and are problematic (Ruppé 1980; Hardin and Russo 1987; Lawrence 1989; Custer and Doms 1990).

The most common model suggests that prehistorically oysters were exploited during winter because during hot summer months they yield less nutrients and are subject to disease during spawning. Seen as a cold weather resource, oysters are the draw that brought prehistoric people to the coast, but only seasonally during cold weather when other resources were less abundant (Milanich and Fairbanks 1980:150; McMichael 1982:81; Steinen 1984:169; Crook 1986:25). In contrast to this view, it has been suggested that oysters are capable of providing protein, fat, carbohydrates, and trace elements in nutritionally beneficial amounts (Watt and Merrill 1975) regardless of the time of year (cf., Larson 1980:226; Russo 1991a, 1996b).

The direct measure of incremental growth structures in oysters has been a long-sought goal characterized in the past by failures to observe measurable increments (Lutz 1976; Palmer and Carriker 1979). More recently there have been successes (Kent 1988; Custer and Doms 1990) some of which are not always replicable (Quick and Mackin 1971; Ruppé 1980; Lawrence 1988) due to limited geographic applicability or inadequate detailing of method. The assumption that incremental breaks in oyster shell correlate with annual breaks in growth (Stenzel 1971; Sambol and Finks 1977; Waselkov 1982) has recently been observed in the ligostracum of the hinge of the oyster (Kent 1988; Lawrence 1988; Custer and Doms 1990). Kent (1988) has successfully retrodicted season of oyster collection from historic assemblages of subtidal shell from Maryland using a method of measuring annual growth similar to that described for quahogs. Not all oysters, however, are measurable. A minimum requirement is that oysters be at least three to five years in age in order to compare the annual phases of growth to previous yearly averages. Unfortunately, farther south in Florida, oysters experience a faster

| Growth Increment (G.I.) | Phase | Radial cross-section of the ventral margin | Description of growth phase |
|---|---|---|---|
| G.I. 1 Translucent | T1 |  | G.I. 1 forming on marginal edge |
| | T2 |  | G.I. 1 half complete |
| | T3 |  | G.I. 1 complete |
| G.I. 2 Opaque | O1 |  | G.I. 2 forming on marginal edge |
| | O2 |  | G.I. 2 half complete |
| | O3 |  | G.I. 2 complete |

**Figure 3.** Growth increments in Quahogs. After Quitmyer et al. 1985.

growth rate which allows individuals to reach edible size in one to two years (Quick 1972), and few oysters in archaeological middens have attained the required age to be effectively read. To date, no application of the method put forward by Kent (1988; Custer and Doms 1990:153–154) has been successfully applied to Florida zooarchaeological collections.

## Boonea impressa as a Seasonal Indicator of Oyster Collection

The impressed odostome (*Boonea impressa*) is an ectoparasitic gastropod commonly found in the shallow-water oyster reef communities of the eastern Atlantic and Gulf coasts of the United States. Distribution and behavior in nature suggest that the primary host of the odostome is the common eastern oyster

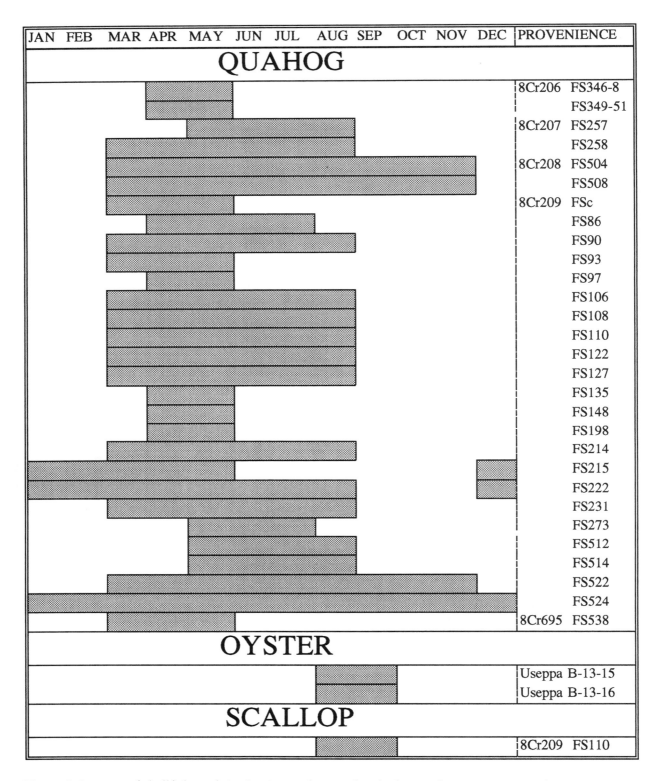

**Figure 4.** Seasons of shellfish exploitation in southwest Florida during the preceramic Archaic.

(Robertson and Mau-Lastovicka 1979; White et al. 1984). Archaeological faunal assemblages in the Southeast support this association. When excavation methods are adequate for the recovery of the small snails, the odostome is often the most common gastropod in oyster middens (Quitmyer 1985:98–111; Hardin and Russo 1987; Russo 1991a).

The close association of the parasite with oysters makes the impressed odostome an ideal subject for studying the seasonal oyster collection pattern of prehistoric peoples. The general pattern of *B. impressa* growth is similar across a wide geographical range of studies from North Carolina to Texas (Russo 1991a). Cohorts of impressed odostome live for approximately one year. The principal cohort begins life in the late spring and early summer months of May and June. The average size of *B. impressa* increases throughout the year until spring of the following year when the previous year's cohort made up of large and moribund individuals dies off and the new year's cohort (young-of-the-year) is recruited (fig. 5).

Samples of the impressed odostome were meager from collections made at Horr's Island despite the fact that oysters were the most abundant shellfish in all middens and the standard recovery technique employed 1/64" mesh at all sites. However, to test McMichael's (1982:81) hypothesis that oysters were a winter resource, measures of impressed odostomes were applied to two samples recovered from late Archaic contexts on Useppa Island. These reveal that both collections of oyster were made in the late summer (fig. 4).

These data, combined with similar data from elsewhere in Florida, suggest that the idea that oysters are inedible during the summer was not practiced prehistorically. Based on their numbers in prehistoric middens and the direct measure of their seasonality, oys-

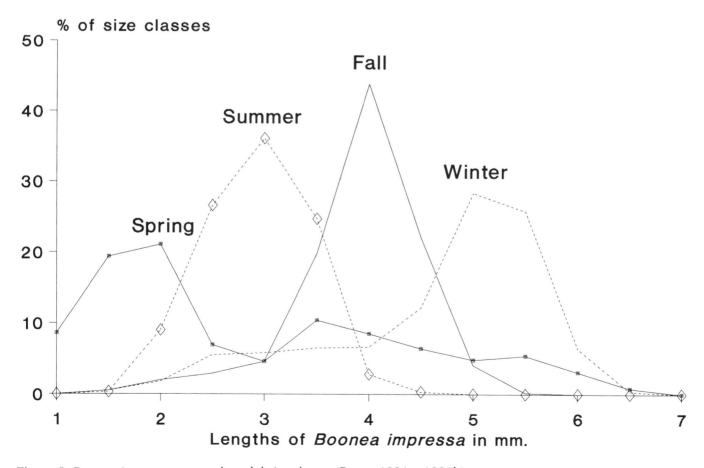

Figure 5. *Boonea impressa* seasonal modal size classes (Russo 1991a, 1991b).

ters served as a cold-weather, warm-weather, and year-round resource for prehistoric populations in Florida and Georgia (Russo 1993). There is no a priori reason to believe that oyster consumption was limited to cold weather during the Archaic in southwest Florida.

### Seasonal Measures of Scallops

Growth patterns of scallops have long been studied in eastern North America, but somewhat more limited numbers of studies have been conducted on the bay scallops (*Argopecten irradians concentricus*), the scallop most commonly exploited in southwest Florida. Most claims that bay scallops migrate great distances from inland estuaries and lagoons to deep, open ocean waters in concert with seasonal changes have been put forward by fishermen and have not been sub-

stantiated by scientific studies (Broom 1976; Winter and Hamilton 1985). Along the Gulf Coast of Florida, the bay scallop has been shown to be present in the estuaries throughout the year, but its abundance and size classes change with the seasons (Barber and Blake 1983). The annual cycle of growth commences during winter with slow growth associated with cold water temperatures and the size of scallops averaging less than 20 mm in height (fig. 6). Rapid growth proceeds as water temperatures increase in early spring (March) and continues through June when average shell height reaches 50 mm. Growth continues through September when shell height averages 60 mm until spawning occurs in October. After spawning, mass mortality occurs with few scallops living into a second year. During the winter, the growth cycle begins again (Barber and Blake 1983).

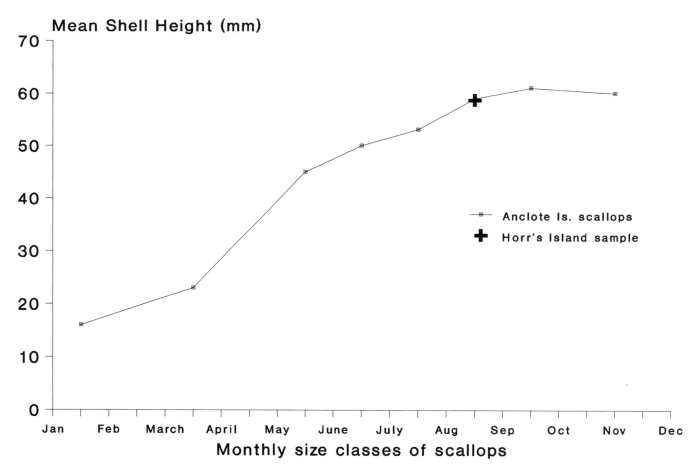

**Figure 6.** Monthly mean size class for bay scallops (*Argopecten irradians*) from Anclote Island, Florida compared to archaeological sample (F.S. 110) from Horr's Island (Russo 1991b).

Large Florida bay scallops are not abundant enough to make their exploitation profitable from late fall to early spring. Further, their growth cycle suggests that from late spring to fall the mean size of scallops increases steadily, allowing prediction of the month of capture of a randomly collected sample of scallops (Austin and Russo 1989; Russo and Quitmyer 1996).

The area around Horr's Island represents the southern distribution limit of the bay scallop. Just north of the area, Late Archaic populations extensively exploited the scallop (Bullen and Bullen 1976; Russo and Quitmyer 1996). The farther south the scallop lives, however, it becomes subject to increasing energetic requirements associated with higher mean annual water temperatures. This probably lessened its ability to reproduce (Barber and Blake 1983) at Horr's Island. Nonetheless, excavations at Horr's Island suggest that the scallop was exploited throughout the Late Archaic occupation in relatively small amounts, and these amounts help establish a warm weather occupation of the site. Calculating the average size of scallops from FS 110, Unit 1, Level 11, a small locus (less than 25 cm in diameter) within a living floor of 8Cr209, and comparing the mean to those shown in figure 6 yields a collection date during the summer (fig. 4).

## Seasonal Measures of Hardhead Catfish

The Late Archaic populations on Horr's Island spent a great deal of subsistence effort on the capture of fish. A wide diversity of species were exploited, most typically those inhabiting estuarine and lagoonal environments. Three species were abundant enough across numerous archaeological proveniences to yield important seasonal data. These species are the hardhead catfish, the most frequently collected species at Horr's Island, pinfish, and threadfin herring.

The use of the *presence* of hardhead or sea catfish in coastal middens as a seasonal indicator of collection in the Southeast has been cautioned against (Reitz 1982:81; Sigler-Eisenberg and Russo 1986:27) based on biological literature suggesting that seasonal movements of the catfish in and out of the estuary are variable from year to year and among locales (Dahlberg 1972; Muncy and Wingo 1983). The relative abundance of certain size classes of the hardhead catfish in coastal estuaries, however, has been noted by researchers (Muncy and Wingo 1983). Pristas and Trent (1978) noted that catfish in southwest Florida estuaries were found in greater numbers in warmer weather, with adults leaving for deeper, offshore

waters during extremes of cold weather. This does not mean that adult catfish abandon estuaries in winter. As Gunter and Hall (1965) note, adults and juveniles are found in the shallow waters of estuaries and lagoons throughout the year.

Size-class population structure within estuaries, however, does vary throughout the year, and thus a measure of modal size classes can be used to determine season of collection. Wang and Raney (1971) have traced shifts in modal size classes as young-of-the-year grow. Like odostomes and scallops, age zero, or young-of-the-year, dominate the population structure in typical estuarine settings. Unlike odostomes and scallops, sea catfish have a life expectancy greater than one year. Most sea catfish, however, do not live longer than two years, although they can live as long as eight. The result is that in any given year, the age-zero class of fish will dominate a population and can be measured for their modal size to determine what time of year a midden faunal assemblage was collected.

Lengths of fish were estimated from zooarchaeological remains using linear allometric formulae (Russo 1991b). Comparison of 11 samples from 8Cr209, 8Cr696 (fig. 7), and 8Cr695 to population distributions obtained by Wang and Raney (1971) from Charlotte Harbor clearly show that young-of-the-year were the primary target size. Adults, classified here as over 150 mm in length (Muncy and Wingo 1983:4), were rarely captured. The most frequently occurring size class indicates that the fish were typically caught sometime in the fall, around September or October (fig. 8). A smaller number of samples indicate a late summer collection.

## Seasonal Measures of Pinfish

Evidence from Horr's Island presented here and elsewhere (McMichael 1982) and from sites in the Charlotte Harbor area (Milanich et al. 1984; Walker 1992) suggests that pinfish were commonly captured and consumed, then deposited and preserved in aboriginal middens (cf., Widmer 1988:51). These relatively small fish typically inhabit the shallow sandflats and mangrove swamps surrounding Horr's Island where seagrass is abundant, and in the more northern sections of Florida where mangroves are not present, they can be found throughout the estuaries. Weinstein et al. (1977) note that a distinct seasonal distribution of size classes occurs within the estuaries. Zero-age-class pinfish are most abundant from January to July when the modal size class increases from around 13 mm to 50

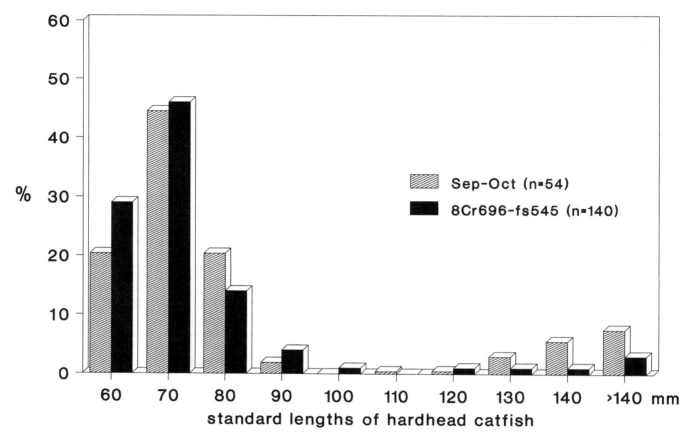

**Figure 7.** Comparison of an archaeological sample of hardhead catfish (*Ariopsis felis*) from a Horr's Island Archaic site to known seasonal modal-size-class distributions from southwest Florida (Russo 1991b).

mm. Pinfish largely abandoned the estuaries in the fall and early winter, with relatively few large (above 86 mm) individuals remaining. Having grown throughout the year, most individuals have matured by winter and leave the estuary to spawn in deeper ocean waters. Although pinfish can live up to three years, most second-year pinfish do not return to the shallow inland bays and estuaries (Darcy 1984:10). Wang and Raney's (1971) data from Charlotte Harbor confirm this general pattern in which small fish dominate a population in the spring and to a lesser extent winter, while fall populations attained their largest modal sizes before leaving the estuary.

Estimates of pinfish lengths from zooarchaeological samples were obtained through the allometric measurement of atlases (Russo 1991b). By comparing the general pattern observed in modern studies and the specific size classes from Charlotte Harbor (fig. 9)

to those pinfish data obtained from Horr's Island, a reliable retrodiction of the season of capture can be estimated. Figure 8 demonstrates that, like the hardhead catfish, most pinfish were captured in the fall and late summer sometime between August and November, with some being collected in midsummer. The size range of fish caught is similar to that of the small catfish recovered, standard length 20–200 mm (Russo 1991b).

## Seasonal Measures of Threadfin Herring

A distinct seasonality for threadfin herring can be found within the estuaries and other shallow coastal waters of southwest Florida. However, most literature on threadfin herring is linked to the offshore fisheries. Threadfin herring most frequently inhabit shallow off-

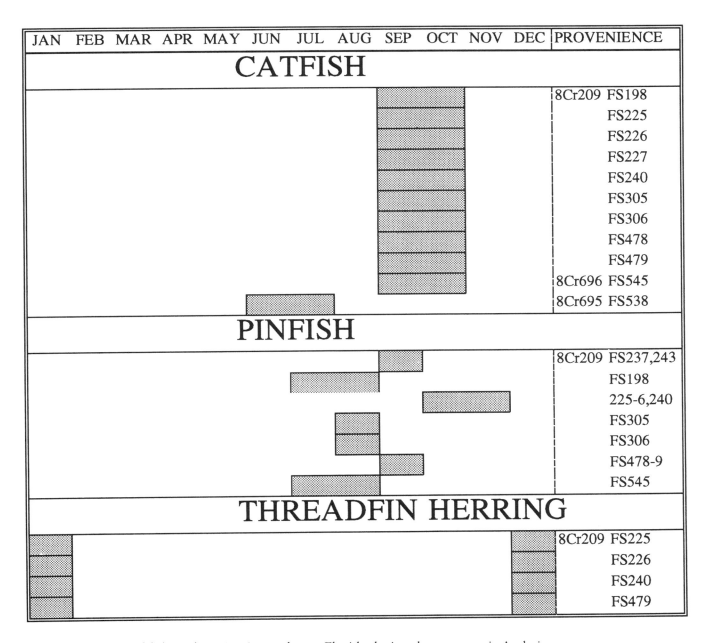

**Figure 8.** Seasons of fish exploitation in southwest Florida during the preceramic Archaic.

shore coastal waters, migrating from the north to south in the Florida Gulf waters and from inshore to offshore waters in the fall and through the winter (Kinnear and Fuss 1971; Finucane and Vaught 1986). Most spawning occurs offshore from February to September with a concentration of activity occurring from March to July or August (Fuss et al. 1969; Prest 1971; Houde 1977;

Finucane and Vaught 1986). At age one, threadfin herring are about 110 mm fork length and reach sexual maturity from 110 to 145 mm fork length (Finucane and Vaught 1986:3–4).

The specific times and degree to which herring occupy shallow intracoastal waters like those that surround Horr's Island is unclear. Most literature relates

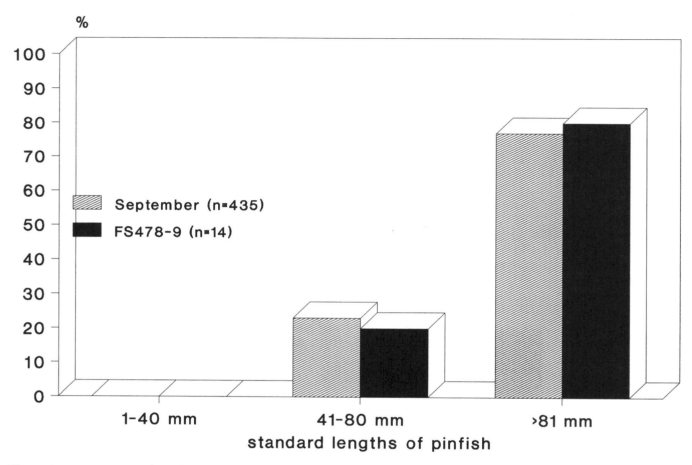

**Figure 9.** Comparison of an archaeological sample of pinfish (*Lagodon rhomboides*) from a Horr's Island Archaic site to known seasonal modal-size-class distribution from southwest Florida (Russo 1991b).

data pertinent to offshore fisheries where spawning, eggs, larva, juveniles, and adults are commonly found together (Finucane and Vaught 1986). Nonetheless, threadfin herring have been reported among the seagrass beds and intracoastal Gulf waters of Florida (Reid 1954; Carr and Adams 1973). Reid (1954:17–18) anecdotally reports large numbers near Cedar Key in September 1951. Threadfin herring were common in collections consisting mostly of spotfin mojarra and scaled sardines I took with a 1/8" mesh drag net pulled through seagrass at San Carlos Pass, Sanibel Island in August 1990 (Russo 1991b). Wang and Raney (1971) collected small numbers in Charlotte Harbor from August to January. The data from Wang and Raney have been used below to provide a tentative seasonal distribution for southwest Florida.

There seems to be a general pattern of increased sizes from late summer to winter within the estuary. In August and September most threadfin herring are below the 110 mm standard length. By December and January the majority are above 110 mm in length (Russo 1991b:237). Archaeological atlases of threadfin herring from Horr's Island were measured and estimates of live lengths allometrically determined (Russo 1991b). By comparing the modern population distribution to that exhibited by four Late Archaic samples from Horr's Island, a winter period of collection seems to have been a common strategy (figure 8). The small sizes of the herring are similar to those of the catfish and pinfish.

## CONCLUSIONS

The goal of this chapter has been to establish reliable and rigorous tests of the season of collection of fisheries resources at Horr's Island during the Late Archaic. Such tests provide empirical data and methods for testing previously untestable hypotheses concerning seasonality and sedentism. The important archaeological problem of distinguishing permanently settled occupations from seasonally settled occupations may ultimately be resolved only with quantifiable measures that can determine seasonal and annual periods of occupation.

Only a few of the faunal resources identified from over 200 species recovered from Horr's Island and other Archaic sites in southwest Florida can, as yet, provide retrodictions of seasonal subsistence strategies. However, these measures demonstrate that key resources were collected throughout the year with seasonal peaks of collection for one resource occurring at different times than that for others. Quahogs were primarily a spring/summer resource but were also collected in other seasons. Scallops were a summer resource. Catfish, pinfish, and threadfin herring were collected mainly in the fall but also in winter and summer. At Horr's Island this seasonal evidence suggests that occupations were not seasonal in the sense of periodic returns at only one time of year as suggested by earlier interpretations of the site (McMichael 1982). The evidence demonstrates that at least some segment of the population was occupying the island and exploiting its abundant coastal fauna throughout the year.

Seasonality data from Useppa Island and mainland Archaic sites indicate that at smaller sites, shellfish were being collected at least during the summer and spring. More numerous Archaic sites exist on the nearby Key Marco, although the seasonality of these sites has not been tested. One possibility is that Archaic settlement in the coastal region was predominated by these small settlements, most of which have not been recognized or have not been preserved due to rising sea level. Whatever the cause for their relative scarcity, it is clear from the limited evidence that the small, seasonal sites surrounding Horr's Island likely articulated with the larger, year-round settlement at Horr's Island. The central, ringed village at Horr's Island provided the seasonality data for this study, indicating year-round occupation. Significant, but less dense midden deposits extend east and west of the central village and have not been tested for their seasons of occupation. It is possible that these areas were home to seasonal visitors who

did not come from interior regions of peninsular Florida, but were relatives and friends who occupied the smaller sites surrounding the village.

The presence of numerous structures, ceremonial mounds, storage pits, the extensive areal distribution of the village—all traditional markers of sedentism—combined with evidence presented above for the year-round collection of fauna supplies substantial evidence that Horr's Island represents a permanent, albeit unexpectedly early, preagricultural, year-round settlement in the Southeast. However, sedentary fisheries-based societies are not unknown for the prehistoric United States. In fact, the heartland of one of the best known permanently settled, mound-building, hierarchically ranked, nonagricultural, fisheries-dependent cultures surrounded the former Archaic occupations of Horr's Island. Here, during the protohistoric period, the Calusa Indians flourished and held hegemony over all of southern Florida where they ruled with armies and marriage alliances and fed their empire on the fisheries resources of marine environments.

In its shell tool technology, dependence on fisheries resources, year-round settlement, and presence of ritual mounds, the Archaic Horr's Island site is like the ceremonial and village settlements of the later Calusa. In fact, because of its size and mounds, it was initially misidentified as a Calusa settlement (McMichael 1982). But it is also different. The fish that supported the village are very small. Unlike Calusa sites, small fish supported the economy to the virtual exclusion of larger fish. The Archaic fishing strategies were designed to exploit the shallow seagrass beds and shoreline mangrove fringes that served as nurseries for small fish and habitats for shallow-water shellfish. Because of their small size, the fish were likely collected with mass capture techniques such as fine nets and scoop baskets.

The Calusa and their immediate ancestors, on the other hand, were less dependent on a single strategy, employing large mesh nets, hooks, composite hooks, gorges, harpoons, diving, leisters, and spears to capture a wider range and large sizes of fish (Walker 1992). Because of our use of fine-mesh screen, the Horr's Island zooarchaeological collection included nearly 200 faunal taxa, the most diverse array of species from any Southeastern archaeological site. Many of the species recovered were nonfood commensal species. Of the food species identified, less then half were subsistence items (Russo 1991b) and of these, only a handful, those used in the seasonality analysis as well as a few other mollusks, provided the major contribution to subsistence. In other words, although the Horr's Island

Archaic had virtually the same tool technology to exploit as wide a range of species and sizes as the later sedentary Calusa cultures, they focused on a few specific species of fish and shellfish.

It is tempting to speculate that the Archaic Horr's Island people's narrow subsistence focus doomed their culture—with the abandonment of Horr's Island, nothing of its size or likeness followed for over 3,000 years. After all, the intensive capture of young-of-the-year fish seems a foolhardy strategy, potentially crippling the fish species' ability to reproduce, and thus limiting the ability of human populations, which survived on the fish, to persist. But human populations were small along the southwest Florida coast during the Archaic, with Horr's Island being the only known large settlement. It is doubtful that intensive or overexploitation of particular species would have done any long term damage to regional fisheries, and the Ten Thousand Islands' estuaries that surround Horr's Island could have supported the island community during any serious local shortfall.

In the end, the long-term, continuous occupation of the site over hundreds of years bespeaks of an efficient, durable subsistence strategy that sustained a community sufficiently large and sedentary to provide the labor to construct ceremonial mounds. I come full circle and ask again the question posed at the start of this chapter—what are the markers of sedentism in the Southeast United States? In short, the data from Horr's Island supports the long held Southeastern view that large mounds are one marker of sedentism—even when they are not built by horticulturalists. It is the seasonality of fauna that tell us that this is so.

## BIBLIOGRAPHY

Abrams, E. M.
 1989 "Architecture and Energy: An Evolutionary Perspective," in *Archaeological Method and Theory*, vol. 1, M. B. Schiffer, ed., pp. 47–88. University of Arizona Press, Tucson.

Austin, R. J., and M. Russo
 1989 "Limited Excavations at the Catfish Creek Site (8So608), Sarasota County, Florida." Report submitted to Palmer Venture, Inc. by Piper Archaeological Research, Inc., St. Petersburg, Florida.

Barber, B. J., and N. J. Blake
 1983 "Growth and Reproduction of the Bay Scallop, Argopecten irradians at its Southern Distributional Limit." *Journal of Experimental Marine Biology and Ecology* 66:247–256.

Broom, M. J.
 1976 *Synopsis of Biological Data on Scallops*. FAO Fisheries Synopsis, no. 114, Food and Agriculture Organization of the United Nations. Rome, Italy.

Bullen, R. P., and A. K. Bullen
 1976 *The Palmer Site*. Florida Anthropological Society Publications, no. 8. Florida Anthropological Society, Gainesville.

Carr, W. E., and C. A. Adams
 1973 "Food Habits of Juvenile Marine Fishes Occupying Seagrass Beds in the Estuarine Zone Near Crystal River, Florida." *Transactions of the American Fisheries Society* 102:511–540.

Clark, G. R., II
 1979 "Seasonal Growth Variations in Shells of Recent and Prehistoric Specimens of *Mercenaria mercenaria* from St. Catherines Island, Georgia." *Anthropological Papers of the American Museum of Natural History* 56:161–172.

Cockrell, W. A.
 1970 "Glades I and Pre-Glades Settlement and Subsistence Patterns on Marco Island (Collier County, Florida)." Master's thesis, Florida State University, Tallahassee.

Crook, M.
 1986 *Mississippi Period Archaeology of the Georgia Coastal Zone*. Georgia Archaeological Research Design Paper, no. 1. University of Georgia, Athens.

Custer, J. F., and K. R. Doms
 1990 "Analysis of Microgrowth Patterns of the American Oyster (*Crassostrea virginica*) in the Middle Atlantic Region of Eastern North America: Archaeological Applications." *Journal of Archaeological Science* 17:151–160.

Dahlberg, M. D.
 1972 "An Ecological Study of Georgia Coastal Fishes." *Fishery Bulletin* 70(2):323–353.

Darcy, G. H.
1984 "Synopsis of Biological Data on the Pinfish, *Lagodon rhomboides* (Pisces:Sparidae)." NOAA Technical Report NMFS 23, FAO Fisheries Synopsis, no. 141. National Oceanic and Atmospheric Administration, National Marine Fisheries Service, Seattle, Washington.

DePratter, C. B.
1979 "Shellmound Archaic on the Georgia Coast." *South Carolina Antiquities* 11(2):1–69.

Estabrook, R.
1989 "Cultural Resource Assessment Survey of the Pelican Bay Development Site, Collier County, Florida." Piper Archaeological Research, Inc., St. Petersburg, Florida. Unpublished manuscript.

Finucane, J. H., and R. N. Vaught
1986 "Species Profile of Atlantic Thread Herring, *Opisthonema oglinum* (Lesueur 1818)." NOAA Technical Memorandum NMFS-SEFC-182. National Oceanic and Atmospheric Administration, National Marine Fisheries Service, Southeast Fisheries Center, Panama City Laboratory, Panama City, Florida.

Fuss, C. M., Jr., J. A. Kelly, Jr., and K. W. Prest, Jr.
1969 "Gulf Thread Herring: Aspects of the Developing Fishery and Biological Research." *Proceedings of the Gulf and Caribbean Fisheries Institute* 21:111–125.

Gibson, J. L.
1973 "Social Systems at Poverty Point: An Analysis of Intersite and Intrasite Variability." Ph.D. diss., Southern Methodist University.
1996 "Poverty Point and Greater Southeastern Prehistory: The Culture that Did Not Fit," in *Archaeology of the Mid-Holocene Southeast*, K. E. Sassaman and D. G. Anderson, eds. University Press of Florida, Gainesville.

Goggin, J. M.
1948 "Florida Archeology and Recent Ecological Changes." *Journal of the Washington Academy of Sciences* 38:225–233.
1952 *Space and Time Perspectives in Northern St. Johns Archeology, Florida.* Yale University Publications in Anthropology, no. 47. Yale University Press, New Haven.

Goodyear, A., S. Upchurch, and M. Brooks
1979 *Laurens-Anderson: An Archaeological Study of the Inter-Riverine Peidmont.* Anthropological Studies 4. Institute of Archeology and Anthropology, University of South Carolina.

Griffin, J. B.
1952 "Culture Periods in Eastern United States Archeology," in *Archeology of Eastern United States*, James B. Griffin, ed., pp. 352–364. University of Chicago Press, Chicago.

Gunter, G., and G. E. Hall
1965 "A Biological Investigation of the Caloosahachee Estuary of Florida." *Gulf Research Report* 2(1):1–71.

Hardin, K., and M. Russo
1987 *Phase II Test Excavations at the Piney Point Site, 8Na31, Amelia Island Florida.* Report Submitted to the Amelia Island Plantation, Florida by Piper Archaeological Research, Inc., St. Petersburg, Florida.

Houde, E. D.
1977 "Abundance and Potential Yield of the Atlantic Thread Herring, *Opisthonema Oglinum*, and Aspects of its Early Life History in the Eastern Gulf of Mexico." *Fishery Bulletin* 75(3):493–512.

Jones, D. S., I. R. Quitmyer, W. S. Arnold, and D. C. Marelli
1990 "Annual Shell Banding, Age, and Growth Rate of Hard Clams (*Mercenaria* spp.) from Florida." *Journal of Shellfish Research* 9(1):215–225.

Kent, B. W.
1988 *Making Dead Oysters Talk: Techniques for Analyzing Oysters from Archaeological Sites.* Maryland Historical Trust, Jefferson Patterson Park and Museum, St. Marys City.

Kinnear, B. S., and C. M. Fuss, Jr.
1971 "Thread Herring Distribution off Florida's West Coast." *Commercial Fisheries Review* 33(7–8): 27–39.

Larson, L. H.
1980 *Aboriginal Subsistence Technology on the Southeastern Coastal Plain During the Late Prehistoric Period.* University Presses of Florida, Gainesville.

Lawrence, D.
1988 "Oysters as Geoarchaeologic Objects." *Geoarchaeology* 3:267–274.
1989 "Oyster Seasonality, Source Environment, and Processing," in *An Archaeological Study of the Minim Island Site: Early Woodland Dynamics in Coastal South Carolina*, C. Espenshade and P. Brockington, Jr., eds., pp. 33–34. Contract No. DACW60-87-C-0005, Department of Army, Corps of Engineers, Charleston.

Lutz, R.
    1976 "Annual Growth Patterns in the Inner Shell of *Mytilus edulis.*" *Journal of the Marine Biological Association* 56:723–731.

McMichael, A. E.
    1982 "A Cultural Resource Assessment of Horr's Island, Collier County, Florida." Master's thesis, University of Florida, Gainesville.

Milanich, J. T., and C. H. Fairbanks
    1980 *Florida Archaeology.* Academic Press, New York.

Milanich, J. T., J. Chapman, A. S. Cordell, S. Hale, and R. A. Marrinan
    1984 "Toward an Understanding of the Prehistoric Development of Calusa Society in Southwest Florida: Excavations on Useppa Island, Lee County," in *Perspectives in Gulf Coast Prehistory*, David D. Davis, ed., pp. 258–314. Ripley P. Bullen Monographs in Anthropology and History, no. 5. University Presses of Florida, Gainesville.

Miller, J.
    1980 "Coquina Middens on the Florida East Coast." *Florida Anthropologist* 33(1):2–16.

Monks, G. C.
    1981 "Seasonality Studies," in *Advances in Archaeological Method and Theory*, vol. 4, M. B. Schiffer, ed., pp. 177–240. Academic Press, New York.

Muncy, R. J., and W. Wingo
    1983 *Species Profiles: Life Histories and Environmental Requirements of Coastal Fishes and Invertebrates (Gulf of Mexico)—Sea Catfish and Gafftopsail Catfish.* Fish and Wildlife Service, U.S. Department of the Interior, Washington D.C.

Neill, W. T., H. J. Gut, and P. Brodkorb
    1956 "Animal Remains from Four Preceramic Sites in Florida." *American Antiquity* 21(4):383–395.

Palmer, R., and M. Carriker
    1979 "Effects of Cultural Conditions on the Morphology of the Shell of the Oyster *Crassostrea virginica.*" *Proceedings of the National Shellfish Association* 69:58–72.

Prest, K. W.
    1971 *Fundamentals Of Sexual Maturation, Spawning, and Fecundity of Thread Herring (Opisthonema oglinum) in the Eastern Gulf of Mexico.* National Marine Fishing Service, St. Petersburg Beach, Florida.

Pristas, P., and L. Trent
    1978 "Seasonal Abundance, Size, and Sex Ratio of Fishes Caught in Gillnets in St. Andrew Bay, Florida." *Bulletin of Marine Science* 28(3):581–589.

Quick, J., Jr.
    1972 "Oyster Parasitism by Labyrinthomyxa marina in Florida." Master's thesis, University of South Florida, Tampa.

Quick, J., Jr., and J. Mackin
    1971 *Oyster Parasitism by Labyrinthomyxa marina in Florida.* Florida Department of Natural Resources Marine Research Laboratory Professional Papers, no. 13. St. Petersburg.

Quitmyer, I.
    1985 "Aboriginal Subsistence Activities in the Kings Bay Locality," in *Aboriginal Subsistence and Settlement Archaeology of the Kings Bay Locality*, W. Adams, ed., pp. 73–91. Report of Investigations, no. 25. University of Florida, Gainesville.
    1990 "The Periodicity of Incremental Shell Growth in the Hard Clam *Mercenaria* spp. in the Southern Portion of its Range and Archaeological Site Paleoseasonality." Paper Presented at the 6th International Conference of the International Council for Archaeozoology, Smithsonian Institute, Washington, D.C.

Quitmyer, I., and D. Jones
    1988 "Calendars of the Coast: Seasonal Growth Increment Patterns in Shells of Modern and Archaeological Southern Quahogs, *Mercenaria campechiensis*, from Charlotte Harbor, Florida." Unpublished manuscript.

Quitmyer, I., S. Hale, and D. S. Jones
    1985 "Paleoseasonality Determination Based on Incremental Shell Growth in the Hard Clam *Mercenaria mercenaria*, and its implications for the Analysis of Three Southeast Georgia Coastal Shell Middens." *Southeastern Archaeology* 4:27–40.

Reid, G. K.
    1954 "An Ecological Study of the Gulf of Mexico Fishes in the Vicinity of Cedar Key, Florida." *Bulletin of Marine Science in the Gulf and Caribbean* 7(1):1–94.

Reitz, E.
    1982 "Vertebrate Fauna from Four Coastal Mississippian Sites." *Journal of Ethnobiology* 2(1):39–61.

Robertson, R., and T. Mau-Lastovicka
1979 "The Ectoparasitism of *Boonea* and *Fargoa* (Gastropoda: Pysramidellidae)." *Biological Bulletin* 157:320–333.

Ruppé, T.
1980 "Analysis of the Mollusks from the Venice Beach Site." *Bureau of Historic Sites and Properties Bulletin* 6:61–69.

Russo, M.
1988 "Coastal Adaptations in Eastern Florida: Models and Methods." *Archaeology of Eastern North America* 16:159–176.
1989 *Faunal Analysis of the Bayhead Camp Site, 8Cr225.* Report submitted to Piper Archaeological Research, Inc., St. Petersburg, Florida.
1991a "A Method for the Measurement of Season and Duration of Oyster Collection: Two Case Studies from the Prehistoric Southeast U.S. Coast." *Journal of Archaeological Science* 18:205–221.
1991b "Archaic Sedentism on the Florida Coast: A Case Study from Horr's Island." Ph.D. diss., University of Florida, Gainesville.
1993 *The Timucuan Ecological and Historic Preserve Phase III Final Report.* Report submitted to Southeast Archeological Center, National Park Service, Tallahassee.
1994a "A Brief Introduction to the Study of Archaic Mounds in the Southeast." *Southeastern Archaeology* 13:89–93.
1994b "Why We Don't Believe in Archaic Ceremonial Mounds and Why We Should: The Case from Florida." *Southeastern Archaeology* 13:93–109.
1996a "Southeastern Mid-Holocene Coastal Settlements," in *Archaeology of the Mid-Holocene Southeast,* K. E. Sassaman and D. G. Anderson, eds. University Press of Florida, Gainesville.
1996b "Southeastern Archaic Mounds," in *Archaeology of the Mid-Holocene Southeast,* K. E. Sassaman and D. G. Anderson, eds. University Press of Florida, Gainesville.

Russo, M., and I. Quitmyer
1996 "Sedentism in Coastal Populations of South Florida," in *Case Studies in Environmental Archaeology,* E. J. Reitz, L. A. Newsom, and S. J. Scudder, eds., pp. 215–231. Plenum Publishing Corporation, New York.

Russo, M., and D. Ste. Claire
1993 "Tomoka Stone: Archaic Period Coastal Settlement in East Florida." *Florida Anthropologist* 45(4):336–346.

Sambol, M., and R. Finks
1977 "Natural Selection in a Cretaceous Oyster." *Paleobiology* 3:1–16.

Sassaman, K. E.
1993 *Early Pottery in the Southeast: Tradition and Innovation in Cooking Technology.* University of Alabama Press, Tuscaloosa.

Saunders, J., and T. Allen
1991 "Evaluation of a Preceramic Mound in Northeast Louisiana." Paper presented at the 48th Annual Meeting of the Southeastern Archaeological Conference, Jackson, Mississippi.

Saunders, J., T. Allen, and R. T. Saucier
1994 "Four Archaic? Mound Complexes in Northeast Louisiana." *Southeastern Archaeology* 13:134–153.

Saxon, A., and C. Higham
1969 "A New Research Method for Economic Prehistorians." *American Antiquity* 34:303–311.

Sigler-Eisenberg, B., and M. Russo
1986 "Seasonality and Function of Small Sites on Florida's Central-East Coast." *Southeastern Archaeology* 5(1):21–31.

Smith, B.
1986 "The Archaeology of the Southeastern United States: From Dalton to DeSoto, 10,500 B.P.–500 B.P." *Advances in World Archaeology* 5:1–92.

Steinen, K.
1984 "Cultural Occupation of the Georgia Coastal Marsh." *Southeastern Archaeology* 3:164–172.

Stenzel, H.
1971 "Oysters," in *Treatise on Invertebrate Paleontology,* pt. N3, Mollusca 6, Bivalvia, R. C. Moore, ed., pp. N953–N1224. University of Kansas Press, Lawrence.

Steponaitis, V.
1986 "Prehistoric Archaeology in the Southeastern United States 1970–1985." *Annual Review of Anthropology* 15:363–404.

Stoltman, J. B.
1978 "Temporal Models in Prehistory: An Example form Eastern North America." *Current Anthropology* 19:703–746.

Torrence, C. M.
   1992 "More than Midden: Opening the Shell around Late Archaic Lifeways." Paper Presented at the 49th meeting of the Southeastern Archaeological Conference, Little Rock, Arkansas.

Trinkley, M.
   1980 "Investigation of the Woodland Period Along the South Carolina Coast." Ph.D. diss., University of North Carolina.

Walker, K. J.
   1992 "The Zooarchaeology of Charlotte Harbor's Prehistoric Maritime Adaptation: Spatial and Temporal Perspectives," in *Culture and Environment in the Domain of the Calusa*, W. H. Marquardt, ed., pp. 265–366. Monograph 1, Institute of Archaeology and Paleoenvironmental Studies. University of Florida, Gainesville.

Wang, J. C. S., and E. C. Raney
   1971 *Distribution and Fluctuations in the Fish Fauna of the Charlotte Harbor Estuary, Florida.* Charlotte Harbor Estuarine Studies, Mote Marine Laboratory, New City Island, Sarasota, Florida.

Waselkov, G.
   1982 "Shellfish Gathering and Shell Midden Archaeology." Ph.D. diss., University of North Carolina.

Watt, B., and A. Merrill
   1975 *Handbook of the Nutritional Contents of Food.* United States Department of Agriculture, Dover Publications, New York.

Weinstein, M. P., C. M. Courtney, and J. Kinch
   1977 "The Marco Island Estuary: A Summary of Physicochemical and Biological Parameters." *Florida Scientist* 40(2):97–124.

White, M., E. Powell, and C. Kitting
   1984 "The Ectoparisitic Gastropod *Boonea (=Odostomia) impressa*: Population Ecology and the Influence of Parasitism on Oyster Growth Rates." *Marine Ecology* 5:283–299.

Widmer, R. J.
   1974 *A Survey and Assessment of Archaeological Resources on Marco Island, Collier County, Florida.* Miscellaneous Projects Report Series, no. 19, Florida Division of Archives, History, and Records Management, Tallahassee.
   1988 *The Evolution of the Calusa: A Nonagricultural Chiefdom on the Southwest Florida Coast.* The University of Alabama Press, Tuscaloosa.

Willey, G. R., and P. Phillips
   1958 *Method and Theory in American Archaeology.* University of Chicago Press, Chicago.

Winter, M. A., and P. V. Hamilton
   1985 "Factors Influencing Swimming in Bay Scallops, *Argopecten irradians* (Lamarck 1819)." *Journal of Experimental Biology and Ecology* 88:227–242.

CHAPTER 10

# Seasonality in the Tropical Lowlands of Northwestern South America: The Case of San Jacinto 1, Colombia

*Augusto Oyuela-Caycedo*

*Instituto de Investigaciones Amazonicas de la Universidad Nacional de Colombia*

## INTRODUCTION

Seasonality in the tropics is regulated by precipitation. Rainy seasons regulate flooding and changes in the landscape of stream and river channels. As a result, rainfall generates different strategies of human mobility, depending on the rain's unimodal or bimodal distribution on the landscape. In the present paper I deal with two problems relating to mobility strategies in tropical environments. The first is the effect that rainy and dry seasons have on the location of sites of mobile populations and of more sedentary occupations. The second problem is how to recognize the frequency of site reoccupation during a season and what kinds of patterns we should look for to demonstrate frequent reoccupation or continual occupation of a site during a season. This second problem is considered in more detail in the second half of this paper.

I argue that there is a direct relation between rainy and dry seasons and the location of sites for mobile as well as sedentary populations. I propose that risk management of such seasonal changes in the tropics generates two patterns of landscape occupation. Sites of residentially and logistically mobile hunter-gatherers most likely will be located on unstable terrain such as point bars or active stream terraces (T0) during the dry season, when there is no risk to occupation and the payoff of the locations is very high (see Kelly 1991, 1992:46–48). During the rainy season, a preference for stable areas (river terraces [T1, T2, T3], hill tops, ridges, rock shelters) is predicted (table 1). More sedentary populations will tend to select more stable land-

scapes during both seasons in order to avoid seasonal flooding and constant destruction of settlements.[1]

These seasonal variations act as constraints and affect the archaeological recovery of base camps or other kinds of sites created by mobile populations during the dry season (see Johnson and Logan 1990:293–295). Dry season sites would be strongly underrepresented in the archaeological record as a result of the natural dynamic of alluvial landscapes. Contrarily, as a result of more stable landscape preference during the rainy season, evidence of camps or special purpose sites of collectors and foragers and even early sedentary populations would be highly represented at these locations.

As a case study, I consider the chance discovery of the Late Archaic site of San Jacinto 1. The lack of comparative sites in the neotropics similar to San Jacinto 1 illustrates the problem of underrepresentation of dry season sites expected in the variable pattern of mobility of foragers and collectors (Kelly 1983). I address the nature of seasonal occupation at San Jacinto 1 through the climatic and landscape context of the site's formation.

## THE CASE: SAN JACINTO 1

San Jacinto 1 is located in a synclinal valley that runs in a south-north direction parallel to the anticline of the Serranía de San Jacinto. The site is at an altitude of 210 meters above sea level in a small alluvial floodplain. The valley is cut by a west to east stream channel

TABLE I

**Seasonal risk variation in alluvial environments**

| | Season | Unstable | Stable |
|---|---|---|---|
| Mobile (residential or logistic) | rainy | avoid | prefer |
| | dry | prefer | avoid |
| Sedentary | rainy | strongly avoid | strongly prefer |
| | dry | weakly prefer | weakly avoid |

known as the "quebrada San Jacinto" (figs. 1–2) (see Instituto Geografico Agustín Codazzí 1975, 1977, 1982; Ballesteros 1983).

This site was initially evaluated in 1986 (Oyuela 1987). As a result of the preliminary work, the importance of the site was seen not so much in its early fiber-temper pottery (the earliest in the continent, see Hoopes 1994; Oyuela 1995) but because it was the starting point for the study of inland adaptations in the neotropics and for testing models relating to the origins of food production and sedentism (Oyuela 1993, 1996). San Jacinto 1 was expected to indicate very different strategies of adaptation from those described for coastal and riverine sites in the tropics. The site was covered by approximately four meters of alluvial soils. A deep open area of 75 square meters (figs. 3–4) was excavated between 1991 and 1992 (seven months). A program of augering, using computer assisted interpo-

lation of the stratigraphic data from each auger hole, permitted a visual reconstruction of the site paleotopography. This information was used to define the size of the site as well as to decide where to excavate. The excavation represents a 20 percent sample of the site. The purpose of exposing a relatively large area was to recover enough data to evaluate models of mobility and food production as well as of household structure. The site provides a starting point for the analysis of the strategies developed by humans in an inland transitional zone of dry forest, wet forest, and savanna environments, which should be very different from those described for coastal adaptations (Gordon 1957; Hammond 1980).

Evidence of dwellings indicates ephemeral structures like windbreaks or temporary shelters. During the most extensive occupation, the cultural activity area was approximately 380 square meters and may have accommodated a population of between 10 to 15 people (stratum 9). From the spatial context, it is clear that pottery was not used as the primary means for daily cooking (Oyuela 1993, 1995). The San Jacinto economy appears to have revolved around harvesting and processing seeds of wild plants by means of an expedient ground-stone lithic technology (Bonzani 1995). These resources were cooked mainly in roasting or fire pits. The diet may have been supplemented by hunting deer, tapir, and small animals such as mud turtles and grassland turtles, as well as iguanas and small fishes

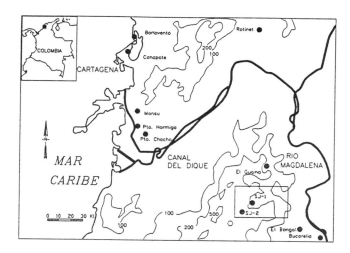

Figure 1. Location of the study region and Early Formative sites.

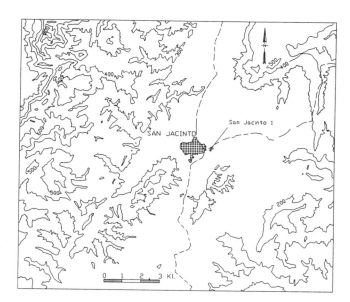

Figure 2. Location of the San Jacinto 1.

**Figure 3.** General view of the San Jacinto 1 floodplain and new channel cut.

**Figure 4.** General view of feature distribution (pits) at San Jacinto.

(few bone remains were recovered in contrast to the abundant carbonized plant remains). These animals were procured and processed with a diverse assemblage of unifacially flaked stone tools. All the raw materials employed for lithics at the site are found in the region in a radius of five to ten kilometers (Castro 1994). There is no evidence of exotic materials or exploited resources that indicate an extensive circuit of mobility. Instead, mobility seems to have been very restricted to a territory that may not have been larger than ten kilometers in radius.

How did the climatic and hydraulic conditions at the site operate in the past? In general, it is accepted that in tropical areas glacial climatic changes had little effect on temperature below an altitude of 2,000 meters. Fluctuations in temperature are thought to have been only 1° or 2° C above or below the present-day normal (Van der Hammen 1986:571). The sedimentation rates and the definition of dry periods during the Holocene in this part of the tropics have been addressed for the lower part of the Magdalena River and the Cauca and San Jórge Rivers (Plazas et al. 1988). These changes seem to correlate well with more distant areas such as the Caquetá River in the Amazon (Van der Hammen et al. 1991). In this context, San Jacinto 1 was occupied during a progressively drier period of the Holocene, but with another important component indicated by sea level data: a lower stream-level gradient (Oyuela 1996).

## RAINS AND STREAM FLOODING AS SEASONAL FACTORS IN THE SAN JACINTO 1 FORMATION PROCESSES

The Serranía is mainly affected by the climatic conditions of the *Deprecíon Momposina* (Mompos Depression) where the Cauca and San Jórge Rivers join the Magdalena River. This depression is characterized by large water surfaces forming cienagas (shallow lagoons). The highly humid environment of the depression favors the formation of saturated clouds that, when pushed by the winds in a northwestern direction, develop into torrential storms. The Serranía operates as a barrier, favoring strong rains in a short amount of time. The pluvial spatial variation of the region is demonstrated by the fact that only ten kilometers from the site is the Cerro Maco (850 meters above sea level), an area that because of its elevation maintains a tropical humid forest and has an annual precipitation of

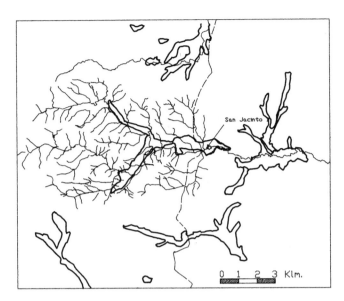

**Figure 5.** Stream catchment and alluvial floodplains (thick line).

close to 2,000 mm. The rest of the lower part of the Serranía is drier. In this sense San Jacinto 1 is located marginally to the waters and humid environment of the depression as well as to the main area of precipitation of the Serranía.

The San Jacinto zone has an annual mean precipitation of 1,097 mm (based on data from 1931–1987) and a mean annual temperature of 27.5 degrees Celsius with a small fluctuation of three degrees. The zone has two major seasons: rainy and dry. The first rainy period starts in late April–June, followed by a small dry month around July–August (Veranillo de San Juan). After this, precipitation increases until the end of November, reaching a peak in October. Then the rains stop in early December, leaving the driest times in January and February, with some years having no precipitation at all. This climatic regime drastically changes the green landscape of November into a dry environment of dead grasses from January to March. This bimodal climatic regime also has a strong impact on the availability of fruits and the growth cycle of annuals and perennials (see Walsh 1981; Bonzani 1995), as well as on the cycles of animal availability (for example, mud turtles, iguanas, and fluvial and land snails).

As a consequence of this climatic regime, today the alluvial floodplain of the San Jacinto stream is affected by flooding episodes during the torrential storms. The flooding episodes last for short amounts of time, such as a few hours, and occur when the stream channel

cannot cope with the waters of the upper part of the drainage system (see fig. 5). The chances of flooding are especially high during the months of April to November. It is important to note that even if flooding is likely during these months, most of the year is characterized by a water deficit in the region (fig. 6), which favors the concentration of resources around streams during the dry season.

Much of the depositional and postdepositional history of the San Jacinto site seems to have been affected by the same kind of processes that modify the landscape today. The floodplain where the site is located is very small and parallel to the entrenched stream of San Jacinto, extending no more than 500 meters from the channels (see fig. 5). The catchment area of the San Jacinto stream is located close to the site of San Jacinto 1 in a radius of two kilometers to the west. Most of the streams that contribute water and form the main stream are seasonal. The only permanent water is of aquifer origin and supplies the main stream even during the driest months (January–February).

What kind of material is carried by the stream and runoff episodes that produced the sedimentation at the site? The exposed material is from sedimentary rocks of marine origin. In relation to the pedogenesis of the site, San Jacinto 1 was possibly located at different moments of its depositional sedimentary history in a stream forest gallery, close to a savanna woodland, or in an open savanna (Oyuela 1993).

A total of 26 layers or strata and facies were defined during systematic augering of the site and its surroundings. These strata where numbered from top or surface to bottom. Evidence of anthropic activity is found in nine layers. The most recent corresponds to the present topsoil or humus, called stratum 1. The second period of human activity is registered in stratum 5, which developed between 2120±90 B.P. (Beta 79780) and 1750±80 B.P. (Beta 78619). The most ancient period of anthropic soils, and the subject of this paper, occurred in strata 9, 10, 12, 14, 16, 18, and 20. According to three radiocarbon dates, these anthropic soils were formed between 5300 B.P. and 6000 B.P. (based on ten uncalibrated radiocarbon dates; see Oyuela 1996:table VII).

The physical and chemical analyses of the soils (fig. 7) indicate that the human activity of the early occupation (strata 9, 10, 12, 14, 16, 18, and 20) developed beside and/or close to the channel of a stream. With the help of a computer program that extrapolates data from the augering it was possible to establish the spatial distribution of stratum 9, confirming an oval form for the settlement and reconstructing a U-shaped

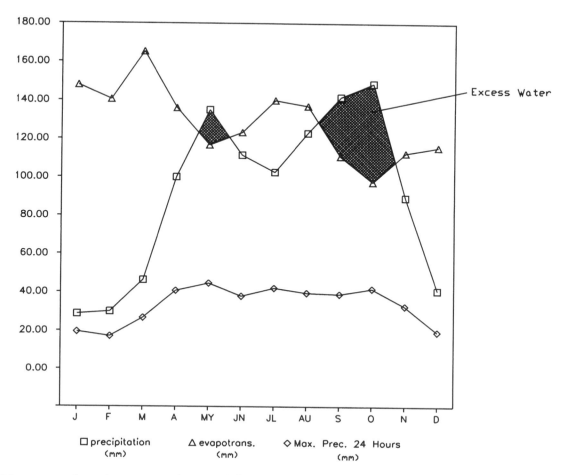

**Figure 6.** Mean annual precipitation and water deficit in mm. Lower distribution is maximum monthly precipitation in 24-hour period (mean values).

dumping area. By considering the stratigraphy, the paleotopography, and the spatial distribution of sediments and soils, I conclude that the early human occupation was located on a point bar of a meandering stream system (Oyuela 1993).

Given the stratigraphic sequence and process of formation, the relationship of the soil with flooding episodes is the major factor of accretion. The process of soil and sediment formation at San Jacinto 1 seems to be similar to that of other alluvial systems studied around the world (see Gladfelter 1985; Hassan 1985; Ferring 1986; Guccione et al. 1988; Mandel 1992). Considering the known models of soil deposition of point bars (Reineck and Singh 1975; Collinson 1986), it was expected that the excavation would yield evidence of characteristic features in the development of a

point bar such as lateral accretional (epsilon) cross-bedding related to the migration of the point bar in a meander and the current of the water (see Brooks and Sassaman 1990). There was some evidence of epsilon formations in the augering, but its confirmation was obtained only during the excavation. Based on these results, an interpretation of the pedogenic changes that occurred at San Jacinto 1 are presented in table 2. As noted in table 2, the accretional sequence depended mainly on flooding during the rainy season and the mobility of the stream channel.

In conclusion, from the geoarchaeological perspective alone, it can be said that: (1) the people settled in a point bar environment, (2) flooding was a variable that affected the site during the rainy season, making it too risky to be occupied at those times, and (3) the

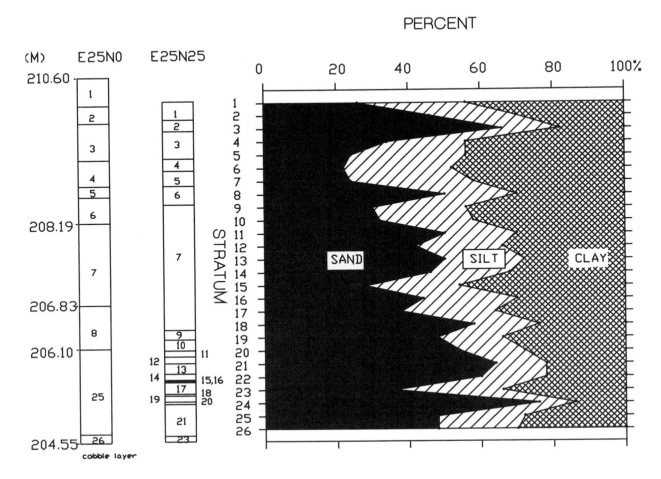

**Figure 7.** Physical and chemical characteristics of strata.

migration of the channel was a variable that affected the development of living floors, producing cross-bedding stratigraphy. The end of the human reoccupation of the site was very likely the result of a displacement of the stream by a neck cutoff process or avulsion.

In synthesis, the major factor that regulated the occupation and formation process of the site was the rainy season. The high risk of flooding inhibited the occupation of such areas during those times. Furthermore, during the dry season, due to the deficit of water in the region, these areas became optimal locations for the concentration of subsistence resources.

Let us now ask how frequent and for how long the point bar was occupied during the dry season. To answer this question a new approach and methodology is required.

## FEATURE DENSITY AND DISTRIBUTION AS AN INDICATOR OF SEASONAL OCCUPATION

It is argued that the variation in the pattern of distribution of features is directly related to the frequency of occupation and indeed even to the strategy of mobility. Features as a unit of analysis have the advantage of not being distorted by redeposition, which affects artifacts and other remains. Features are affected by the rates of sedimentation and geomorphological dynamics of their site location. Even in environments of high sedimentation rates, geological events occur at a slower rate than does feature formation by human activity. Therefore, two different occupations of a site in the same season are not recognizable in the archaeological

TABLE 2

Soil formation sequence of San Jacinto 1

| Formation Sequence Units | Stratum | Characteristics |
|---|---|---|
| IVd | 1, 2 | Flood basin, slow rate of sedimentation, development of organic soils. |
| IVc | 3 | Single flooding event, high rate of sedimentation. |
| IVb | 4–6 | Flood basin, low accretion and rate of sedimentation, development of organic soils. |
| IVa | 7 | Flood basin, medium rate of sedimentation of fine materials (finely laminated). |
| III | 8 | Abandoned channel is filled with fine sediments of flood basin, medium rate of sedimentation. |
| IIc | 9–20 | Upper point bar, epsilon, foreset beds of cross stratification, high rate of sedimentation. |
| IIb | 21–23 | Lower point bar accretion, high rate of sedimentation. |
| IIa | 24 | Lower point bar-scour pool, high rate of sedimentation, single flooding event. |
| Ib | 25–26 | In-channel deposits, coarse/fine material. |
| Ia | 27 | Channel floor. |

record. Accepting this, the alternative to studying this problem is to look for patterns that show the asynchronic effect of different events that are the product of occupations within and between seasons. The following analysis explores this approach.

The study of patterns of feature distribution as a function of hunter-gatherer seasonal behavior is important since it contributes to (1) defining the kind of mobility pattern that most likely produced the observed synchronic pattern of features, (2) refining the relationship of mobility strategies and environmental seasonality of the area, if there is one, (3) establishing the frequency of site reoccupation within a season, and (4) defining the probable seasons of reoccupation.

Binford (1983, 1989) considers the patterns that we should expect in archaeological assemblages of different kinds of camps. One of the variables he discusses is the degree of assemblage redundancy generated by logistically mobile populations (Binford 1983:357–378, 1989:223–263). In his analyses, "assemblage" is used

to indicate artifactual remains and may apply to ecofactual remains as well. "Redundancy" indicates the amount or quantity of reoccurrence of an artifact type. The pattern of assemblage redundancy is interpreted according to a "middle range theory" that is very limited in its development. The most useful components of it are based on studies of the logistically mobile Nunamiut, a population that depends to a high degree on hunting (Binford 1978). Before reviewing this pattern, we must consider whether the interpretation of assemblage redundancy creates a problem when the population in the case study more likely has plant resources as its major food supply. It seems not. Other studies conducted in relation to foraging hunter-gatherers in Africa and Australia (see Gould and Yellen 1987; O'Connell 1987; Gamble and Boismier 1991; Kroll and Price 1991; cf. Ebert 1992) seem to corroborate and refine the interpretation of the reoccupation of sites from assemblage redundancy and feature density.

Considering that the variation of the spatial distribution of assemblages reflects the function of a site (e.g., base camp, special-purpose camps) and that it is directly related to mobility strategy (Binford 1983, 1989), increases in assemblage redundancy are expected more often in what are generally referred to as special-purpose locations and least likely to occur in residential camps of logistically mobile groups. Residential base camps are relatively long occupations in which the full array of daily activities takes place each day until the occupation is abandoned. Special-purpose camps are short-term occupations in which only specific tasks, for instance resource acquisition, are performed. Residential base camps are generally occupied for longer periods of time and contain a greater array of activity types than do special purpose sites. Further, in the considered ethnoarchaeological cases it is rare for one base camp to be directly on top of another. Instead different types of occupations tend to occur in the archaeological sequence of a site. Special-purpose sites, however, do tend to occur in the same locations due to the patterning of the required resource. With these considerations in mind, variation of the artifact assemblage is expected to be greater in base camp sites than at special-purpose locations (Binford 1983:328). Assemblage redundancy is expected for special purpose locations.

Residential sites are more flexible in their location and more variable in their content. Special-purpose locations are more discrete in their location and more redundant in their use and contents (Binford 1983:330). [Furthermore,] . . . systemic characteristics of an adaptation will condition not only variability among sites in their contents, but it will also equally condition the pattern of redundancy or variance in the sequence of archaeological remains that accumulate through multiple occupations at a single site (Binford 1983:331).

The variation and/or redundancy in assemblages allows for the diagnosis of the strategies of seasonal mobility that most likely generated the archaeological record under study (Binford 1980; O'Connell 1987). The set of relationships proposed can be synthesized as follows in table 3.

From this perspective, the development of a concept of redundancy by taking into consideration the spatial configuration of features seems to be the way to approach the diagnosis of the kinds of occupations at San Jacinto 1. It also permits the anticipation of the kinds of sites that are expected in a region with a variable system of logistic mobility (see Ebert 1992:127–156). Furthermore, this analysis of redundancy of features allows for the differentiation between features generated by residential mobility in contrast to those generated by logistic mobility, at least at the two extremes of the mobility spectrum prior to sedentism.

The term "feature" is used to refer to the material (artifacts, ecofacts, or soils) manifestation of a discreet activity. Redundancy of features refers to the reoccurrence of that feature type as defined by its material components, spatial patterning, and density. The concept is important because as the reader will note in table 3, the degree of assemblage redundancy at permanent camps or special purpose sites of sedentary populations seems not to differ from redundancy at the corresponding sites produced by logistically mobile populations. When addressing how to differen-

tiate the assemblage redundancy generated by sedentary populations of hunter-gatherers from that produced by logistically mobile populations, the answer logically appears to exist at the level of feature spatial patterning and density. Thus feature spatial distribution as well as feature type (or diversity) must be incorporated into the definition of redundancy when discussing features.

Before passing to the analysis of the case of San Jacinto 1, it is important to consider that there are factors that may affect the visibility of the spatial arrangement of features in the archaeological record. It is necessary to acknowledge that the pattern of feature density variations can also be the result of unknown activities unrelated to the type of occupation. The problem is that so far, ethnoarchaeological studies of the behaviors that can produce alternative effects on feature density and spatial arrangement are still very poorly developed.

In order to analyze the degree of redundancy, each cultural stratum must be studied in its own context. It is in this vertical context that it might be possible to see variation in the strategies of seasonal occupation and mobility. Interpreting Binford's (1983, 1989) argument of assemblage redundancy and the ethnoarchaeological work of O'Connell (1987), I propose the following. (1) If the settlement formation process is the result of a permanent year-round occupation lasting for several years, we should expect nonredundant behavior in the base camps, nonredundant feature types, and a spatial pattern of aggregated or clustered features with low density as a consequence of the reuse

TABLE 3

**Relationship between mobility strategy, variation of sites, seasonal reoccupation, and assemblage redundancy**

| Mobility strategy | Variation between sites | Seasonal reoccupation of sites | Degree of assemblage redundancy |
|---|---|---|---|
| Residential | low | none or low for base camps | low or none |
| Logistic | high | none or low for base camps | low |
| | | high for special-purpose sites | high |
| Sedentism | high | permanent camp | low or none |
| | | permanent special-purpose sites | high |

of features and of the spatial differentiation of activities that can take place. In the case of special purpose sites generated from a permanent camp, there should be high redundancy of the archaeological assemblage, but the density of features associated with the function of the site will be low as a consequence of feature maintenance and reuse. Clearer spatial differentiation of activity areas also should exist. (2) If the site is an accumulation of seasonal special-purpose camps, which in general are reoccupied several times during the same season (with resources moved to the base camp), we should expect high redundancy of the activities and, as a consequence, redundancy of feature type and a random spatial distribution of features related to the opportunistic behavior of gathering resources when available. There would be little concern for reuse of features and no clear definition of activity areas would occur. The density of such features should increase in direct relation to the number of times the site is reoccupied within a season as well as with the number of seasons of occupation. (3) In the case of seasonal base camps of a logistically mobile group, we should expect nonredundant behavior, nonredundant feature types, low feature density, and a near random spatial distribution of features. Furthermore, there should be observable differentiation of activity areas. These expectations can be restated in a simplistic and operational form presented in table 4.

In this study I assume the following. (1) The density of features has a relation with the length of occupation of a site. The longer the continual occupation of the site, the more likely the continual reuse of facilities or features and, as a consequence, the lower the density of features. In an inverse relationship, the shorter and more frequent reoccupation of the site during each season, the higher the density of features. (2) A base camp will have more variation in feature types as a consequence of more diverse activities. In a special-purpose

site the diversity of feature types is less as a consequence of more specific activities.

To assess the lithic assemblage redundancy, Binford (1978:495–497, reinterpreting the work of Vierra 1975) suggests the use of factor analysis. Binford argues that techniques such as factor analysis can help in understanding the degree of redundancy of a site. Using this technique, he suggests that if a site was a seasonal base camp, then significant changes in the activities of the site are expected, and variability among the assemblages in each stratum would be explained by different factors. Contrarily, if the continual reuse of the site for the same seasonal special purpose occurred, then the variation of the assemblage by strata would be explained by a single factor.

For San Jacinto 1, a site that seems not to have a long sequence of occupation, factor analysis may be useful. The only problem with this technique is that it does not give us a definition of the degree of spatial patterning and the redundancy of this patterning. It is for this reason that other techniques such as nearest-neighbor statistics seem more appropriate. Nearest-neighbor statistics can give a measure of the degree of spatial feature distribution departure from randomness toward clustering or regularity in space. It measures the spatial relationship between items. The data used are the exact horizontal locations of features. It has the power to detect patterns of clustering or regularity of any size or scale.

The basic equations of nearest neighbor statistics have been described elsewhere (Clark and Evans 1954:447; Pielou 1959; for a review, see Earle 1976:197–200; Wilson and Melnick 1990). For the present research the methodology and equations described by Whallon (1974) have been followed, using corrections for the boundary effect proposed by Pinder, Shimada, and Gregory (1979). These calculations were made using the computer program elaborat-

TABLE 4

**Feature redundancy and mobility**

| Feature Characteristics | Sedentary Sites | Logistic Base Camps | Logistic Special-Purpose Camps |
| --- | --- | --- | --- |
| Degree of Redundancy | Low | Low | High |
| Special Pattern | Clusters or Agglomerations | Random | Random |
| Density | Low | Low | High |

ed by Drennan (1986). In basic outline, the nearest-neighbor statistics can be interpreted as follows. The statistics of a random distribution are 1. A lower value, down to a minimum of 0, indicates agglomeration or clustering of items. A higher value, up to a maximum of 2.15, indicates more regular spacing. This value has to be interpreted with respect to the significance of the pattern and degree of departure from randomness (see Pinder et al. 1979:fig. 5). As mentioned above, each site type should generate a unique spatial distribution of features. Specifically, special-purpose camps of logistically mobile hunter-gatherers are expected to generate a random distribution of features as a consequence of the multiple reoccupations of a site and repetition of the behavior of the group (within the same season or during the same season year after year).

Features such as cooking pits, storage pits, or any other kind of pit in general are well represented in the archaeological record. In the present case, all the pits found at San Jacinto 1 seem to relate to food-processing activities (see fig. 8). Since pits reflect the kind of subsistence activities performed at a site, this makes it

easy to differentiate special-purpose sites from base camps. The function of the pits is irrelevant to this part of the research; the aim is merely to establish their spatial arrangement. The data are the locations of all pits encountered in the excavation in their stratigraphic contexts. Only strata 10 and 12 are useful for this analysis because only a small sample of pits were found in the other strata (three in stratum 5, three in stratum 9, and four in stratum 14). The low number of pits in those strata is interpreted as being the result of a different occupational pattern at the site (the pits in stratum 14 are the product of other factors), which is considered in more detail at the end of this chapter. The thickness of each of the cultural strata ranges between 6 and 27 centimeters (see figs. 4, 9). The results of the nearest neighbor analysis are presented below (for the data, see fig. 10).

A total of 45 pits were excavated in stratum 10. The density of pits is 0.6 per square meter. The average observed distance from each pit to its nearest neighbor is 0.734 meters with a standard deviation of 0.335. The expected distance from each pit to its neighbor in a random distribution is 0.691 with a standard error of 0.059 meters. The ratio of the observed pit distance to the expected average nearest-neighbor distance is 1.063. This ratio means that the mean nearest-neighbor distance is only slightly different from that expected in a random distribution. The significance of this slight departure from the expected distance is also very low (df=44, t=0.729, p<0.5).

**Figure 8.** Detail of feature 57 (E24N38).

**Figure 9.** Southern section of the excavation; note overlapping features from strata 10, 12, and 14.

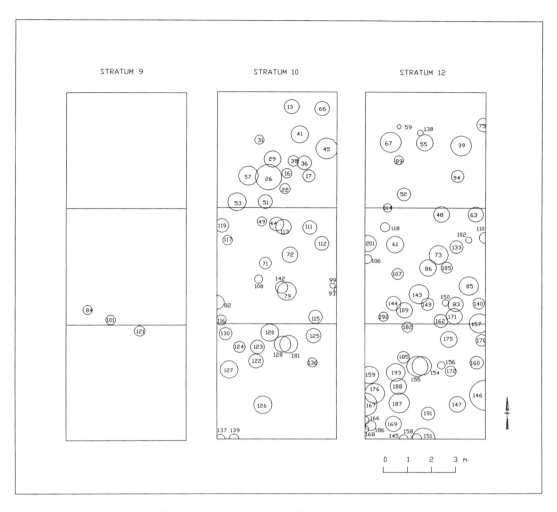

**Figure 10.** Distribution of pits in strata 9, 10, and 12.

A total of 60 pits were excavated in stratum 12. The density of pits is 0.8 per square meter. The average observed distance from each pit to its nearest neighbor is 0.711 meters with a standard deviation of 0.289; the expected distance from each pit to its neighbor in a random distribution is 0.592 with a standard error of 0.044 meters. The ratio of the observed pit distance to the average nearest-neighbor distance is 1.201. This ratio means that the observed nearest-neighbor distance differs from that expected in a random distribution in the direction of more regular spacing. The significance of this departure from the expected distance is high (df=59, t=2.705, p<0.01).

The result of the nearest-neighbor analysis reveals that there is enough evidence to suggest that the high density and near random distribution of features is indicative of redundant behavior and very likely was the result of seasonal reoccupations of the site in which new features were produced with each reoccupation and without regard to previously emplaced ones. In other words, the results follow the expectations of a pattern that is very likely the product of a logistically mobile group that used the site as a seasonal special-purpose camp. Further, it is very likely that the site was occupied for a few days at a time but on several occasions during a season.

The tendency toward regular spacing or symmetry in the distribution of features in stratum 12 may be explained as a consequence of the lateral and frontward accretion of the point bar. As the point bar grew to the north, activities and feature emplacement moved northward as well. By the time of the occupations in Strata 10 and 9, point bar accretion northward would have been slower as the meander was cut off. It is also important to note that in each occupation there was a strong emphasis against the reuse of pits. This can be understood in terms of the function of the pits (as roasting and/or fire pits) and explains why the pits were refilled after each occupation.

It is further interesting to note that the mean distance between features is extremely low in comparison to that observed from ethnographic work on base camps in Africa and Australia. For the !Kung and desert Australian aboriginals (groups with residential mobility), for example, the distance between hearths range between 4.65 meters and 11.52 meters, and the distance between roasting pits is even higher (O'Connell 1987). The nearest-neighbor analysis conducted for such groups indicates that there is no relationship between distance between hearths and length of occupation or the size of household (Gould and Yellen 1987). As has been described elsewhere, features such as hearths are associated with activities that require less space than pits because most of the activities conducted around them are done by individuals that sit around the fire. Contrarily, pits require extensive activity areas, as they generally involve activities that are performed standing up. Binford (1988:169) estimates that an area of around 17–24 square meters of space is required for a pit. This ethnoarchaeological information gives us a clear idea of how a pattern of pits such as is observed in San Jacinto 1 is very likely associated with a logistically mobile group who performed the same activities at the same site, season after season.

This interpretation seems to be valid for strata 10 and 12, but what happened with strata 9 and 14 where pits were also found in lower densities? In the case of stratum 14, this is understandable because the stratum is a facie that only becomes differentiated in the secondary refuse area of the stream channel. In the case of stratum 9, the distribution of features as well as the spatial distribution of artifacts suggest a totally different pattern than that described above. The occupation of the site in this stratum seems to have more of the characteristics of a continual seasonal base camp occupied during the dry season, where activity areas were clearly differentiated. Stratum 9 is the only layer that permits the reconstruction of activity areas during the season of site occupation. The clustering of features, as well as activities (see distribution of fire-cracked rocks and pottery in Oyuela 1993), suggests that the site was occupied as a base camp for a longer period of time,

very likely the whole dry season. It is interesting to note that no burials were found in any part of the early stratigraphic sequence. Human remains of an adult were found dispersed on the "living floor" of stratum 9, however.

## FINAL COMMENTS

The results from San Jacinto 1 complicate the traditional view that we have for the lowlands of the neotropics. This is mainly a consequence of the fact that for the first time we have started to look at sites that correspond to the variability expected in strategies of hunter-gatherer adaptations in this environment. The recognition of one kind of site with seasonal occupation (dry season), which is not very likely to be found due to natural high sedimentation conditions and instability of the landscape, shows the importance of recognizing the problem of seasonal variability in the archaeological assemblage of mobile hunter-gatherers in the tropics. After indicating with hard climatological data the importance of the rainy and dry seasons in the tropics, this work has shown that seasonality caused by precipitation can be expected to be a major factor in regulating the variation in hunter-gatherer mobility strategies in regions such as that illustrated in the case of San Jacinto 1. This is compatible with the basic structure of the mobility strategies proposed by Binford (1980) and Kelly (1991). It is in this context that research on the tropics may contribute to the understanding of the different strategies that hunter-gatherers may have developed in the past.

The use of concepts such as feature redundancy seems to be very useful for the recognition of patterns of camp variability as well as for confirming feature distribution patterns in terms of seasonality of occupation. Nearest-neighbor statistics seem also to be a powerful measure of spatial structure, facilitating the interpretation of the seasonal behavior that explains the distribution of features at San Jacinto 1. In this regard, the results presented here are still very preliminary. The final confirmation of the interpreted pattern can only be assessed more securely by finding and excavating other sites that correspond to different points in the cycle of collecting and seasonality. In this regard, only a regional study may contribute to a better understanding of the seasonal behavior of tropical hunter-gatherers.

Finally, the preliminary results from the research on the San Jacinto region has led to some speculations. One of these is that more sedentary populations may only occupy landscapes of high risk when a reduction in mobility pushes populations to intensify in such areas. The process of intensification would require mass modification of the environment by artificial construction that reduces the risk of seasonal flooding or by new construction technologies and more complex forms of social and political organization such as in the Sinú area and western llanos of Colombia and Venezuela (see Plazas and Falchetti 1981; Zucchi 1985). With future work in the region we hope to have more hard evidence to test some of the models proposed for the origin of sedentism as well as to refine the interpretation of the subsistence strategies in time and space.

## Acknowledgments

The fieldwork at San Jacinto 1 was made possible thanks to funding from a National Science Foundation Dissertation Improvement Grant given to the author under the direction of Dick Drennan, *mecenas* and teacher. The fieldwork responsibilities were shared with Renée M. Bonzani who collaborated on the project with the support of a Fulbright Commission grant for her dissertation and who helped with the editing of this paper. Thanks are extended to Jaime Castro, collaborator and research assistant of the project, and to Santiago Madriñan, the late Gerardo Reichel-Dolmatoff, and Alicia Dussan, friends who shared with us very fascinating moments of archaeological theoretical discussion during our stays at Cambridge, Cartagena, and Bogotá.

## Note

1. Sedentary populations are defined as those that have a permanent camp as a base during a whole year.

## BIBLIOGRAPHY

Ballesteros Torres, C. I.
1983 *Reseña Explicita del Mapa Geológico Generalizado del Departamento de Bolivar.* Instituto Nacional de Investigaciones Geológico-Minerales, Mapa escala 1:500.000. Ministerio de Mínas y Energía, Bogotá.

Binford, L. R.
1978 *Nunamiut Ethnoarchaeology.* Academic Press, Orlando.
1980 "Willow Smoke and Dogs' Tails: Hunter-Gatherer Settlement Systems and Archaeological Site Formation." *American Antiquity* 45(1):4–20.
1983 *Working at Archaeology.* Academic Press, Orlando.
1988 *In Pursuit of the Past.* Thames and Hudson, New York.
1989 *Debating Archaeology.* Academic Press, Orlando.

Bonzani, R. M.
1995 "Seasonality, Predictability and Plant Use Strategies at San Jacinto 1, Northern Colombia." Ph.D. diss., University of Pittsburgh, Pittsburgh.

Brooks, M. J., and K. E. Sassaman
1990 "Point Bar Geoarcheology in the Upper Coastal Plain of the Savannah River Valley, South Carolina: A Case Study", in *Archaeological Geology of North America*, N. P. Lasca and J. Donahue, eds., pp. 183–197. Centennial Special Volume 4. Geological Society of America, Boulder, Colorado.

Castro, J.
1994 "La Actividad de Molienda en San Jacinto 1, los Liticos de Moler." Tesis de grado, Departamento de Antropología, Universidad de Los Andes, Bogotá.

Clark, P. J., and F. C. Evans
1954 "Distance to Nearest Neighbor as a Measure of Spatial Relationships in Populations." *Ecology* 35:445–453.

Collinson, J. D.
1986 "Alluvial Sediments," in *Sedimentary Environments and Facies*, 2d ed., H. G. Reading, ed., pp. 20–62. Blackwell Scientific Publications, Boston.

Drennan, R. D.
1986 "Nearest Neighbor Program." Department of Anthropology, University of Pittsburgh, Pittsburgh. Unpublished manuscript.

Earle, T. K.
1976 "A Nearest-Neighbor Analysis of Two Formative Settlement Systems," in *The Early Mesoamerican Village*, K. V. Flannery, ed., pp. 196–223. Academic Press, Orlando, Florida.

Ebert, J. I.
1992 *Distributional Archaeology*. University of New Mexico Press, Albuquerque.

Ferring, R. C.
1986 "Rates of Fluvial Sedimentation: Implications for Archaeological Variability." *Geoarchaeology* 1(3):259–274.

Gamble, C., and W. A. Boismier
1991 *Ethnoarchaeological Approaches to Mobile Campsites*. International Monographs in Prehistory, Ann Arbor, Michigan.

Gladfelter, B.
1985 "On the Interpretation of Archaeological Sites in Alluvial Settings," in *Archaeological Sediments in Context*, J. K. Stein and W. R. Farrand, eds., pp. 41–52. Center for the Study of Early Man, vol. 1. Orono, Maine.

Gordon, B. L. R.
1957 *Human Geography and Ecology in the Sinú Country of Colombia*. University of California Press, Berkeley and Los Angeles.

Gould, R. A., and J. E. Yellen
1987 "Man the Hunted: Determinants of Household Spacing in Desert and Tropical Foraging Societies." *Journal of Anthropological Archaeology* 6:77–103.

Guccione, M. J., R. H. Laggerty, II, and L. S. Cummings
1988 "Environmental Constraints of Human Settlement in an Evolving Holocene Alluvial System, the Lower Mississippi Valley." *Geoarchaeology* 3(1):65–84.

Hammond, N.
1980 "Prehistoric Human Utilization of the Savanna Environments of Middle and South America," in *Human Ecology in Savanna Environments*, D. R. Harris, ed., pp. 73–105. Academic Press, New York.

Hassan, F. A.
1985 "Fluvial Systems and Geoarchaeology in Arid Lands: With Examples from North Africa, the Near East and the America Southwest," in *Archaeological Sediments in Context*, J. K. Stein and W. R. Farrand, eds., pp. 53–68. Center for the Study of Early Man, vol. 1. Orono, Maine.

Hoopes, J. W.
1994 "Ford Revisited: A Critical Review of the Chronology and Relationships of the Earliest Ceramic Complexes in the New World, 6000–1500 B.C." *Journal of World Prehistory* 8(1):1–49.

Instituto Geografico Agustín Codazzi
1975 *Estudio General de Suelos de los Municipios de Carmen de Bolívar, San Jacinto, San Juan Nepomuceno, Zambrano, El Guamo y Cordoba (Departamento de Bolívar)*. Bogotá.
1977 *Carta Ecológica*. Subdirección Agrológica.
1982 *Bolívar, Aspectos Geográficos*. Editorial Andes, Bogotá.

Johnson, W. C., and B. Logan
1990 "Geoarchaeology of the Kansas River Basin, Central Great Plains," in *Archaeological Geology of North America*, N. P. Lasca and J. Donahue, eds., pp. 267–299. Centennial Special Volume 4. Geological Society of America, Boulder, Colorado.

Kelly, R. L.
1983 "Hunter-Gatherer Mobility Strategies." *Journal of Anthropological Research* 39(3):277–306.
1991 "Sedentism, Sociopolitical Inequality, and Resource Fluctuations," in *Between Bands and States*, S. A. Gregg, ed., pp. 135–158. Center for Archaeological Investigations Occasional Paper 9. Southern Illinois University, Carbondale.
1992 "Mobility/Sedentism: Concepts, Archaeological Measures, and Effects." *Annual Review of Anthropology* 21:43–66.

Kroll, E. M., and T. D. Price, eds.
1991 *The Interpretation of Archaeological Spatial Patterning*. Plenum Press, New York.

Mandel, R. D.
1992 "Soils and Holocene Landscape Evolution in Central and Southwestern Kansas: Implications for Archaeological Research," in *Soils in Archaeology*, V. T. Holliday, ed., pp. 41–100. Smithsonian Institution Press, Washington, D. C.

O'Connell, J. F.
1987 "Alyawara Site Structure and its Archaeological Implications." *American Antiquity* 52(1):74–108.

Oyuela-Caycedo, A.
1987 "Dos Sitios Arqueológicos con Degrasante de Fibra Vegetal en la Serrania de San Jacinto (Departamento de Bolívar)." *Boletín de Arqueológia* 2(1):5–26.

1993 "Sedentism, Food Production and Pottery Origins in the Tropics." Ph.D. diss., University of Pittsburgh, Pittsburgh.

1995 "Rocks vs. Clay: The Evolution of Pottery Technology in the Case of San Jacinto 1 (Colombia)," in *The Emergence of Pottery*, W. K. Barnett and J. W. Hoopes, eds., pp. 133–144. Smithsonian Institution Press, Washington, D.C.

1996 "The Study of Collector Variability in the Transition to Sedentary Food Producers in Northern Colombia." *Journal of World Prehistory* 10(1):49–93.

Pielou, E. C.
1959 "The Use of Point-to-Plant Distances in the Study of the Patterns of Plant Populations." *Journal of Ecology* 47:607-613.

Pinder, D., I. Shimada, and D. Gregory
1979 "The Nearest-Neighbor Statistics: Archaeological Application and New Developments." *American Antiquity* 44(3):430–445.

Plazas, C., and A. M. Falchetti de Saenz
1981 *Asentamientos Prehispanicos en el Bajo San Jorge*. Banco de la República, Bogotá.

Plazas, C., A. M. Falchetti, T. van der Hammen, and P. Botero
1988 "Cambios Ambientales y Desarrollo Cultural en el Bajo Rio San Jorge." *Boletin Museo del Oro* 20:55–88.

Reineck, H. E., and I. B. Singh
1975 *Depositional Sedimentary Environments*. Springer-Verlag, New York.

Van der Hammen, T.
1986 "Datos Sobre la Historia de Clíma, Vegetación y Glaciación de la Sierra Nevada de Santa Marta," in *Studies on Tropical Andean Ecosystems: La Sierra Nevada de Santa Marta*, T. Van der Hammen and P. M. Ruiz, eds., pp. 561–580. J. Cramer, Berlin-Stutgart.

Van der Hammen, T., J. F. Duivenvoorden, J. M. Lips, L. E. Urrego, and N. Espejo
1991 "Fluctuaciones del Nivel del Agua del Río y de la Velocidad de Sedimentación Durante los Ultimos 13000 Años en el Area del Medio Caquetá (Amazonia Colombiana)." *Colombia Amazonica* 5(1):91–118.

Vierra, B. J.
1975 "Structure versus Function in the Archaeological Record." Ph.D. diss., University of New Mexico, Albuquerque.

Walsh, R. P. D.
1981 "The Nature of Climatic Seasonality," in *Seasonal Dimensions to Rural Poverty*, R. Chambers, R. Longhurst, and A. Pacey, eds., pp. 11–29. Frances Pinter Ltd., London.

Whallon, R., Jr.
1974 "Spatial Analysis of Occupation Floors II: The Application of Nearest Neighbor Analysis." *American Antiquity* 39(1):16–34.

Wilson, S. M., and D. J. Melnick
1990 "Modelling Randomness in Locational Archaeology." *Journal of Archaeological Science* 17:403–412.

Zucchi, A.
1985 "Recent Evidence of Pre-Columbian Water Management Systems in the Western Llanos of Venezuela," in *Prehistoric Intensive Agriculture in the Tropics*, vol. 1, S. Farrington, ed., pp. 167–180. British Archaeological Reports, International Series 232. Oxford.

# CHAPTER 11

# Measures of Mobility and Occupational Intensity in Highland Peru

*Katherine M. Moore*

*Bentley College*

## Abstract

Preceramic (9000–3800 B.P.) and Formative (3800–1500 B.P.) occupations on the Junín puna of Peru reflected local adaptations to a climate where daily temperature changes are severe but where there is only minor seasonal variation. Archaeologists have directed attention toward whether this pattern led to a relatively nonseasonal or possibly sedentary prehistoric occupation. In this study, faunal remains are used to test some hypothesized differences in length or intensity of occupation at Panaulauca, a deeply stratified cave site in Junín, Peru. Fragmentation and alteration of animal bone is used as an indirect measure of mobility to and from the site. Two distinct patterns emerge: an early period of moderate occupational intensity followed by a period of heightened occupational intensity. Qualitative indicators of seasonality from bones in the same layers confirm this interpretation.

## INTRODUCTION

Patterns of prehistoric mobility are taken to reflect responses to seasonal changes in climate and available resources, especially when those patterns are marked and predictable. Such predictable patterns are seen in the Levant (discussed by both Lieberman and Valla in this volume) and the American Southwest (discussed by Adams and Bohrer, and Rocek in this volume). Near the equator, patterns of climatic variation may be much less strongly marked and less predictable from year to year. Any pattern of prehistoric mobility and resource choice should be considered in the light of a specific environment.

The region described in this paper is equatorial, though it is relatively cold and severe. The central Andes of western South America have patches of high grassland called the "puna" or "altiplano" at altitudes between the treeline and the glaciated or rocky peaks. Along most of the central Andes, these puna regions are relatively narrow and scattered between valleys and peaks. In Junín (around Lake Junín) and in Puno (around Lake Titicaca), these grasslands are extensive. The area considered here is the high puna of Junín, extending in altitude from about 3,900 m to about 4,500 m (fig. 1). In the center of this puna is Lake Junín (Chinchaychocha in Quechua), the source for the Mantaro River. Many smaller springs, lakes, and marshy areas are located between the lower limits of the surrounding glaciers and the lake. The rockshelter site of Panaulauca (at 4,150 m) is in a small valley along a small, perennial stream that flows into the Mantaro.

### Climate

The climate on the Junín puna is cold (mean annual temperature 5 to 7 degrees C) with abundant precipitation (859 mm/year). (Other puna areas to the south are much drier.) Daily temperatures on the puna vary widely, 15 or 20 degrees C between midnight and midafternoon, but monthly mean temperatures vary by less than 4 degrees C across the year (ONERN 1976). The strongest annual pattern is in precipitation. June and July are the driest and coldest months (during the

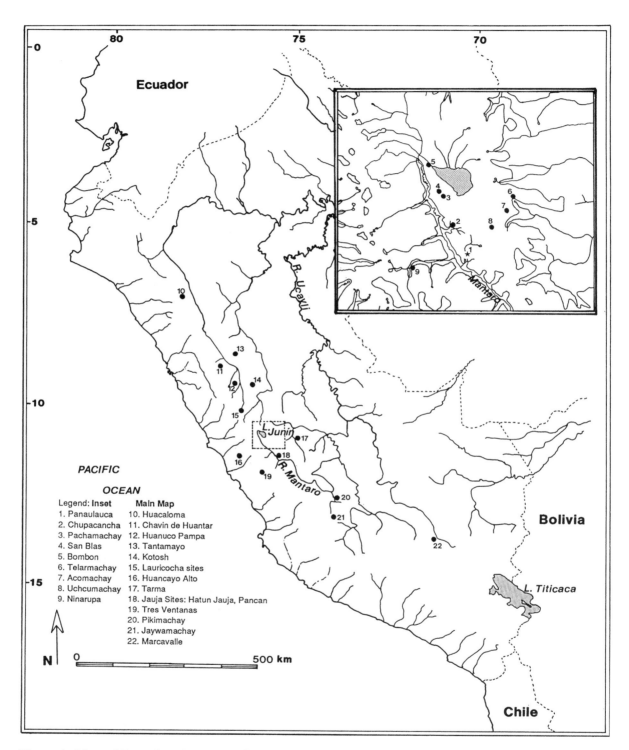

**Figure 1.** Map of Peru showing research area (inset) and other sites relating to Panaulauca.

austral winter), and February is the wettest and warmest month (during the austral summer). Frost, snow, hail, and rain are possible in every month, but snow rarely lays on the ground for more than a few days in any season. Variation between years complicates this pattern, as years of record high or low rainfall for one small area are not the same for an area only 15 or 20 km away.

## Land Use and Plant Resources

The Junín puna is intensively grazed today by sheep and camelids (domesticated llamas and alpaca and wild vicuna, where protected), but no crops are grown. Archaeological and ethnohistoric records suggest, however, that frost resistant tubers and seeds were grown there in precontact times. Observers from other climates may overemphasize the contrast between the so-called wet and dry seasons, especially as roads become impassable to vehicles during the wet season. Contemporary herders in villages and on isolated estancias (small ranch stations) occupy the area year round, though there is some shift in population to and from villages in response to cycles of pastoral and ritual activities and the school calendar (Tsopick 1947). To prehistoric people on foot, the differences between the two seasons would have been differently perceived.

Ethnobotanist Deborah Pearsall carefully studied the seasonal patterns of growth, flowering, and maturity of the important food and forage plants. Her surveys of stream side, lake shore, and upland areas suggested that while overall productivity of edible plant foods is low compared to other regions, foods such as grass seeds, several starchy tubers, greens, and cactus fruits would have been available at all seasons of the year. Dried fruits and tubers could have been used across several seasons. During the wet season, herbs, roots, tubers, and fruits would have been most abundant. Grass seeds mature during the dry season, and some tubers and roots would have been available at this time (Pearsall 1986; Pearsall 1989:326).

## Animal Resources

Native vicuna, guanaco, and deer graze on natural puna pasture year-round, though sheep dominate these environments today. The focus of this discussion is on the vicuna, which was the dominant wild species in prehistoric times. New pasture production peaks at the end of the wet season when the bunch grasses mature, but the seasonality of vicuna forage plants taken together is less pronounced. Other important forage plants for the vicuna include tender grasses that grow beneath and between bunches of the dominant grasses, and other perennially green forbs and cushion plants by streams and springs. The basic social unit of the vicuna is a single-male family group, or harem. Some family groups have defended feeding territories located around permanent sources of water and separate sleeping territories away from water. Vicuna are obligate drinkers, so nonterritorial family groups and larger, looser groups of bachelor males must risk vigorous defense displays of the territorial males to reach water every day (Franklin 1978, 1983). The stability of vicuna family-group territories throughout the year indicates that water availability, rather than forage availability, is more important. The reproductive cycle of the vicuna is strongly seasonal, however, with the birth of young coinciding with the warmest nighttime temperatures and most abundant forage in February and March.

Guanaco (and deer) can survive on water obtained in forage, and their range includes areas with little surface water. The guanaco prefer a diet of grasses and forbs. Like the vicuna, their breeding is seasonal, with the young born in April and June (Menard 1982:22; Menard 1984). Deer feed at slightly lower altitudes than the camelids, and their diet usually includes some woody browse as well as grasses (Merkt 1987). Some evidence from other regions suggests that deer move higher into the puna during the wet season, taking advantage of more abundant forage (Roe and Reese 1976).

## Potential of the Puna to Support Human Occupation

Could the Junín puna have been occupied year-round by foragers or early herders? The spatial stability of the main prey animals is one important justification for a postulated permanent or nonseasonal occupation on the puna. Another supporting condition is provided by the continuously available sources of plant food. Overall yield of biomass in this cold, high region is low, however, and the numbers of people who could be supported in this way may have been small. Alternatively, periodic short trips to high-altitude pastures to hunt vicuna, guanaco, and deer could have been part of a foraging routine that included stays at camps in regions at lower altitudes, where wild plant foods would have been more abundant. Very little of such a midvalley occupation has been identified for the preceramic periods in the Junín region (see Moore 1989:43–52 for a summary) though, leading to the suggestion that the hunters of the puna may have been permanently located there (Rick 1980, 1986). Partly in order to examine this proposition, excavations at Panaulauca were carried out during the 1970s and early 1980s under the direction of J. Rick, and I undertook analysis of the animal bone.

Three possibilities are considered in this study: (1) that occupations were seasonal and periodic, (2) that they were nonseasonal and periodic, and (3) that they were nonseasonal and relatively prolonged. One goal of this study of the animal bones was to develop descriptive measures that could address the issues of seasonality of occupation independently of length of occupation. Using material from only one site, it is not possible to establish *where* people were located when they were not at Panaulauca. They could have been at other sites on the puna (smaller ones or at another of the known larger cave sites) or at sites at lower elevation. Other data sets from this site and region do have some bearing on this issue though, in particular, patterns of style and raw material of the chipped stone tools, patterns of availability of storable plant food, and stable-isotopic data from the human skeletons from the site.

## RESEARCH AT PANAULAUCA

The site of Panaulauca is a series of deeply stratified deposits around the mouth of a shallow limestone cave (fig. 2). Excavation and surveys of sites in the surrounding area indicate that Panaulauca was one of the first sites occupied in the immediate region and remained one of the largest sites in the region from 7500 B.C. to 500 B.C. From that time until the Spanish conquest of the region, Panaulauca was a less important, specialized encampment in an expanding settlement system, with clear cultural and economic connections with populations at lower altitudes. Excavations were made in the living floors under the cave overhang, on the talus slope of the main cave, and in smaller deposits at either side of the cave. This study is based only on the excavations of the main cave and the cave talus deposit, not on any of the smaller sheltered areas away from the mouth of the main cave.

An important measure of cultural activity used in our analysis was artifact density, that is, the weight of different kinds of cultural material divided by the volume of archaeological deposit that produced it. Implicit in this measure is the assumption that the accretion of fine particles of soil took place at a constant rate, and changes in artifact density reflect changes in depositional rates resulting from human activity. A specific sedimentological test of this assumption is lacking, but the fact that the climate of the region has remained stable for the period of the site's occupation and that the topography of the cave floor has been regular (based on coring and three deep test excavations), indicate that this is an acceptable assumption.

General site patterns of density of stone tools, debitage, and ceramics show three sharp peaks in artifact densities, the first at about 6000 B.C., the second at 3500 B.C. in the later preceramic, and the third at about 1800 B.C., just at the end of the preceramic and beginning of the Formative (fig. 3). It is difficult to tell from these densities, though, if the accretion of artifacts results from several prolonged occupations or many brief ones. The structure of animal bone densities in the same levels allows further insights into the intensity and duration of different occupations.

## Panaulauca Bone Assemblage

The faunal remains in this study came from two deep test columns, one in the cave and one in talus slope deposits, and a sample of six living floors (of a total of 16 excavated) in the cave. About a million bone fragments are included in this sample. The assemblage of identifiable bones is dominated by three groups of large mammals. The first group is the taruca and possibly the white tailed deer. The second two groups are two size classes of native camelids, one small (the wild vicuna and later a domesticated form similar in size to the modern alpaca), and one large (the guanaco and later the domesticated llama). In every phase, the abundance of small camelids overwhelms the abundance of deer and large camelids. The deer had greatest economic importance in the early phases (1–2B), but were reduced in importance for the rest of the sequence. The bones are well preserved according to Behrensmeyer's (1978) typology of bone destruction, predominantly showing weathering stage 0 or 1. One region of the site, along the dripline, showed a very low density of bone and heavy erosion of bone surfaces from dissolution and tumbling, so the results from these excavation units are not treated as reflecting

| Phase | Time Period | Cave Levels and Radiocarbon Dates B.P. Living Floor Sample* | Radiocarbon Years | Talus Levels |
|---|---|---|---|---|
| 8 | 350 b.c.- A.D. 1200 | 7   750±50  (WSU 2996)<br>8   1095±65  (WSU 2997)<br>9 | A.D.1195±50<br>A.D. 858±60 | 3 |
| 7 | 1050 b.c.- 350 b.c. | 10   2680±95 (WSU 2998)<br>11 *<br>12 | 730±95 B.C | 4<br>5<br>6 |
| 6 | 1620 b.c- 1050 b.c. | 12B<br>13   3150±60 (WSU 2999)<br>14<br>15<br>16 ceramic * | 1200±60 B.C | 7<br>8<br>9<br>10 |
| 5 | 2640 b.c.- 1620 b.c. | 16 pre-ceramic*  3630±90 (WSU 3000)<br>17<br>18*   4040±60 (WSU 3001)<br>19 | 1680±90 B.C<br><br>2090±60 B.C | 11<br>12<br>13 |
| 4 | 3800 b.c.- 2640 b.c. | 20<br>21*   5135±75 (WSU 2938)<br>22<br>23<br>24<br>25<br>26<br>27 | 3185±75 B.C | 14<br>15<br>16<br>17<br>18 |
| 3 | 5000 b.c.- 3800 b.c. | 28<br>29<br>30   5990±90  (WSU 3002)<br>31<br>32 | 4040±90 B.C | 19<br>20 |
| 2B | 5900 b.c.- 5000 b.c. | 33<br>34 7650±95  (WSU 2939)<br>35 | 5700±95 B.C | 21<br>22 |
| 2A | 7050 b.c.- 5900 b.c. | 36<br>37<br>38<br>39 8350±140 (Beta 7724) | 6210 ±145 B.C. | 23 |
| 1 | 7700 b.c.- 7050 b.c. | 40 9650±145 (WSU 2940)<br>41 | 7700 ±140 B.C. | 24 |
| Pre-1 | ? No Extinct Fauna | 42<br>43 | | |

**Figure 2a.** Cross section of Panaulauca deposits. Faunal remains described in this paper came from shaded layers. Note relationship of deep stratigraphic columns Unit 1/9 in the cave and Unit 35 on the talus.

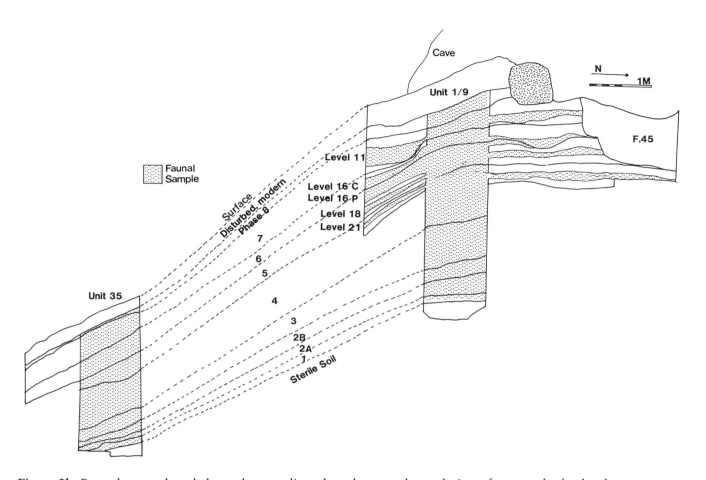

**Figure 2b.** Panaulauca cultural chronology, radiocarbon dates, and correlation of cave and talus levels.

the original deposition. All of the deposits were recovered using standard one-quarter-inch hardware cloth screens, with subsamples passed through one-sixteenth-inch window screen.

Collecting bone with standard screens increases and improves the sample recovered. The practice of screening reveals cases when small fauna (especially fish or rodents), whose bones are seldom noticed during excavation, were an important part of an assemblage. At Panaulauca, screening and fine-screening programs document that these smaller taxa, while present, were never important in the human diet.

Another well-established benefit of using screen samples is that it increases the reliability of estimates of body-part representation of larger animals (Payne 1972; Watson 1972). At Panaulauca, comparisons of grab samples to screen samples from the same units show that the reliability of body-part sampling was an important benefit of the screening program.

A third benefit of screening realized at Panaulauca was the ease of obtaining a complete, or nearly complete, sample of unidentifiable bone. To some zooarchaeologists, this may seem a limited, even perverse, goal. We know that the most accurate and complete identification possible of taxon age, sex, and so on, is necessary to be able to reconstruct hunting patterns, herd management, or environmental conditions from bone. Analysis of animal *use*, however, must take into account the bone that has been fragmented beyond identification of taxon or element, but can still be identified to, for example, vertebrate class or size class, and type of bone tissue (rib fragment, long bone shaft fragment, spongy bone, etc.). The fact that this bone is still present in the assemblage is important information about consumption and discard. Analysis of general body-part *type*, for example, can suggest whether "missing" bones of a particular animal were transported from the site or were merely processed so complete-

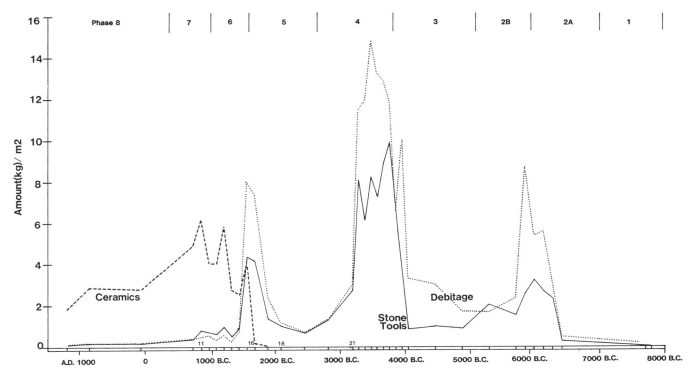

**Figure 3.** Density of artifacts (weight in kg of artifact/cubic meter of deposit) in Panaulauca cave deposits.

ly that they are no longer "identifiable." When only the identifiable specimens are analyzed, only the earliest stages of animal processing may be detected. Ignoring the bulk of unidentifiable fragments ignores subsequent decisions of the site's occupants about whether to either eat, transport, or abandon the food still available from animals already procured. The least unidentifiable bones are the archaeological food remains deposited last, and possibly closest in time to the moment of site abandonment or burial by sediment.

The less diverse the identifiable component of the remains in terms of species richness, the more potentially useful will be the *un*identifiable fragments. Where the overall assemblage is relatively diverse (many birds, smaller mammals, or fish, for example), variation within the unidentifiable category may be less interpretable. At Panaulauca, the assemblage was not fundamentally diverse (six possible large-mammal species of similar body weight provided virtually all meat). Identifiability of all large-mammal bone was low, due to possible confusion between the four possible camelids species and the two possible deer species. Still, I was concerned that lumping all large-mammal

bone into a single animal type would obscure a pattern of differential use of parts of different animal species. Patterns of density of deer and camelid bone across living surfaces at Panaulauca did not differ, however. This suggests that the behaviors of preparing and discarding bone did not distinguish between types of animal, though the human behavior used to obtain these animals must have been different. Patterns of different fragment-size classes did vary strongly across living floors, indicating that discard practices for different fragment types reflected the structure of the site while in use.

In summary, no matter how little information may be obtainable about animal procurement from an unidentifiable sample, the spatial pattern of these remains is part of the archaeological, diagenetic, and geological context of the larger, still-identifiable bones. Even though these fragments may be laborious to pick out, heavy to ship, and individually meaningless to the study of animal procurement, they cannot be ignored as artifactual remains of distinctive and important behaviors.

The bones recovered from the one-quarter-inch screen were sorted through a one-half-inch screen before they were analyzed. The larger screen fraction (larger than one-half inch) contained most of the "identifiable" (to mammalian subfamily or genus) bone and many large pieces of long bones, vertebrae, and skull, and sections of rib, which were not identifiable. The small screen fraction (one-half to one-quarter inch in two dimensions) was made up of splinters of long-bone shafts and crushed spongy bone from long-bone ends, vertebrae, and ribs, and occasional complete carpals or tarsals, sesamoids, and incisor teeth. So little of it was "identifiable" (to taxon) that I sorted only a 25 or 50 percent sample of larger samples, seeking in each case to analyze at least 1,000 of these small fragments from every excavation unit.

## MODELS FOR INTENSITY OF ANIMAL USE

Using ethnographic accounts of bone fragmentation, I relate characteristics of the bone assemblage to a hypothetical sequence of consumption practices. Four stages of use and discard can be proposed.

(1) Whole carcasses arrive at the site and are skinned and dismembered. Body-part representation at Panaulauca indicates that no parts were left behind at a kill or primary processing location; the animals are too small (40–80 kg) to require this step. At this point, some bones are removed from the carcass unbroken and remain whole until burial. Evidence for this derives from finds of articulated sections of feet, neck, or back, presumably deposited fresh, perhaps even with the skin still on. Bones discarded whole represent the abandonment of the food value contained within them.

(2) Meat is stripped off bone and large bones are broken to remove the marrow contained within them. At this stage, most of the long bones are broken across the shaft to remove marrow, and a few become singed in cooking fires. Many of the smaller bones are still whole. Some bones (either broken or still whole) may be discarded at this stage, even though they still contain considerable food value (mostly fat held in spongy bone). Some meat (some containing bones, especially ribs) may be dried for storage.

(3) Bones are fragmented to remove fat and shreds of meat, either while still fresh or after having been dried. Toe bones, ribs, and vertebrae are crushed, and long bone ends are pounded into a loose mass. Some of the small bits of meat may have been eaten as a soup or

stew (Leechman 1951; Binford 1978), but bone grease could be prepared by heating and then pounding long bone ends (Bridges 1949). These fragments, while they provide valuable dietary fats, are, as Bonnichsen (1973:13) puts it, "smashed beyond recognition." At Panaulauca, the proportions of proximal (fat-rich) to distal (fat-poor) humeri fragments (27.7 percent in the phase 4 and 5 samples from the talus) and proximal (fat-rich) to distal (fat-poor) tibiae (25.7 percent in the same sample) are low, showing this destruction to have been a general and effective practice. Bone waste from this process, as meal waste or latrine deposit, is represented by the small unburned fragments.

(4) Further episodes of burning, unrelated to cooking or eating, seem to have produced the small fragments of burned bone. Their incidence was the result of accidental burning or site clearance (Stiner et al. 1995:234). At sites with different depositional environments, further weathering could also lead to noncooking fragmentation, but this does not appear to have been the case at Panaulauca.

Here, I suggest that the small size class of fragments had already been reduced to that size at the time that they were burned, and that their small size was the factor that led them to be swept into heat features rather than tossed into a pit or onto the talus. In contrast, Mary Stiner and colleagues (Stiner et al. 1995) have conducted experiments that suggest to them that burning itself is an important agent of fragmentation. According to their study, bone burned only to the partially black stage was significantly fragmented as a result. I do not dispute the observations of Stiner et al., but I point out that the category of small unburned bone is so abundant at Panaulauca that there must have been significant forces at work (presumably humans but possibly some other unidentified process) that acted to reduce the size of fresh, unburned bone fragments.

Thus the relative amounts of different kinds of bone fragments reflect the amount of processing that each animal received as it was being butchered and eaten. This handling, sorting, saving, and reuse of bone as further and further amounts of food are wrung out of individual animals reflects the length of the occupation that followed a particular kill. As occupations were prolonged, more different kinds of bone scrap would have been mixed together and tossed away from the living floors onto the talus slope. In contrast, shorter occupations would be reflected by a truncated fragmentation sequence, with bones abandoned as larger fragments or carried to another location for further storage or processing. In a brief occupation, more bone would be left on the living floor rather than being tossed outside the cave.

The match between characteristics of this bone assemblage and contemporary bone assemblages must be carefully assessed. It is important to note here that few ethnoarchaeological accounts of bone fragmentation describe as fragmented an assemblage as was recovered at Panaulauca (though some ethnographic accounts do suggest this level of fragmentation). The assumption that fragmentation is a direct result of human intensity of food utilization has been generally accepted but seldom directly examined (Marshall 1986; Todd and Rapson 1988; Enloe 1993; Oliver 1993). To apply this assumption, it is important to exclude other processes that might have acted to accentuate fragmentation. Weathering of bone exposed on the ground surface has been unimportant except in a few isolated cases, based on evidence for rapid burial and sod formation. Plow damage or other mechanical damage is irrelevant, as the living floors and features are intact. Dog and other carnivore damage has been observed in most levels, but a tiny minority of fragments seem to have been affected by either gnawing or swallowing; humans appear to have been the last user in the vast majority of cases.

It is also important to consider other aspects of material culture that could be relevant in this case, specifically the availability of pottery or other vessel technology and the equipment for dismembering animals and crushing bone.

## MODELS FOR SEASONALITY OF OCCUPATION

At Panaulauca it would be possible to document an occupation that took place during the wet season using remains of the many plants that are available during this time. It is much more difficult to document occupation during a time of dormancy or slowed production of plant foods. One focus of research on the animal remains was on developing a positive archaeological indicator for occupations during the dry season.

Estimates of season of death (and by extension, season of occupation) come from three sources. First, the patterns of eruption and wear of teeth of very young camelids and deer were recorded and compared to dental patterns of known-age animals from similar environments (Wheeler 1982; Moore 1989). The results are presented as percentages of 13 possible age

classes. The youngest five age classes (0=late fetal to birth; 1=birth to 1 month; 2=1 month to 3 months; 3=3 months to 9 months; 4=9 months to 18 months) represent short enough periods of time to be used to estimate season of death (fig. 4a). One problem in using age-at-death estimates to determine seasonality is that long periods (sometimes hundreds of years) must be assumed to be characterized by a single seasonal pattern of occupation. To strengthen the claim for possible seasonal identifications, I compiled predicted assemblages of animals that would have been alive at the same time (fig. 4a). Note that animals of age class 0 and 1 might co-occur with animals of age class 4, but would not, at a single moment, co-occur with animals of age class 3. Thus very late fetal animals should be found with animals in the nine- to eighteen-month age class. Similarly, an assemblage with animals in both age classes 1 and 3 must have included occupation in both the wet and dry seasons. The proportions of young animals for each phase were matched to these assemblages to determine the seasons in which they might have co-occurred or could not have co-occurred (fig. 4b).

In the earliest phases (1–2B), there is strong evidence for occupation during the wet season, indicated by the incidence of one-month-old animals (age class 1). This birth peak for the camelids would also have been the time of peak availability of some plant foods. The first evidence for dry season occupation comes during phase 3 (after about 5000 B.C.). The two subsequent phases 4 and 5 have an even and complete representation of age-class assemblages, documenting occupation at all seasons of the year. In phases 6 and 7, evidence for occupation in the later dry season and early wet season are missing, despite large sample sizes. During phase 8, when the site appears to have become a specialized camp, the occupation appears to have been restricted once again to the wet season.

Second, the annual cycle of deer antler development was used as a rough indicator of season of occupation. Male deer develop bony antlers during the months preceding the breeding season, which loosen and drop off after the rut. Here the presence of antler still attached to the skull is used as an indicator of a kill during the late wet to mid-dry season (March–June); dropped antlers (or skulls with scars of shedding) are used as an indicator of a find or kill during the later dry season (Roe and Reese 1976; Merkt 1987; see Moore 1989:34). Shed antler may be stored, transported, or found some time after it has been dropped, so shed antlers cannot be used as a positive indication of the season of antlerless deer. Samples in phases 1, 2A, 2B,

| Year since birth | Dec | Jan | Feb | Mar | April | May | June | July | Aug | Sept | Oct | Nov |
|---|---|---|---|---|---|---|---|---|---|---|---|---|
| **Year of birth** | Age class 0 → | 0 | Age class 1 | Age class 2→ | 2 | Age class 3→ | 3→ | 3→ | 3→ | 3→ | 3→ | Age class 4 ← |
| **Year 1** | ↙ 4→ | 4→ | 4→ | 4→ | 4→ | 4→ | 4→ | 4 | Age Class 5→ | 5→ | 5→ | 5 ← |
| **Year 2** | ↙ 5→ | 5→ | 5→ | 5→ | 5→ | 5→ | 5→ | 5 | Age class 6→ | 6→ | 6→ | 6 ← |
| **Year 3** | ↙ 6→ | 6→ | 6 | Age class 7 | 7→ | 7→ | 7→ | 7→ | 7→ | 7→ | 7→ | 7 |
| **Season** | Mid | Wet | Birth Peak | Late | Wet | Early | | Dry | Late | Dry | Early | Wet |

**Figure 4a.** Seasonal calendar of camelid dental development. Age classes of camelids are determined by comparison of dental eruption and wear from a known-age sample (age class 0: late fetal; age class 1: 0–1 month; age class 2: 1–3 months; age class 4: 3–9 months; age class 5: 18–30 months; age class 6: 2.5–3 years; age class 7: 3–4 years; mature age classes based exclusively on tooth wear not shown). Animals born in the current year (top row) will co-occur with immature animals born in previous years (subsequent rows). Seasons of the year, indicated in the bottom row, should be associated with distinctive combinations of young age classes. These expectations are used to assign seasons or ranges of seasons of occupation from the archaeological assemblages of camelid mandibles from Panaulauca (fig. 4b).

and 8 are too small to be meaningful (n=61 specimens for which seasonality could be determined in this comparison). In phase 3 and again in phase 7, attached antler is more abundant than shed antler. In those phases, the associated dental remains also indicate that the emphasis in occupation was on late wet season to early dry season. During phases 4, 5, and 6, where dental remains indicate a less seasonal deposit, shed antler is more abundant (Moore 1989:215). It is unclear if the association of shed antler with less seasonal occupations relates to a less seasonal practice of hunting deer or the importance of antler to the technology of a more permanent campsite.

The third indicator of seasonality draws from the biology of birds in the area. Specimens from phases 2B, 3, and 4 were identified as bones of the Andean goose (*Cloephagea*), specifically goslings that would have still been in the nest in the late wet season (Johnsgaard 1978:104). Another specimen from phase 5 at Panaulauca was from a cormorant (*Phalacrocorax*), a bird that nests in the Junín area only during the wet season (Morrison 1939).

All of these estimates depend on a somewhat variable natural process to track human action in the past, and so the three indicators taken together should be more reliable than any one alone. Of these three measures, the dental evidence provides the only measure that can be used to estimate the *rank* of importance of the occupations at different seasons. Dental remains were abundant at Panaulauca (unusually so), and so the sample is reliable in size. The other measures (antler, birds) are used as presence/absence indicators of the possibility of occupation at different seasons. Further weaknesses of the second two measures are the

| Phase | Camelid Dental Age Classes | | | | | | | | MNI | Seasonal Diagnosis |
|---|---|---|---|---|---|---|---|---|---|---|
| | 0 (late fetal) | 1 (Birth to 1mo) | 2 (1-3mo) | 3 (3-9mo) | 4 (9-18mo) | 5 (18-30 mo) | 6 (2.5-3 years) | 7 (3-4 years) | | |
| 8 350 b.c.-A.D. 1200 | | 45 | | | | 25 | 12 | | 9 | Mid-Wet |
| 7 1050 b.c.-350 b.c. | | 31 | 5 | 5 | | 12 | | | 39 | Midwet to early dry |
| 6 1620 b.c.-1050 b.c. | | 30 | 2 | 2 | 4 | | | | 48 | Birth peak; early Dry |
| 5 2640 b.c.-1620 b.c. | 2 | 15 | | 4 | 12 | 9 | 13 | 4 | 99 | All year |
| 4 3800 b.c.-2640 b.c. | 2 | 16 | 4 | 2 | 4 | 6 | 22 | 4 | 82 | All year |
| 3 5000 b.c.-3800 b.c. | 2 | 32 | 5 | 4 | | 5 | | | 37 | Mid-late Wet;Dry |
| 2B 5900 b.c.-5000 b.c. | | 15 | | | | 2 | 15 | | 26 | Mid-late Wet |
| 2A 7050 b.c.-5900 b.c. | | 15 | | | | 15 | 15 | | 8 | Mid Wet |
| 1 7700 b.c.-7050 b.c. | | 33 | | | | | 33 | | 3 | Mid Wet |

**Figure 4b.** Mortality by age class and seasonality of occupation at Panaulauca. Percentages of immature age classes based on tooth eruption and wear are shown for each of the phases at Panaulauca. Using patterns of seasonal co-occurrence of age classes shown in figure 4a, a range of seasons is given for occupations in each phase.

fact that they depend on sampling relatively rare finds, and the fact that different states observed do not vary continuously during the year.

## OCCUPATION AT PANAULAUCA

The analysis here focuses on cultural practices that took place after a carcass arrived at the site but before it became part of the archaeological deposit. Relevant data are the abundance (count or NISP, except that taxonomic identifications were not made), average fragment weight (in grams), and density of the burned and unburned large (greater than one half-inch) and small (between one-half and one-quarter inch) bone fragments (expressed as kilograms of bone divided by cubic meters of deposit).

The density of bone fragments varied from almost zero to more than 120 kg per cubic meter of excavated deposit. Generally, higher densities of bone were found on the talus away from the main living floors and features, indicating that a storage/trash zone was only a few meters from the focus of occupation. Generally, burned fragments are less common than unburned fragments, and burned bones are not strongly associated with the hearths where they had been burned. Variation in the weight of the large bone fragments was considerable, since there were many almost complete bones. The small size class of fragments varied in weight according to shape, heavier bones being long, narrow splinters that could fit through the one-half-inch mesh, and the lighter bones being rounded crumbs of spongy bone.

Correlations of densities of fragment types in the two parts of the site for all time periods taken together show some interesting patterns that suggest the events that created the deposits (table 1). The relationship between large, unburned bone and small fragments is strong on the cave floor but much weaker in the talus, indicating that bones that were spatially associated (during use? upon discard?) have become separated from one another during the process of discard outside the cave. A similar pattern occurs with the association of large and small burned fragments; inside the cave burned fragments are highly correlated (spatially close to the site of burning), but they have been separated on the talus. The small size class of fragments shows low correlation within the cave between burned and unburned fragments, but outside the cave on the talus slope, these fragments are much more likely to be found together, presumably because the fragments have been size sorted after deposition on the talus. The location of these small fragments is no longer related to the context of their use, but rather reflects dumping well after use.

Correlations of fragment types between cave and talus environments for individual time periods are limited to comparisons of groups of deposits that have been assigned to phase, since individual levels cannot be correlated (see fig. 2, table 1). Roughly similar densities of large unburned fragments are found in cave and talus deposits, indicating that the source of this primary scrap on the talus is the activity on the cave floor. Small unburned fragments do not show such a similar pattern, a clue that specific clearing or dumping events produced the pattern of tiny fragments. Patterns of burned bone show even greater differences. Large burned bones, likely to have been primary food waste, are patterned much differently than small burned fragments, which appear to have been much-handled trash. Calcined (whitened) bone, which forms when bone is burned in an open fire at relatively high temperatures (Shipman et al. 1984; Nicholson 1993), was found only in the talus trash deposits, further indicating that these fragments had been handled and processed many times.

The sequence of occupations at the cave begins with layers of low bone and artifact density, interpreted as the results of relatively brief occupations (fig. 5). We have only a small sample of remains from the earliest "peak" of occupational intensity, in our phases 2B and 3. The bones from this level, though, indicate that while many animals were brought to the cave in a short time, the use of any individual animal was not prolonged or intense. The weights of fragments are relatively high, and little of the bone is burned. This era of apparently intense hunting is associated with biological evidence of only wet-season kills (fig. 4). The summary

## TABLE I

### Comparison of fragment type associations in cave and on talus

| Pairs of Different Bone Fragment Types | Correlation Coefficients for Each Depositional Zone | |
| --- | --- | --- |
| | Cave | Talus |
| Large Unburned:Large Burned | .32 | .27 |
| Large Unburned:Small Unburned | .78 | .37 |
| Large Unburned:Small Burned | .12 | .05 |
| Large Burned:Small Burned | .90 | .59 |
| Small Unburned:Small Burned | .17 | .48 |

Comparisons are for the unit 9/1 test column (37 level samples; total n=166,947 fragments) for the cave sample and the unit 35 test column for the talus sample (22 level samples; total n=301,755 fragments).

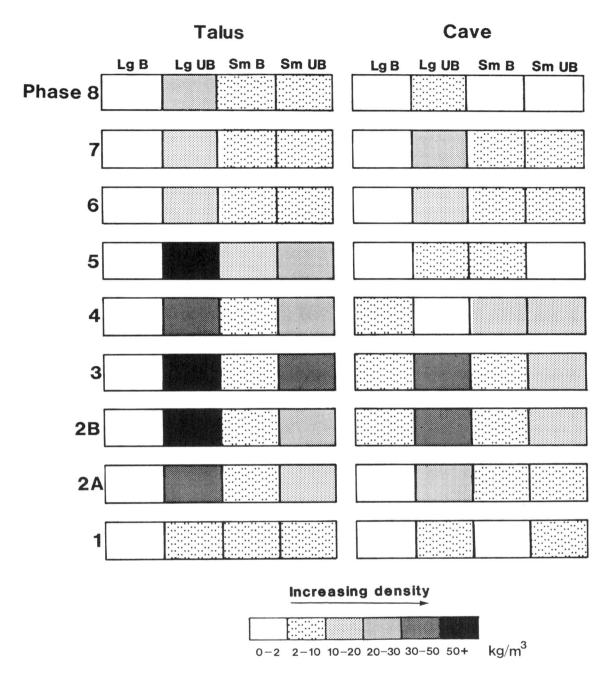

**Figure 5.** Summary of spatial patterns in fragmentation and burning. Intensity of shading indicates increasing density of bone (weight of bone in kg/cubic meter of deposit) in talus and cave deposits. Each column of shaded boxes indicates a different fragment type (LgB-1/2"+ size fraction, burned; LgUb-1/2"+ size fraction, unburned; SmB-1/4-1/2" size fraction, burned; SmUb-1/4-1/2" size fraction, unburned).

picture of this use of the cave is of frequent but short occupations during only one season of the year.

The occupation of the cave shifted in phases 4 and 5. Here, despite the fact that overall bone densities are not as high as in phases 2 and 3, there is intense use of the animals that were taken, according to several measures. The small-screen fraction of bone fragments is a high proportion of all fragments (about 60 percent by weight), and these individual fragments are smaller than in any other deposits at the site, reflecting intense use of fat from spongy bones. The deposition of burned fragments, especially small, burned fragments, also became particularly intense. The features and structures on the living floors of these phases also give a sense of the relatively prolonged occupations that produced the remains. The clearest signal of changing mobility, though, is the first indications in the sequence that the cave was occupied during the dry season of the year. In fact, dental remains provide positive documentation of occupation during each of the seven periods of the year that can be distinguished. Even despite this assemblage of seasonality and intensity indicators, we cannot call this a permanent or year-round occupation, since the remains represent such a long span of time. There is, however, a lack of seasonal focus to this tradition of relatively prolonged visits to the site.

During the subsequent phases 6 to 8, analysis of the bone remains shows that domestic camelids had begun to be kept by the occupants of the cave, even while many wild animals were still being hunted. The determination of domesticated status cannot be effectively combined with seasonality indicators to determine if occupation by hunters came at different seasons than occupation by herders. In these later phases, overall densities of bone wane, indicating a less intense occupation. Evidence for the seasonality of the occupation increasingly is restricted to the wet season, and evidence for dry-season occupations is missing altogether by phase 8. The pattern of bone fragmentation and discard, however, is different from the pattern seen when the cave was a wet-season hunting camp in Phases 2 and 3. In phase 7 and 8, overall densities are low but the size of all bone fragments increases (fig. 6). Much less of the bone has been burned. The occupants apparently dumped large bone fragments, ones that would have still been usable according to former standards. I speculate that this wasteful discard was associated with brief stays in which few animals were hunted or slaughtered during a particular visit. Other substantial parts of the seasonal cycle were probably spent at lower altitudes at agricultural settlements. One possible nutritional implication of this shift is that the care-

ful extraction of fats from bone that is documented for the early phases had become less important as cereals and tubers cultivated at lower altitudes became more important in the diet.

## CONCLUSIONS

Using a combination of seasonality indicators and measures indicating the duration and intensity of occupation, it has been possible to evaluate the three possibilities suggested earlier in this paper for Panaulauca. The first possibility, that the occupations were seasonal and periodic, is suggested by the earliest occupation and some of the latest occupation. During the middle phases at the site, seasonal indicators show a lack of seasonality in visits to the cave. The question then arises whether the visits were prolonged in duration, or whether they were short, perhaps frequent, and occurring at all seasons of the year. A detailed examination of the fragmentation data suggests that the patterns of bone breakage and discard are not consistent with the comparable measures for earlier or later patterns. These occupations, occurring from 3800 to 1600 B.C., were distinctively prolonged and intense. The lack of strong seasonality in the availability of key resources makes this a plausible reconstruction. The relatively low primary productivity and severe climate of this region force us to carefully examine how foragers and hunters would have met their basic needs living for long periods at Panaulauca. The current consensus of archaeological indicators from Panaulauca and nearby sites that there was very limited interaction with sites at lower, warmer locations during this period needs to be continually evaluated as more data become available.

Three general points may be drawn from this specific case and considered in wider geographical perspective:

(1) Degrees of mobility reconstructed for hunter-gatherers should be reconstructed independent of patterns of season of occupation. In this case, the indications of occupational intensity provide stronger evidence of mobility or sedentism than traditional biological markers, but the biological markers provide important further details.

(2) The rates at which different classes of material remains were deposited should not be assumed to be similar or related if, in fact, the most common activities at a site change over time. At Panaulauca, the intense and prolonged occupations of the middle phases 4 and

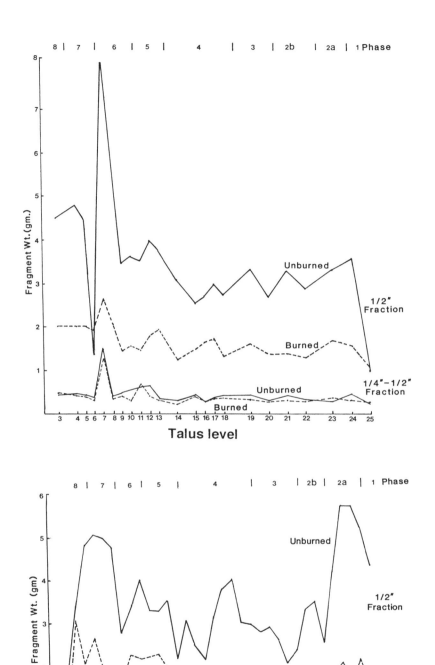

**Figure 6.** Size (weight in gm) of bone fragments by level for cave and talus deposits. Cultural phases of both samples are arranged on the same horizontal scale, correlation of individual levels is approximate. Fragment types are as given in figure 5.

5 are marked by the peak densities of stone tools and debitage. At the same time, bone densities are declining, and the flow of meat and bone to the site has slowed in comparison to previous phases. Looking at only a single class of artifact as a measure of occupational intensity would obscure such revealing differences.

(3) More than 90 percent of the bone fragments mentioned here qualify as unidentifiable large-mammal bones, a category of faunal remains that is often ignored when animal *procurement* is at issue. Even so, these bones are an important class of archaeological information about animal *use*, in particular the shifting utilization of meat and within-bone nutrients. In a further stage of this analysis, I hope to combine information about which bones were being fragmented with these basic fragmentation data to better understand the nutritional implications of the process.

Not all sites will have the kind of spatial and depositional uniformity that allowed us to make heavy use of densities as measures of intensity at Panaulauca. Nor do all sites provide such uniformly good bone preservation over many millennia. Even so, faunal remains should always be recognized as artifactual debris as well as food remains, in order to best understand their significance to cultural adaptations.

## Acknowledgments

I gratefully acknowledge financial support from the University of Michigan, Bentley College, and Sigma Xi in undertaking this research. Further, I would like to thank John Rick, Kent Flannery, Susan Scott, Richard Redding, the editors and discussants of this volume, and an anonymous reviewer for generous commentary and assistance.

## BIBLIOGRAPHY

Behrensmeyer, A. K.
1978 "Taphonomic and Ecologic Information from Bone Weathering." *Paleobiology* 4(2):150–162.

Bonnichsen, R.
1973 "Some Operational Aspects of Human and Animal Bone Alteration," in *Mammalian Osteoarchaeology: North America*, B. M. Gilbert, ed., pp. 9–24. Missouri Archaeological Society, Columbia.

Binford, L.
1978 *Nunamiut Ethnoarchaeology.* Academic Press, New York.

Bridges, L.
1949 *Uttermost Ends of the Earth.* Dutton, London.

Enloe, J. C.
1993 "Ethnoarchaeology of Marrow Cracking: Implications for the Recognition of Prehistoric Subsistence Organization," in *From Bones to Behavior: Ethnoarchaeological and Experimental Contributions to the Interpretation of Faunal Remains*, J. Hudson, ed., pp. 82–97. Center for Archaeological Investigations Occasional Paper 21. Southern Illinois University, Carbondale.

Franklin, W. L.
1978 "Socioecology of the Vicuna." Ph.D. diss., Utah State University.
1983 "Contrasting Socioecologies of South America's Wild Camelids: The Vicuna and the Guanaco," in *Advances in the Study of Mammalian Behavior*, J. F. Eisenberg and D. G. Kleinmann, eds., pp. 573–629. Special Publication of the American Society of Mammalogists, no. 7. Shippensburg, Pennsylvania.

Johnsgaard, P. A.
1978 *Ducks, Geese, and Swans of the World.* University of Nebraska Press, Lincoln.

Leechman, D.
1951 "Bone Grease." *American Antiquity* 16:355–356.

Marshall, F.
1986 "Implications of Bone Modification in a Neolithic Faunal Assemblage for the Study of Early Hominid Butchery and Subsistence Practices." *Journal of Human Evolution* 15:661–672.

Menard, N.
1982 "Quelques Aspects de la Socioecologie de la Vicogne (*Lama vicugna*)." *Revue Ecologique (Terre et Vie)* 36:15–35.
1984 "Le Regime Alimentaire de Vicognes (*Lama vicugna*) Pendent une Periode de Secheresse." *Mammalia* 48(4):529–539.

Merkt, J.
1987 "Reproductive Seasonality and Grouping Patterns of the North Andean Deer or Taruca (*Hippocamelus antisensis*) in South Peru," in *Biology and Management of the Cervidae*, C. M. Wemmer, ed., pp. 388–401. Smithsonian Institute Press, Washington, D.C.

Moore, K. M.
1989 "Hunting and the Origins of Herding in Prehistoric Highland Peru." Ph.D. diss., University of Michigan.

Morrison, A.
1939 "Notes on the Birds of Lake Junín, Central Peru." *Ibis* 3(4):643–653.

Nicholson, R. A.
1993 "A Morphological Investigation of Burnt Animal Bone and an Evaluation of its Utility in Archaeology." *Journal of Archaeological Science* 20:411–428.

Oliver, J. S.
1993 "Carcass Processing by the Hadza: Bone Breakage from Butchery to Consumption," in *From Bones to Behavior: Ethnoarchaeological and Experimental Contributions to the Interpretation of Faunal Remains*, J. Hudson, ed., pp. 200–227. Center for Archaeological Investigations Occasional Paper 21. Southern Illinois University, Carbondale.

ONERN (Oficina Nacional de Evaluacion de Recursos Naturales)
1976 "Inventorio y Evaluacion de los Recursos Naturales de la S.A.I.S. 'Tupac Amaru.'" Estudios ONERN, no. 41. Lima, Peru.

Payne, S.
1972 "Partial Recovery and Sample Bias—The Results of Some Sieving Experiments," in *Papers in Economic Prehistory*, E. S. Higgs, ed., pp. 49–64. Cambridge University Press, Cambridge.

Pearsall, D. M.
1986 "Interpreting the Meaning of Macroremain Abundance: The Impact of Source and Context," in *Current Paleoethnobotany; Analytical Methods and Cultural Interpretations of Archaeological Plant Remains*, C. A. Hastorf and V. S. Popper, eds., pp. 97–118. University of Chicago Press, Chicago.
1989 "Adaptation of Prehistoric Hunter-Gatherers to the High Andes: The Changing Role of Plant Resources," in *Foraging and Farming: The Evolution of Plant Exploitation*, D. R. Harris and G. C. Hillman, eds., pp. 318–332. One World Archaeology, no. 13. Unwin Hyman, Winchester, Massachusetts.

Rick, J. R.
1980 *Prehistoric Hunters of the High Andes*. Academic Press, New York.
1986 *Chronologia, Clima y Subsistencia en el Preceramico Peruano*. INDEA, Lima.

Roe, N. A., and Reese W. E.
1976 "Preliminary Observations of the Taruca (*Hippocamelus antisensis*: Cervidae) in Southern Peru." *Journal of Mammology* 57(4):722–730.

Shipman, P., G. Foster, and M. J. Schoeninger
1984 "Burnt Bones and Teeth: An Experimental Study of Colour, Morphology, Crystal Structure, and Shrinkage." *Journal of Archaeological Science* 11:307–325.

Stiner, M., S. L. Kuhn, S. Weiner, and O. Bar-Yosef
1995 "Differential Burning, Recrystallization, and Fragmentation of Archaeological Bone." *Journal of Archaeological Science* 22:223–237.

Todd, L. C., and D. J. Rapson
1988 "Long Bone Fragmentation and Interpretation of Faunal Assemblages: Approaches to Comparative Analysis." *Journal of Archaeological Science* 15:307–325.

Tsopick, H.
1947 *Highland Communities of Central Peru*. Institute of Social Anthropology Publication 5. Smithsonian Institution, Washington, D.C.

Watson, J. P. N.
1972 "Fragmentation Analysis of Animal Bone from Archaeological Sites." *Archaeometry* 14:21–228.

Wheeler, J. C.
1982 "Aging Llamas and Alpacas from Their Teeth." *Llama World* 1(2):12–17.

# CHAPTER 12

# Pithouses and Pueblos on Two Continents: Interpretations of Sedentism and Mobility in the Southwestern United States and Southwest Asia

*Thomas R. Rocek*

*University of Delaware*

## Abstract

Interpretations of the sequence of settlement changes associated with the transition to agriculture in Levantine Southwest Asia and in the U.S. Southwest suggest a major contrast. In the Levant, village sedentism preceded agriculture; in the U.S. Southwest, villages and sedentism came after agriculture. However, the settlement patterns of the early villages in the two regions appear to be similar.

Here, I compare site size, architecture, and storage technology to test the view that settlement in the agricultural Southwestern sites and preagricultural Levantine villages was similar. The results of the comparison are consistent with this view. I find a fair, though imperfect, similarity between Levantine Natufian sites and the larger of the ceramic period pithouse sites of the Southwest. This similarity fits the interpretation that the sites represent comparable settlement patterns despite their very different subsistence economies.

The analysis also has implications for interpretations of settlement patterns *within* each region, however. Current interpretations emphasize evidence of sedentism in the Natufian sites but seasonal mobility in the Southwest. The comparability of the Natufian and Southwestern sites suggests that the arguments for high mobility at the latter and full sedentism at the former may be overstated.

A comparison of site characteristics such as those examined here is not a substitute for biological measures of site seasonality and can not demonstrate the existence of a particular settlement pattern. However, it provides information complementary to other assessments of settlement in the two regions, helps narrow the range of likely interpretations, and suggests directions for research in both areas.

## INTRODUCTION

Settlement variability is a critical factor for understanding the correlated developments of agriculture and sedentism. Although the link between sedentism and agriculture was once viewed as simple and invariant, research in the last several decades has demonstrated the complexity of the relationship (e.g., Price and Brown 1985; Flannery 1986). While studies within particular regions demonstrate this complexity, comparative analyses of the subsistence-mobility relationship *between* regions can contribute important insights into the diversity of independent developmental trajectories and the effects of differing environments (Fish and Fish 1991).

In this paper, I compare cultural features of sites in the U.S. Southwest and in Southwest Asia to assess similarities and contrasts in the relationship between changes in mobility and the appearance of agriculture in the two regions. In the section that follows, I describe how the changing site characteristics in the two regions have been interpreted to show agriculture preceding sedentism in the U.S. Southwest and following sedentism in Southwest Asia. Next, I compare site size, architecture, and storage technology in the two areas. In each of these characteristics, I identify significant, though imperfect similarities between the larger of the ceramic period agricultural pithouse villages in the U.S. Southwest and the villages of the Levantine Natufian. I argue that this finding supports the view that agriculture preceded sedentism in the U.S. Southwest and followed after it in Southwest Asia. However, the similarities also suggest that previous interpretations of high mobility in the pithouse villages in the U.S. Southwest and of full sedentism in the Natufian have both been overstated. I conclude with a discussion of methodological issues raised by the comparative settlement analysis.

## INTERPRETATIONS OF SETTLEMENT CHANGE IN THE TWO REGIONS

In the U.S. Southwest, where agriculture was imported about 3,500 years ago, the appearance of villages and substantial indications of sedentism follow after the start of agriculture; even evidence of food storage is not widespread until the arrival of cultigens (e.g., Wills 1988:461). This contrasts with the pattern in Southwest Asia where substantial communities with well developed storage technology existed in the Natufian, prior to the appearance of agriculture (e.g., Perrot 1966; see also papers by Lieberman and by Valla in this volume).

Despite these contrasts, the sequence of development in the two areas and some of the physical remains themselves are strikingly similar (Fish and Fish 1991). In both regions, rounded, usually semisubterranean structures are succeeded by multiroom rectilinear surface dwellings (the pithouse-to-pueblo transition in the Southwest [Gilman 1987] and the Natufian and Pre-Pottery Neolithic A (PPNA) versus later Neolithic architecture in the Levant [Aurenche 1981b]). In both areas, the traditional interpretation of pithouse villages (Natufian or Basketmaker) has emphasized occupation permanence, but in both regions recent interpretations have raised questions regarding this view (e.g., Carmichael 1981; Gilman 1987; Byrd 1989a; Edwards 1989; Olszewski 1991). And in both areas, the transition to rectilinear surface architecture occurs at *approximately* the same period as an increase in agricultural dependence and in sedentism.

## U.S. Southwest

In the U.S. Southwest, agricultural pithouse settlements (such as the aceramic Basketmaker II [BMII, ca. 500 B.C.–A.D. 400] and the ceramic Basketmaker III [BMIII, ca. A.D. 400–750]) were initially assumed to represent a transitional stage in the emergence of sedentary villages, with fully sedentary life developing during either the late pithouse period (BMIII) or the transition to surface dwellings (Pueblo I [PI, ca. A.D. 750–900]) (e.g., Amsden 1949; Powell 1990).

Research in the last decade, however, has suggested substantial mobility associated with some or all pithouse villages and has demonstrated considerable variability; even the degree of sedentism at some later pueblo sites is at issue (e.g., Carmichael 1981, 1990; Powell 1983; Nelson and Leblanc 1986; Gilman 1987; Wills and Windes 1989). Thus arrival of agriculture before sedentism is generally accepted, but the connection between the pithouse-to-pueblo transition and increasing sedentism is uncertain.

In the Southwest, questions of mobility have primarily been studied using architecture, site features, and site layout as indicators of seasonality and settlement pattern (e.g., Carmichael 1981; Powell 1983; Lightfoot and Jewett 1984, 1986; Gilman 1987; Wills and Windes 1989; Schlanger 1990; Wills 1992; see also Minnis and Redman [1990] for an overview). Faunal and ethnobotanical evidence are occasionally cited (see e.g., Adams and Bohrer, this volume), but these biologically based measures of seasonality have not been well developed in the region.

## Southwest Asia

The Epipaleolithic (ca. 20,000–10,200 b.p.) is the period preceding the appearance of agriculture in the Levant. For most of its duration, Epipaleolithic sites preserve no architecture or only ephemeral traces. When first studied, the whole period was viewed as an example of mobile hunter-gatherer lifeways. However, with the recognition of the large scale of occupation at some Natufian (late Epipaleolithic, ca. 12,500–10,200 b.p.) sites in the 1950s and 1960s, the view of the late Epipaleolithic shifted to one of sedentism (e.g., Perrot 1966; see discussions in Bar-Yosef and Belfer-Cohen 1989; Edwards 1989; Belfer-Cohen 1991). Despite some dissent (e.g., Edwards 1989), most recent syntheses emphasize evidence of sedentism on at least some Natufian sites (e.g., Tchernov 1984, 1991; Bar-Yosef and Belfer-Cohen 1989; Henry 1989; Hillman et al.

1989; Lieberman 1993). This interpretation places sedentism before the appearance of agriculture in the PPNA (ca. 10,200–9500 b.p.) and before the pithouse-to-pueblolike architectural shift in the Pre-Pottery Neolithic B (PPNB, ca. 9500–8000 b.p.).

A growing awareness of chronological change within the Epipaleolithic sequence has also suggested that the transition from a mobile to sedentary lifeway need not be unidirectional—the most convincing evidence for sedentism derives from the Early (or "ancient," ca. 12,500–11,000 b.p.) and Late (or "recent," ca. 11,000–10,500 b.p.) Natufian, as opposed to the Final (ca. 10,500–10,200 b.p.) Natufian period (Valla 1987; Belfer-Cohen 1991).

In Southwest Asia, many recent studies of mobility have used detailed rigorous analyses of faunal and ethnobotanical evidence of seasonality of occupation (e.g., Tchernov 1984, 1991; Hillman et al. 1989; Pichon 1991; Lieberman 1993 and this volume; see also Monks 1981). However, many of the site attributes used in examining settlement in the Southwest can and have also been applied in the Levant (e.g., Byrd 1989a; Edwards 1989).

## SITE COMPARISONS

Fish and Fish (1991) have pointed out some of the general issues of geographic and temporal scale that emerge from comparisons between the Levant and the Southwest. An archaeological entity such as the late Epipaleolithic Natufian and Harifian combined covers an area comparable to the historic distribution of the Piman language group in the U.S. Southwest—a group with considerable cultural diversity (Fish and Fish 1991:404–406) (see figs. 1–2). This magnitude of ethnographic variation serves as a warning regarding broad generalizations about the terminal Epipaleolithic cultures. Similarly, the roughly two-and-a-half-thousand-year chronological span of the Natufian would encompass the U.S. Southwestern sequence from late Archaic times up to European contact. The chronological subdivisions of all but the Final Natufian remain on a long time scale: 1,500, 500, and 300 years for the Early, Late, and Final Natufian respectively (Valla 1987; Belfer-Cohen 1991:172–173). So, analysis of cultural processes in the Epipaleolithic and Neolithic operate at a coarse temporal resolution that may miss some of the kinds of changes that are documented in the American data (Fish and Fish 1991:406–407).

Beyond these general observations on chronological and spatial scale, more specific issues of site variability and *similarity* in settlement strategy are brought out by a comparison of the physical characteristics of sites in the two areas. While a comparison of cultural features of settlements is not a substitute for biological measures of seasonality at sites in each region (e.g., Bar-Yosef and Meadow 1995), it complements them by constraining alternative interpretations and drawing attention to potential biases and sources of variation. I examine in particular three of the sets of site characteristics that are most commonly used to argue for greater or lesser degrees of sedentism:

(1) Site size. This variable has not been widely used in the U.S. Southwest but has often been cited in Southwest Asia (e.g., Byrd 1989a, with references).

(2) The presence of pithouses (Gilman 1987) and the labor investment in structure construction as measured by characteristics such as size, depth, and numbers of postholes (Lightfoot and Jewett 1984, 1986).

(3) The presence of extramural storage pits (e.g., Gilman 1987; Wills and Windes 1989; Wills 1992).

## Site Size

Site size is a function of a range of factors including duration of occupation, number of occupants, and kinds of activities carried out at a site. Size provides one of many possible general measures of the multiple dimensions of "intensity" of occupation. Figure 3 (and table 1) shows site surface area from a sample of Southwest Asian and U.S. Southwest sites.[1] The sites are divided into time periods in each case: Basketmaker II through Pueblo II in the U.S. Southwest[2] and late Epipaleolithic Natufian through late Pre-Pottery Neolithic B in Southwest Asia.

Although these data have serious limitations, several significant patterns emerge. In the Southwest, the earliest period, the aceramic BMII, is represented almost entirely by small sites—only one attains half a hectare in size. This pattern contrasts with the succeeding periods (BMIII through PII), where most sites remain small, but the overall distribution broadens to include occasional sites of well over a hectare.

In Southwest Asia, despite a drastically smaller sample of sites, the Pre-Pottery Neolithic periods show a substantially greater range in site sizes than any of the American time periods. In particular, the number of large sites over a hectare in size is striking. This pattern is already present in the PPNA and persists into the early PPNB. In the late PPNB, the pattern is further complicated by the appearance of some very large sites, over 10 ha (see also Aurenche 1981a, 1981b). Thus sites in all of the Southwest Asian Neolithic periods appear to represent a substantially different and more intensive pattern of occupation than the American sites.

In contrast, the late Epipaleolithic sites are smaller.[5] Natufian sites—Rosh Horesha, Ain Mallaha, Beidha, and Hayonim—fall within the upper end of the BMIII or even BMII size range. Thus the site sizes *do* suggest comparability in the intensity of occupation represented in the Natufian and the larger ceramic period pithouse sites.

If true, this result is important but must be viewed with caution due to several biases and complexities that affect data from both areas. The sites in either area are not in any sense random samples. In both regions, preservation ensures that sampling is inherently biased against smaller and older sites, since they are harder to find and harder to date.

Several methodological issues that apply to both areas are clearer in the more extensive U.S. Southwest data. For instance, table 1 shows that on Black Mesa, site-size estimates from sites that were excavated are substantially larger than size estimates based only on survey data—mean-size estimates for excavated sites range from two to eight times as large as survey data for a given time period. The Southwestern data also demonstrate the level of regional variation: the Dolores and Black Mesa patterns differ greatly (table 1).

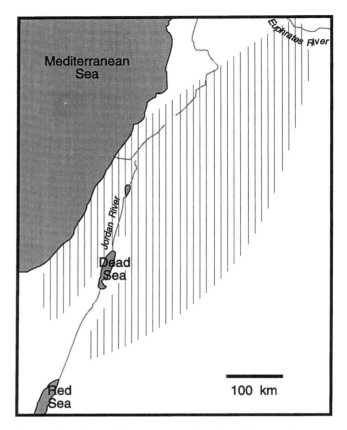

**Figure 1.** Map of Southwest Asia. Hatching indicates approximate distribution of Late Epipaleolithic Sites (Natufian or related). To same scale as figure 2. After Byrd (1989a) and Henry (1989).

TABLE I

**U.S. Southwest and Southwest Asian mean site surface area (by data set and time period)**

| Period | U.S. SOUTHWEST | | | SOUTHWEST ASIA | |
| | BMAP Survey | BMAP Excavation | Dolores Survey | Period | SW Asia Excavation |
| --- | --- | --- | --- | --- | --- |
| BMII | .018±.034 [.01] n=88 | .144±.139 [.11] n=33 | | Epipal. | 1.420±2.51 [.40] n=5 |
| BMIII | .036±.042 [.01] n=36 | .125±.067 [.15] n=9 | .433±.906 [.12] n=41 | PPNA | 1.983±2.15 [1.0] n=15 |
| PI | .048±.069 [.02] n=297 | .103±.090 [.07] n=24 | .363±.716 [.21] n=73 | e PPNB | 1.488±1.13 [1.2] n=8 |
| PII | .052±.085 [.02] n=633 | .101±.078 [.07] n=30 | .555±.799 [.24] n=13 | 1 PPNB | 4.958±5.68 [1.9] n=12 |

Areas in ha. ± 1 standard deviation; numbers in brackets are medians; n is sample size. BM = Basketmaker, P = Pueblo, Epipal. = Epipaleolithic, PPNA = Pre-Pottery Neolithic A, e PPNB = early Pre-Pottery Neolithic B, l PPNB = late Pre-Pottery Neolithic B. The Southwest Asian figures are from Aurenche (1981a), Byrd (1989b), Lechavallier et al. (1989), Kozlowski and Kempisty (1990), and Bar-Yosef (1991a).[3] Most of the Southwest Asian sites have been partially excavated. The American sites include survey data from the Dolores Archaeological Program in southwest Colorado (Kane et al. 1986:260–263), survey data from the 1979–1983 seasons of the Black Mesa Archaeological Project in northeast Arizona, and excavated sites from the 1977–1983 seasons of the latter project (Klesert 1978; Klesert and Powell 1979; Powell et al. 1980; Andrews et al. 1982; Smiley et al. 1983; Nichols and Smiley 1984; Christenson and Parry 1985).[4]

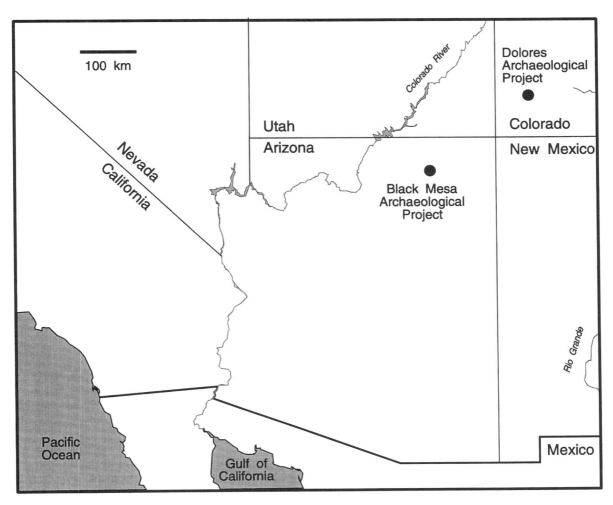

**Figure 2.** Map of the U.S. Southwest showing Dolores and Black Mesa Archaeological Projects. To same scale as figure 1.

Undoubtedly a combination of survey techniques (particularly differences in site boundary definitions) and actual differences between the two regions (Black Mesa is noted for its modest scale of occupation) contribute to the contrast.

These same sorts of biases and sources of variation apply to the Southwest Asian data. The factors that obscure small sites in the American data are bound to be more severe on the much older Levantine sites (Byrd 1989a). Furthermore, the Southwest Asian data used here derive mostly from excavated sites classified as "base camps," or similarly identified as extraordinary; hence they represent the large end of the site-size distribution. In fact, Southwest Asian sites are known to cover a wider range of sizes, at least in certain areas (e.g., Bar-Yosef and Belfer-Cohen 1992:29).

Chronological and regional variation adds a critical dimension to the data. For instance, some of the relatively early "core" Natufian sites most commonly cited as examples of Natufian sedentism, such as Ain Mallaha and Hayonim, are considerably smaller than the later and architecturally less substantial Negev highlands site of Rosh Horesha.

Finally, the site-size distributions from both regions exhibit heavy positive skewing (distributions with many small sites and a "tail" of a few large ones). A comparison of measures of central tendency (mean or median) of the Southwest Asian and U.S. Southwest

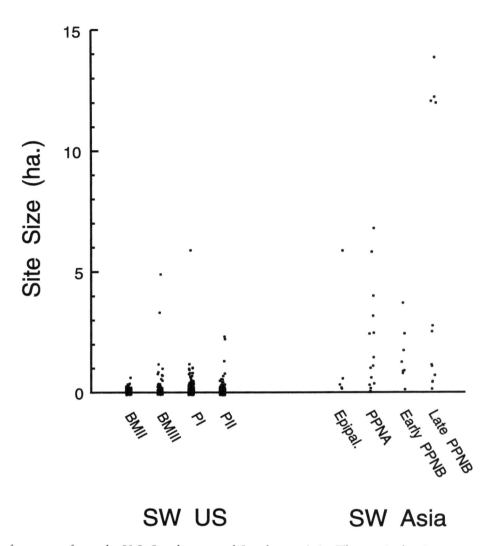

**Figure 3.** Site surface areas from the U.S. Southwest and Southwest Asia. The vertical axis represents site size in hectares; different periods within the U.S. Southwest and Southwest Asia are represented along the horizontal axis. The data have been "jittered"; that is moved slightly in random directions to make superimposed data points more apparent (Wilkinson 1990).

sites, as in table 1, suggests that the former are substantially bigger. This is because the numerous small sites recovered in the U.S. Southwest are missing from the Southwest Asian sample. This difference is almost certainly a product of the greater age-induced bias against small sites and the limited, excavation-based nature of the Southwest Asian sample used here.

Thus the available data can not show how comparable the *overall distributions* of site sizes in the Levant and Southwest may be. The analysis suggests that smaller Natufian sites may be underrepresented, giving an exaggerated impression of prolonged settlement at a few large sites. Despite the biases, the Natufian sites *do* fit within the size range of BMIII through early Pueblo sites in the Southwestern sample.

This overlap in size range fits the interpretation of the relative timing of sedentism and agriculture in Southwest Asia and the Southwest. Given the data biases, the large Natufian sites do not, however, demonstrate a greater level of occupation permanence for the preagricultural Natufian than for the agricultural BMIII pithouse sites in the Southwest. Instead, the overlapping site-size distributions are compatible with the view that settlement in the Natufian and the BMIII *was* similar.

## Architecture

Architecture provides a second basis for addressing questions of mobility in the two regions. In both areas, rounded pithouse architecture precedes rectilinear surface construction.[6] Both the round shape and the underground construction of these pithouses have been noted to correlate ethnographically with nonsedentary settlement (Flannery 1972, with references; Gilman 1987). The reasons for this correlation have yet to be explained (Edwards 1989), however, and the existence of counterexamples shows that the correlation is imperfect. Consequently, archaeological examples of pithouse architecture can not automatically be interpreted as residences of mobile groups.

A complementary approach to the architectural data is offered by McGuire and Schiffer's (1983; see also Binford 1990; Diehl 1992, 1994) argument that substantial investment in domestic architecture correlates with anticipated prolonged use of the structures. This correlation is one that can be used to compare archaeological cases such as pithouses in the Southwest and in Southwest Asia.

Natufian pithouses range up to eight m or more in internal diameter (e.g., Valla 1981), though most range from three to four m (Olszewski 1991). Some have stone and/or plaster linings, large internal hearths, and are dug half a meter to over a meter deep. In one somewhat atypical D-shaped structure at Ain Mallaha, stone-outlined postholes running 30 to 50 cm deep and holding posts perhaps 15 to 20 cm in diameter indicate the roofing technique. A reconstruction of the structure suggests use of a total of 11 posts and several fairly long beams to support the roof (fig. 4) (Valla 1981, 1988).

Although many Natufian sites have little or no known architecture, the largest site (Ain Mallaha) has up to 18 houses (Valla 1981; Olszewski 1991). Many of these structures are superimposed; for the Early Natufian, for instance, Valla (1987:278) suggests a maximum of three or four contemporary structures at Ain Mallaha and six at Hayonim Cave. Admittedly the number of structures may be underrepresented, since only portions of the sites have been excavated,

but the total number of contemporaneous dwellings is likely low.

Natufian architecture is very different from that of the aceramic Basketmaker II sites in the Southwest. Basketmaker II houses are often at the middle or smaller end of the Natufian size range (averaging four meters diameter or less) and are notably ephemeral in construction, usually lacking a regular outline, plastering, stone linings, or (in most cases) deep postholes (e.g., fig. 6). Southwestern aceramic sites in general contain no more than one or two structures, though they do range up to as many as 12 houses on Black Mesa (Powell 1984).

Southwestern architectural similarity to Natufian houses is much closer in the ceramic period. Well constructed formalized structures, often 4.5 m or more in diameter, with substantial postholes, prepared hearths, and in some cases even stone linings are fairly common in many parts of the Southwest. Average sites remain small, but sites with upwards of 50 structures also occur in areas beyond the sample examined here (e.g., fig. 7) (see e.g., Lightfoot and Jewett 1986:34; Blinman et al. 1988:615; Wills 1992:165). Contemporaneity of dwellings is again uncertain, but given the total numbers, the counts of contemporary structures is probably at least as high or higher than in the Natufian.

The Southwestern ceramic period sites lack one set of features found on several Natufian sites: stone terrace retaining walls and stone pavements. Although these features involve substantial construction effort, it is unlikely that either of them represents significantly greater labor investment than pithouse construction (quantitative data on labor requirements are needed). So despite the lack of these features in the Southwest, there is a fair degree of similarity between the architectural investment at sites in the two regions.

With the shift to the PPNA in Southwest Asia, the similarity with the Southwestern pithouse sites disappears. Most notable is the change in architectural technology to mud brick and stone superstructures (though cf. Kozlowski and Kempisty 1990), in contrast to the perishable superstructures of the Southwest and of Epipaleolithic times. This technological shift suggests greater energy investment and permanence. Also in the PPNA, the site of Jericho begins a striking development in architectural complexity (Kenyon 1981; Bar-Yosef 1986). The investment in the construction of a large stone wall and tower, as well as a bewildering array of overlapping house construction, is unparalleled in the pithouse settlements in the Southwest. Still, the multimillennial occupation of Jericho exaggerates the impression of massive scale. How many houses were in

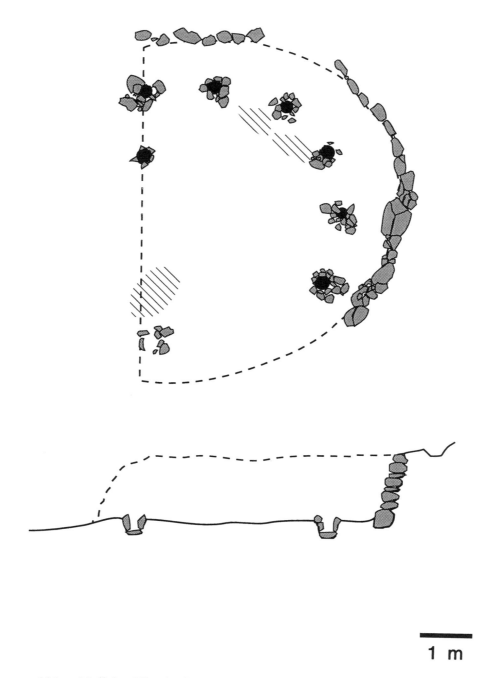

1 m

**Figure 4.** Structure 131 at Mallaha. The shading indicates rocks, hatched areas are hearths, and black features are known posthole locations. Dashing indicates approximate structure outline. Plan view on top, cross-section below. To same scale as figure 6. After Valla (1988).

simultaneous use at any point in Jericho's occupation is unknown, and its overall areal extent of around two and a half hectares, within the range of BMIII sites, is a reminder that it was still a small town (Aurenche 1981a). Furthermore, contemporary PPNA sites are much smaller and have small numbers of houses.

Clearly variability within a given period is great among sites in both the Southwest and the Levant (see Bar-Yosef 1991a; Fish and Fish 1991). Given the long duration of the PPNA, it is very likely that transformation towards increasing complexity and permanence occurred over the course of the early PPNA. The best

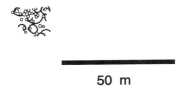

**50 m**

**Figure 5.** Plan of a portion of Ain Mallaha. After Perrot (1989). Dark lines are house outlines, thinner lines are pits. To same scale as figure 7, though this figure shows a smaller portion of Ain Mallaha than figure 7 shows of Shabik'eschee Village. Note the numerous overlapping pits and rebuilt houses.

analogues to the processes involved in the American pithouse to pueblo transition may lie within the temporal and regional variability of the early PPNA, perhaps in the Khiamian, even though the architectural similarity to pueblos does not develop until the succeeding PPNB.

Overall, the architectural comparison supports the view suggested by site areal extent: the more substantial ceramic period pithouse sites in the Southwest are similar in scale of occupation to the Natufian sites and the pattern of anticipated mobility at these sites may be comparable. The patterns of settlement changes in the two regions in the succeeding periods are difficult to compare given the high diversity and coarse chronological resolution, particularly in the Levant.

## Storage

In addition to architecture, one of the most visually striking similarities of some Levantine late Epipaleolithic and Southwestern pithouse period sites is the parallel in storage technology (fig. 8). The underground straight walled to bell-shaped pits in both the Southwest and the Levant fit the ethnographically recognized characteristics of storage pits (DeBoer 1988) used worldwide for grain storage (among other things; see Raymer 1990). They are also comparable in size; for instance the pits at Ain Mallaha average one m diameter and their preserved depth ranges up to 80 cm (Perrot 1966:460); the preserved portions of BMII bell-shaped pits on Black Mesa average about 1.10 m in diameter and 80 cm in depth (Smiley 1985:299).

The Natufian pits are part of the evidence for the presumed heavy use of wild cereals (but cf. Cauvin 1989), and part of the overall view of an "agricultural-

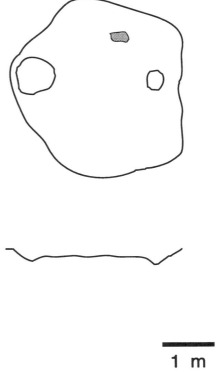

**1 m**

**Figure 6.** A Basketmaker II pithouse from Black Mesa. Shading indicates a piece of burnt sandstone. The two internal features are shallow basin-shaped depressions, possibly postholes. Contrast figure 4 (same scale). After Reed and Landreth (1983).

ist-like" adaptation that allowed sedentism prior to the adoption of agriculture. Soffer (1989) points out that except in a "Garden of Eden" setting (such as has never been observed ethnographically), storage is necessary for sedentism.

However, ethnographic data suggest that these underground storage features are indicative of food caching usually associated with seasonal site *abandonment* rather than year-round sedentism (Gilman 1987; DeBoer 1988; Wills and Windes 1989; Wills 1992; but cf. Raymer 1990). This argument applies to extramural storage pits that are most effectively used by being sealed for prolonged periods and opened only intermittently.

The occurrence of storage pits varies through time in the Levant. They are rare in the Epipaleolithic and occur in low numbers per site, being identified with confidence only at Ain Mallaha, Nahal Oren, and Hayonim Terrace (Byrd 1989a:185; Olszewski 1991:331).

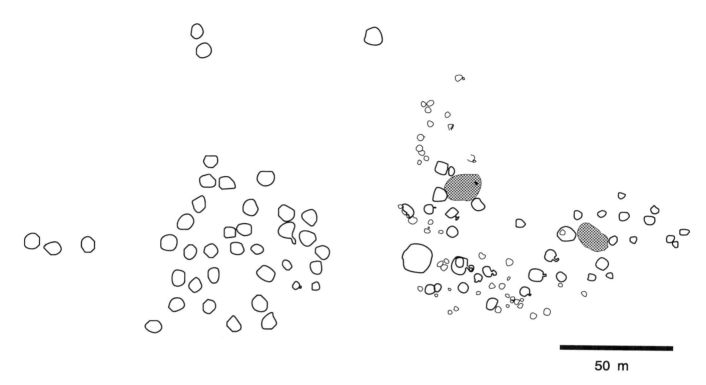

**Figure 7.** Map of Shabik'eschee Village, a Basketmaker III site. Thick lines represent houses, thin lines storage features, and shaded areas are midden mounds. Map is approximate (locations within about 10 m), but to same scale as figure 5. Most of the map represents structures visible on the surface, but a portion of the site (near the right end of the figure) was excavated, and storage features are only recorded in that area. Note large size (site area is over 7 ha [Wills and Windes 1989]) and the relatively lower level of superposition of features compared to the pattern at Ain Mallaha (fig. 5). Still, the area of Ain Mallaha shown in figure 5 is comparable to the portion of Shabik'eschee on the right where detailed excavation data were collected. After Wills and Windes (1989).

Possible storage pits occur at a number of other sites such as Jericho and Abu Hureyra (Edwards 1989:26).

The greatest concentration of these features is associated with the early and particularly the middle period of occupation at Ain Mallaha. None of the pits can be shown to be located inside of a contemporary structure (Valla 1981:415–417); instead, most or all appear to lie outside the dwellings. These houses, with their substantial construction and intense occupation, have often been cited as evidence of sedentism (e.g., Perrot 1966). Given the ethnographic evidence of the association of extramural storage pits and mobility, their presence may in fact be a fairly strong argument for seasonal occupation instead. The caches of ground-stone that occur at some of the major Natufian sites (e.g., Perrot 1966:fig. 10; Bar-Yosef 1991b:89; Edwards 1991:131) might also suggest periodic aban-

donment. The external pits disappear from many areas in the PPNA and are replaced by storage rooms and/or bins and surface silos (e.g., Bar-Yosef 1991a).[7]

In the Southwest, storage pits are fairly widespread in the aceramic pithouse period. As in the Natufian, the pits are not ubiquitous; despite excavation strategies designed to find extramural features, well under half of BMII sites on Black Mesa yielded unambiguous large underground storage features. In the ceramic pithouse period, some sites in some regions have numerous external storage pits, while others (for instance, the Dolores BMIII sites) have few or none but are instead associated with above-ground storage features and/or internal pits (Wills 1992).

Thus if outdoor underground storage technology suggests nonsedentary settlement, then its occurrence at major Natufian and Southwestern pithouse sites

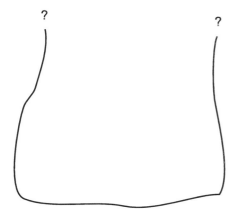

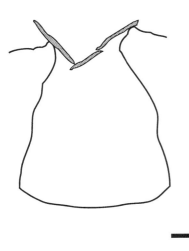

**1 m**

**Figure 8.** (Top) Bell-shaped pit at Ain Mallaha. After Perrot 1989. (Bottom) Bell-shaped pit at a Basket-maker II site on Black Mesa. After Leonard et al. (1985). Shaded areas are stone slabs.

## Discussion

The preceding analyses have demonstrated that archaeological sites in the Southwest and the Levant are comparable in overall site area, architectural style, level of labor investment, number of houses, and storage technology, though significant contrasts also exist. The greatest similarity links the more elaborate of the Natufian settlements (particularly from the Early and Late, as opposed to the Final, periods) and large ceramic period pithouse occupations such as those of the BMIII. These similarities might also extend into some of the earliest PPNA sites, though the shift to more durable architecture differs from the pattern in the Southwest.

The resemblances between the sites indicate similar scales of site occupation, levels of labor investment, and storage strategies and are consistent with the existence of comparable settlement systems. It must be acknowledged, however, that these data do not conclusively demonstrate this interpretation. Edwards (1989) has shown convincingly that measures of site characteristics such as the ones I have discussed are unlikely to distinguish certain kinds of mobile settlement from various forms of sedentism (see also Bar-Yosef and Meadow 1995). For instance, he cites numerous ethnographic examples of nonsedentary groups, such as the complex hunter-gatherers of the American Northwest Coast, who produced sites far larger in areal extent than any of the Natufian, PPNA, or pithouse period sites considered here.

But Edwards (1989:32–33) also warns of the danger of site seasonality interpretations based on the inventory of season-specific botanical or faunal remains, since they can be mislead due to the reuse of locations at different seasons and over many years (see also Rocek 1988). That is, the archaeobotanical and faunal records may be palimpsests of multiple site visits (see also Binford 1982), and thus may accumulate seasonal resources from the whole year without anyone actually occupying them year-round.

While the site characteristics do not conclusively resolve this problem, the comparisons discussed here help to narrow the likely settlement patterns in both regions to two (not mutually exclusive) options: year-round sedentism or anticipated long use of facilities at a stable location.

In the first case, the previously mentioned indicators of occupation intensity (site size, construction of substantial architecture) fit an interpretation of small-scale sedentary hamlet or village life, although the outdoor underground storage pits are atypical. The Natu-

supports the view of periodic site abandonment in both regions. The transition away from underground pits in both areas in the succeeding periods may reflect a change to decreased mobility.

fian sites lie at the upper end of the range of ceramic period pithouse communities in size and appearance of permanence. Large, late pithouse sites in the Southwest may reflect a shift to a substantially reduced level of mobility or a mixture of settlement strategies, in contrast to more mobile, earlier, and/or smaller communities (Wills and Windes 1989; Wills 1992; Diehl 1994).

The second alternative, large-scale investment in facilities at seasonal sites, is the one that raises more intriguing issues. This is the interpretation that many would accept for some Southwestern pithouse sites, but that is less widely accepted for the large Natufian or PPNA settlements.

Perhaps most intriguing is the question of what kind of adaptation seasonal use of a site with heavy investment in facilities would represent. An interpretation suggesting part-time seasonal mobility would have to be evaluated with respect to the specific environmental conditions and the particular seasonality indicators available for each region. But the ethnographic data suggest that seasonal sites with heavy investment in facilities represent a distinctive group of adaptations and settlement patterns.

While some ethnographic examples of large-scale construction, such as Nunamiut stone hunting drive lanes (Binford 1978; Edwards 1989), are made by small and highly mobile populations, these cases generally involve the building of nonhabitation facilities. Ethnographic examples of heavy investment in *domestic architecture* by nonsedentary groups (e.g., villages of the North American Northwest Coast, the Ainu, the Missouri River) suggest that although these groups do not spend the whole year in one place, they exhibit many of the social and economic characteristics of sedentary village dwellers. Thus, if we conclude that the archaeological settlement systems considered here were nonsedentary, this does not mean that they represent small-scale, highly mobile groups (see also Belfer-Cohen 1991:177). If they resemble modern hunter-gatherers, they resemble "complex" hunter-gatherers (Price and Brown 1985), not small-scale bands.

Other measures of site use not considered here may be helpful in examining how such complex groups organized their settlements over the course of the year. In addition to biological seasonality indicators, these include the proportion of outdoor relative to interior space (Powell 1983), the number and composition of indoor versus outdoor features such as hearths (Powell 1983; Lightfoot and Jewett 1984, 1986), the depth and placement of midden areas (Carmichael 1981; Blomberg 1983; Lightfoot and Jewett 1984, 1986), the diversity and density of architectural and artifact

assemblages (Powell 1983; Lightfoot and Jewett 1984, 1986), and the organization of lithic reduction (Parry and Christenson 1987; Parry and Kelly 1987) as well as procurement strategy.[8]

The other major source of information on mobility strategies is intersite variability (Fish and Fish 1991). As Byrd (1989a) points out for the Levant and Gilman (1990) for the Southwest, the only resolution to the ambiguity of individual seasonality and mobility indicators is a shift from concentration on evidence of sedentism at a few large sites to examination of the range of sites comprising settlement systems (see also Rafferty 1985:136). The site-size distributions suggest that coverage of variation is particularly limited in Southwest Asia (though a range of site sizes *is* recognized there [e.g., Bar-Yosef and Belfer-Cohen 1992:29]), and additional work is required in both regions.

## Conclusion

Comparisons of site cultural characteristics in the Levant and U.S. Southwest indicate significant, though imperfect, similarities between the larger sites of the ceramic period, agricultural, pithouse villages in the U.S. Southwest and the villages of the Levantine Natufian. To the extent that these resemblances reflect similar scales of occupation, patterns of labor investment in housing, and storage strategies, they also suggest a degree of similarity in settlement systems.

The similarity of the sites from these periods is of considerable interest, since it supports the view that these two strikingly different economic systems—an adaptation in the Southwest with a 2,000-year record of agricultural use and an occupation that predates plant domestication in the Levant—had comparable settlement systems. Once agriculture appeared in Southwest Asia (or perhaps even before domestication occurred; see Watkins 1990; Bar-Yosef 1991a:14–15), sites changed rapidly to a pattern quite different from that found in the pithouse period in the Southwest.

Given the evidence from biological seasonality indicators in the Natufian (e.g., Tchernov 1984, 1991; Hillman et al. 1989; Pichon 1991; Lieberman 1993 and this volume) as well as the evidence of the cultural features of the Natufian sites themselves, it is clear that substantial periods of site occupation—over many months and multiple years—characterized these sites. This conclusion raises the likelihood that the large ceramic period pithouse villages of the Southwest that resemble these Natufian sites may also have had relatively reduced seasonal as well as interannual mobility. On the other hand, given the arguments for seasonal abandonment of the Southwestern pithouse villages, their similarity to the Natufian communities suggests that perhaps the argument for full, year-round sedentism at the latter sites may be overstated, and that examination of the full settlement pattern (including particularly the less visible smaller sites) may indicate a more complex seasonal round, even if heavily tethered to the major sites.

The site attributes considered here are in no sense a substitute for rigorous biological measures of seasonality, and the sites found most comparable (Early and Late Natufian and BMIII) need not represent identical settlement systems. However, the comparison of site characteristics helps to limit the range of likely settlement patterns in each area, draws attention to likely biases in site samples, and serves as a cross-check for inferences based on other sources of data. Using a comparison of cultural remains such as considered here, as well as specific seasonality indicators such as discussed elsewhere in this volume, and studying a range of sites comprising a settlement pattern, is the strategy most likely to resolve the question of changing mobility patterns in the Old World and the New World.

## Acknowledgments

I am very grateful for numerous comments on the manuscript by Jill Neitzel, Karen Rosenberg, and John Speth. They get to keep the good parts; remaining errors and the conclusions are, of course, my own.

## Notes

1. The Southwest Asian discussion focuses on Levantine sites, though I make reference to other regions as well (fig. 1). In the U.S. Southwest, my discussion refers in fairly general terms to the highland regions (Colorado Plateau and adjacent mountainous country), but I draw most of my examples from two particular sets of sites (fig. 2). My analysis does not draw on data from the lower elevation desertic regions of the Southwest (see table 1 for additional information about the samples).

2. For multicomponent sites in the American data, the earliest period of site occupation is used to classify the sites.

3. For the Natufian period on which much of the following discussion concentrates, the sites included in the sample are: Beidha, Hayonim, Ain Mallaha, Rosh Horesha, and Zawi Chemi. For a full list of the sites in the later time periods, consult the sources listed above.

4. The Black Mesa survey and excavation data used here are restricted to sites which were (1) clearly classified by time period in the report and (2) for which site area could readily be determined either from the text or from the map, without excessive guesswork. These criteria eliminated data from the early field seasons at Black Mesa (pre-1977 excavation and pre-1979 survey), as well as several large sites from the 1977–1978 excavation reports (which had complicated maps for which surface area was difficult to determine). Subsequent reports were more consistent in describing site area. The result is probably some bias against large excavated sites, particularly since the Black Mesa project in its early years investigated several large sites, whereas it made a conscious effort in later years to sample a range of site sizes and types.

5. One site outside of the Levant, Zawi Chemi Shanidar in northern Iraq, is an outlier of nearly six hectares, but the single structure known from the Epipaleolithic occupation at that site is ephemeral and does not make a strong argument for sedentism [Solecki 1981].

6. The term "pithouse" is generally used for the semisubterranean early structures in the Southwest. In Southwest Asia, the term is less widely used. However, most Epipaleolithic structures as well as many of the early Neolithic dwellings are constructed with their floor surfaces below the level of the surrounding ground (Aurenche [1981b:1:96–98] in fact suggests that this is true for *all* of the Epipaleolithic structures). The construction is variable, ranging from deep round pits at Ain Mallaha (Perrot 1966) to shallow excavations leveling a floor into the side of a slope; this latter pattern is particularly common (Aurenche 1981b:1:96–98). Walls were sometimes constructed within the floor pit or sometimes built around it. A wide range of construction techniques also occurs in the U.S. Southwest.

7. In Southwest Asia, underground storage features continued in use in later periods, but generally in indoor or courtyard contexts that made concealment of the stores during site abandonment unlikely (e.g., Watson 1979).

It must be noted that a few possible surface storage features are also present in the Natufian (e.g., Feature 55 at Mallaha [Perrot 1966]), and it is possible that some of the structures served storage functions

(Henry 1989:212). Positive identification of the latter structures would be of particular interest in interpreting storage strategy.

8. The use of reduction strategies to examine settlement in the Americas (Parry and Christenson 1987; Parry and Kelly 1987) is particularly intriguing, since parallel (but quite different) lines of argument to interpret settlement based on reduction have been developed for the Southwest Asian data (Byrd 1989a:185–186; Belfer-Cohen 1991:177–178). In the American case, the view is that biface reduction, which represents a systematic reduction strategy aimed at conserving portable lithics, differs from an expedient reduction strategy used on sedentary sites. In the Southwest Asian data, where bifaces are never important, the argument emphasizes the more thorough and systematic reduction of lithics on the presumably more sedentary Natufian sites in contrast to the less thorough reduction at more mobile sites. The overall lithic technology differs greatly in the two areas, but comparing the underlying assumptions about stone tool use in the two cases might well prove productive. In addition, examination of changing patterns of raw material transport in both Southwest Asia and the Southwest could be elaborated to more thoroughly tackle the question of mobility.

# BIBLIOGRAPHY

Amsden, C. A.
    1949 *Prehistoric Southwesterners from Basketmaker to Pueblo*. Southwest Museum, Los Angeles.

Andrews, P. P., R. Layhe, D. Nichols, and S. Powell, eds.
    1982 *Excavations on Black Mesa, 1980: A Descriptive Report*. Center for Archaeological Investigations, Research Paper 24. Southern Illinois University, Carbondale.

Aurenche, O.
    1981a "Essai de Demographie Archeologique. L'Example Des Villages du Proche Orient Ancien." *Paléorient* 7(1):93–105.
    1981b *La Maison Orientale: L'Architecture du Proche Orient Ancien des Origines au Milieu du Quatrieme Millenaire*. Librairie Orientaliste Paul Geuthner S.A., Paris.

Bar-Yosef, O.
    1986 "The Walls of Jericho: An Alternative Interpretation." *Current Anthropologist* 27(2):157–162.
    1991a "Neolithic: The Early Neolithic of the Levant: Recent Advances." *The Review of Archaeology* 12(2):1–18.
    1991b "The Archaeology of the Natufian Layer at Hayonim Cave," in *The Natufian Culture in the Levant*, O. Bar-Yosef and F. R. Valla, eds., pp. 81–92. International Monographs in Prehistory, Archaeological Series 1. Ann Arbor, Michigan.

Bar-Yosef, O., and A. Belfer-Cohen
    1989 "The Origins of Sedentism and Farming Communities in the Levant." *Journal of World Prehistory* 3(4):447–498.
    1992 "From Foraging to Farming in the Mediterranean Levant," in *Transitions to Agriculture in Prehistory*, A. B. Gebauer and T. D. Price, eds., pp. 21–48. Prehistory Press, Madison, Wisconsin.

Bar-Yosef, O., and R. H. Meadow
    1995 "The Origins of Agriculture in the Near East," in *Last Hunters—First Farmers: New Perspectives on the Prehistoric Transition to Agriculture*, T. D. Price and A. B. Gebauer, eds., pp. 39–94. School of American Research Press, Santa Fe, New Mexico.

Belfer-Cohen, A.
    1991 "The Natufian in the Levant." *Annual Review of Anthropology* 20:167–186.

Binford, L. R.
    1978 *Nunamiut Ethnoarchaeology*. Academic Press, New York.
    1982 "The Archaeology of Place." *Journal of Anthropological Archaeology* 1:5–31.
    1990 "Mobility, Housing and Environment: A Comparative Study." *Journal of Anthropological Research* 46(2):119–152.

Blinman, E., C. J. Phagan, and R. H. Wilshusen
    1988 *Dolores Archaeological Program: Supporting Studies: Additive and Reductive Technology*. United States Department of the Interior, Bureau of Reclamation, Engineering and Research Center, Denver, Colorado.

Blomberg, B.
    1983 *Mobility and Sedentism: The Navajo of Black Mesa, Arizona*. Center for Archaeological Investigations, Research Paper 32. Southern Illinois University, Carbondale.

Byrd, B. F.
    1989a "The Natufian: Settlement Variability and Economic Adaptations in the Levant at the End of the Pleistocene." *Journal of World Prehistory* 3(2):159–198.

1989b *The Natufian Encampment at Beidha: Late Pleis-tocene Adaptations in the Southern Levant.* Excavations at Beidha 1, Jutland Archaeological Society, pub. 23(1). Arhus, Denmark.

Carmichael, D. L.
1981 "Non-residential Occupation of the Prehistoric Southern Tularosa Basin, New Mexico." *Artifact* 19(3–4):51–68.
1990 "Patterns of Residential Mobility and Sedentism in the Jornada Mogollon Area," in *Perspectives on Southwestern Prehistory*, P. E. Minnis and C. L. Redman, eds., pp. 122–134. Westview Press, Boulder, Colorado.

Cauvin, J.
1989 "La Neolithisation au Levant et sa Premiere Diffusion," in *Neolithisations*, O. Aurenche and J. Cauvin, eds., pp. 3–36. British Archaeological Reports, International Series 516. Oxford.

Christenson, A. L., and W. J. Parry, eds.
1985 *Excavations on Black Mesa, 1983: A Descriptive Report.* Center for Archaeological Investigations, Research Paper 46. Southern Illinois University, Carbondale.

DeBoer, W. R.
1988 "Subterranean Storage and the Organization of Surplus: The View From Eastern North America." *Southeastern Archaeology* 7(1):1–20.

Diehl, M. W.
1992 "Architecture as a Material Correlate of Mobility Strategies: Some Implications for Archaeological Interpretation." *Behavior Science Research* 26:1–35.
1994 "Subsistence Economies and Emergent Social Differences: A Case study from the Prehistoric North American Southwest." Ph.D. diss., State University of New York, Buffalo.

Edwards, P. C.
1989 "Problems of Recognizing Earliest Sedentism: The Natufian Example." *Journal of Mediterranean Archaeology* 2(1):5–48.

Fish, S. K., and P. R. Fish
1991 "Comparative Aspects of Paradigms for the Neolithic Transition in the Levant and the American Southwest," in *Perspectives on the Past: Theoretical Biases in Mediterranean Hunter-Gatherer Research*, G. A. Clark, ed., pp. 396–410. University of Pennsylvania Press, Philadelphia.

Flannery, K. V.
1972 "The Origins of the Village as a Settlement Type in Mesoamerica and the Near East: A Comparative Study," in *Man, Settlement and Urbanism*, P. J. Ucko, R. Tringham, and G. W. Dimbleby, eds., pp. 23–53. Duckworth, London.
1986 *Guila Naquitz, Archaic Foraging and Early Agriculture in Oaxaca, Mexico.* Academic Press, Orlando.

Gilman, P. A.
1987 "Architecture as Artifact: Pit Structures and Pueblos in the American Southwest." *American Antiquity* 52:538–564.
1990 "Settlement Patterns and the Seasonal Use of Pit Structures." Paper presented at the 55th Annual Meeting of the Society for American Archaeology, Las Vegas, Nevada.

Henry, D. O.
1989 *From Foraging to Agriculture: The Levant at the End of the Ice Age.* University of Pennsylvania Press, Philadelphia.

Hillman, G. C., S. M. Colledge, and D. R. Harris
1989 "Plant-food Economy during the Epipalaeolithic Period at Tel Abu Hureyra, Syria: Dietary Diversity, Seasonality, and Modes of Exploitation," in *Foraging and Farming, The Evolution of Plant Exploitation*, D. R. Harris and G. C. Hillman, eds., pp. 240–268. One World Archaeology, no. 13. Unwin Hyman, Winchester, Massachusetts.

Kane, A. E., W. D. Lipe, T. A. Kohler, and C. K. Robinson
1986 *Dolores Archaeological Program: Research Designs and Initial Survey Results.* United States Department of the Interior, Bureau of Reclamation, Engineering and Research Center, Denver, Colorado.

Kenyon, K. M.
1981 *Excavations at Jericho.* Vol. 3, *The Architecture and Stratigraphy of the Tell.* British School of Archaeology in Jerusalem, London.

Klesert, A. L., ed.
1978 *Excavation on Black Mesa, 1977: A Preliminary Report.* Center for Archaeological Investigations, Research Paper 1. Southern Illinois University, Carbondale.

Klesert, A. L., and S. Powell, eds.
1979 *Excavation on Black Mesa, 1978: A Preliminary Report.* Center for Archaeological Investigations, Research Paper 8. Southern Illinois University, Carbondale.

Kozlowski, S. K., and A. Kempisty
1990 "Architecture of the Pre-Pottery Neolithic Settlement in Nemrik, Iraq." *World Archaeology* 21(3):348–362.

Lechevallier, M., D. Philibert, A. Ronen, and A. Samzun
1989 "Une Occupation Dkiamienne et Sultanienne a Hatoula (Israel)?" *Paléorient* 15(1):1–10.

Leonard, R. D., P. H. McCartney, M. Gould, J. Carucci, and G. D. Glennie
1985 "Arizona D:11:449," in *Excavations on Black Mesa, 1983: A Descriptive Report*, A. L. Christenson and W. J. Parry, eds., pp. 125–154. Center for Archaeological Investigations, Research Paper 46. Southern Illinois University, Carbondale.

Lieberman, D. E.
1993 "The Rise and Fall of Seasonal Mobility among Hunter-Gatherers: The Case of the Southern Levant." *Current Anthropology* 34(5):599-634.

Lightfoot, K. G., and R. Jewett
1984 "The Occupation Duration of Duncan," in *The Duncan Project: A Study of the Occupation Duration and Settlement Pattern of an Early Mogollon Pithouse Village*, K. G. Lightfoot, ed., pp. 47–82. Anthropological Field Studies, no. 6. Office of Cultural Resource Management, Department of Anthropology, Arizona State University, Tempe.
1986 "The Shift to Sedentary Life: A Consideration of the Occupation Duration of Early Mogollon Pithouse Villages," in *Mogollon Variability*, B. Charlotte and S. Upham, eds. pp. 9–43. The University Museum Occasional Papers, no. 15. New Mexico State University, Las Cruces.

McGuire, R. H., and M. B. Schiffer
1983 "A Theory of Architectural Design." *Journal of Anthropological Archaeology* 2:277–303.

Minnis, P. E., and C. L. Redman, eds.
1990 *Perspectives on Southwestern Prehistory*. Westview Press, Boulder, Colorado.

Monks, G. G.
1981 "Seasonality Studies." *Advances in Archaeological Method and Theory* 4:177–240.

Nelson, B. A., and S. A. LeBlanc
1986 *Short-Term Sedentism in the American Southwest: The Mimbres Valley Salado*. University of New Mexico Press, Albuquerque.

Nichols, D. L., and F. E. Smiley, eds.
1984 *Excavations on Black Mesa, 1982: A Descriptive Report*. Center for Archaeological Investigations, Research Paper 39. Southern Illinois University, Carbondale.

Olszewski, D. I.
1991 "Social Complexity in the Natufian? Assessing the Relationship of Ideas and Data," in *Perspectives on the Past: Theoretical Biases in Mediterranean Hunter-Gatherer Research*, G. A. Clark, ed., pp. 322–340. University of Pennsylvania Press, Philadelphia.

Parry, W. J., and A. L. Christenson
1987 *Prehistoric Stone Technology on Northern Black Mesa, Arizona*. Center for Archaeological Investigations, Occasional Paper 12. Southern Illinois University, Carbondale.

Parry, W. J., and R. L. Kelly
1987 "Expedient Core Technology and Sedentism," in *The Organization of Core Technology*, J. K. Johnson and C. A. Morrow, eds., pp. 285–304. Westview Special Studies in Archaeological Research. Westview Press, Boulder.

Perrot, J.
1966 "Le Gisement Natoufien De Mallaha (Eynan), Israël." *L'Anthropologie* 70(5–6):437–484.
1989 "Les Variations du Mode de Sepulture dans le Gisement Natoufien de Mallaha (Eynan), Israel," in *Investigations in South Levantine Prehistory/Prehistoire du Sud-Levant*, O. Bar-Yosef and B. Vandermeersch, eds., pp. 289–296. British Archaeological Reports, International Series 497. Oxford.

Pichon, J.
1991 "Les Oiseaux au Natoufien, Avifaune et Sédentarité," in *The Natufian Culture in the Levant*, O. Bar-Yosef and F. R. Valla, eds., pp. 371–380. International Monographs in Prehistory, Archaeological Series 1. Ann Arbor, Michigan.

Powell, S.
1983 *Mobility and Adaptation. The Anasazi of Black Mesa, Arizona*. Southern Illinois University, Carbondale.
1990 "Sedentism or Mobility: What do the Data Say? What Did the Anasazi Do?" in *Perspectives on Southwestern Prehistory*, P. E. Minnis and C. L. Redman, eds., pp. 92–102. Westview Press, Boulder, Colorado.

Powell, S., ed.
1984 *Excavations on Black Mesa 1971–1976: A Descriptive Report.* Center for Archaeological Investigations, Research Paper 48. Southern Illinois University, Carbondale.

Powell, S., R. Layhe, and A. L. Klesert, eds.
1980 *Excavation on Black Mesa, 1979: A Descriptive Report.* Center for Archaeological Investigations, Research Paper 18. Southern Illinois University, Carbondale.

Price, T. D., and J. A. Brown, eds.
1985 *Prehistoric Hunters and Gatherers: The Emergence of Cultural Complexity.* Academic Press, Orlando.

Rafferty, J. E.
1985 "The Archaeological Record on Sedentariness: Recognition, Development, and Implications." *Advances in Archaeological Method and Theory* 8:113–156.

Raymer, L. E.
1990 "The Form and Function of Subterranean Food Storage Structures: An Ethnoarchaeological Study of the Social and Environmental Determinants of Pit Storage." Master's thesis, University of Oklahoma, Norman.

Reed, P. K., and G. K. Landreth
1983 "Arizona D:11:2067," in *Excavations on Black Mesa, 1981: A Descriptive Report,* F. E. Smiley, D. L. Nichols, and P. P. Andrews, eds., pp. 209–216. Center for Archaeological Investigations, Research Paper 36. Southern Illinois University, Carbondale.

Rocek, T. R.
1988 "The Behavioral and Material Correlates of Site Seasonality: Lessons from Navajo Ethnoarchaeology." *American Antiquity* 53(3):523–536.

Schlanger, S. H.
1990 "Introduction: Transitions to Sedentism," in *Perspectives on Southwestern Prehistory,* P. E. Minnis and C. L. Redman, eds., pp. 103–121. Westview Press, Boulder, Colorado.

Smiley, F. E
1985 "The Chronometrics of Early Agricultural Sites in Northeastern Arizona: Approaches to the Interpretation of Radiocarbon Dates." Ph.D. diss., University of Michigan, Ann Arbor.

Smiley, F. E, D. L. Nichols, and P. P. Andrews, eds.
1983 *Excavations on Black Mesa, 1981: A Descriptive Report.* Center for Archaeological Investigations, Research Paper 36. Southern Illinois University, Carbondale.

Soffer, O.
1989 "Storage, Sedentism and the Eurasian Palaeolithic Record." *Antiquity* 63:719–732.

Solecki, R. L.
1981 *An Early Village Site at Zawi Chemi Shanidar.* Bibliotheca Mesopotamica, vol. 13. Undena Publications, Malibu, California.

Tchernov, E.
1984 "Commensal Animals and Human Sedentism in the Middle East," in *Animals and Archaeology.* Vol. 3, *Early Herders and their Flocks,* J. Clutton-Brock and C. Grigson, eds., pp. 91–115. British Archaeological Reports, International Series 202. Oxford.
1991 "Biological Evidence for Human Sedentism in Southwest Asia during the Natufian," in *The Natufian Culture in the Levant,* O. Bar-Yosef and F. R. Valla, eds., pp. 315–340. International Monographs in Prehistory, Archaeological Series 1. Ann Arbor, Michigan.

Valla, F. R.
1981 "Les Etablissements Natoufiens dans le Nord D'Israel," in *Prehistoire du Levant: Chronologie et Organisation de L'Espace Depuis les Origines Jusqu'au Vie Millenaire,* J. Cauvin and P. Sanlaville, eds., pp. 409–419. Colloques Internationaux du Centre National de la Recherche Scientifique 598. Editions du Centre National de la Recherche Scientifique, Paris.
1987 "Chronologie Absolue et Chronologie Relative dans le Natoufien," in *Chronologies in the Near East,* O. Aurenche, J. Evin, and F. Hours, eds., pp. 267–294. British Archaeological Reports, International Series 379. Oxford.
1988 "Aspects du Sol de L'Abri 131 de Mallaha (Eynan)." *Paléorient* 142(2):283–296.
1991 "Les Natoufiens de Mallaha et l'Espace," in *The Natufian Culture in the Levant,* O. Bar-Yosef and F. R. Valla, eds., pp. 111–122. International Monographs in Prehistory, Archaeological Series 1. Ann Arbor.

Watkins, T.
1990 "The Origins of House and Home?" *World Archaeology* 21(3):336–347.

Watson, P. J.

1979 *Archeological Ethnography in Western Iran.* Viking Fund Publication 57. University of Arizona Press, Tucson.

Wilkinson, L.

1990 *Sygraph: The System for Graphics.* Systat, Inc., Evanston, Illinois.

Wills, W. H.

1988 "Early Agriculture and Sedentism in the American Southwest: Evidence and Interpretations." *Journal of World Prehistory* 2(4):445–488.

1992 "Plant Cultivation and the Evolution of Risk-Prone Economies in the Prehistoric American Southwest," in *Transitions to Agriculture in Prehistory*, A. B. Gebauer and T. D. Price, eds., pp. 153–176. Monographs in World Archaeology 4. Prehistory Press, Madison, Wisconsin.

Wills, W. H., and T. C. Windes

1989 "Evidence for Population Aggregation and Dispersal during the Basketmaker III Period in Chaco Canyon, New Mexico." *American Antiquity* 54(2):347–369.

# CHAPTER 13

# Remarks on *Seasonality and Sedentism: Archaeological Perspectives from Old and New World Sites*

*James L. Phillips*

*University of Illinois at Chicago*

## INTRODUCTION

The organizers and contributors of this volume are concerned with discerning the development of techniques for establishing an understanding of seasonality and sedentism in the archaeological record. Over the past two decades or so, numerous techniques have been perfected for recovery of data previously deemed unobtainable. This has led to greater concerns by prehistorians about the nature of settlement and mobility amongst prehistoric hunters and gatherers. The question which seems to be ubiquitous is: *how can we recognize sedentism or the season of occupation in the archaeological record, specifically when dealing with earliest farmers and/or hunters and gatherers?* One can understand the concern of the authors when the very definition of sedentism is subject to numerous debates, in print and in private discussions, and several definitions have been introduced into the literature that have in turn led to further debate. Keeley (1992, 1995) and Bar-Yosef and Meadow (1995) present evidence for farmers who leave villages, and hunters and gatherers, such as the Chumash, who live in one village for 11 months of the year. Thus to be sedentary may carry a different connotation in different environmental and cultural contexts.

Most archaeologists working in Pleistocene or early Holocene prehistory are interested in establishing the season of occupation at a site in order to facilitate the prediction of the mobility and settlement system of the local archaeological culture, while those interested in the origins and development of settled life need to understand how and by what process(es) the hunters and gatherers who became permanent settlers, in both the Old and New World, elaborated this subsistence strategy. For, of course, the origins of sedentism are cloaked in the process by which hunters and gatherers developed new settlement and subsistence systems that could accommodate spending more and more time in a specific location, rather than scheduling regular moves for the purpose of obtaining resources. The process by which hunters and gatherers became subsistence farmers included changes in the social systems of these groups in order to accommodate the necessity of occupying a locale for a longer duration with greater population densities.

It must be understood that the rationale for the development of techniques for identifying sedentism and seasonality must ultimately lie in the anthropological significance of the questions raised by their identification. That is, we must understand the seasonal occupation and reoccupation of sites in terms of their mobility and economic systems, represented in the archaeological patterning of a group or groups of hunters-gatherers moving through a mosaic landscape on a yearly basis. For if we view the recognition of seasonality for its own sake, we obviate the use of that knowledge for purposes of anthropological endeavor. Similarly, the identification and understanding of the process of sedentism is intimately involved in understanding developments in cultural complexity which led to the establishment of village life.

In the past decade, the edited volume of Doug Price and Jim Brown (1985) was a major forerunner and impetus to the present volume; those editors and contributors attempted to present methodological and theoretical strategies for dealing with these topics (in addition to others), specifically how they were related to the emergence of cultural complexity in the prehistoric record. Thus the understanding of seasonality and sedentism may lead to the development of models that can help us understand the process by which hunters and gatherers developed settled life, became farmers and herders, and subsequently evolved the concepts of states and empires.

The variety of papers and areas covered in this volume is most impressive. Almost all continents are discussed, as are areas within different topographical and climatological zones, such as the South American lowlands and Andean highlands, the Mediterranean zone, represented by the Levant and the Balkans, the North American Southwest, and so on. All in all, I was very impressed by the work represented in this volume.

# THE PAPERS

With the above in mind I would like to address some of the questions that arose from listening to the papers and reading the re-edited, or, in some cases, rewritten works, and present my take on the discussion that followed the presentation of these papers at the Society for American Archaeology meeting in which they were presented. The first and foremost question that has not been answered by any of these authors, although they are certainly cognizant of my concern, is: how can we deal with complex hunter-gatherers with underground storage facilities. Another major question that arises from the papers is how can we best use the archaeozoological and archaeobotanical data in determining seasonality and sedentism.

The idea of using a faunal assemblage for establishing seasonality is not a new concept, nor one fraught with major problems. The long-ago-developed basic concept is that if we know the habits of certain species, such as their birthing season, the time of year for losing antlers or shedding skin, and so on, we will be able to predict the season of occupation once we determine the species. Of course, this concept is only as good as our knowledge of the species behavior and during the Pleistocene, these behaviors must be inferred, as many of the species recovered from archaeological sites are extinct. Further, it is clear that microfauna are more easily used than macrofauna for studies of this type.

Using fetal long bones and tooth increments in red deer from the Epipaleolithic site of Badanj in the Adriatic-Mediterranean zone of Bosnia, P. Miracle and C. O'Brien postulate increasing shifts toward seasonal environments and the seasonal use of resources due to the variety of climatic changes occurring during the Late Glacial period, about 13,000–10,000 B.P. The authors suggest that due to "dramatic and widespread environmental changes associated with deglaciation at the end of the Pleistocene . . .," populations in the Adriatic basin modulated their subsistence system toward the more seasonal procurement of subsistence resources. They suggest that ". . . fetal remains can be highly indicative of the season of death of the target species . . ."; increment analysis of tooth cementum "functions as a powerful tool distinguishing aspects of prey seasonality and demography . . . ." By analyzing the fetal bones of red deer, the authors indicate that seasonality becomes more evident as one moves up the sequence at Badanj. Specifically, the fetal remains indicate that the animals were brought to the site in late winter-early spring. Using regression analyses of fetal long bones, the authors claim they can refine the seasons into late winter or early spring. Cementum evidence of *Cervus* incisors indicates that, in the upper levels of the site, summer occupation occurred with frequency.

Overall, the work on the *Cervus* fauna from Badanj indicates a trend toward different, more seasonal occupations from the Late Glacial period onward. Although the authors recognize sample-size variability between levels is important for interpreting their data, they suggest that it is not enough to defer their interpretation. The particular use of different kinds of faunal information at this site is a fine example of using data in interesting ways. I would have liked, however, to have seen more information on the other fauna and to have the investigators mesh this information with the *Cervus* data. Further, red deer as well as carnivore incisors, if they are found loose at the site, may imply collection for purposes of personal adornment (as at Magdalenian sites in France) and would therefore not be indicators of seasonality.

M. Russo's use of fish and shellfish to determine seasonal occupation and/or sedentism at Horr's Island on the southwestern Florida coast stems from his hypothesis that ". . . Archaic period cultures along Florida's southwest coast were sedentary villagers at least 3,000 years before such a settlement pattern was thought to have evolved in the Southeast." Seasonal measures of oysters, quahog clams, bay scallops, herring, and catfish are some of the riverine and marine species used by the author. Based on a series of measurements and seasonal indicators, he suggests that the quahogs were a winter/spring resource, scallops were gathered during the summer, and catfish and other fish were caught in the fall and also in winter and summer. Based on this evidence, he states ". . . that at least some segment of the population was living on the island and exploiting its abundant coastal fauna throughout the year".

What Russo fails to deal with, in my opinion, is the presence of storage facilities at the site. Because a food source is found at a site and the general season of exploitation is established should in no way allow us to identify the site as sedentary. An example of a different scenario would be: people brought the resources from three to ten kms to the site, processed and stored them, and then left the island for mainland hunting and gathering on a seasonal basis, leaving behind a few individuals not able to move easily on the mainland or the infirm. That scenario is more than likely to have occurred time and again in the Archaic period. Does the leaving of some segment of the population make the site a sedentary village as Russo maintains? The definition of the terms sedentism and sedentary, I suggest, has not been fully addressed in this paper, nor in most of the other contributions. This is F. Valla's main concern in his paper, as it is in Kelly's and Rocek's contributions.

When considering seasonal reoccupation of sites in semiequatorial regions, we are faced with another series of problems (see Oyuela-Caycedo, this volume). As there are generally two annual seasons, wet and dry; it may not be efficacious to even try to predict the season of the year except in elevations such as the puna (see Moore, this volume), where camelids do seasonally move through the highlands.

Cases where different conclusions are arrived at using similar data sets are the articles by François Valla and Daniel Lieberman on the Natufian period of the Levant (12,500–10,250 B.P.). The Natufian is represented in the literature (Byrd 1989; Belfer-Cohen 1991; Bar-Yosef and Belfer-Cohen 1992) as the first settled populations, subsisting on stored wild grasses and pulses with occasional foraging for seasonally available resources such as nuts, fish, game, and so on. Valla's contribution to this volume contains evidence of his skepticism in assigning this archaeological culture to a sedentary life. He views the faunal and botanical evidence from Natufian sites as indicating a cyclical acquisition of resources, such as migratory water fowl in the winter, fishing at several times of the year, and hunting of wild boar, goat, and gazelle throughout the

year. His view of the biological information brings him to the conclusion that Natufian populations aggregated and dispersed at several times during the year and that special locales, such as cave terraces (Hayonim, Nahal Oren, El-Wad) or special ecotones, such as above Lake Hula (Mallaha), provided the natural resources for the yearly aggregation of dispersed social units such as nuclear families.

Lieberman, on the other hand, using biological data rescued from the cementum of gazelle teeth, comes to the conclusion that the early Natufian populations in the core zone were sedentary and that a majority of the population stayed in one place throughout the year. This system was able to flower because of the use of storage, mainly for wild cereals such as emmer wheat and two-rowed barley. Thus two different views from one archaeological data set.

As discussed above, ethnographic evidence suggests that farmers can move part of the year, and hunters-gatherers may stay in one place for most of the year. Native American farmers, such as the Iroquois, occasionally planted in the spring, stayed until the crop was viewed as safe, then a majority of the men left to hunt in the forests of the eastern woodlands. On the other hand, California or Northwest Coast hunter-gatherers perhaps moved only twice a year, if that. Thus different patterns of settlement and mobility based on local needs and motivations, perhaps economic, perhaps social, perhaps both.

Robert Kelly's approach of analyzing ethnographic hunter-gatherer mobility patterns, caloric intake, and resource procurement, focusing on the rationale, number, and timing of moves, leads him to the conclusion that ". . . in an environment of homogeneously distributed resources, even if the resources have high return rates, the only apparent reason hunter-gatherers would not move is if there was no place to move to." The implication from this conclusion is that there must have been some type of forcing mechanism that prompted some hunter-gatherers to become sedentary. This forcing factor(s) might be population growth (as Kelly mentions), adaptation to environmental shifts, technological innovation, role and status changes in groups, or, more likely, a combination of them all.

The problem for Kelly and other scholars working in tropical or marginal environments (such as the Great Basin) is that the basis of sedentism, as I see it, is the presence of food resources that could accommodate greater population densities and the processing and storage of these resources during seasonal resource lows. In every case where sedentism develops, such as the Levant or Meso- and South America, grasses either were, or become, the staple food of these sedentary populations. These grasses are not available all through the year but only for a short period and they, along with pulses, nuts, and meat sources, become the normal diet for sedentary populations. In a way, this is similar to the seasonal appearance of salmon in the Columbia River at the Dalles, where native American populations accumulated enormous protein resources for the year, by smoking, freezing or drying them, thus maintaining a seasonally available food source for the entire year.

I differ with Kelly in his assumption that ". . . sedentism is a product of population increase." The data in the Levant, for example, suggests that population densities shifted in the "core" zone from the Geometric Kebaran to the Natufian (i.e., 14,500–10,500 B.P.), but total population did not increase, contra Cohen (1977; see Bar-Yosef and Belfer-Cohen 1992, Keeley 1992). I agree with Kelly, however, that "sedentism resulting from different conditions may have different implications for the evolution of other aspects of forager economy, society, politics." Consequently, universal models for the origins of sedentism are inherently flawed, as the conditions for facilitating this development were themselves different from one another. Therefore, the sedentism in the Archaic Period that Russo postulates along the Florida coasts (see Phillips 1983; Phillips and Gladfelter 1983 for earlier discussions of Archaic Period sedentism) did not develop in the same manner as did the Levantine or Mesoamerican cases, but may be more similar to the Jomon of Japan (see Crawford and Bleed, this volume).

T. Rocek suggests that there can be a valuable analytical tool in linking the site architectural characteristics of Southwestern ceramic period pithouses (Basketmaker III/II–PI/PII) and the biological measures of seasonality in the Natufian and early Neolithic periods of the Levant. Using a series of statistical tests and analyses, such as tests on mean site-surface area, depth of deposits through time (table 1), and the presence of storage facilities, building architecture, and so on, Rocek suggests ". . . sites in the American Southwest and Southwest Asia exhibit a fair, though imperfect, degree of similarity." But, he acknowledges, this comparability does not necessarily imply similar processes of development. He indicates that assessment of mobility as discussed in this volume, as well as specific analyses of seasonality based on biological rationale are more likely to resolve questions of "changing mobility patterns in the Old World and the New ."

Moore and Morales Muñiz, although working in different areas of the world and on different types of fauna, approach their data from a species behavioral point of view. They use mobile or migratory fauna—camelids by Moore, birds by Morales Muñiz—to predict season use of archaeological sites in the highland puna of Peru and the hilly areas of southern Spain, near Málaga. I think that both of these papers have used their respective faunas wisely; that is, the behavior of these species is such that when their remains are found at archaeological sites, the time or season of the year of occupation can be predicted with relative certainty. Based on their strategies, and with comparisons with other sites in the settlement system, archaeologists can begin to define the human population movements in association with the behavior of the animals they are exploiting. Just as reindeer herds break up into smaller units during the stressful winter months, the vicuna herds' need for water obligates their movements throughout the year.

Only one of the articles deals heavily with the implications derived from plants at archaeological sites. Adams and Bohrer discuss the archaeobotanical remains found in sites in the American Southwest, and the pitfalls one must deal with when assigning "seasonality" of occupation solely on the identification of plant remains. They discuss microbotanical remains (pollen) and macrobotanical remains (seeds, etc.) found in hearths, human coprolites, and so on. They caution that these botanical remains are subject to a variety of actions, both natural and cultural, that can alter their receptivity to interpretation. I found this article to be one of the most fascinating and most informative of those in the entire volume.

## CONCLUSIONS

This volume contains a wealth of information on techniques for identifying sedentism and seasonality in archaeological sites. They are mostly directed towards the use of fauna in these endeavors; the papers tend to use the natural historical data as a cynosure for success. More than likely, when we can combine information from the natural world and the cultural domain found at our sites, we can better interpret their context and meaning and develop the necessary testable models for understanding the archaeological record. To place in one volume a group of papers dealing with methods and techniques used in the Old World and the New World was a novel and valuable exercise by the editors. I commend them for it.

# BIBLIOGRAPHY

Bar-Yosef, O., and A. Belfer-Cohen
  1992 "From Foraging to Farming in the Mediterranean
     Levant," in *Transitions to Agriculture in Prehistory*,
     A. B. Gebauer and T. D. Price, eds., pp. 21–48. Pre-
     history Press, Madison, Wisconsin.

Bar-Yosef, O., and R. Meadow
  1995 "The Origins of Agriculture in the Near East," in
     *Last Hunters First Farmers: New Perspectives on
     the Prehistoric Transition to Agriculture*, T. D.
     Price and A. B. Gebauer, eds., pp. 39–94. School of
     American Research Press, Santa Fe, New Mexico.

Belfer-Cohen, A.
  1991 "The Natufian in the Levant." *Annual Review of
     Anthropology* 20:167–186.

Byrd, B.
  1989 "The Natufian: Settlement Variability and Eco-
     nomic Adaptations in the Levant at the end of the
     Pleistocene." *Journal of World Prehistory*
     3(2):159–197.

Cohen, M.
  1977 *The Food Crises in Prehistory*. Yale University
     Press, New Haven, Connecticut.

Keeley, L.
  1992 "The Use of Plant Foods Among Hunter-Gather-
     ers: A Cross-Cultural Survey," in *Préhistoire de
     l'Agriculture*, P. Anderson-Gerfaud, ed., pp. 29–38.
     Éditions CNRS, Paris.
  1995 "Protoagricultural Practices Among Hunter-Gath-
     erers: A Cross-Cultural Survey," in *Last Hunters
     First Farmers: New Perspectives on the Prehistoric
     Transition to Agriculture*, T. D. Price and A. B.
     Gebauer, eds., pp. 243–272. School of American
     Research Press, Santa Fe, New Mexico.

Phillips, J. L.
  1983 "Introduction," in *Archaic Hunters and Gatherers
     in the American Midwest*, J. L. Phillips and J. A.
     Brown, eds., pp. 1–4. Academic Press, New York.

Phillips, J. L., and B. G. Gladfelter
  1983 "The Labras Lake Site and the Paleogeographic
     Setting of the Late Archaic in the American Bot-
     tom," in *Archaic Hunters and Gatherers in the
     American Midwest*, J. L. Phillips and J. A. Brown,
     eds., pp. 197–218. Academic Press, New York.

Price, T. D., and J. A. Brown, eds.
  1985 *Prehistoric Hunter-Gatherers: The Emergence of
     Cultural Complexity*. Academic Press, San Diego.